GREAT MOTHER!

Do your homework!

尾田栄一郎

They say that if you trace the roots of human DNA, it leads to a single woman from a long time ago in Africa. Still, theoretically speaking, that doesn't mean she was the very first human in existence. But such a person must exist! The mother of humanity! I thought it sounded awesome, so I drew a picture of her. All of humanity is one big family. No matter what happens, we're all in this together. Anyway, volume 62 is now starting!

-Eiichiro Oda, 2011

E iichiro Oda began his manga career at the age of 17, when his one-shot cowboy manga **Wanted!** won second place in the coveted Tezuka manga awards. Oda went on to work as an assistant to some of the biggest manga artists in the industry, including Nobuhiro Watsuki, before winning the Hop Step Award for new artists. His pirate adventure **One Piece**, which debuted in **Weekly Shonen Jump** in 1997, quickly became one of the most popular manga in Japan.

ONE PIECE VOL. 62
NEW WORLD PART 2

SHONEN JUMP Manga Edition

This graphic novel contains material that was originally published in English in SHONEN JUMP #107–110. Artwork in the magazine may have been slightly altered from that presented here.

STORY AND ART BY EIICHIRO ODA

English Adaptation/Lance Caselman
Translation/Laabaman, HC Language Solutions, Inc.
Touch-up Art & Lettering/Vanessa Satone
Design/Fawn Lau
Editor/Alexis Kirsch

Printed in the U.S.A.

Published by VIZ Media, LLC
P.O. Box 77010
San Francisco, CA 94107

10 9 8 7 6 5 4 3 2 1
First printing, May 2012

www.viz.com

THE WORLD'S MOST POPULAR MANGA
www.shonenjump.com

SHONEN JUMP MANGA

ONE PIECE

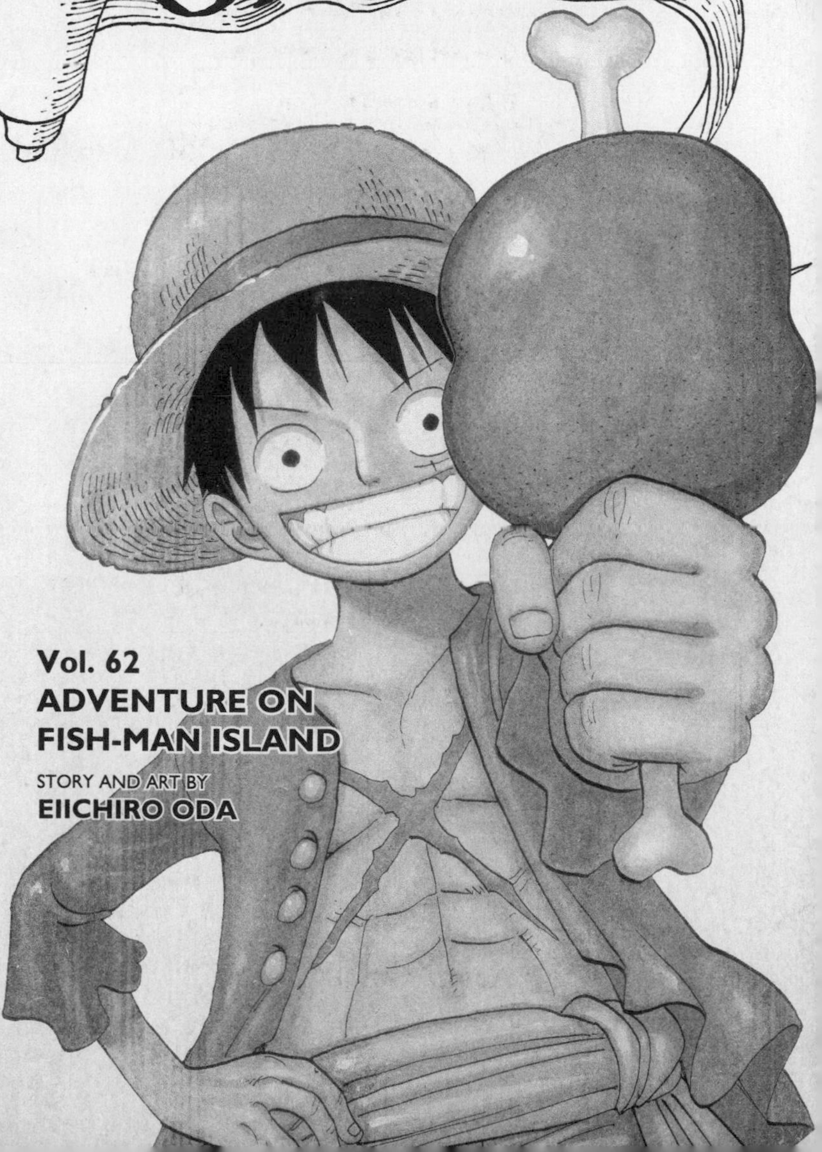

Vol. 62

ADVENTURE ON FISH-MAN ISLAND

STORY AND ART BY
EIICHIRO ODA

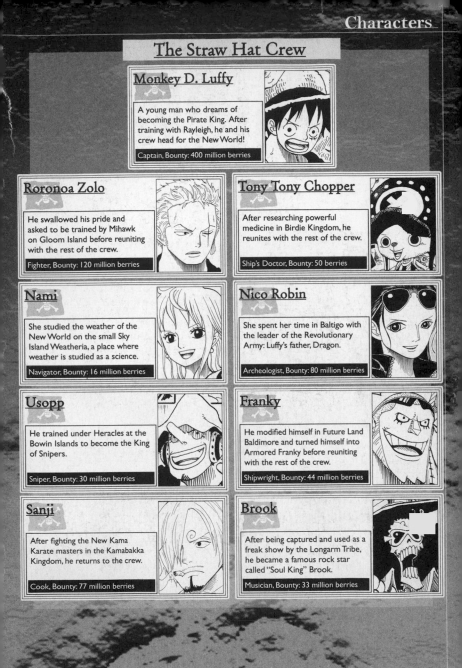

The Straw Hat Crew

Monkey D. Luffy

A young man who dreams of becoming the Pirate King. After training with Rayleigh, he and his crew head for the New World!

Captain, Bounty: 400 million berries

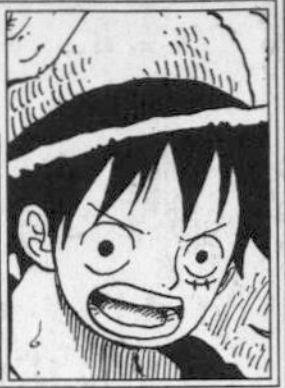

Roronoa Zolo

He swallowed his pride and asked to be trained by Mihawk on Gloom Island before reuniting with the rest of the crew.

Fighter, Bounty: 120 million berries

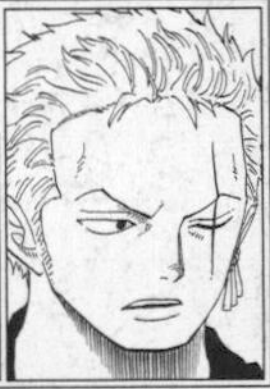

Tony Tony Chopper

After researching powerful medicine in Birdie Kingdom, he reunites with the rest of the crew.

Ship's Doctor, Bounty: 50 berries

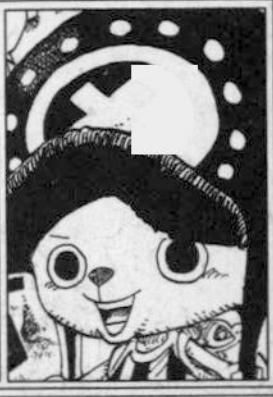

Nami

She studied the weather of the New World on the small Sky Island Weatheria, a place where weather is studied as a science.

Navigator, Bounty: 16 million berries

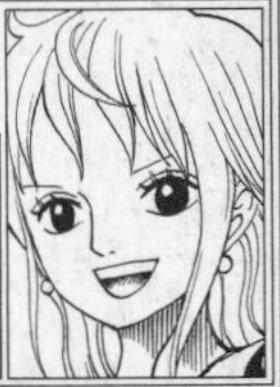

Nico Robin

She spent her time in Baltigo with the leader of the Revolutionary Army: Luffy's father, Dragon.

Archeologist, Bounty: 80 million berries

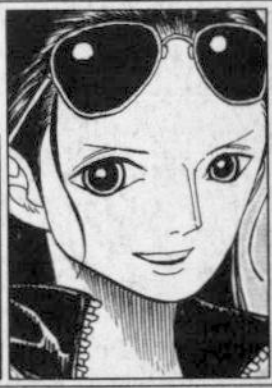

Usopp

He trained under Heracles at the Bowin Islands to become the King of Snipers.

Sniper, Bounty: 30 million berries

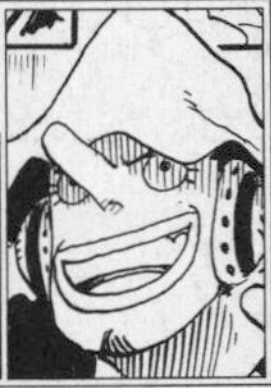

Franky

He modified himself in Future Land Baldimore and turned himself into Armored Franky before reuniting with the rest of the crew.

Shipwright, Bounty: 44 million berries

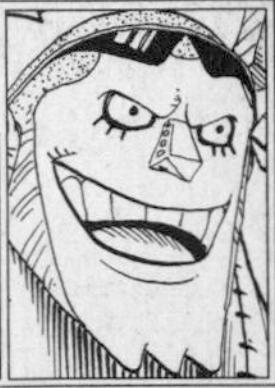

Sanji

After fighting the New Kama Karate masters in the Kamabakka Kingdom, he returns to the crew.

Cook, Bounty: 77 million berries

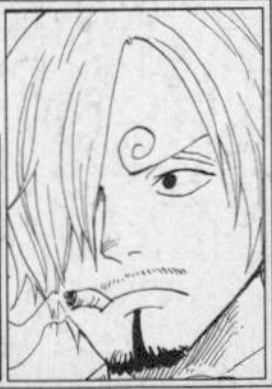

Brook

After being captured and used as a freak show by the Longarm Tribe, he became a famous rock star called "Soul King" Brook.

Musician, Bounty: 33 million berries

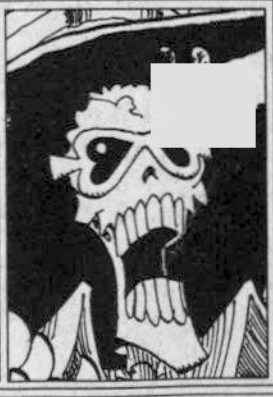

The story of ONE PIECE 1»62

Shanks

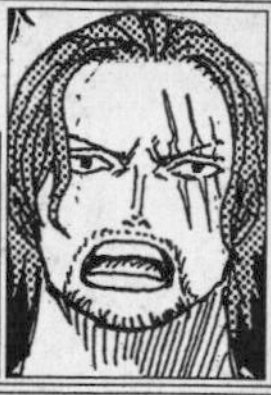

One of the Four Emperors. He continues to wait for Luffy in the second half of the Grand Line, called the New World.

Captain of the Red-Haired Pirates

Jimbei

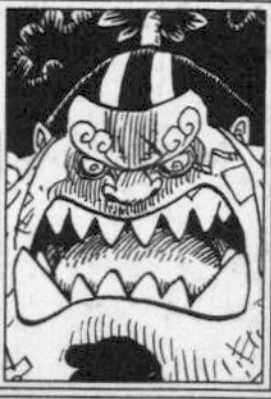

He left Luffy before he started his training and returned to Fish-Man Island.

Former Warlord of the Sea

Blood Splatter Coribou

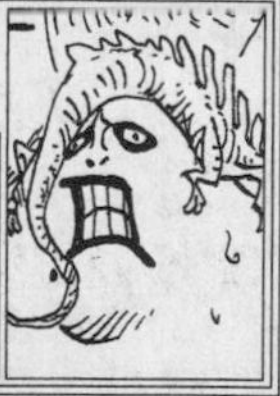

He is currently chasing after the Straw Hats and on the way to Fish-Man Island with his brother Caribou.

Co-captain of the Caribou Pirates (little brother)

Wet-Haired Caribou

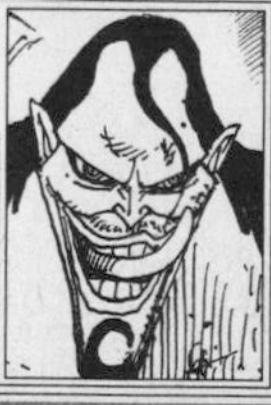

He joined the fake Straw Hats at one point. After escaping the Navy, he chases after Luffy and his crew.

Captain of the Caribou Pirates

Story

When he lost his brother Ace in the Paramount War, Luffy learned just how weak he really was. But Luffy also reconfirmed how important his friends were for him to move forward. Rayleigh visits Luffy and suggests that he train. Agreeing, Luffy sends a message to the rest of his crew to meet again in two years.

After two years, the Straw Hat Pirates meet up once again in the Sabaody Archipelago. They set sail for the New World with a renewed resolve! Though the fake Straw Hats interfere, Luffy's crew strikes them down easily. They are on their way to the underwater Fish-Man Island, but...

Vol. 62
Adventure on Fish-Man Island

CONTENTS

Chapter 604: To the Deep Sea   8

Chapter 605: The Kraken and the Pirates   29

Chapter 606: Deep Sea Adventure   49

Chapter 607: 30,000 Feet Under the Sea   67

Chapter 608: Underwater Paradise   85

Chapter 609: Adventure on Fish-Man Island   102

Chapter 610: Madam Sharley, Fortune-Teller   123

Chapter 611: Hody Jones   139

Chapter 612: Taken by the Shark They Saved   156

Chapter 613: Mermaid Princess of Shell Tower   177

Chapter 614: Too Late Now   195

ONE PIECE

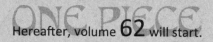

Hereafter, volume 62 will start.

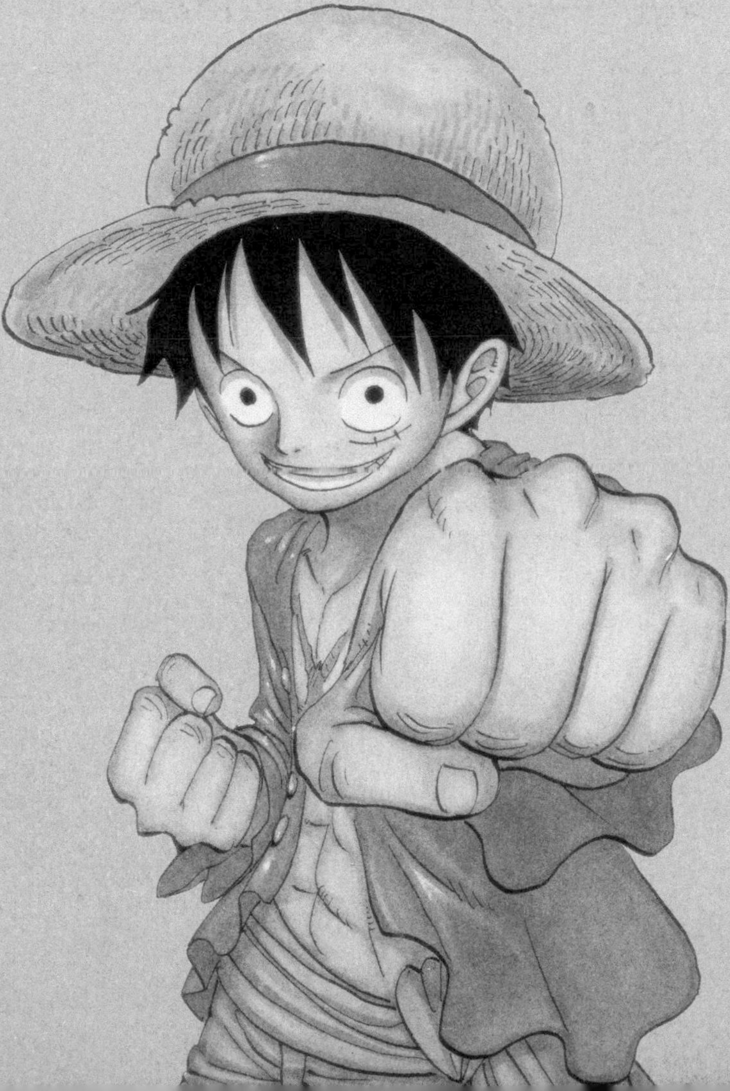

TO THE DEEP SEA

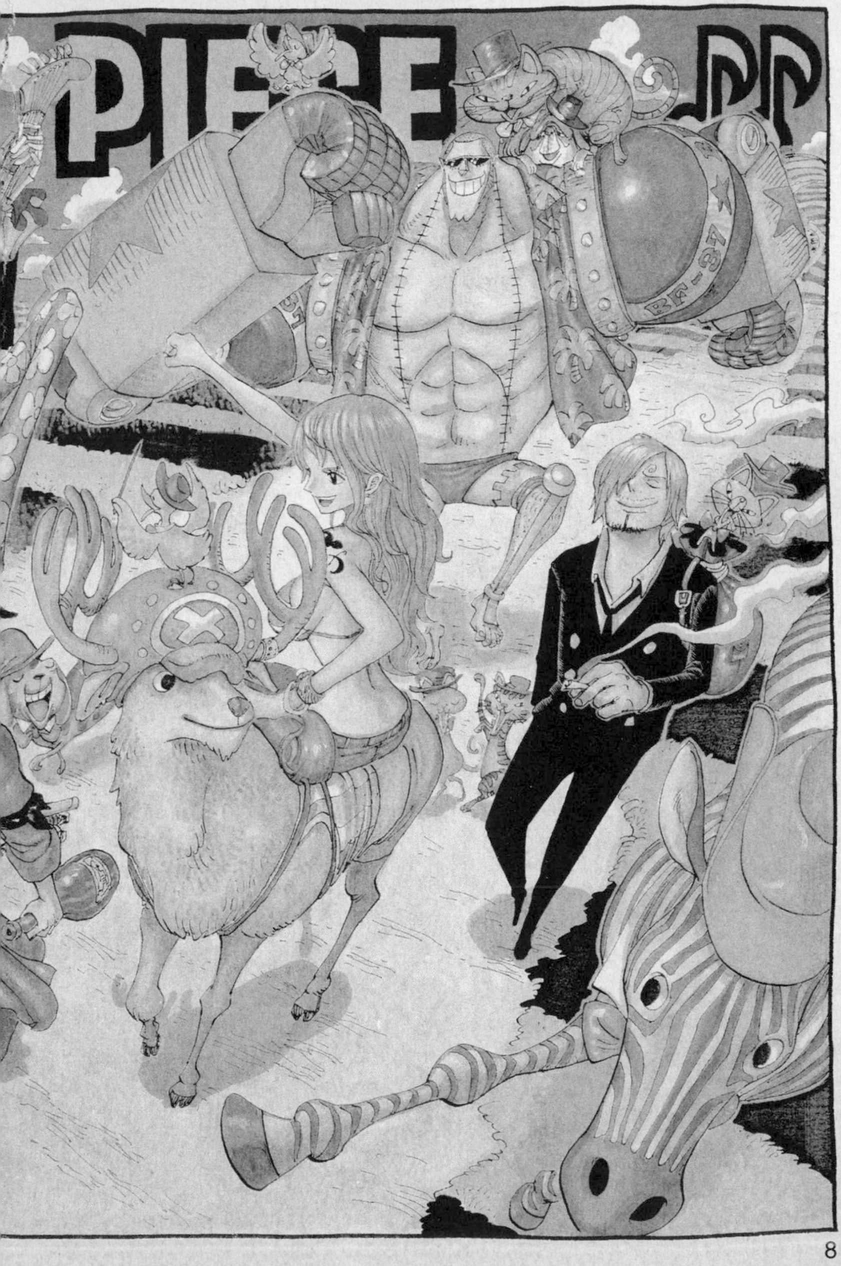

Chapter 604:

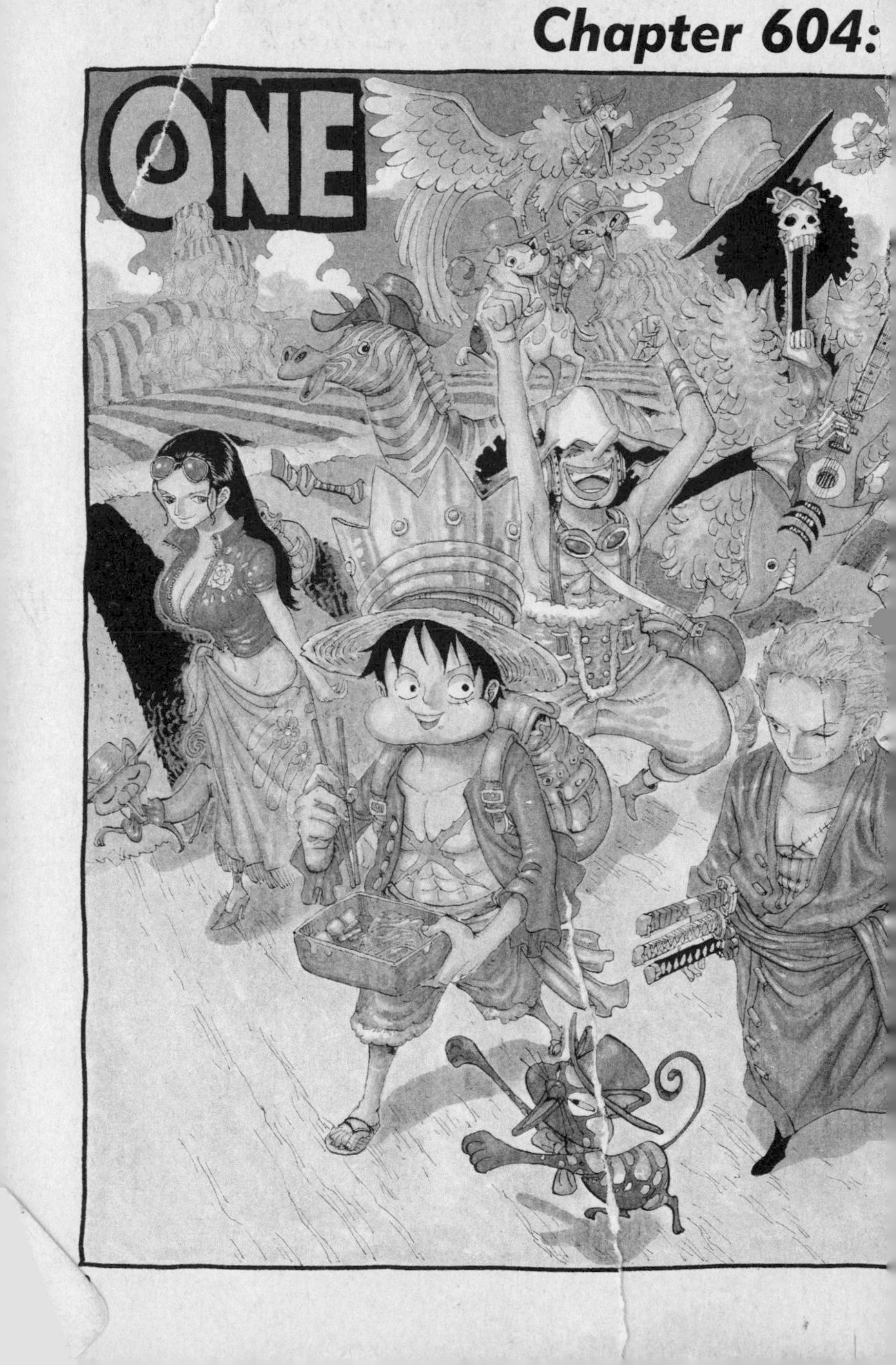
ONE

vol.62
ONE PIECE

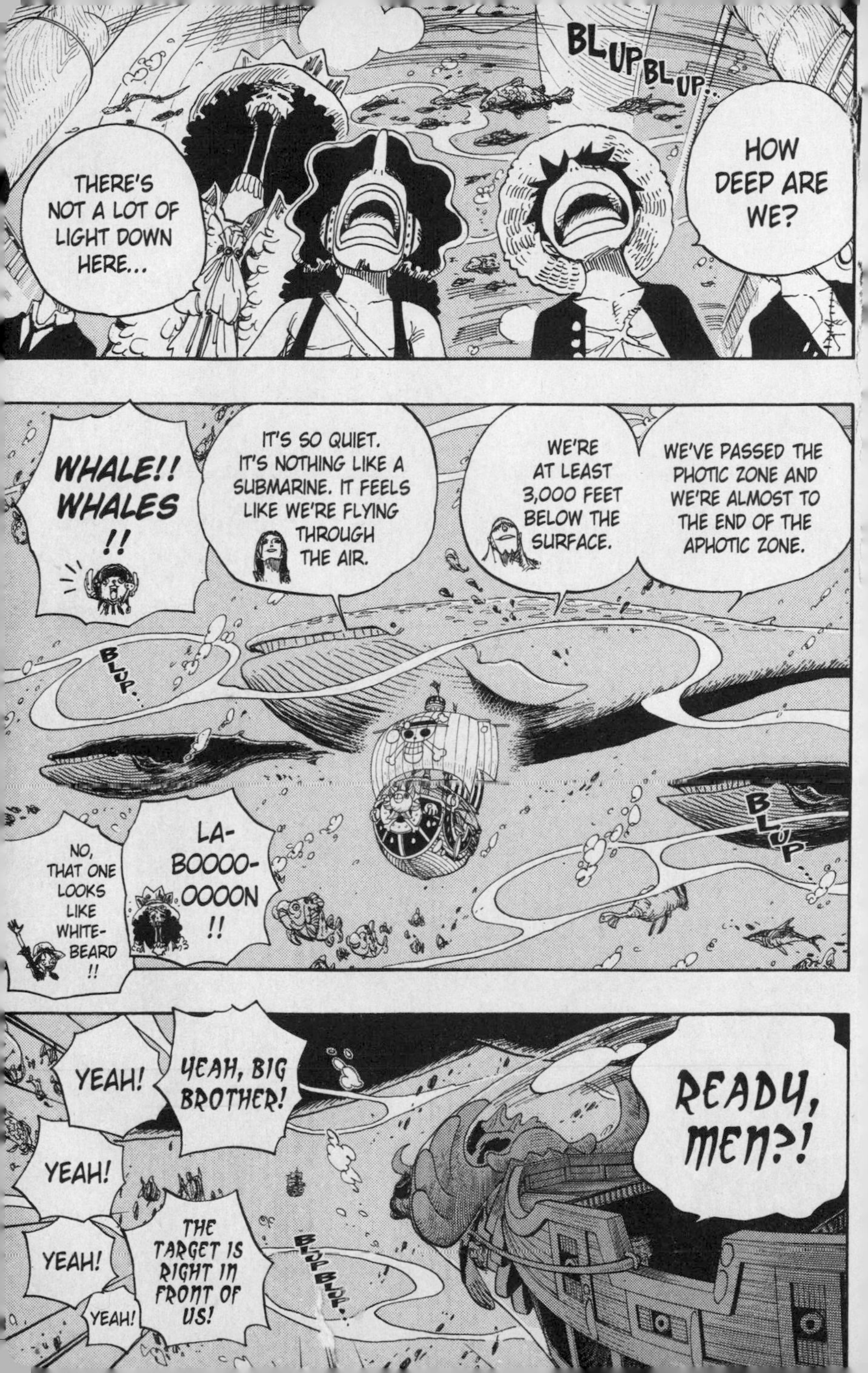
BLUP BLUP...
HOW DEEP ARE WE?
THERE'S NOT A LOT OF LIGHT DOWN HERE...
WE'VE PASSED THE PHOTIC ZONE AND WE'RE ALMOST TO THE END OF THE APHOTIC ZONE.
WE'RE AT LEAST 3,000 FEET BELOW THE SURFACE.
IT'S SO QUIET. IT'S NOTHING LIKE A SUBMARINE. IT FEELS LIKE WE'RE FLYING THROUGH THE AIR.
WHALE!! WHALES!!
BLUP...
BLUP...
LA-BOOOO-OOOON!!
NO, THAT ONE LOOKS LIKE WHITE-BEARD!!
READY, MEN?!
YEAH, BIG BROTHER!
YEAH!
YEAH!
THE TARGET IS RIGHT IN FRONT OF US!
YEAH!
YEAH!
BLUP BLUP...

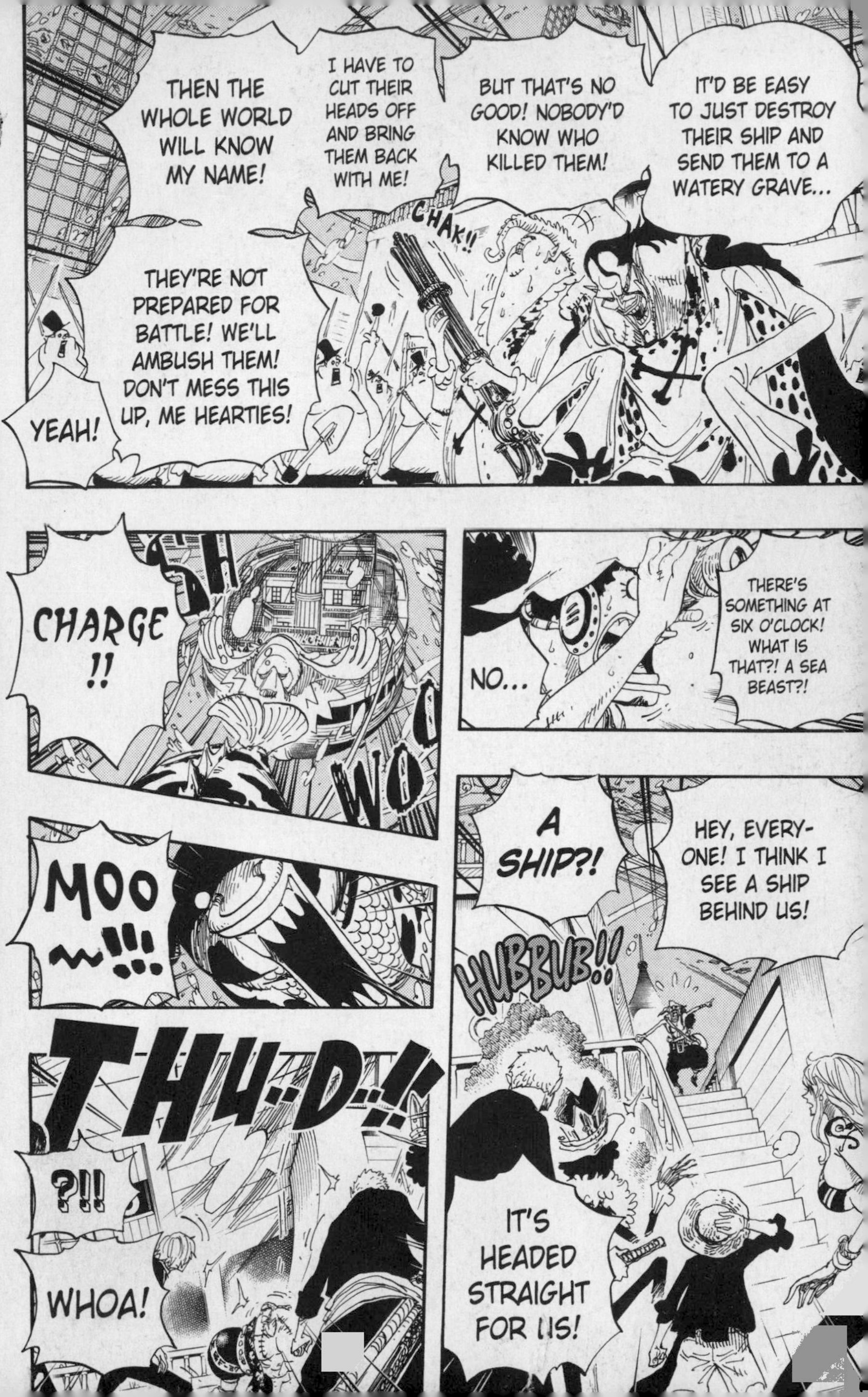
IT'D BE EASY TO JUST DESTROY THEIR SHIP AND SEND THEM TO A WATERY GRAVE...
BUT THAT'S NO GOOD! NOBODY'D KNOW WHO KILLED THEM!
CHAK!!
I HAVE TO CUT THEIR HEADS OFF AND BRING THEM BACK WITH ME!
THEN THE WHOLE WORLD WILL KNOW MY NAME!
THEY'RE NOT PREPARED FOR BATTLE! WE'LL AMBUSH THEM! DON'T MESS THIS UP, ME HEARTIES!
YEAH!
THERE'S SOMETHING AT SIX O'CLOCK! WHAT IS THAT?! A SEA BEAST?!
NO...
HEY, EVERY-ONE! I THINK I SEE A SHIP BEHIND US!
A SHIP?!
HUBBUB!!
IT'S HEADED STRAIGHT FOR US!
CHARGE!!
WO
MOO~!!!
THUD!!
?!!
WHOA!

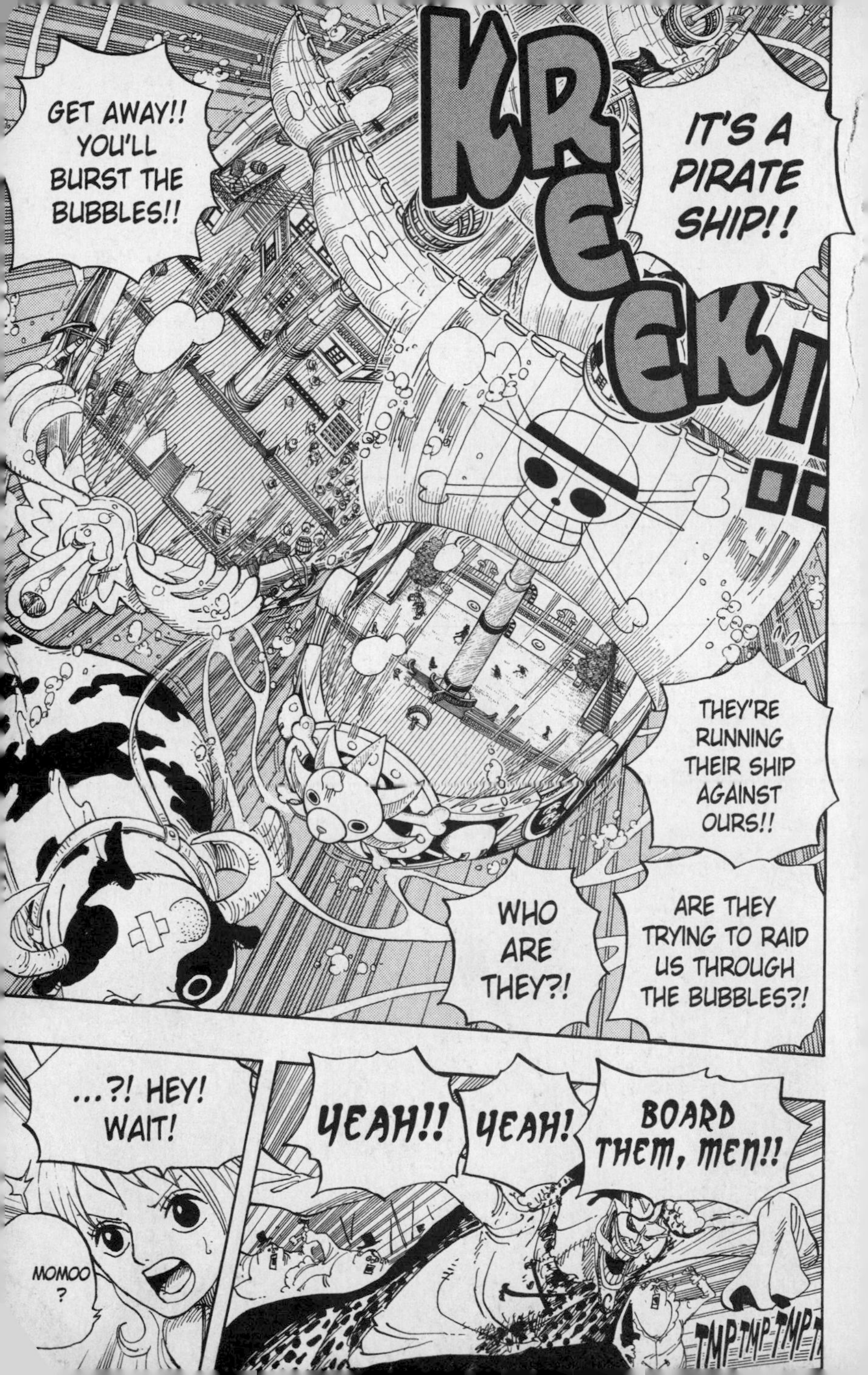
KREEK!!
IT'S A PIRATE SHIP!!
GET AWAY!! YOU'LL BURST THE BUBBLES!!
THEY'RE RUNNING THEIR SHIP AGAINST OURS!!
ARE THEY TRYING TO RAID US THROUGH THE BUBBLES?!
WHO ARE THEY?!
BOARD THEM, MEN!!
YEAH!
YEAH!!
TMP TMP TMP
...?! HEY! WAIT!
MOMOO ?

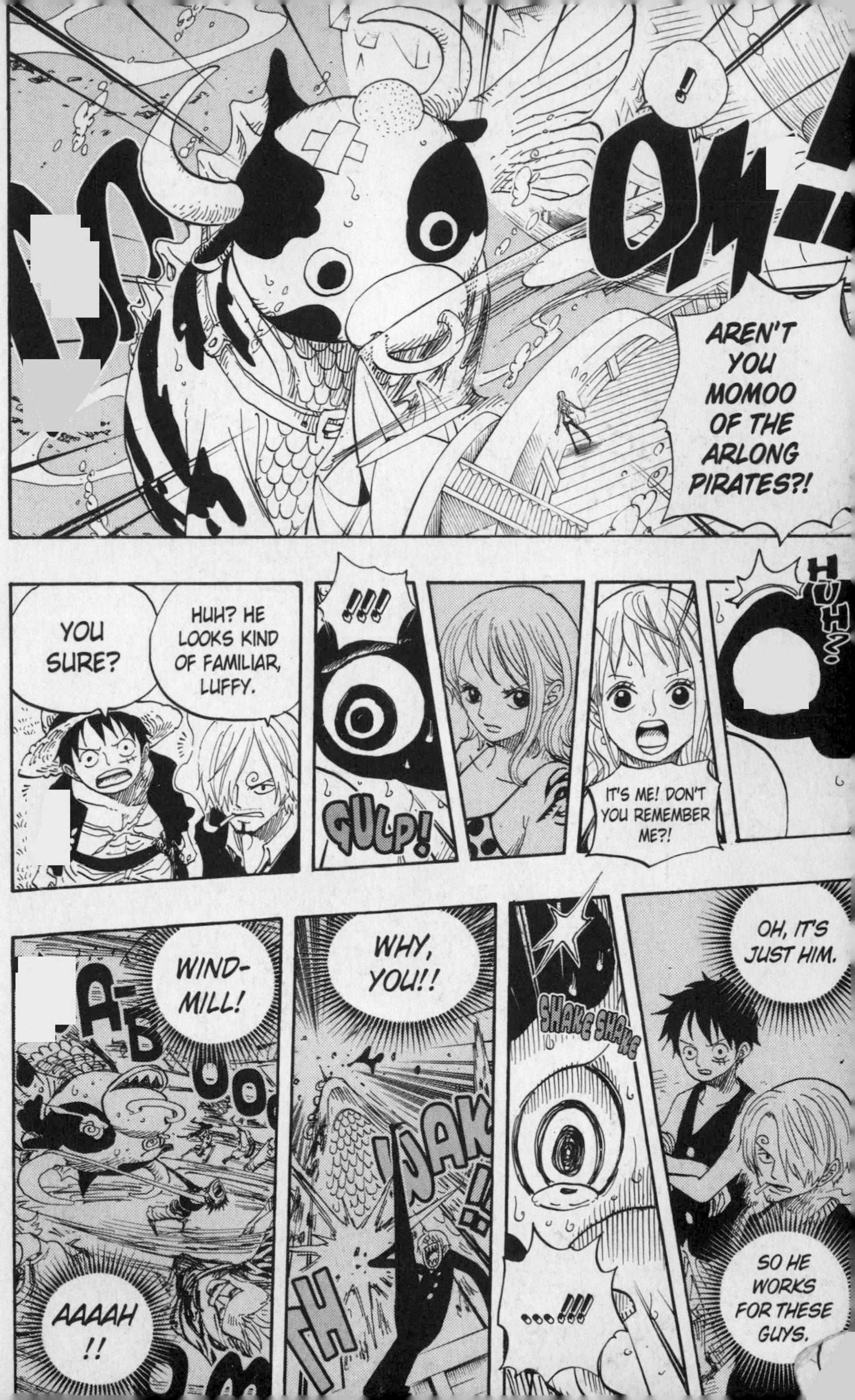
!
ARE'N'T YOU MOMOO OF THE ARLONG PIRATES?!
HUH?
IT'S ME! DON'T YOU REMEMBER ME?!
!!!
GULP!
HUH? HE LOOKS KIND OF FAMILIAR, LUFFY.
YOU SURE?
OH, IT'S JUST HIM.
SO HE WORKS FOR THESE GUYS.
SHAKE SHAKE
...!!!
WHY, YOU!!
WIND-MILL!
AAAAH!!

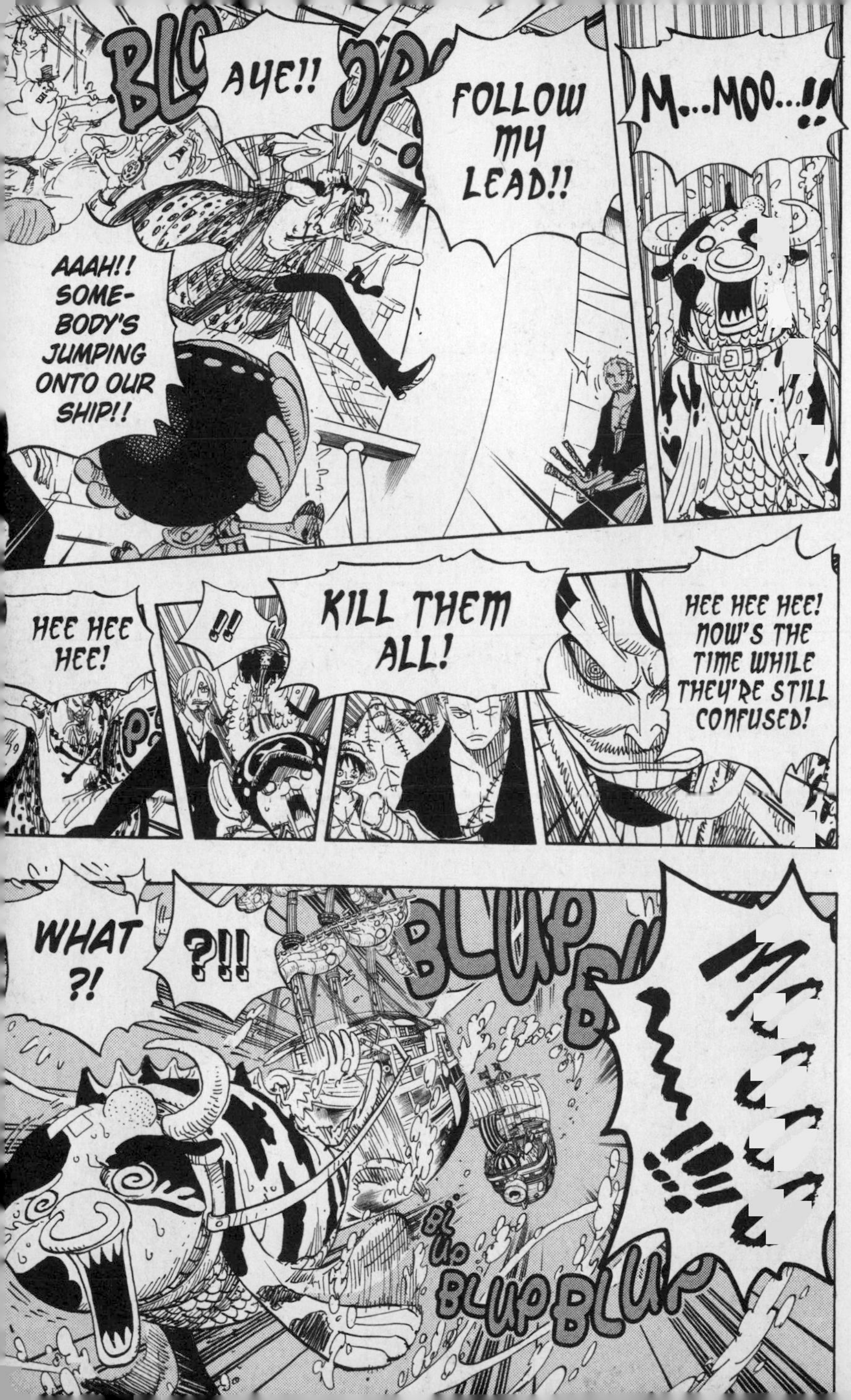
M...MOO...!!
FOLLOW MY LEAD!!
AYE!!
BLO
OP
AAAH!! SOMEBODY'S JUMPING ONTO OUR SHIP!!
HEE HEE HEE! NOW'S THE TIME WHILE THEY'RE STILL CONFUSED!
KILL THEM ALL!
!!
HEE HEE HEE!
?!!
WHAT?!
BLUP
BLUP
BLUP BLUP

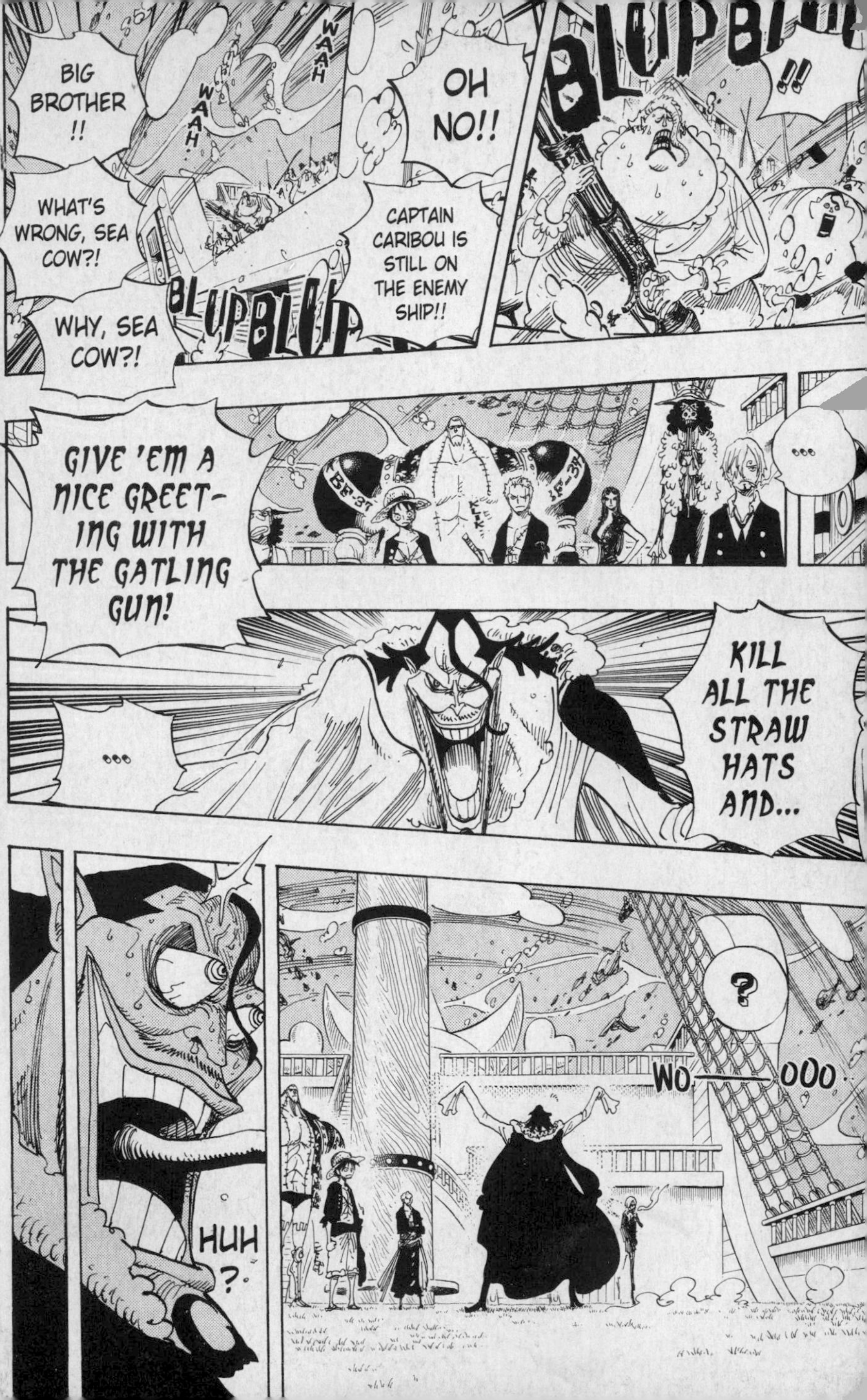
BLUPBLUP
!!
OH NO!!
CAPTAIN CARIBOU IS STILL ON THE ENEMY SHIP!!
BIG BROTHER !!
WAAH
WAAH
WHAT'S WRONG, SEA COW?!
WHY, SEA COW?!
BLUPBLUP
...
GIVE 'EM A NICE GREETING WITH THE GATLING GUN!
KLIK
KILL ALL THE STRAW HATS AND...
...
?
WO——OOO
HUH ?

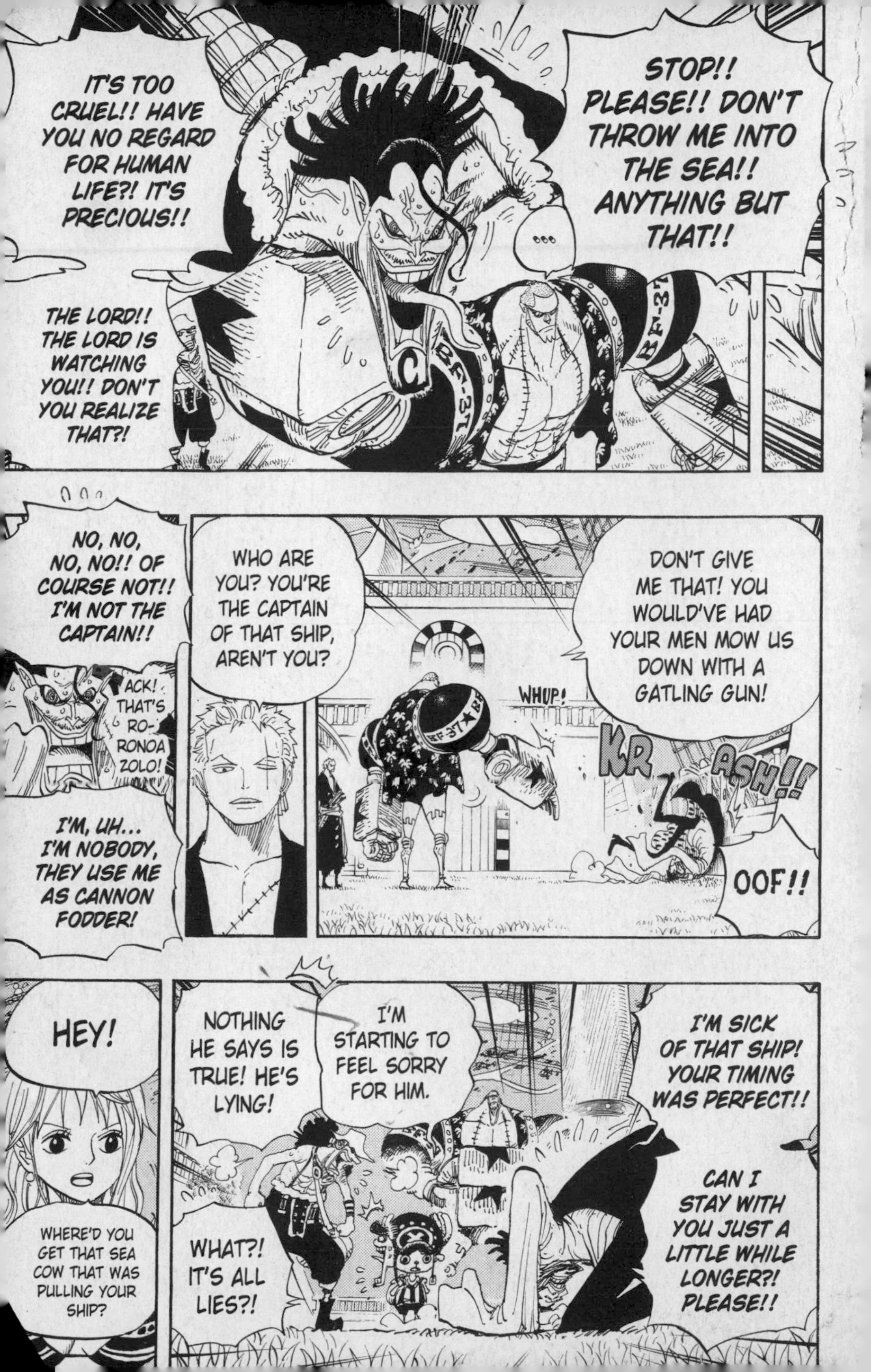
STOP!! PLEASE!! DON'T THROW ME INTO THE SEA!! ANYTHING BUT THAT!!
...
IT'S TOO CRUEL!! HAVE YOU NO REGARD FOR HUMAN LIFE?! IT'S PRECIOUS!!
THE LORD!! THE LORD IS WATCHING YOU!! DON'T YOU REALIZE THAT?!
DON'T GIVE ME THAT! YOU WOULD'VE HAD YOUR MEN MOW US DOWN WITH A GATLING GUN!
WHUP!
KRASH!!
OOF!!
WHO ARE YOU? YOU'RE THE CAPTAIN OF THAT SHIP, AREN'T YOU?
NO, NO, NO, NO!! OF COURSE NOT!! I'M NOT THE CAPTAIN!!
ACK! THAT'S RO-RONOA ZOLO!
I'M, UH... I'M NOBODY, THEY USE ME AS CANNON FODDER!
I'M SICK OF THAT SHIP! YOUR TIMING WAS PERFECT!!
CAN I STAY WITH YOU JUST A LITTLE WHILE LONGER?! PLEASE!!
I'M STARTING TO FEEL SORRY FOR HIM.
NOTHING HE SAYS IS TRUE! HE'S LYING!
WHAT?! IT'S ALL LIES?!
HEY!
WHERE'D YOU GET THAT SEA COW THAT WAS PULLING YOUR SHIP?

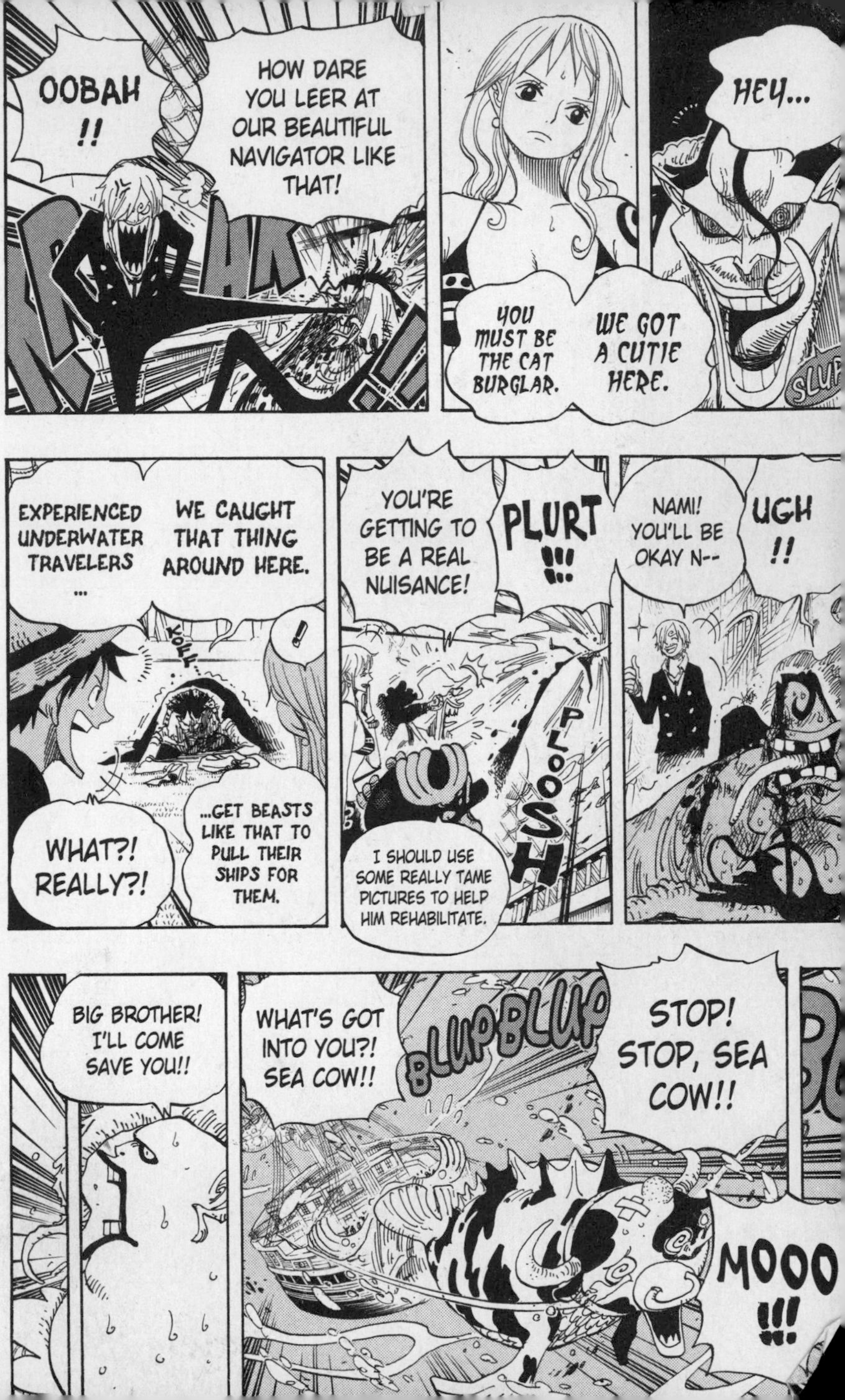
HEY...
WE GOT A CUTIE HERE.
YOU MUST BE THE CAT BURGLAR.
HOW DARE YOU LEER AT OUR BEAUTIFUL NAVIGATOR LIKE THAT!
OOBAH !!
UGH !!
NAMI! YOU'LL BE OKAY N--
PLURT !!!
YOU'RE GETTING TO BE A REAL NUISANCE!
PLOOSH
I SHOULD USE SOME REALLY TAME PICTURES TO HELP HIM REHABILITATE.
WE CAUGHT THAT THING AROUND HERE.
EXPERIENCED UNDERWATER TRAVELERS ...
!
KOFF...
...GET BEASTS LIKE THAT TO PULL THEIR SHIPS FOR THEM.
WHAT?! REALLY?!
STOP! STOP, SEA COW!!
BLUPBLUP
WHAT'S GOT INTO YOU?! SEA COW!!
MOOO !!!
BIG BROTHER! I'LL COME SAVE YOU!!

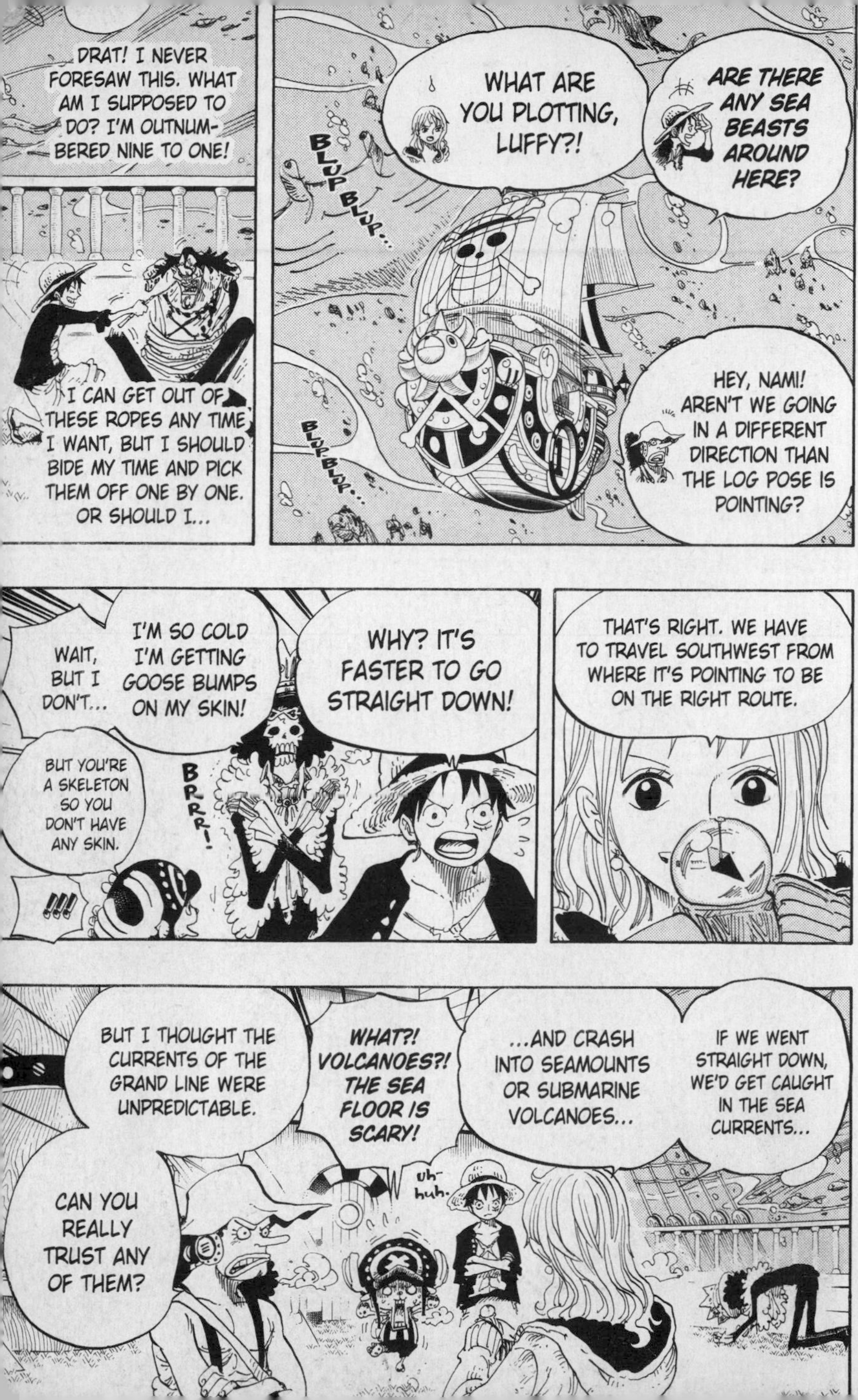
ARE THERE ANY SEA BEASTS AROUND HERE?
WHAT ARE YOU PLOTTING, LUFFY?!
BLUP BLUP BLUP...
HEY, NAMI! AREN'T WE GOING IN A DIFFERENT DIRECTION THAN THE LOG POSE IS POINTING?
BLUP BLUP...
DRAT! I NEVER FORESAW THIS. WHAT AM I SUPPOSED TO DO? I'M OUTNUM-BERED NINE TO ONE!
I CAN GET OUT OF THESE ROPES ANY TIME I WANT, BUT I SHOULD BIDE MY TIME AND PICK THEM OFF ONE BY ONE. OR SHOULD I...
THAT'S RIGHT. WE HAVE TO TRAVEL SOUTHWEST FROM WHERE IT'S POINTING TO BE ON THE RIGHT ROUTE.
WHY? IT'S FASTER TO GO STRAIGHT DOWN!
I'M SO COLD I'M GETTING GOOSE BUMPS ON MY SKIN!
WAIT, BUT I DON'T...
BRRR!
BUT YOU'RE A SKELETON SO YOU DON'T HAVE ANY SKIN.
!!!
IF WE WENT STRAIGHT DOWN, WE'D GET CAUGHT IN THE SEA CURRENTS...
...AND CRASH INTO SEAMOUNTS OR SUBMARINE VOLCANOES...
WHAT?! VOLCANOES?! THE SEA FLOOR IS SCARY!
BUT I THOUGHT THE CURRENTS OF THE GRAND LINE WERE UNPREDICTABLE.
uh-huh.
CAN YOU REALLY TRUST ANY OF THEM?

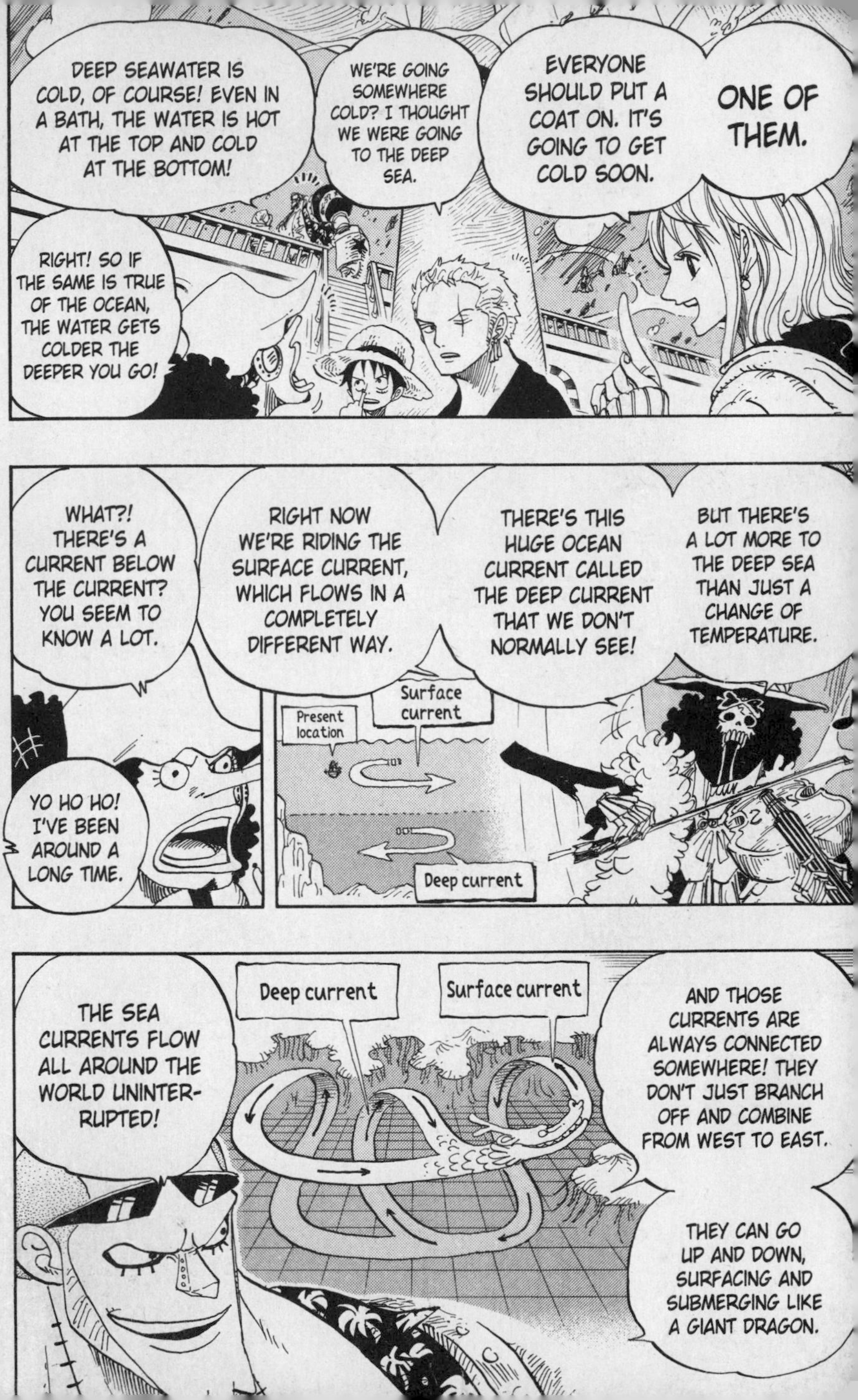
ONE OF THEM.
EVERYONE SHOULD PUT A COAT ON. IT'S GOING TO GET COLD SOON.
WE'RE GOING SOMEWHERE COLD? I THOUGHT WE WERE GOING TO THE DEEP SEA.
DEEP SEAWATER IS COLD, OF COURSE! EVEN IN A BATH, THE WATER IS HOT AT THE TOP AND COLD AT THE BOTTOM!
RIGHT! SO IF THE SAME IS TRUE OF THE OCEAN, THE WATER GETS COLDER THE DEEPER YOU GO!
BUT THERE'S A LOT MORE TO THE DEEP SEA THAN JUST A CHANGE OF TEMPERATURE.
THERE'S THIS HUGE OCEAN CURRENT CALLED THE DEEP CURRENT THAT WE DON'T NORMALLY SEE!
RIGHT NOW WE'RE RIDING THE SURFACE CURRENT, WHICH FLOWS IN A COMPLETELY DIFFERENT WAY.
Surface current
Present location
Deep current
WHAT?! THERE'S A CURRENT BELOW THE CURRENT? YOU SEEM TO KNOW A LOT.
YO HO HO! I'VE BEEN AROUND A LONG TIME.
AND THOSE CURRENTS ARE ALWAYS CONNECTED SOMEWHERE! THEY DON'T JUST BRANCH OFF AND COMBINE FROM WEST TO EAST.
Surface current
Deep current
THE SEA CURRENTS FLOW ALL AROUND THE WORLD UNINTER-RUPTED!
THEY CAN GO UP AND DOWN, SURFACING AND SUBMERGING LIKE A GIANT DRAGON.

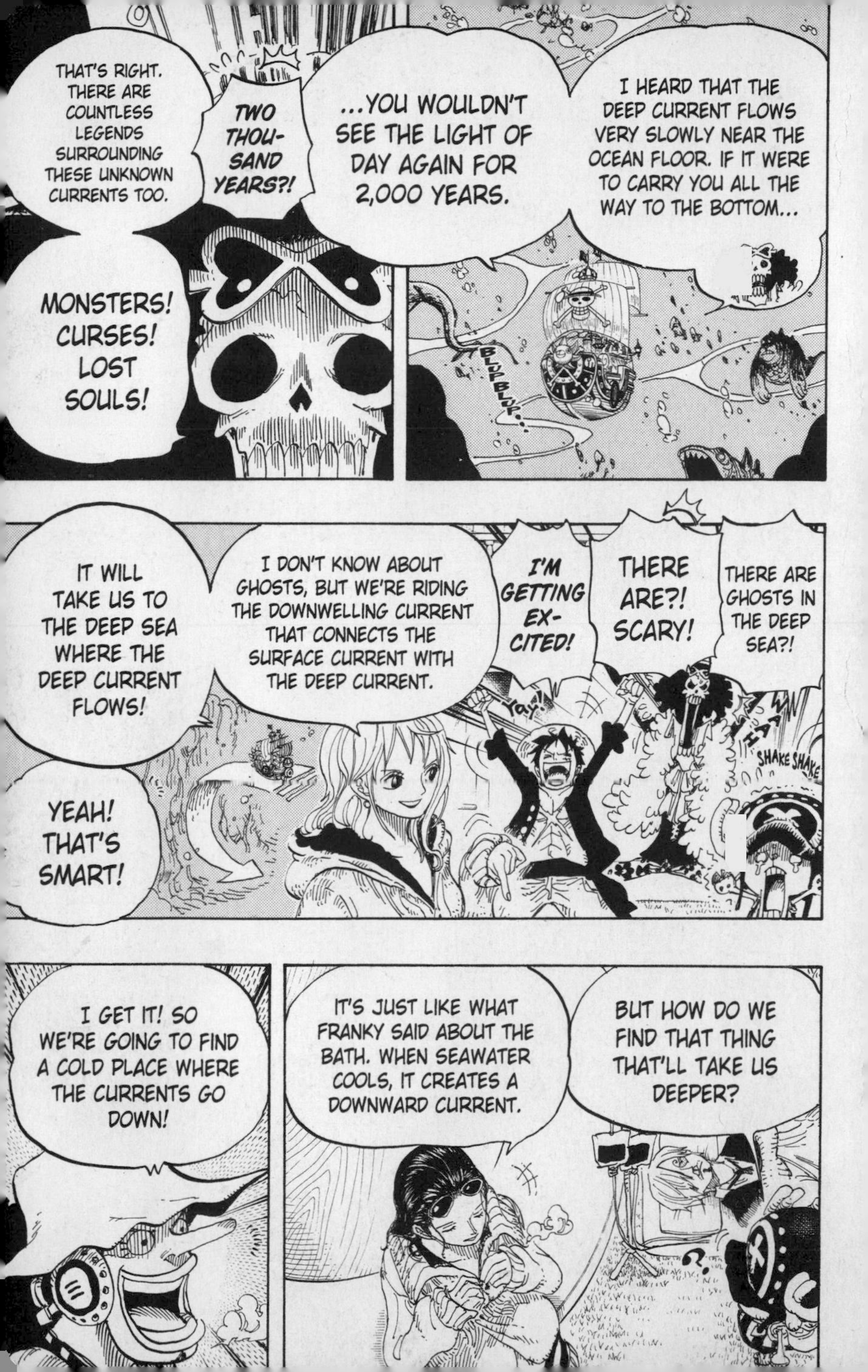
I HEARD THAT THE DEEP CURRENT FLOWS VERY SLOWLY NEAR THE OCEAN FLOOR. IF IT WERE TO CARRY YOU ALL THE WAY TO THE BOTTOM...
...YOU WOULDN'T SEE THE LIGHT OF DAY AGAIN FOR 2,000 YEARS.
BLUP BLUP...
TWO THOU-SAND YEARS?!
THAT'S RIGHT. THERE ARE COUNTLESS LEGENDS SURROUNDING THESE UNKNOWN CURRENTS TOO.
MONSTERS! CURSES! LOST SOULS!
THERE ARE GHOSTS IN THE DEEP SEA?!
SHAKE SHAKE
THERE ARE?! SCARY!
I'M GETTING EX-CITED!
YAY!!
I DON'T KNOW ABOUT GHOSTS, BUT WE'RE RIDING THE DOWNWELLING CURRENT THAT CONNECTS THE SURFACE CURRENT WITH THE DEEP CURRENT.
IT WILL TAKE US TO THE DEEP SEA WHERE THE DEEP CURRENT FLOWS!
YEAH! THAT'S SMART!
BUT HOW DO WE FIND THAT THING THAT'LL TAKE US DEEPER?
IT'S JUST LIKE WHAT FRANKY SAID ABOUT THE BATH. WHEN SEAWATER COOLS, IT CREATES A DOWNWARD CURRENT.
I GET IT! SO WE'RE GOING TO FIND A COLD PLACE WHERE THE CURRENTS GO DOWN!

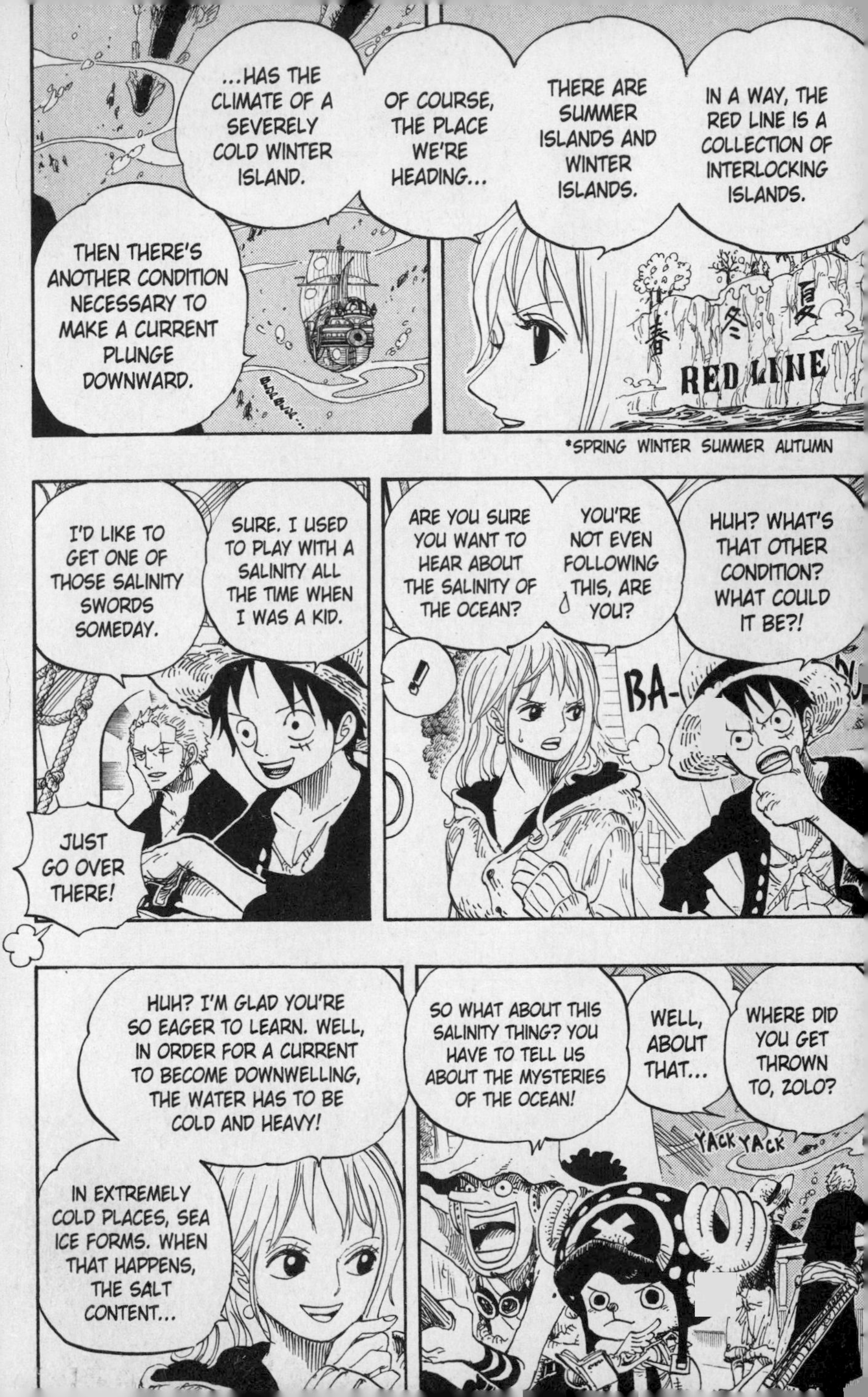
IN A WAY, THE RED LINE IS A COLLECTION OF INTERLOCKING ISLANDS.
THERE ARE SUMMER ISLANDS AND WINTER ISLANDS.
春 冬 夏
RED LINE
*SPRING WINTER SUMMER AUTUMN
OF COURSE, THE PLACE WE'RE HEADING...
...HAS THE CLIMATE OF A SEVERELY COLD WINTER ISLAND.
THEN THERE'S ANOTHER CONDITION NECESSARY TO MAKE A CURRENT PLUNGE DOWNWARD.
HUH? WHAT'S THAT OTHER CONDITION? WHAT COULD IT BE?!
BA-
YOU'RE NOT EVEN FOLLOWING THIS, ARE YOU?
ARE YOU SURE YOU WANT TO HEAR ABOUT THE SALINITY OF THE OCEAN?
!
SURE. I USED TO PLAY WITH A SALINITY ALL THE TIME WHEN I WAS A KID.
I'D LIKE TO GET ONE OF THOSE SALINITY SWORDS SOMEDAY.
JUST GO OVER THERE!
WHERE DID YOU GET THROWN TO, ZOLO?
WELL, ABOUT THAT...
YACK YACK
SO WHAT ABOUT THIS SALINITY THING? YOU HAVE TO TELL US ABOUT THE MYSTERIES OF THE OCEAN!
HUH? I'M GLAD YOU'RE SO EAGER TO LEARN. WELL, IN ORDER FOR A CURRENT TO BECOME DOWNWELLING, THE WATER HAS TO BE COLD AND HEAVY!
IN EXTREMELY COLD PLACES, SEA ICE FORMS. WHEN THAT HAPPENS, THE SALT CONTENT...

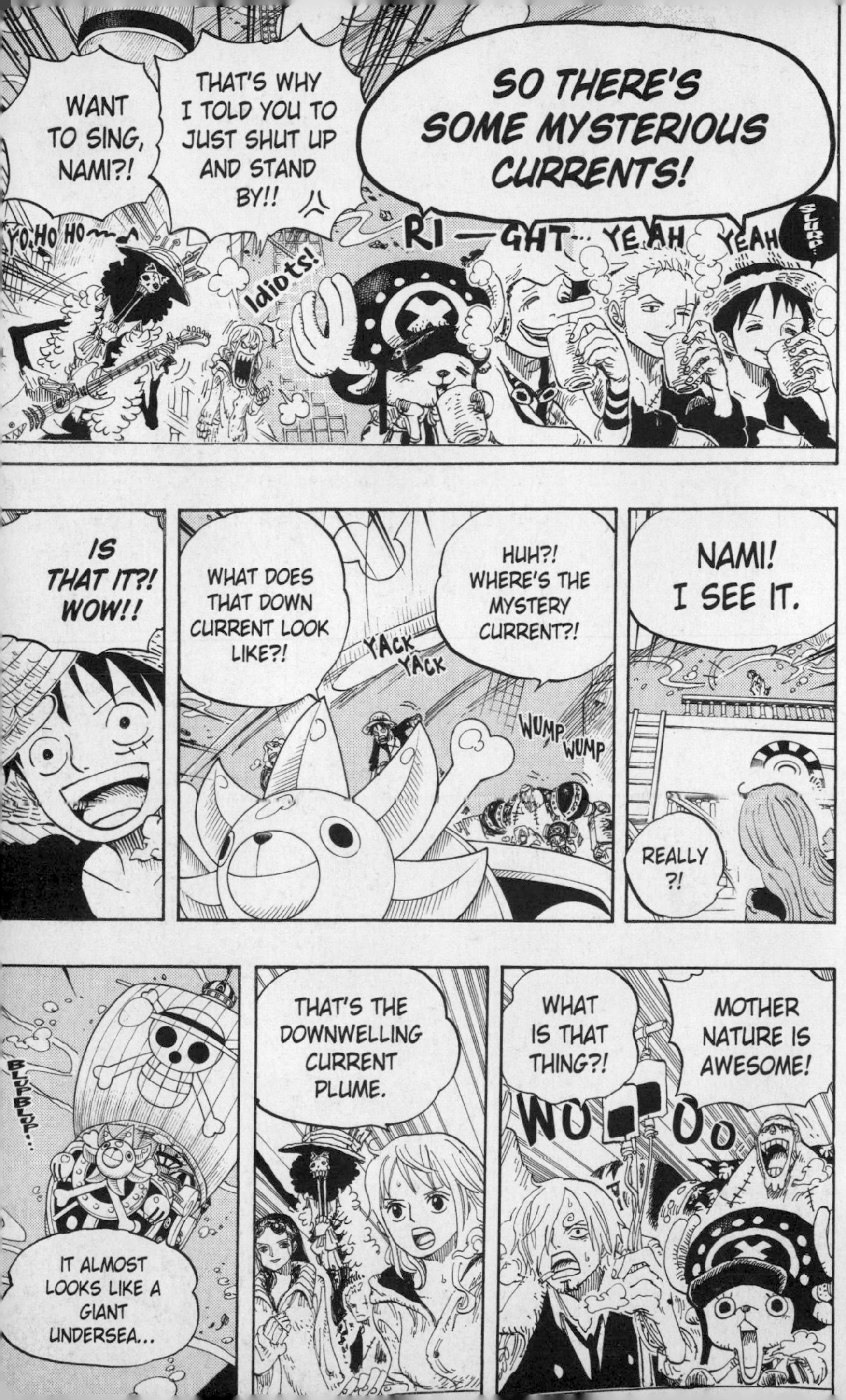
SO THERE'S SOME MYSTERIOUS CURRENTS!
SLURP...
YEAH
YE AH
RI—GHT...
THAT'S WHY I TOLD YOU TO JUST SHUT UP AND STAND BY!!
Idiots!
WANT TO SING, NAMI?!
YO HO HO~
NAMI! I SEE IT.
REALLY ?!
HUH?! WHERE'S THE MYSTERY CURRENT?!
WUMP WUMP
WHAT DOES THAT DOWN CURRENT LOOK LIKE?!
YACK YACK
IS THAT IT?! WOW!!
MOTHER NATURE IS AWESOME!
WHAT IS THAT THING?!
THAT'S THE DOWNWELLING CURRENT PLUME.
BLUPBLUP...
IT ALMOST LOOKS LIKE A GIANT UNDERSEA...

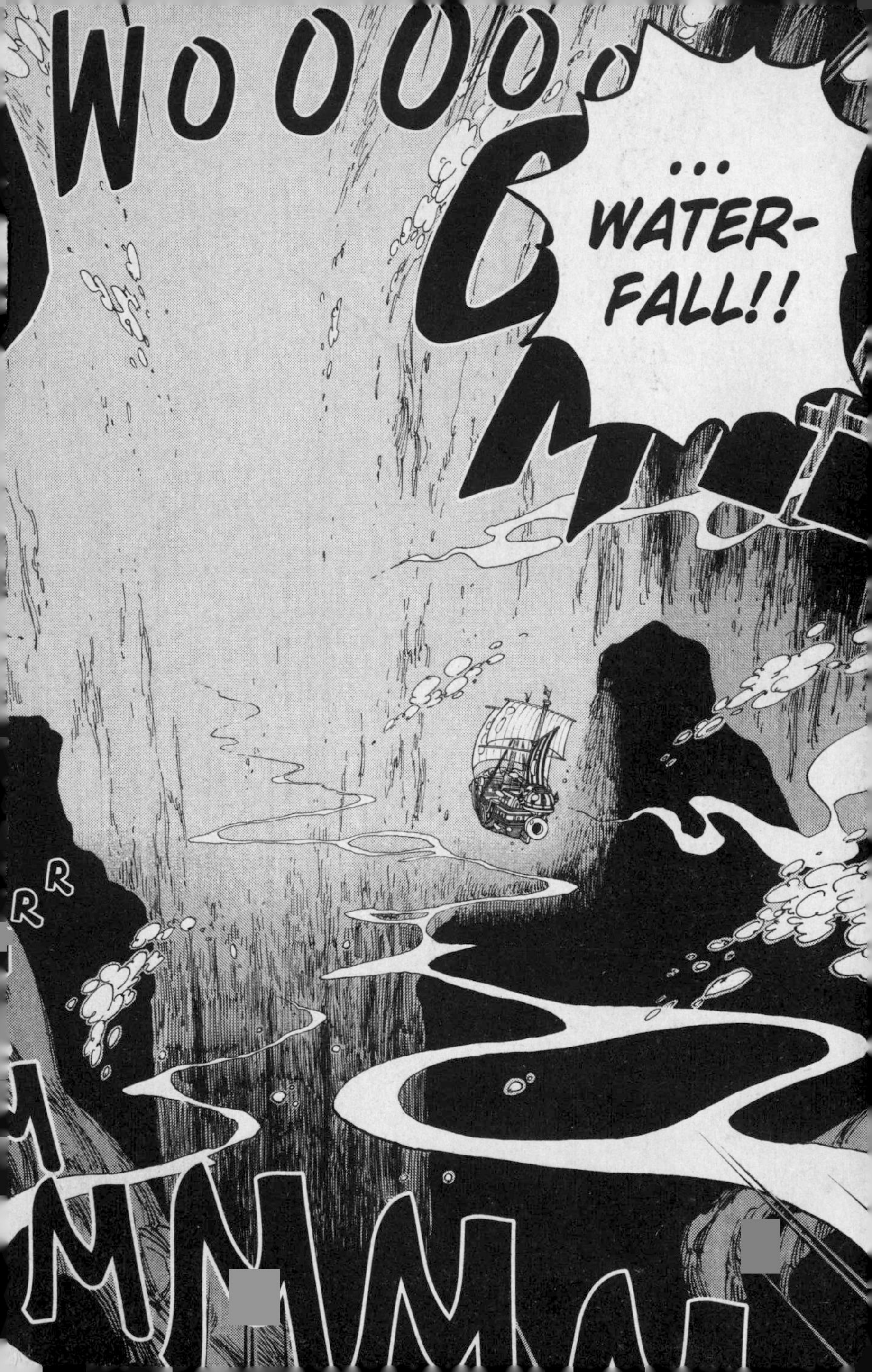
WOOOO
... WATER-FALL!!
RR

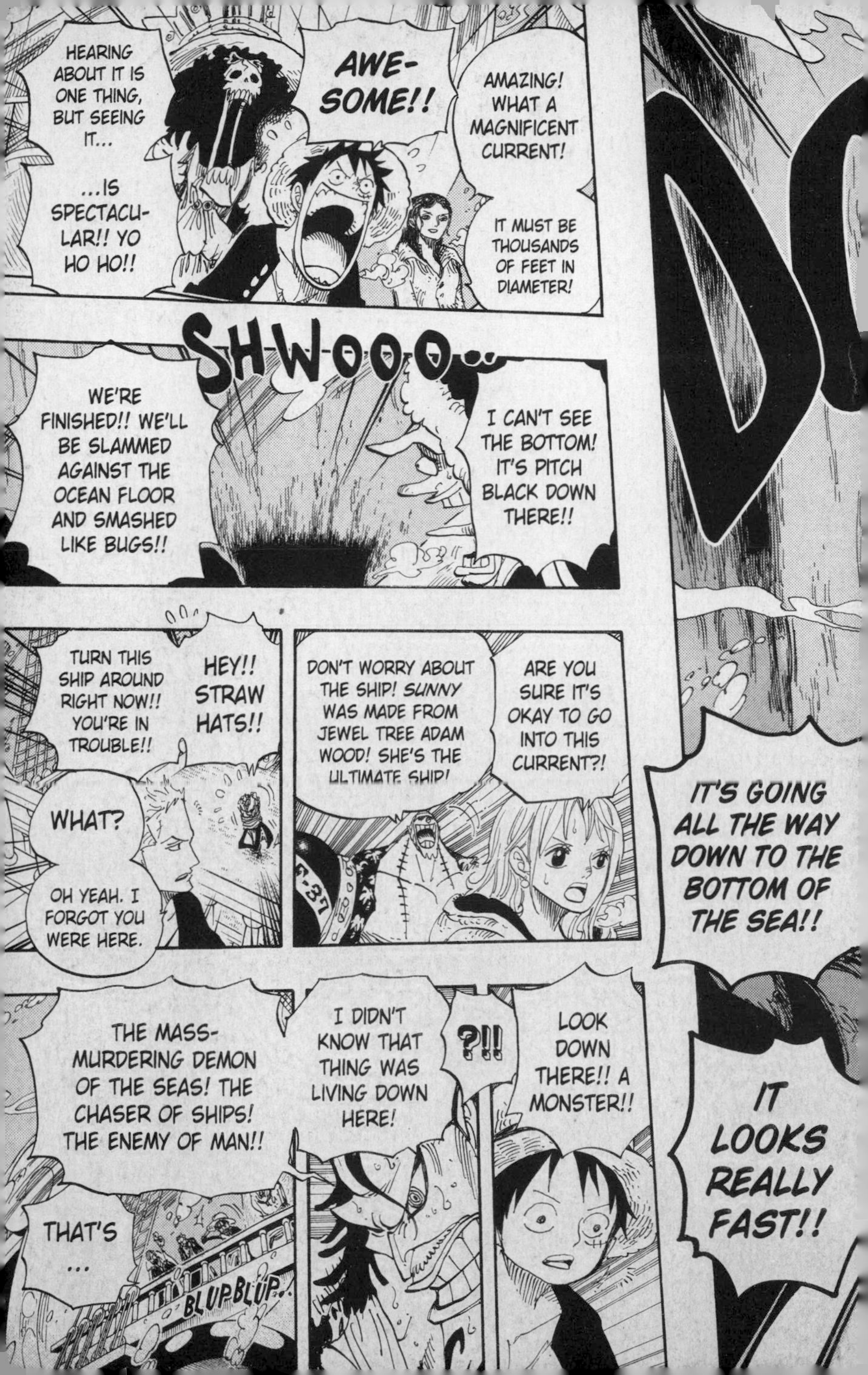
IT'S GOING ALL THE WAY DOWN TO THE BOTTOM OF THE SEA!!
IT LOOKS REALLY FAST!!
AMAZING! WHAT A MAGNIFICENT CURRENT!
IT MUST BE THOUSANDS OF FEET IN DIAMETER!
AWE-SOME!!
HEARING ABOUT IT IS ONE THING, BUT SEEING IT...
...IS SPECTACULAR!! YO HO HO!!
SHWOOO...
I CAN'T SEE THE BOTTOM! IT'S PITCH BLACK DOWN THERE!!
WE'RE FINISHED!! WE'LL BE SLAMMED AGAINST THE OCEAN FLOOR AND SMASHED LIKE BUGS!!
ARE YOU SURE IT'S OKAY TO GO INTO THIS CURRENT?!
DON'T WORRY ABOUT THE SHIP! *SUNNY* WAS MADE FROM JEWEL TREE ADAM WOOD! SHE'S THE ULTIMATE SHIP!
HEY!! STRAW HATS!!
TURN THIS SHIP AROUND RIGHT NOW!! YOU'RE IN TROUBLE!!
WHAT?
OH YEAH. I FORGOT YOU WERE HERE.
LOOK DOWN THERE!! A MONSTER!!
?!!
I DIDN'T KNOW THAT THING WAS LIVING DOWN HERE!
THE MASS-MURDERING DEMON OF THE SEAS! THE CHASER OF SHIPS! THE ENEMY OF MAN!!
THAT'S...
BLUP BLUP...

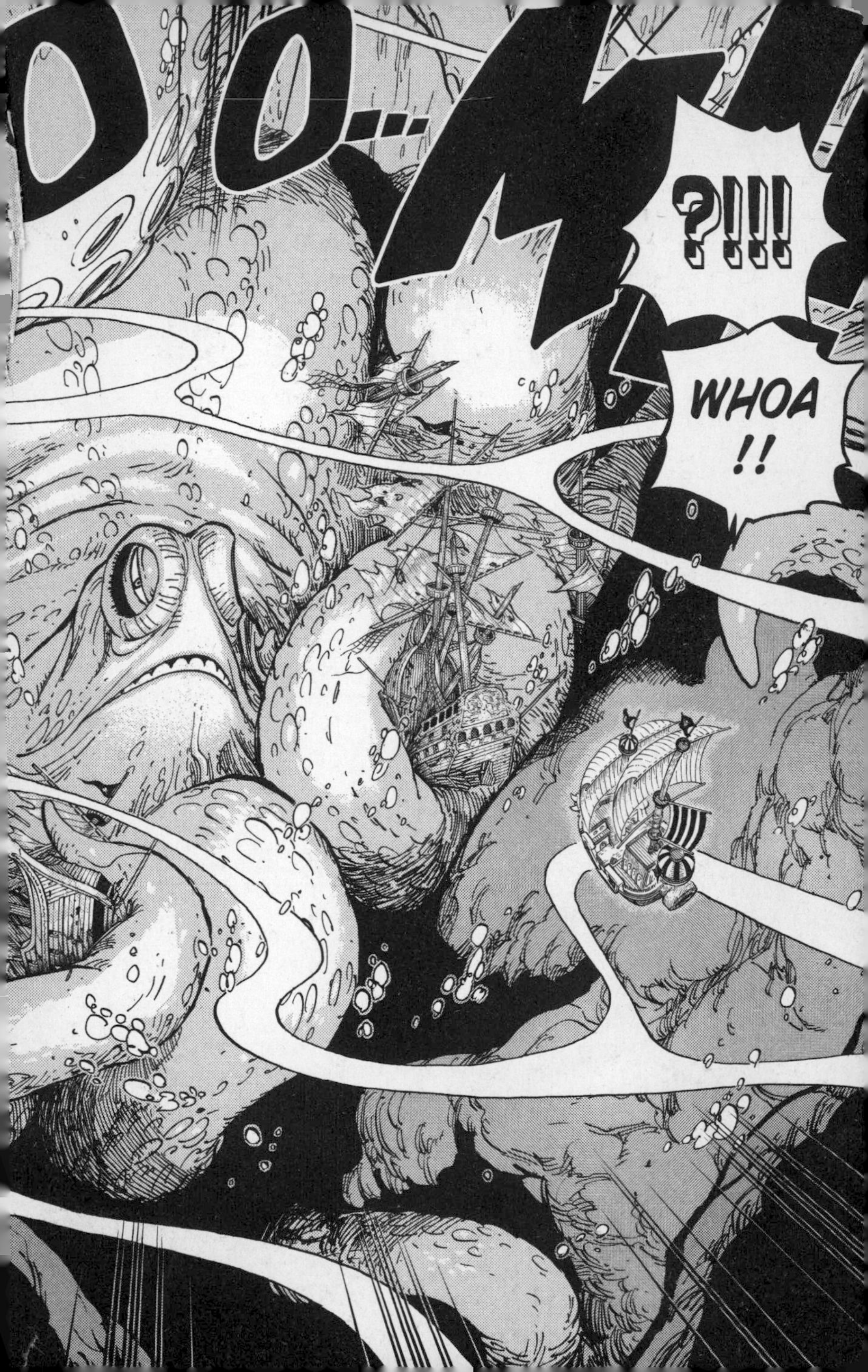
?!!!
WHOA !!

Chapter 605:

THE KRAKEN AND THE PIRATES

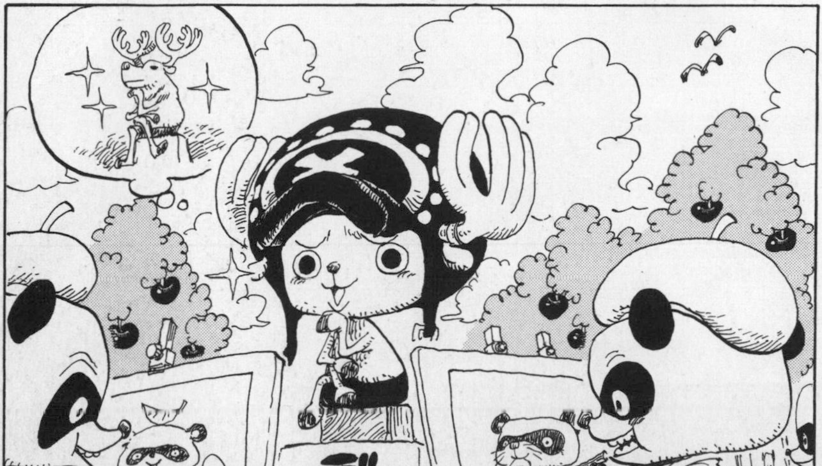

デッサン教室
仲間のデッサン

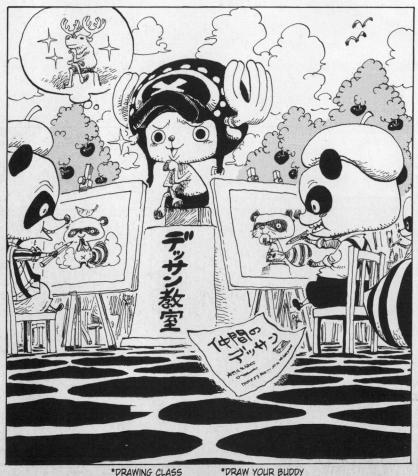

*DRAWING CLASS *DRAW YOUR BUDDY

REQUEST: “CHOPPER BEING SKETCHED BY RACCOON DOGS” BY MOSSARI

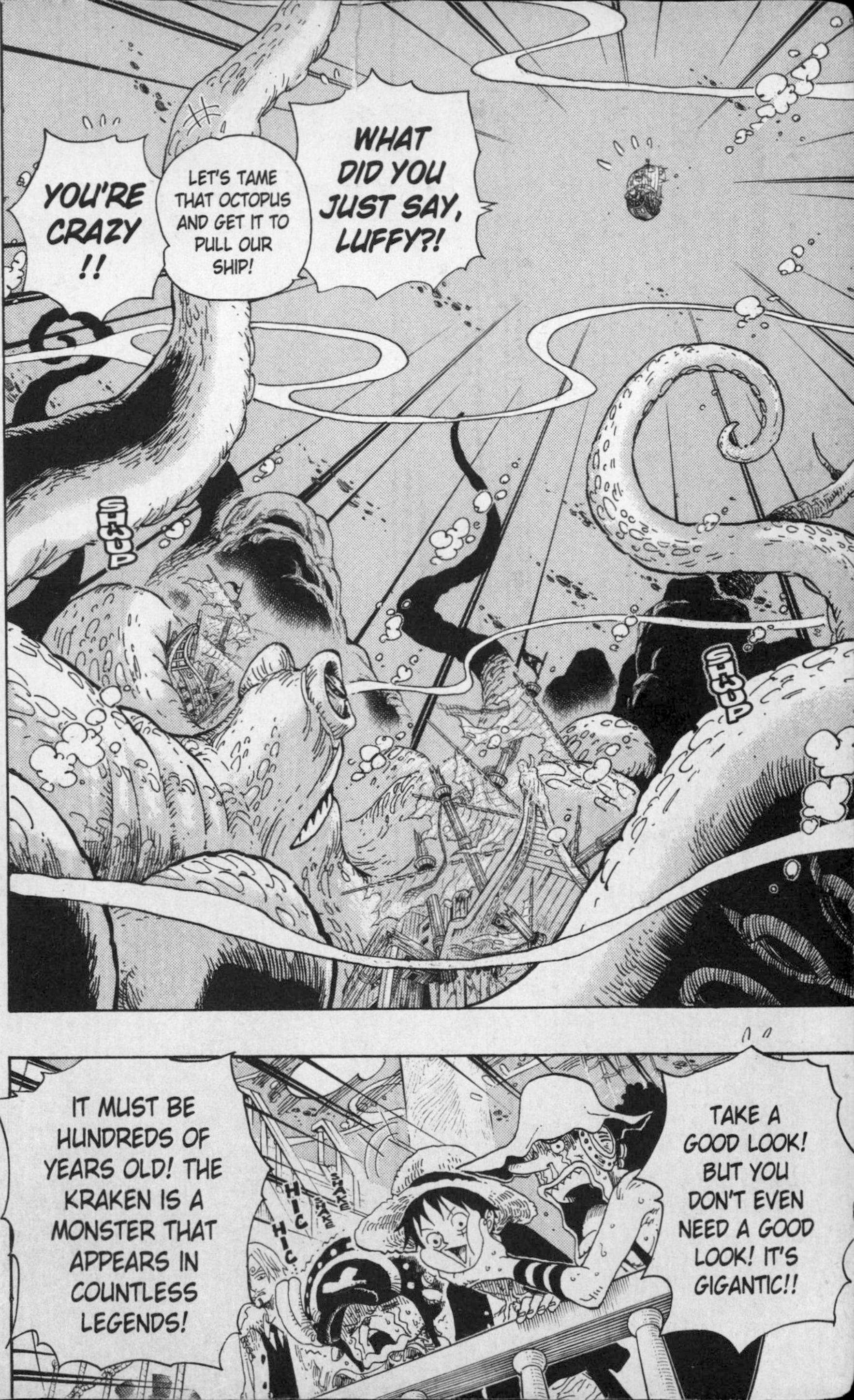
WHAT DID YOU JUST SAY, LUFFY?!
LET'S TAME THAT OCTOPUS AND GET IT TO PULL OUR SHIP!
YOU'RE CRAZY!!
SHWUP
SHWUP
TAKE A GOOD LOOK! BUT YOU DON'T EVEN NEED A GOOD LOOK! IT'S GIGANTIC!!
SHAKE SHAKE
HIC HIC
IT MUST BE HUNDREDS OF YEARS OLD! THE KRAKEN IS A MONSTER THAT APPEARS IN COUNTLESS LEGENDS!

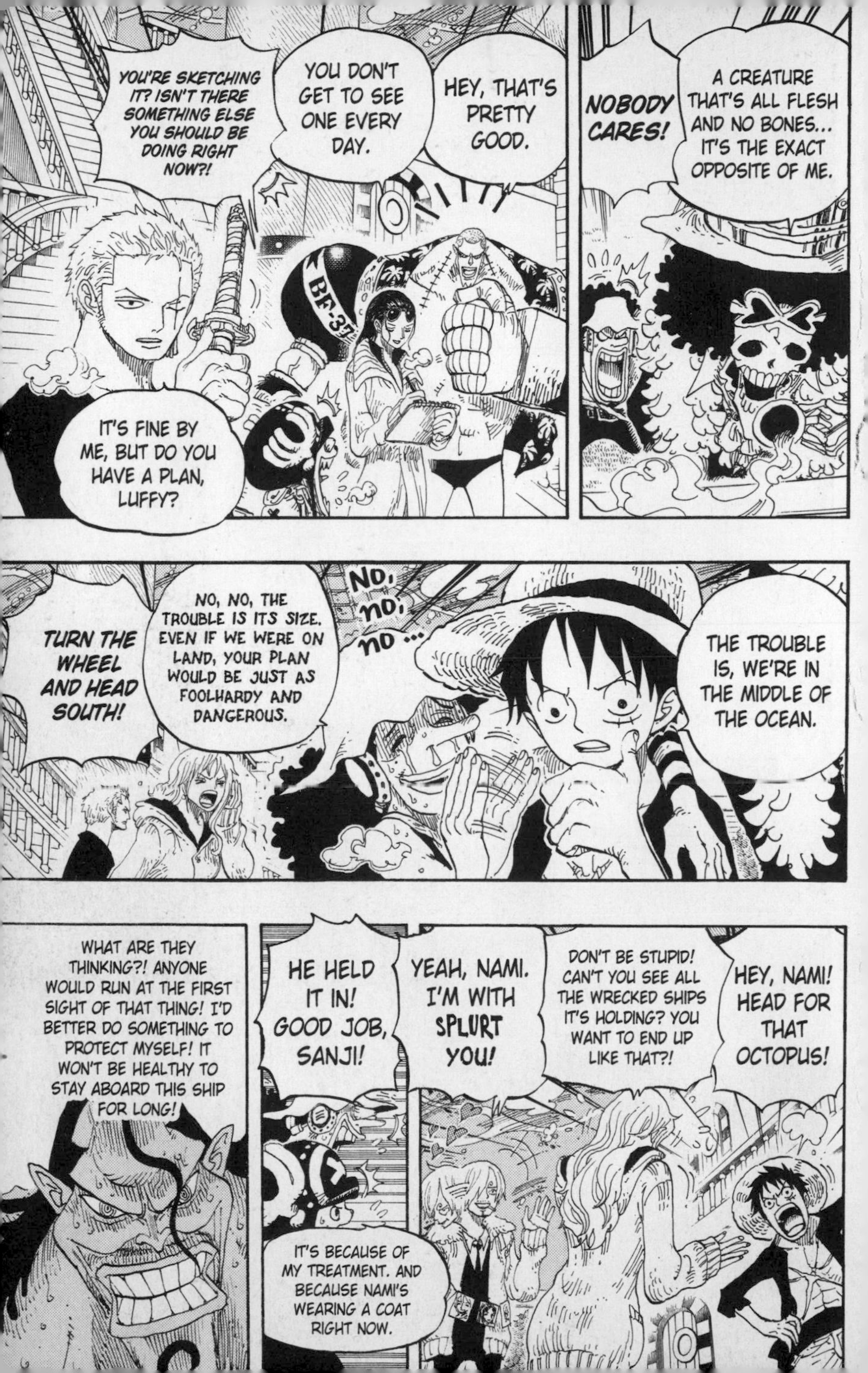

A CREATURE THAT'S ALL FLESH AND NO BONES... IT'S THE EXACT OPPOSITE OF ME.
NOBODY CARES!
HEY, THAT'S PRETTY GOOD.
YOU DON'T GET TO SEE ONE EVERY DAY.
YOU'RE SKETCHING IT? ISN'T THERE SOMETHING ELSE YOU SHOULD BE DOING RIGHT NOW?!
IT'S FINE BY ME, BUT DO YOU HAVE A PLAN, LUFFY?
THE TROUBLE IS, WE'RE IN THE MIDDLE OF THE OCEAN.
NO, NO, NO...
NO, NO, THE TROUBLE IS ITS SIZE. EVEN IF WE WERE ON LAND, YOUR PLAN WOULD BE JUST AS FOOLHARDY AND DANGEROUS.
TURN THE WHEEL AND HEAD SOUTH!
HEY, NAMI! HEAD FOR THAT OCTOPUS!
DON'T BE STUPID! CAN'T YOU SEE ALL THE WRECKED SHIPS IT'S HOLDING? YOU WANT TO END UP LIKE THAT?!
YEAH, NAMI. I'M WITH SPLURT YOU!
HE HELD IT IN! GOOD JOB, SANJI!
IT'S BECAUSE OF MY TREATMENT. AND BECAUSE NAMI'S WEARING A COAT RIGHT NOW.
WHAT ARE THEY THINKING?! ANYONE WOULD RUN AT THE FIRST SIGHT OF THAT THING! I'D BETTER DO SOMETHING TO PROTECT MYSELF! IT WON'T BE HEALTHY TO STAY ABOARD THIS SHIP FOR LONG!

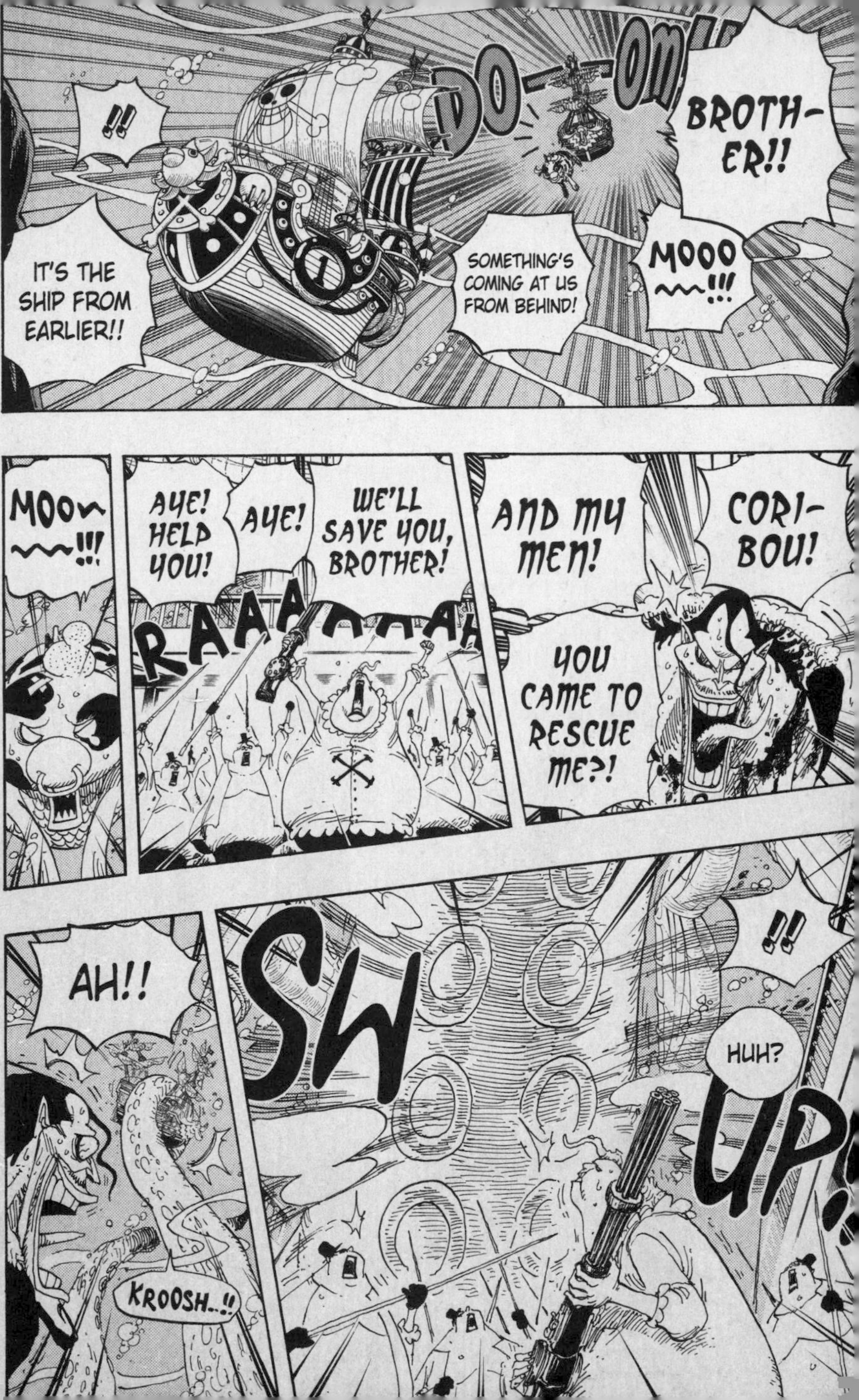
BROTHER!!
DO-OM!!
MOOO~~!!!
SOMETHING'S COMING AT US FROM BEHIND!
!!
IT'S THE SHIP FROM EARLIER!!
CORIBOU!
AND MY MEN!
YOU CAME TO RESCUE ME?!
WE'LL SAVE YOU, BROTHER!
AYE!
AYE! HELP YOU!
RAAAAAAH
MOO~~~!!!
!!
HUH?
SHUP!!
AH!!
KROOSH..!!

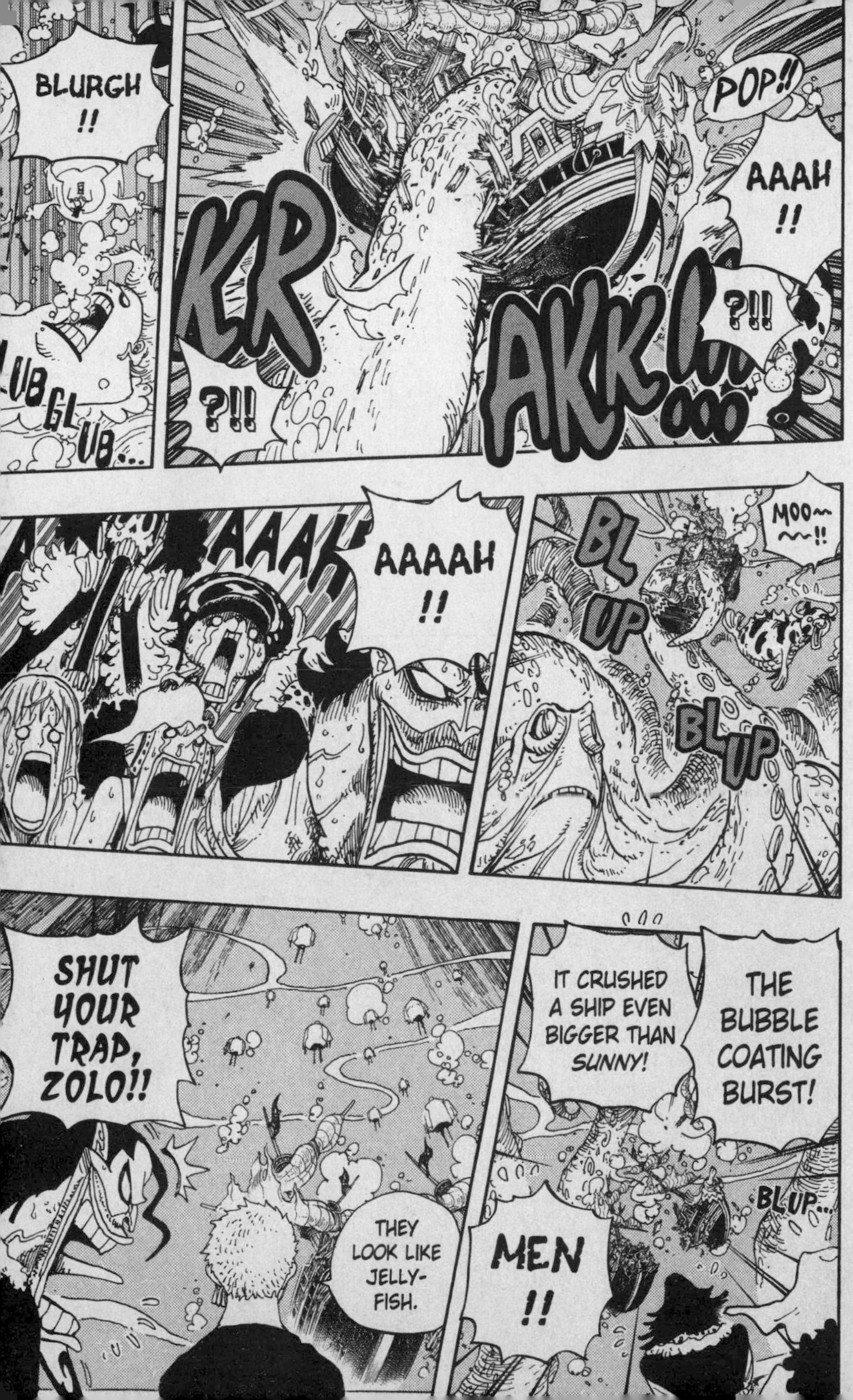
POP!!
AAAH!!
?!!
KR AKK...
?!!
BLURGH!!
GLUB GLUB...
MOO~~~!!
BL UP
BL UP
AAAAH!!
AAAAK
THE BUBBLE COATING BURST!
IT CRUSHED A SHIP EVEN BIGGER THAN SUNNY!
BLUP...
MEN!!
THEY LOOK LIKE JELLY-FISH.
SHUT YOUR TRAP, ZOLO!!

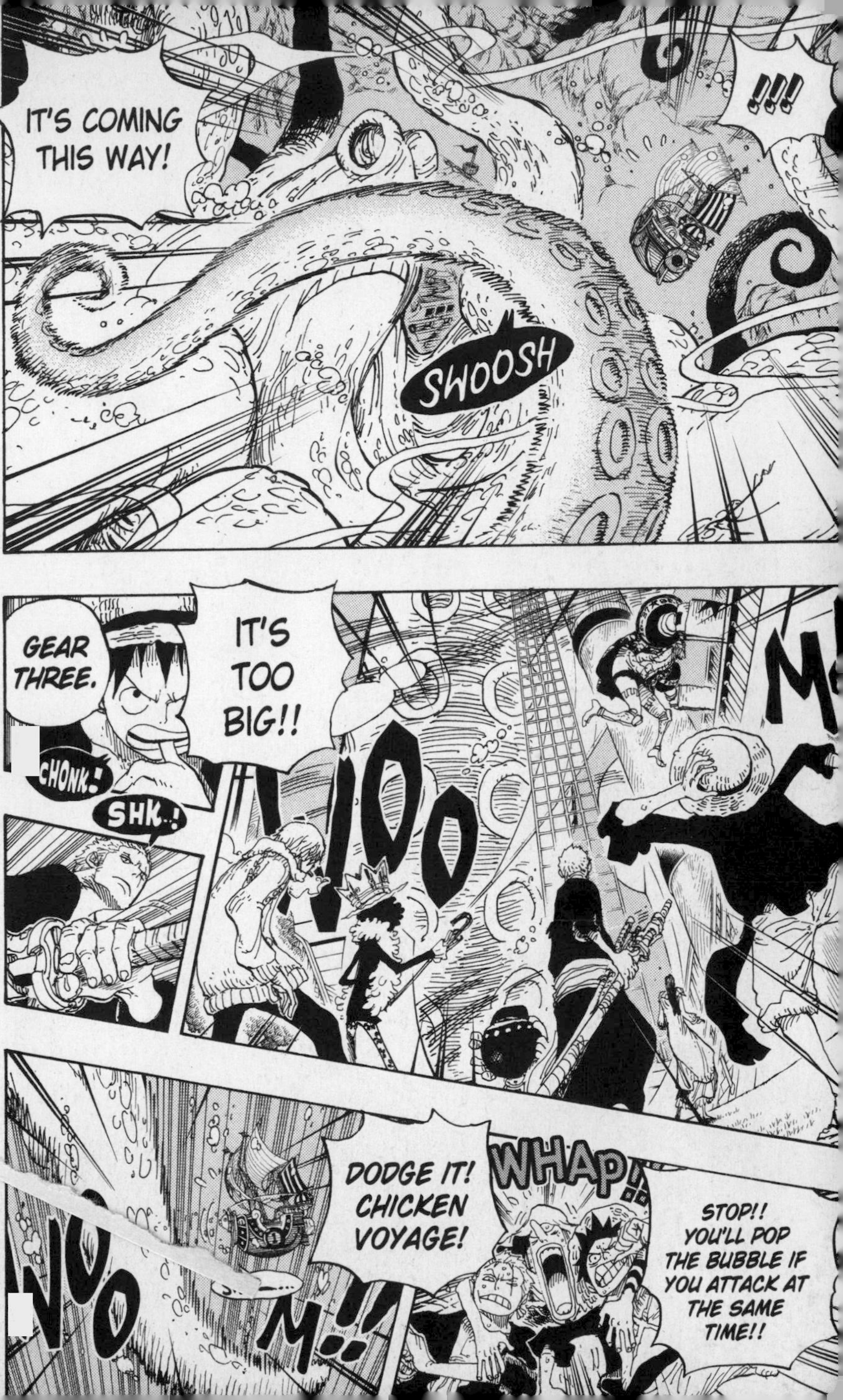
!!!
IT'S COMING THIS WAY!
SWOOSH
IT'S TOO BIG!!
GEAR THREE.
CHONK!
SHK..!
STOP!! YOU'LL POP THE BUBBLE IF YOU ATTACK AT THE SAME TIME!!
WHAP!!
DODGE IT! CHICKEN VOYAGE!
WOO
M!!

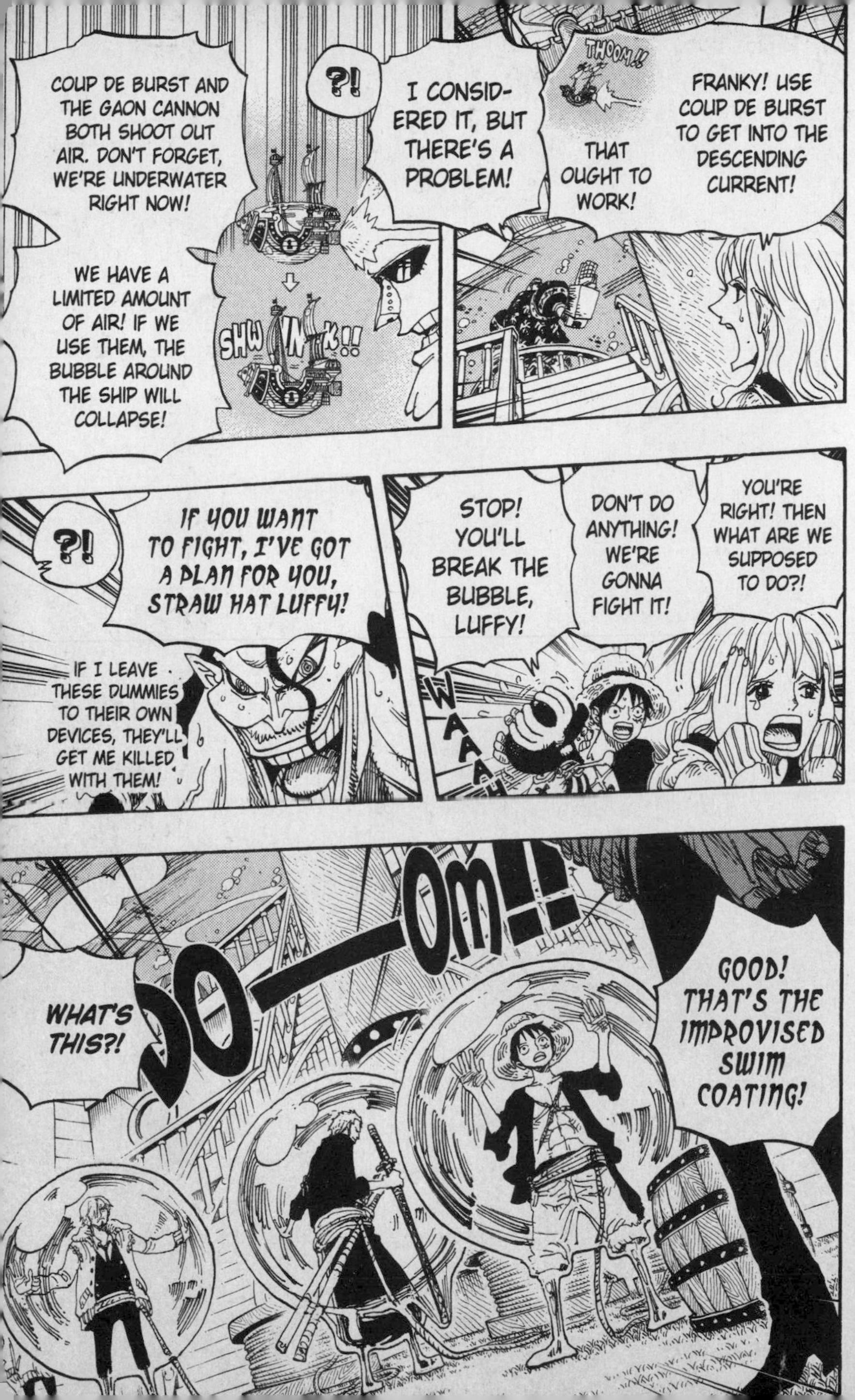
FRANKY! USE COUP DE BURST TO GET INTO THE DESCENDING CURRENT!
THAT OUGHT TO WORK!
THOOM!!
I CONSIDERED IT, BUT THERE'S A PROBLEM!
?!
COUP DE BURST AND THE GAON CANNON BOTH SHOOT OUT AIR. DON'T FORGET, WE'RE UNDERWATER RIGHT NOW!
WE HAVE A LIMITED AMOUNT OF AIR! IF WE USE THEM, THE BUBBLE AROUND THE SHIP WILL COLLAPSE!
YOU'RE RIGHT! THEN WHAT ARE WE SUPPOSED TO DO?!
DON'T DO ANYTHING! WE'RE GONNA FIGHT IT!
STOP! YOU'LL BREAK THE BUBBLE, LUFFY!
WAAAH
IF YOU WANT TO FIGHT, I'VE GOT A PLAN FOR YOU, STRAW HAT LUFFY!
?!
IF I LEAVE THESE DUMMIES TO THEIR OWN DEVICES, THEY'LL GET ME KILLED WITH THEM!
GOOD! THAT'S THE IMPROVISED SWIM COATING!
DO-OM!!
WHAT'S THIS?!

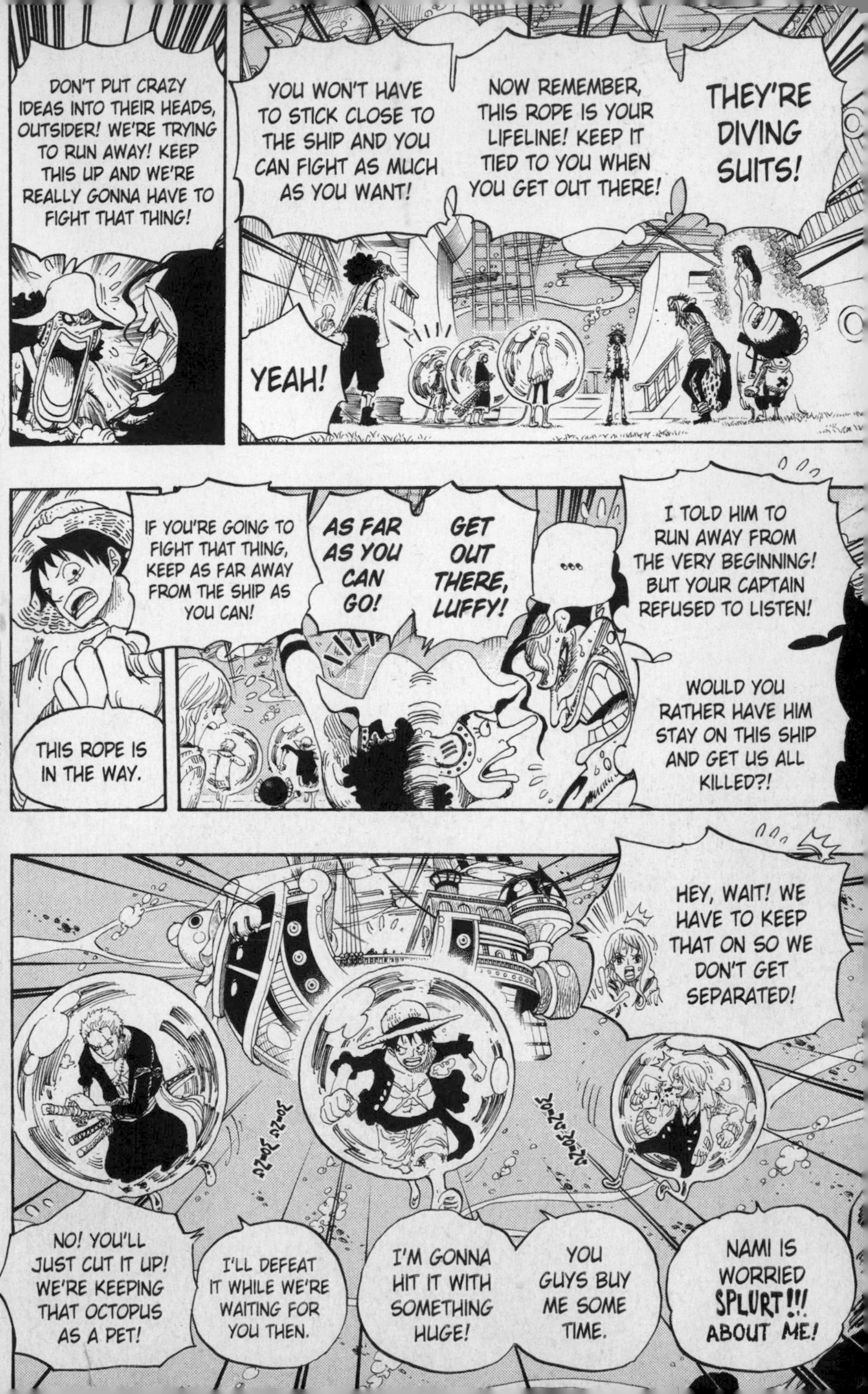
THEY'RE DIVING SUITS!
NOW REMEMBER, THIS ROPE IS YOUR LIFELINE! KEEP IT TIED TO YOU WHEN YOU GET OUT THERE!
YOU WON'T HAVE TO STICK CLOSE TO THE SHIP AND YOU CAN FIGHT AS MUCH AS YOU WANT!
YEAH!
DON'T PUT CRAZY IDEAS INTO THEIR HEADS, OUTSIDER! WE'RE TRYING TO RUN AWAY! KEEP THIS UP AND WE'RE REALLY GONNA HAVE TO FIGHT THAT THING!
I TOLD HIM TO RUN AWAY FROM THE VERY BEGINNING! BUT YOUR CAPTAIN REFUSED TO LISTEN!
WOULD YOU RATHER HAVE HIM STAY ON THIS SHIP AND GET US ALL KILLED?!
GET OUT THERE, LUFFY!
AS FAR AS YOU CAN GO!
IF YOU'RE GOING TO FIGHT THAT THING, KEEP AS FAR AWAY FROM THE SHIP AS YOU CAN!
THIS ROPE IS IN THE WAY.
HEY, WAIT! WE HAVE TO KEEP THAT ON SO WE DON'T GET SEPARATED!
NAMI IS WORRIED SPLURT!!! ABOUT ME!
YOU GUYS BUY ME SOME TIME.
I'M GONNA HIT IT WITH SOMETHING HUGE!
I'LL DEFEAT IT WHILE WE'RE WAITING FOR YOU THEN.
NO! YOU'LL JUST CUT IT UP! WE'RE KEEPING THAT OCTOPUS AS A PET!

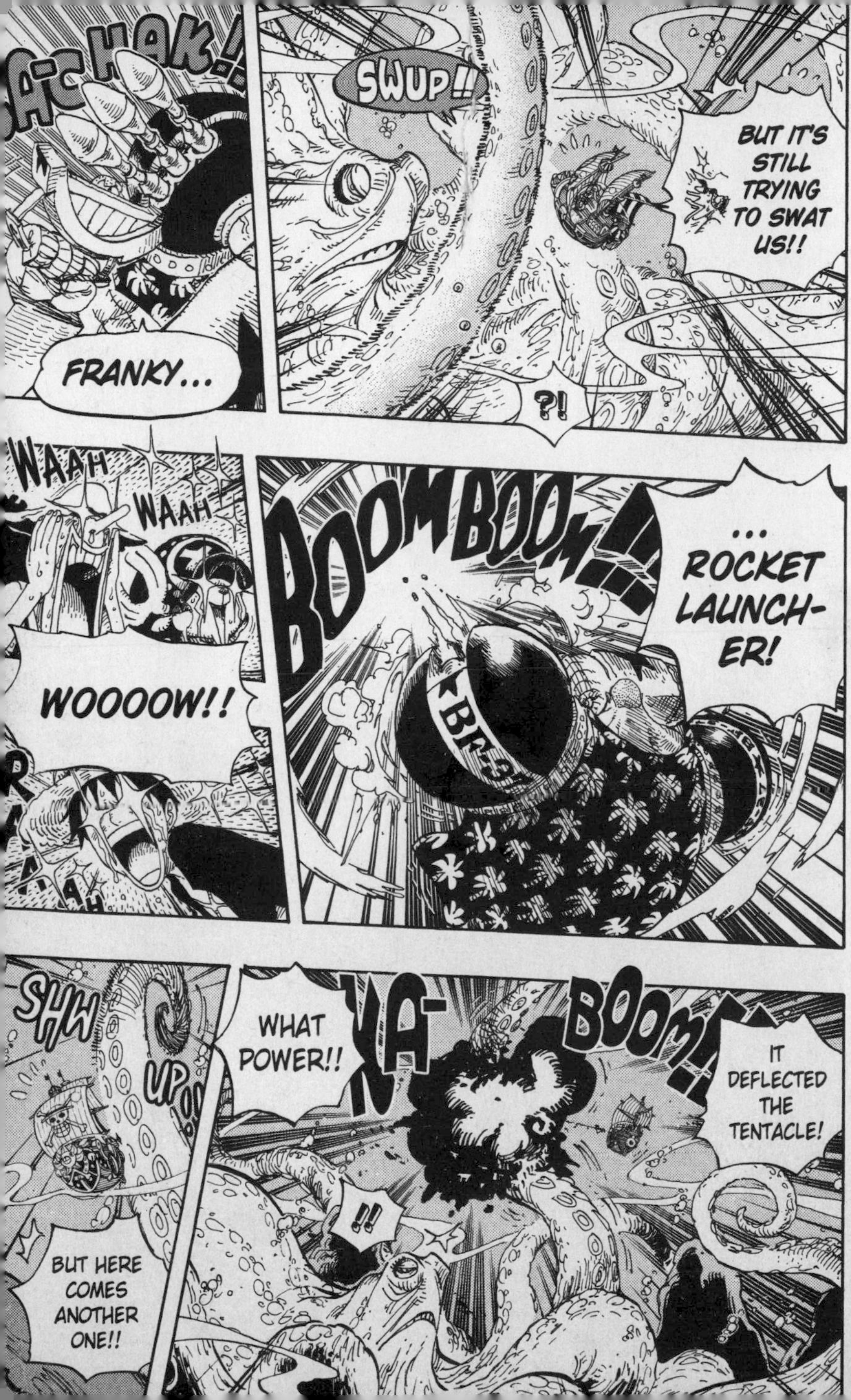
SWUP!!
BUT IT'S STILL TRYING TO SWAT US!!
?!
A-CHAK!!
FRANKY...
BOOMBOOM!!
... ROCKET LAUNCHER!
WAAH
WAAH
WOOOOW!!
KA-BOOM!!
IT DEFLECTED THE TENTACLE!
WHAT POWER!!
!!
SHWUP!!
BUT HERE COMES ANOTHER ONE!!

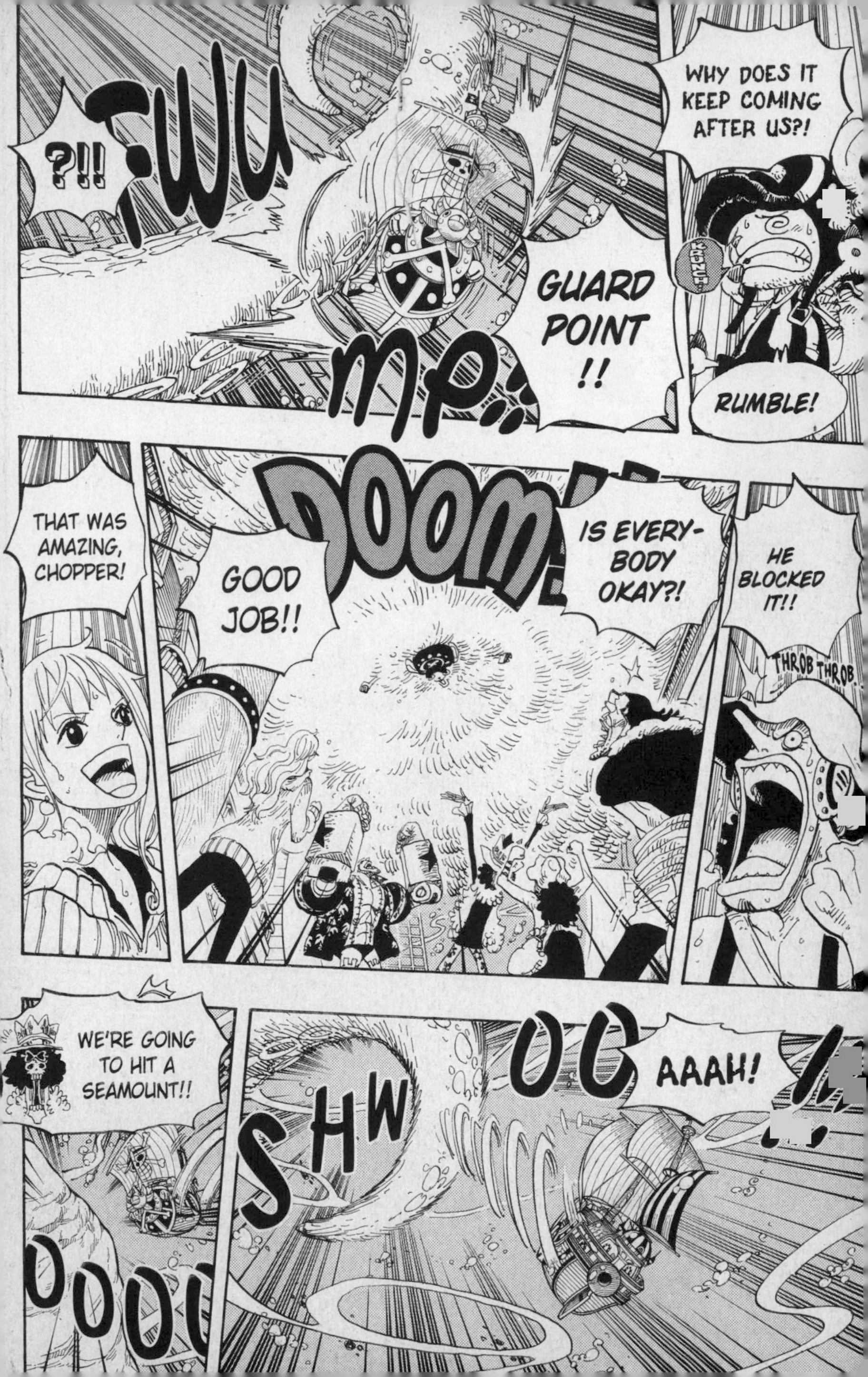
WHY DOES IT KEEP COMING AFTER US?!
RUMBLE!
GUARD POINT !!
?!!
FWU
MP
HE BLOCKED IT!!
THROB THROB
DOOM
IS EVERY-BODY OKAY?!
GOOD JOB!!
THAT WAS AMAZING, CHOPPER!
OO
AAAH!
SHW
WE'RE GOING TO HIT A SEAMOUNT!!
OOOO

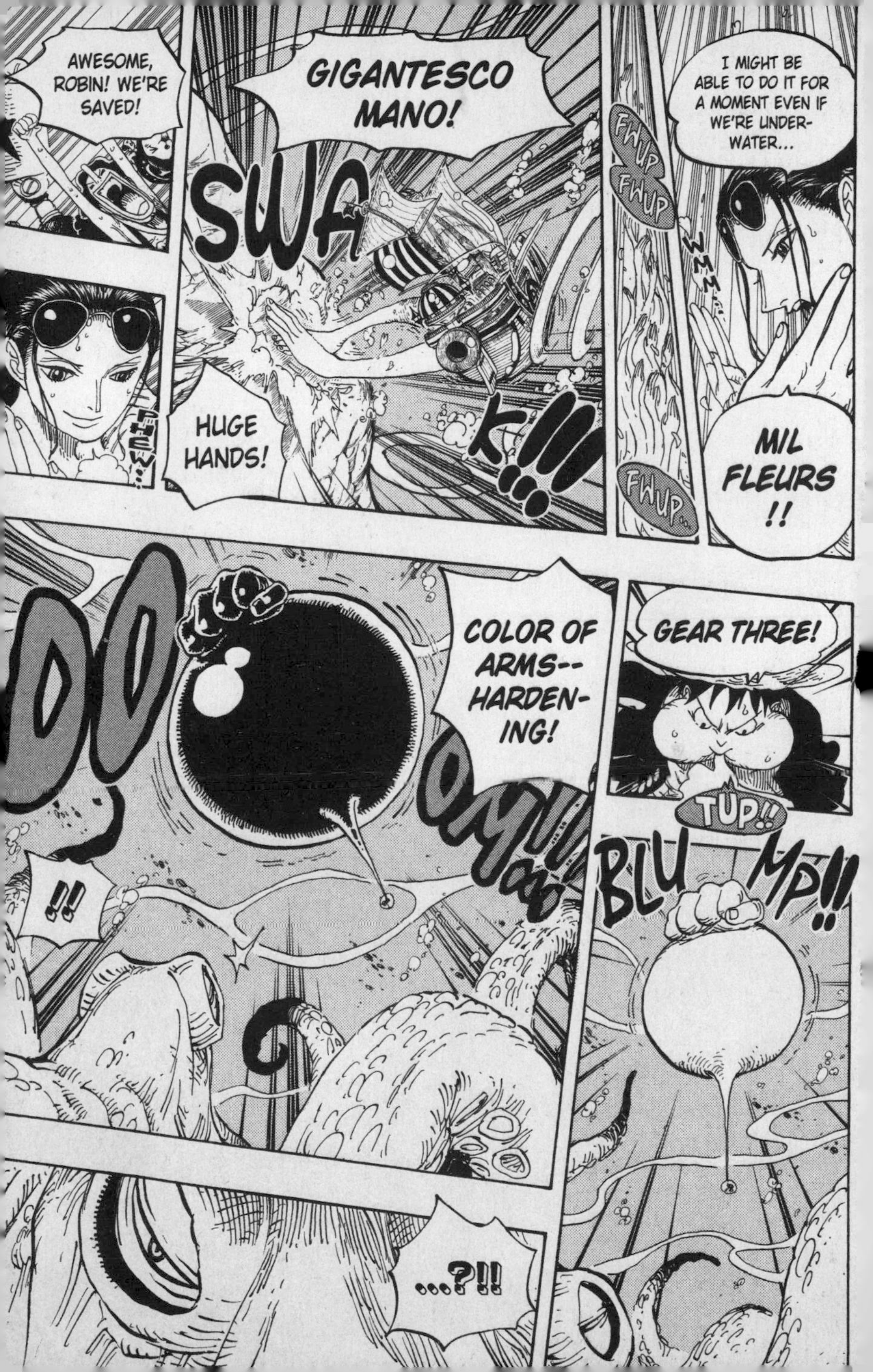
I MIGHT BE ABLE TO DO IT FOR A MOMENT EVEN IF WE'RE UNDER-WATER...
FWUP
FWUP
FWUP...
MIL FLEURS !!
GIGANTESCO MANO!
SWA
K!!!
HUGE HANDS!
AWESOME, ROBIN! WE'RE SAVED!
GEAR THREE!
TUP!!
BLU MP!!
COLOR OF ARMS-- HARDEN-ING!
!!
...?!!

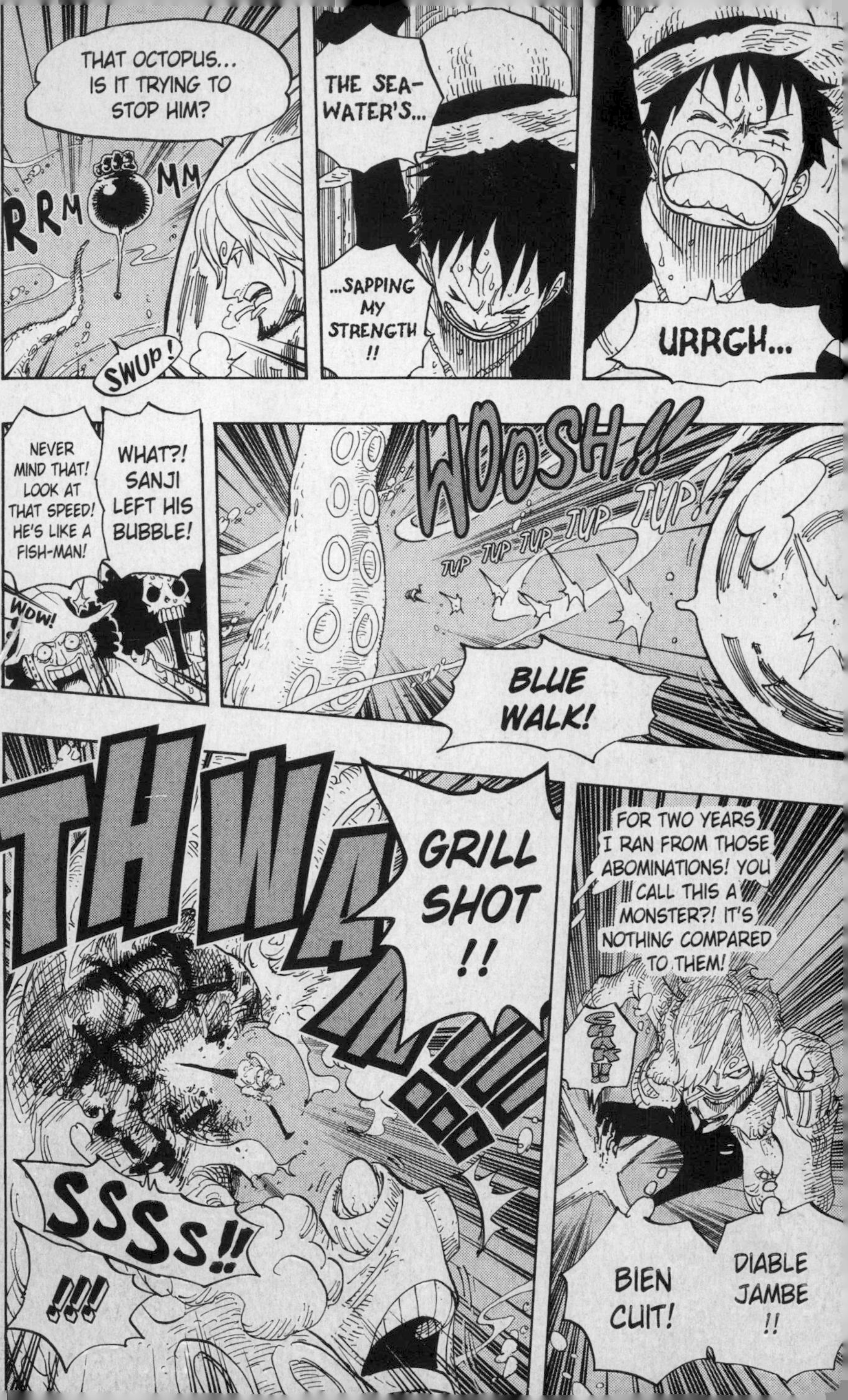
URRGH...
THE SEA-WATER'S...
...SAPPING MY STRENGTH!!
THAT OCTOPUS... IS IT TRYING TO STOP HIM?
RRRMMM
SWUP!
WOOSH!!
TUP TUP TUP TUP TUP TUP!!
BLUE WALK!
WHAT?! SANJI LEFT HIS BUBBLE!
NEVER MIND THAT! LOOK AT THAT SPEED! HE'S LIKE A FISH-MAN!
WOW!
FOR TWO YEARS I RAN FROM THOSE ABOMINATIONS! YOU CALL THIS A MONSTER?! IT'S NOTHING COMPARED TO THEM!
DIABLE JAMBE!!
BIEN CUIT!
GRILL SHOT!!
SSSs!!
!!!

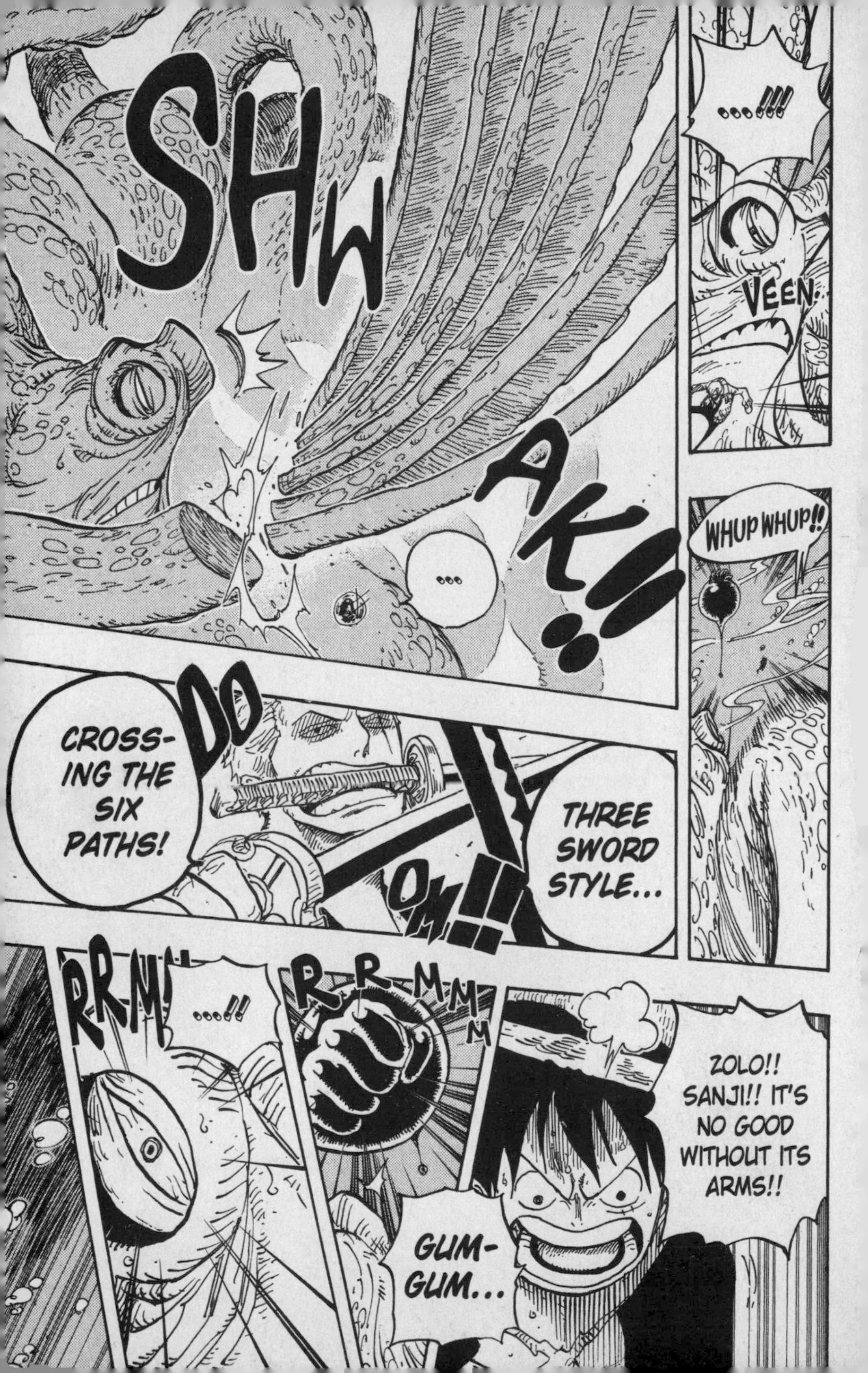
...!!!
VEEN...
WHUP WHUP!!
SHW
AK!!
...
THREE SWORD STYLE...
DO
OM!!
CROSS-ING THE SIX PATHS!
ZOLO!! SANJI!! IT'S NO GOOD WITHOUT ITS ARMS!!
GUM-GUM...
RRRMMMM
RRM!
...!!

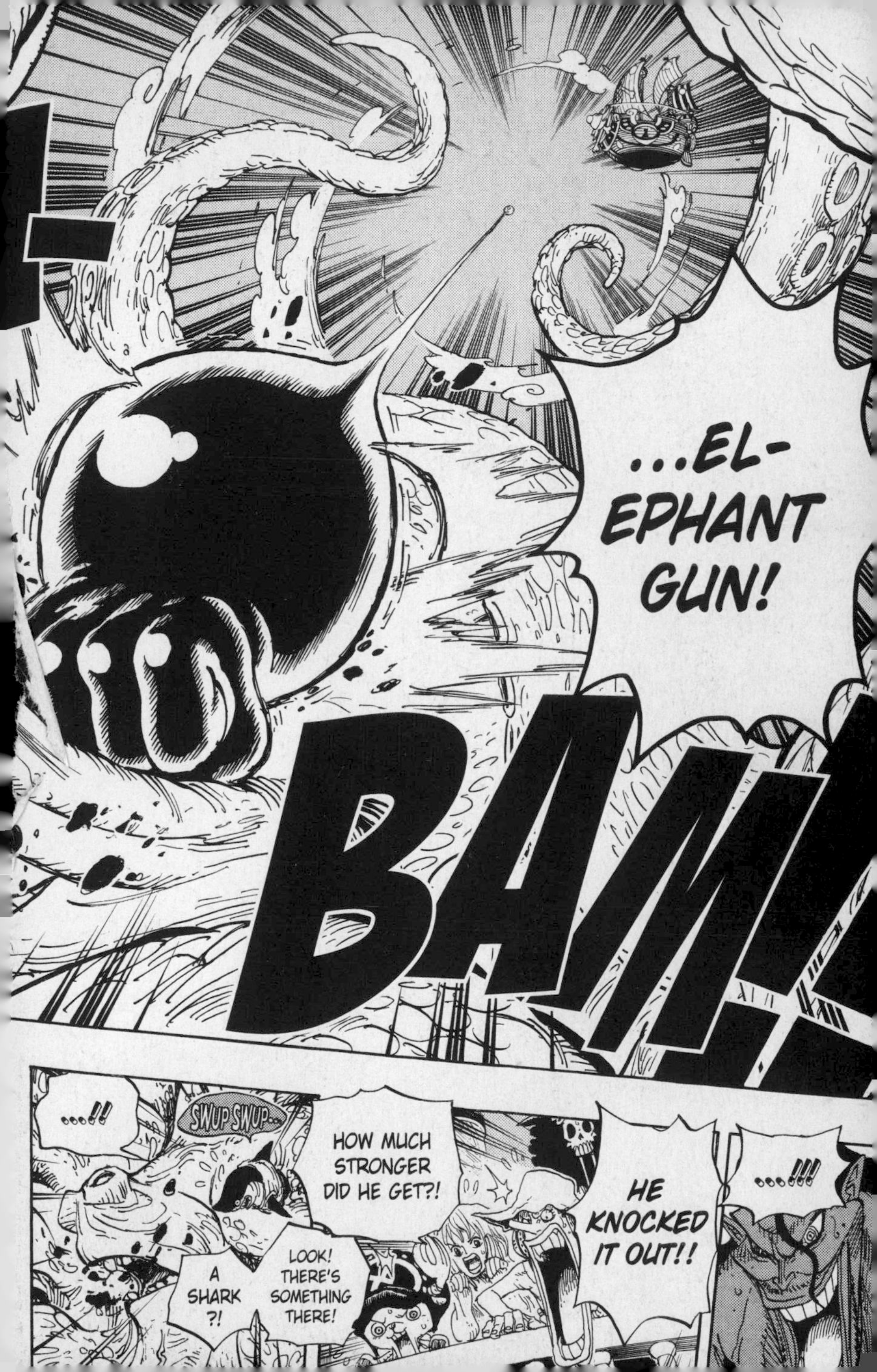

...EL-EPHANT GUN!
BAM
...!!!
HE KNOCKED IT OUT!!
HOW MUCH STRONGER DID HE GET?!
LOOK! THERE'S SOMETHING THERE!
A SHARK?!
SWUP SWUP...
...!!

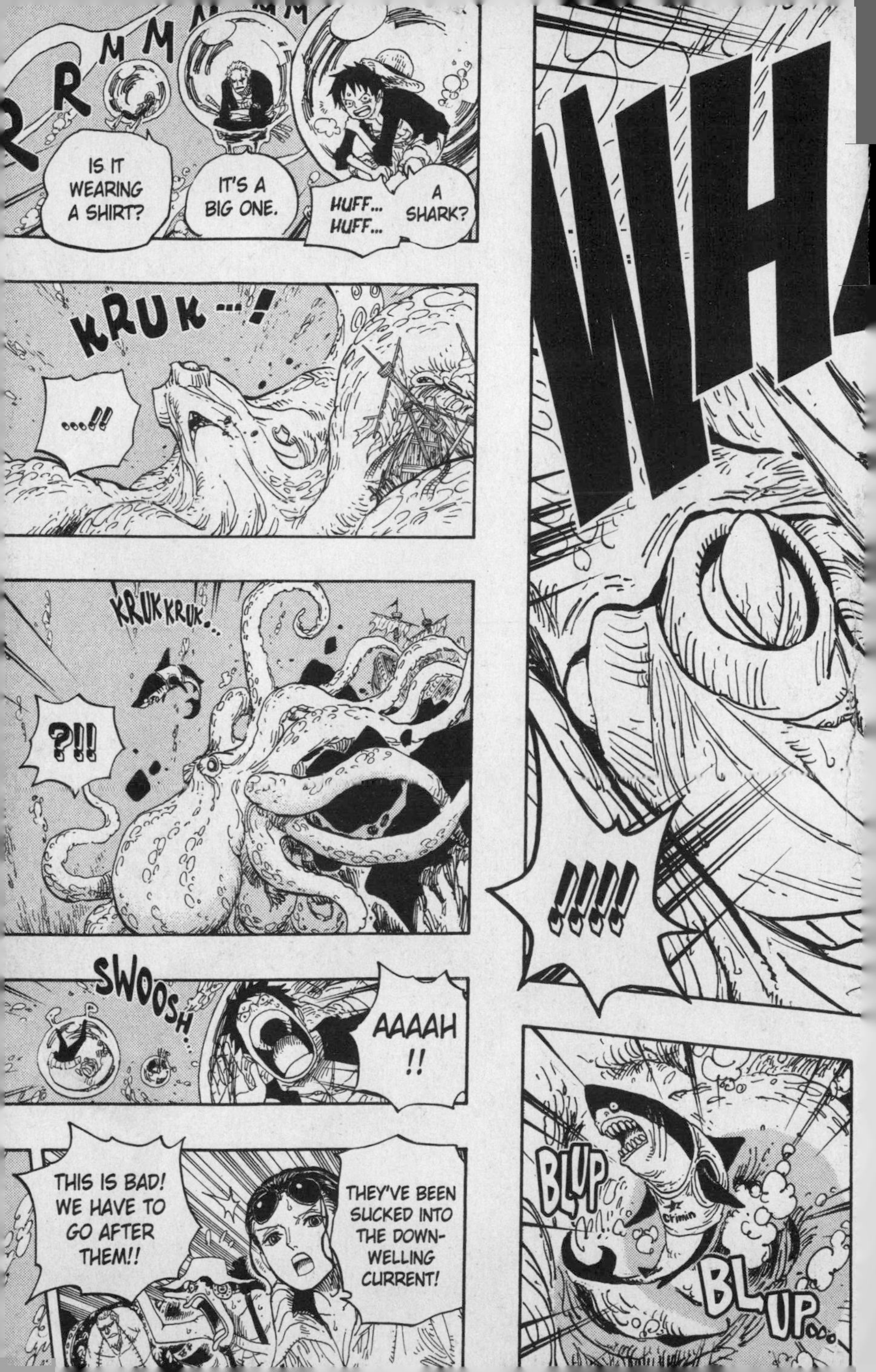
WHA
!!!!
BLUP
BLUP
RRMMMM
A SHARK?
HUFF... HUFF...
IT'S A BIG ONE.
IS IT WEARING A SHIRT?
KRUK...!
...!!
KRUKKRUK...
?!!
SWOOSH...
AAAAH!!
THEY'VE BEEN SUCKED INTO THE DOWN-WELLING CURRENT!
THIS IS BAD! WE HAVE TO GO AFTER THEM!!

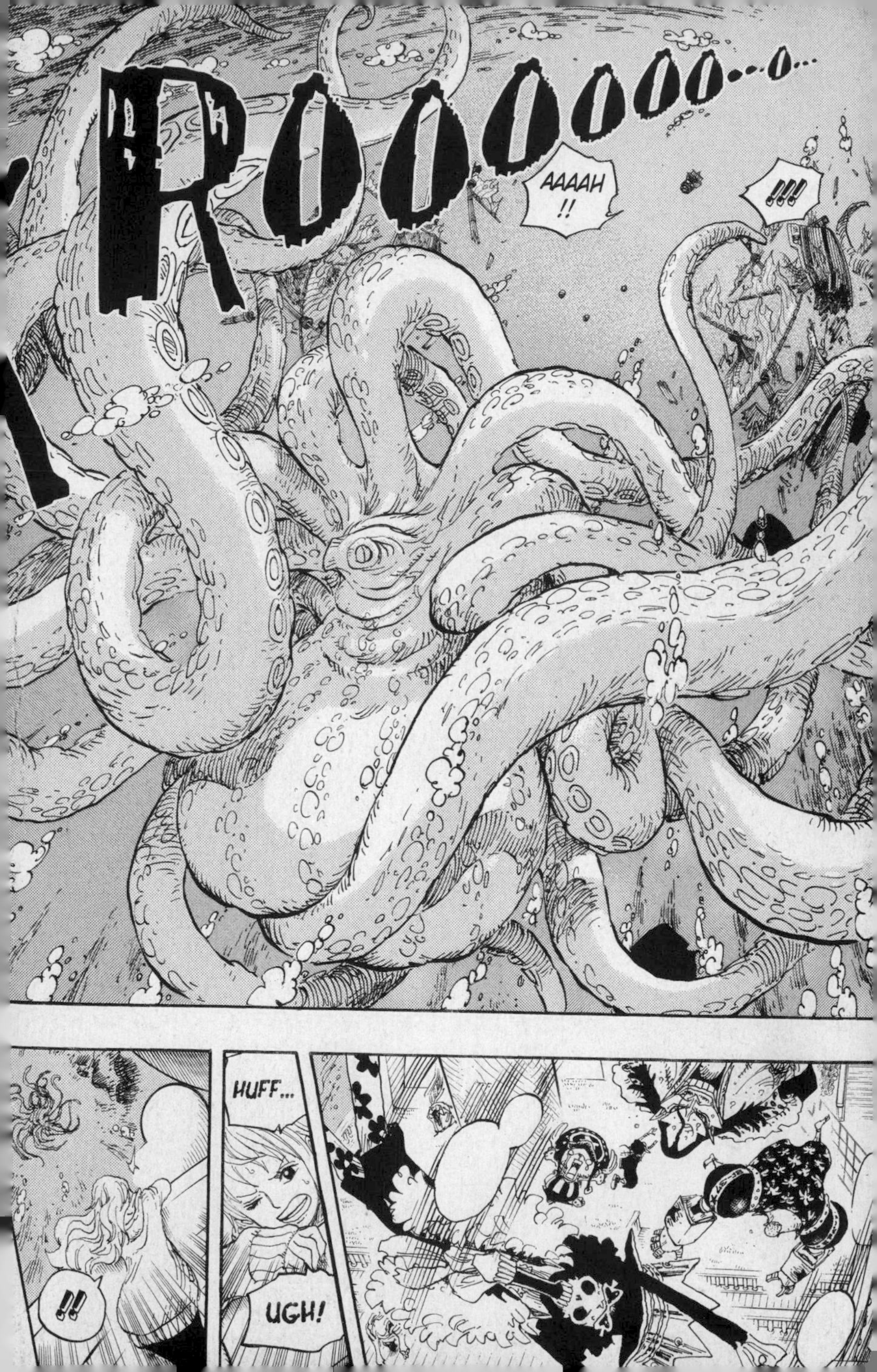
!!!
AAAAH !!
ROOOOOOO...O...
HUFF...
UGH!
!!

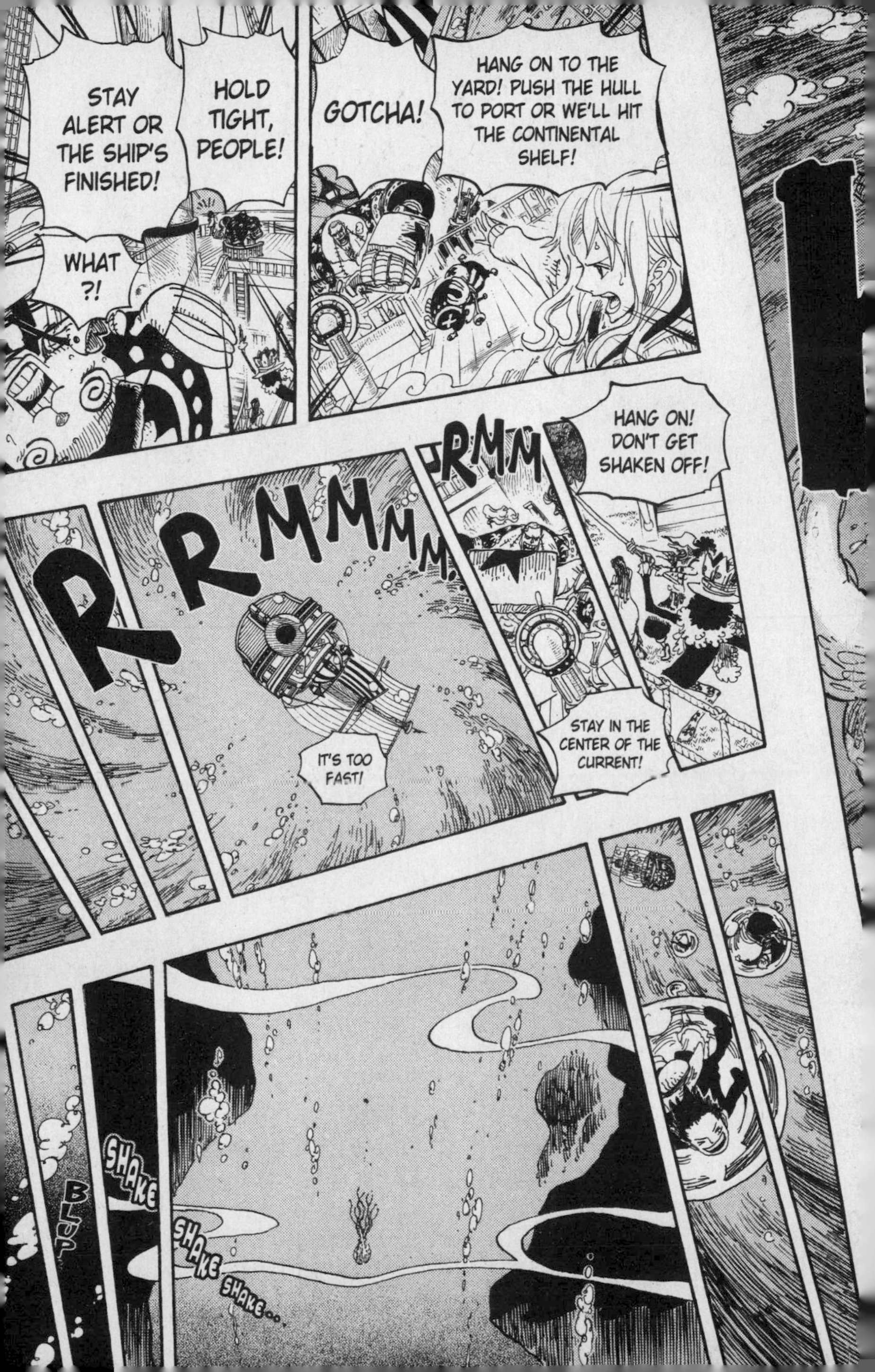
HANG ON TO THE YARD! PUSH THE HULL TO PORT OR WE'LL HIT THE CONTINENTAL SHELF!
GOTCHA!
HOLD TIGHT, PEOPLE!
STAY ALERT OR THE SHIP'S FINISHED!
WHAT ?!
HANG ON! DON'T GET SHAKEN OFF!
RMM
STAY IN THE CENTER OF THE CURRENT!
RRMMMMM
IT'S TOO FAST!
SHAKE
SHAKE
SHAKE...
BLUP

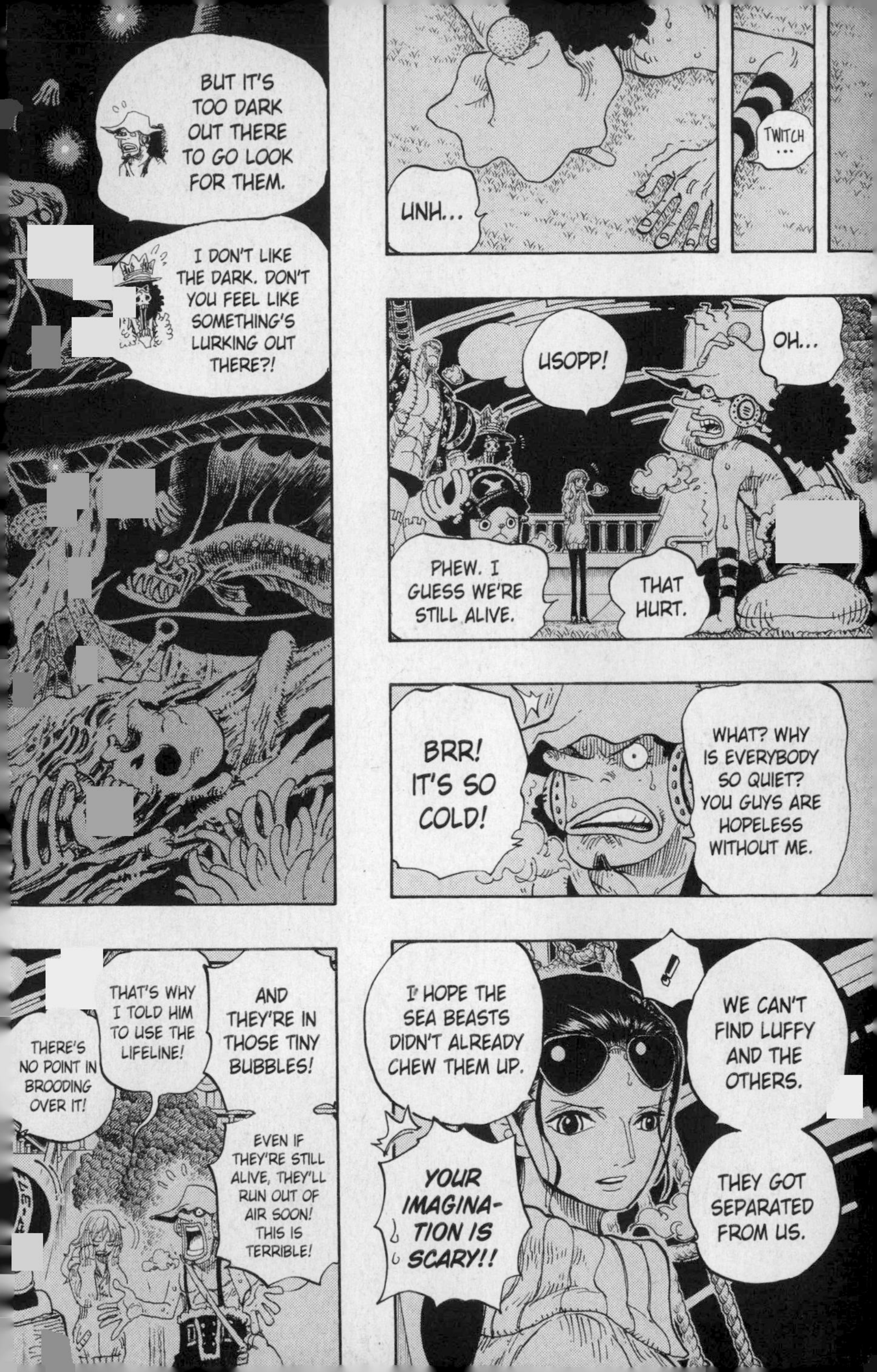
TWITCH...
UNH...
OH...
USOPP!
THAT HURT.
PHEW. I GUESS WE'RE STILL ALIVE.
WHAT? WHY IS EVERYBODY SO QUIET? YOU GUYS ARE HOPELESS WITHOUT ME.
BRR! IT'S SO COLD!
BUT IT'S TOO DARK OUT THERE TO GO LOOK FOR THEM.
I DON'T LIKE THE DARK. DON'T YOU FEEL LIKE SOMETHING'S LURKING OUT THERE?!
!
WE CAN'T FIND LUFFY AND THE OTHERS.
THEY GOT SEPARATED FROM US.
I HOPE THE SEA BEASTS DIDN'T ALREADY CHEW THEM UP.
YOUR IMAGINA-TION IS SCARY!!
AND THEY'RE IN THOSE TINY BUBBLES!
EVEN IF THEY'RE STILL ALIVE, THEY'LL RUN OUT OF AIR SOON! THIS IS TERRIBLE!
THAT'S WHY I TOLD HIM TO USE THE LIFELINE!
THERE'S NO POINT IN BROODING OVER IT!

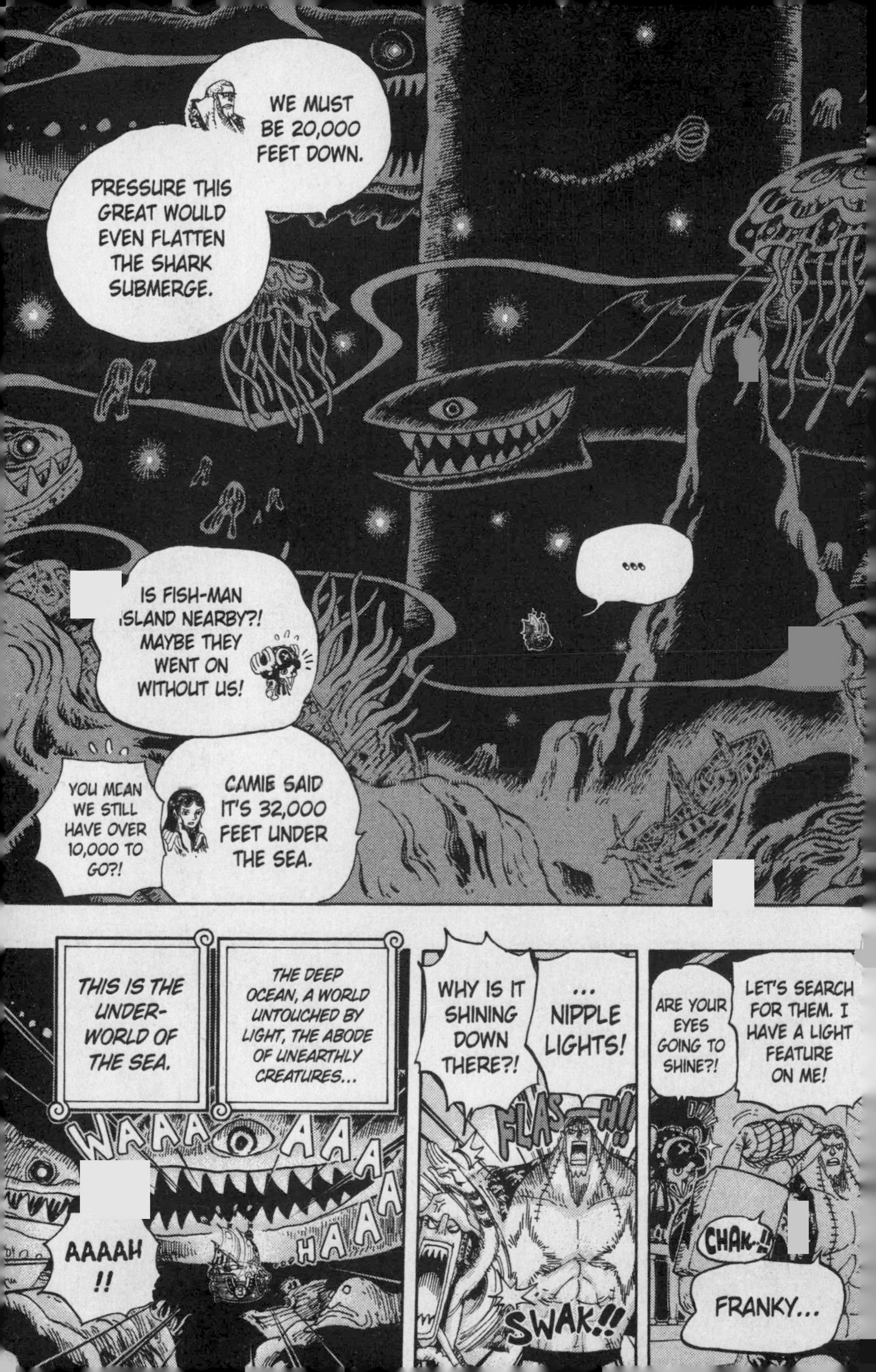
WE MUST BE 20,000 FEET DOWN.
PRESSURE THIS GREAT WOULD EVEN FLATTEN THE SHARK SUBMERGE.
...
IS FISH-MAN ISLAND NEARBY?! MAYBE THEY WENT ON WITHOUT US!
CAMIE SAID IT'S 32,000 FEET UNDER THE SEA.
YOU MEAN WE STILL HAVE OVER 10,000 TO GO?!
LET'S SEARCH FOR THEM. I HAVE A LIGHT FEATURE ON ME!
ARE YOUR EYES GOING TO SHINE?!
CHAK!!
FRANKY...
... NIPPLE LIGHTS!
WHY IS IT SHINING DOWN THERE?!
FLASH!!
SWAK!!
THE DEEP OCEAN, A WORLD UNTOUCHED BY LIGHT, THE ABODE OF UNEARTHLY CREATURES...
THIS IS THE UNDER-WORLD OF THE SEA.
WAAA AAAAAHAA
AAAAH !!

SBS Question Corner

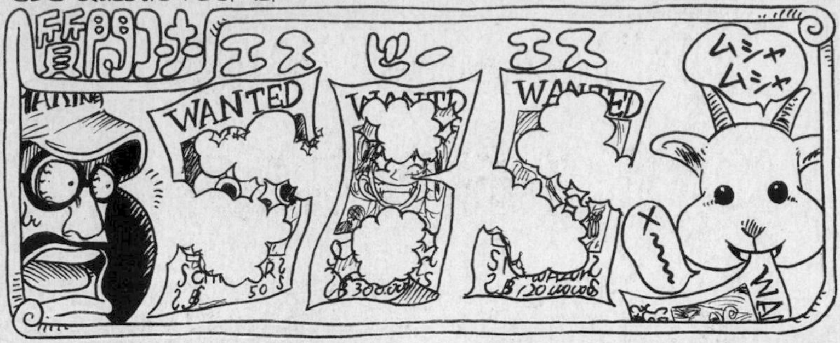
質問コーナー エス ピー エス
WANTED
WANTED
WANTED
ムシャ ムシャ

(Yuki, Nagasaki)

Q: Odacchi! Nice to meet you! This may be sudden, but the covers of volumes 1 and 61 are…
the same! That is all!

--Chi-chan's friend

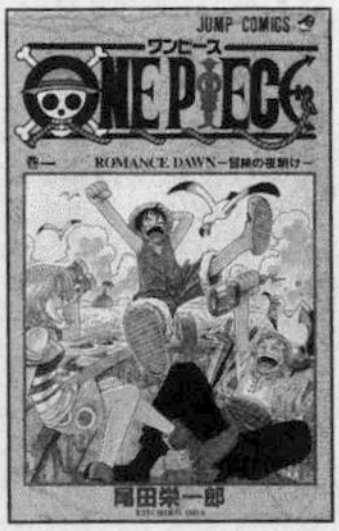
JUMP COMICS
ONE PIECE
ROMANCE DAWN

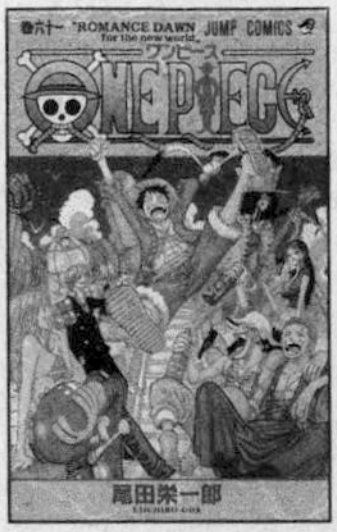
ROMANCE DAWN for the new world
JUMP COMICS
ONE PIECE

A: Whoops! I didn't notice at all! I thought I drew something similar in the past! What a bad mistake! (Note: To my young readers, this is on purpose. I did it on purpose and I pretended that I made a mistake. That's what makes me a funny guy.)

Q: Mr. Oda, I have a question. There was a time when I couldn't hold my pee anymore in class. I asked to go to the bathroom and was really embarrassed because of it. If I had the power of the Flower-Flower Fruit, would I be able to sprout my crotch at the toilet and pee from the classroom?

--Love-kun

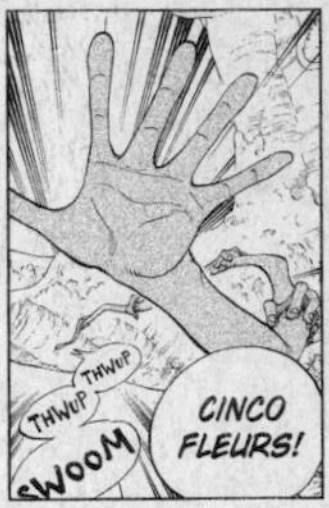
CINCO FLEURS!
THWUP
THWUP
SWOOM

A: What are you talking about? Well, if you consider the power, it is possible. It'll be a "Dinky Fleur!"

Q: Does Killer take his mask off when he eats? Or does he keep it on? If he eats with his mask on, would it become like the picture on the right? ➡ Does he prefer his food in stick form?

--N. Ro

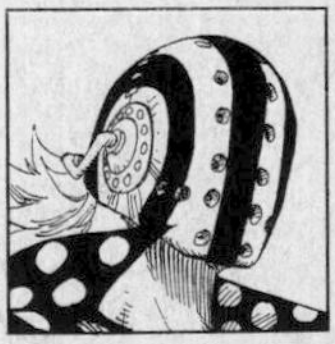

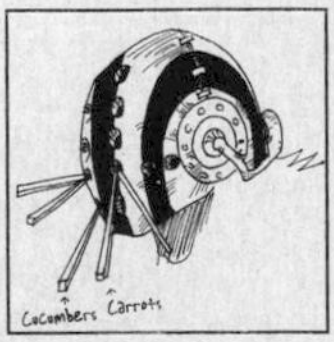
Cucumbers
Carrots

A: Hmm. He probably eats with his mask on. I think he would prefer all his food in stick form, but I hear he likes noodles too. The food he eats most is pasta. Light dishes like spaghetti pepperoncino are among his favorites. Neapolitan or other tomato-sauced based dishes will make his mask all red, so he doesn't like them. By the way, he drinks his alcohol through a straw.

Chapter 606:
DEEP SEA ADVENTURE

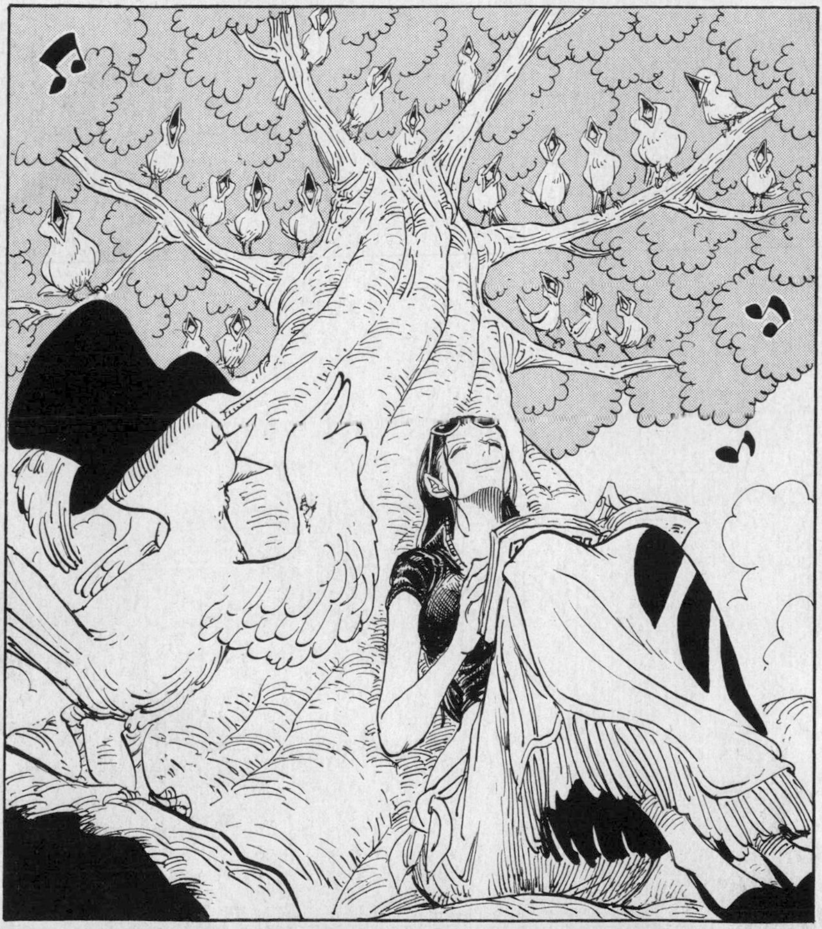

REQUEST: "ROBIN READING A BOOK UNDER A TREE WITH BIRDS THAT LOOK LIKE CANARIES SINGING." BY YUKI I.

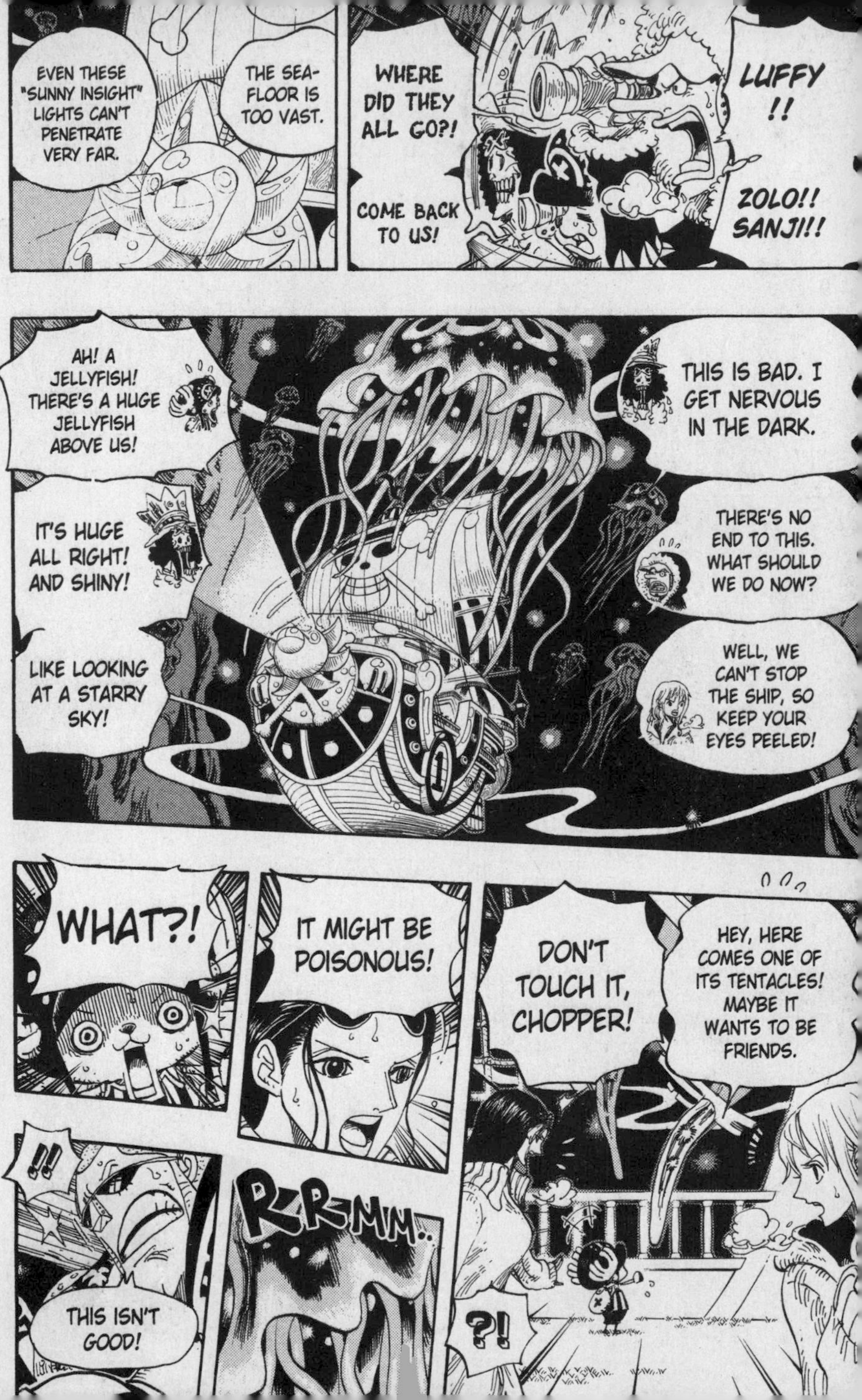
LUFFY!!
ZOLO!! SANJI!!
WHERE DID THEY ALL GO?!
COME BACK TO US!
THE SEA-FLOOR IS TOO VAST.
EVEN THESE "SUNNY INSIGHT" LIGHTS CAN'T PENETRATE VERY FAR.
THIS IS BAD. I GET NERVOUS IN THE DARK.
THERE'S NO END TO THIS. WHAT SHOULD WE DO NOW?
WELL, WE CAN'T STOP THE SHIP, SO KEEP YOUR EYES PEELED!
AH! A JELLYFISH! THERE'S A HUGE JELLYFISH ABOVE US!
IT'S HUGE ALL RIGHT! AND SHINY!
LIKE LOOKING AT A STARRY SKY!
HEY, HERE COMES ONE OF ITS TENTACLES! MAYBE IT WANTS TO BE FRIENDS.
DON'T TOUCH IT, CHOPPER!
?!
IT MIGHT BE POISONOUS!
WHAT?!
R-R-MM..
!!
THIS ISN'T GOOD!

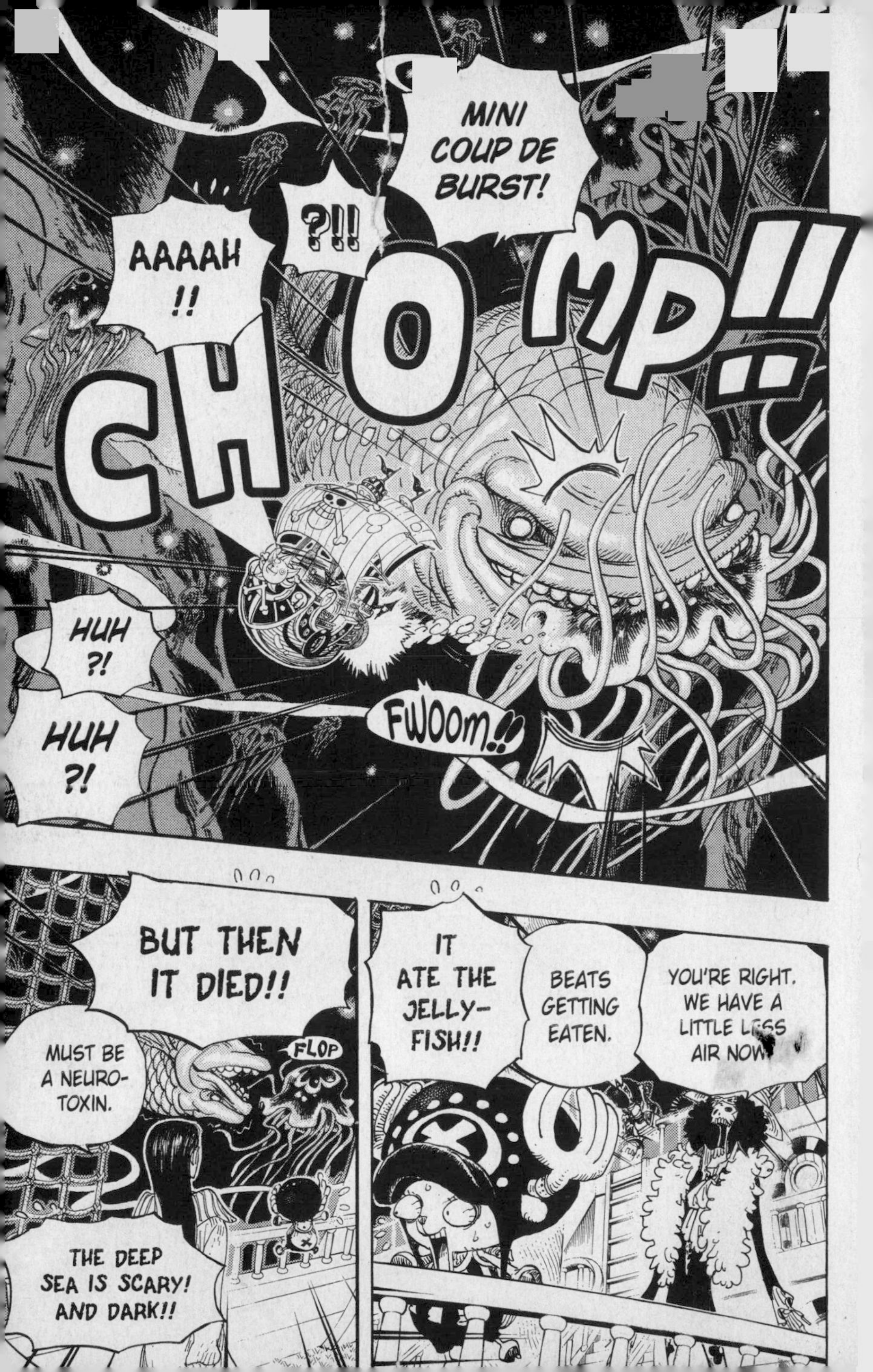
MINI COUP DE BURST!
?!!
AAAAH !!
CHOMP!!
FWOOM!!
HUH ?!
HUH ?!
YOU'RE RIGHT. WE HAVE A LITTLE LESS AIR NOW
BEATS GETTING EATEN.
IT ATE THE JELLY-FISH!!
BUT THEN IT DIED!!
FLOP
MUST BE A NEURO-TOXIN.
THE DEEP SEA IS SCARY! AND DARK!!

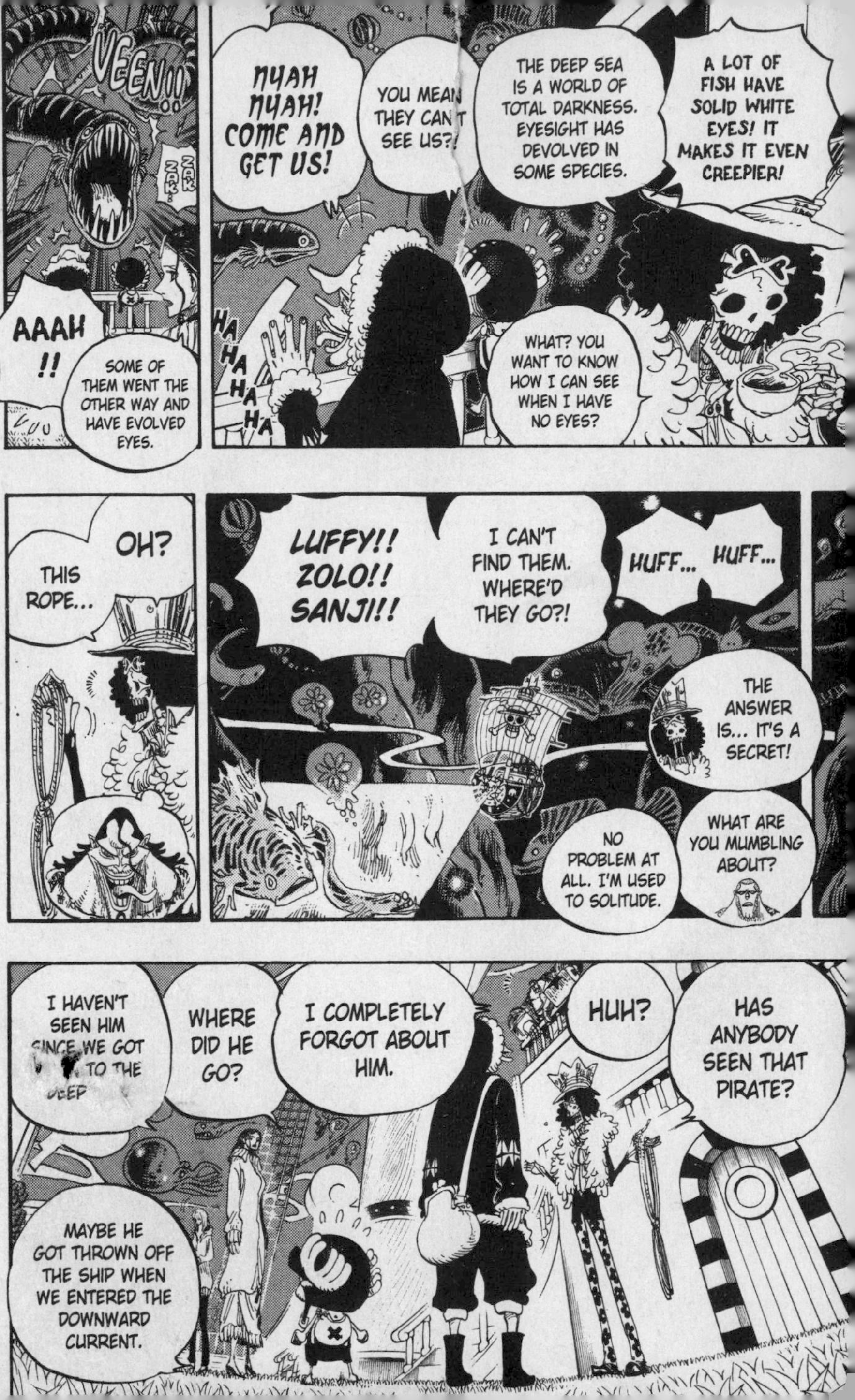
A LOT OF FISH HAVE SOLID WHITE EYES! IT MAKES IT EVEN CREEPIER!
THE DEEP SEA IS A WORLD OF TOTAL DARKNESS. EYESIGHT HAS DEVOLVED IN SOME SPECIES.
YOU MEAN THEY CAN'T SEE US?!
NYAH NYAH! COME AND GET US!
WHAT? YOU WANT TO KNOW HOW I CAN SEE WHEN I HAVE NO EYES?
HA HA HA HA HA
VEEN!!
ZAK ZAK
AAAH!!
SOME OF THEM WENT THE OTHER WAY AND HAVE EVOLVED EYES.
HUFF... HUFF...
THE ANSWER IS... IT'S A SECRET!
I CAN'T FIND THEM. WHERE'D THEY GO?!
LUFFY!! ZOLO!! SANJI!!
WHAT ARE YOU MUMBLING ABOUT?
NO PROBLEM AT ALL. I'M USED TO SOLITUDE.
OH?
THIS ROPE...
HAS ANYBODY SEEN THAT PIRATE?
HUH?
I COMPLETELY FORGOT ABOUT HIM.
WHERE DID HE GO?
I HAVEN'T SEEN HIM SINCE WE GOT TO THE DEEP
MAYBE HE GOT THROWN OFF THE SHIP WHEN WE ENTERED THE DOWNWARD CURRENT.

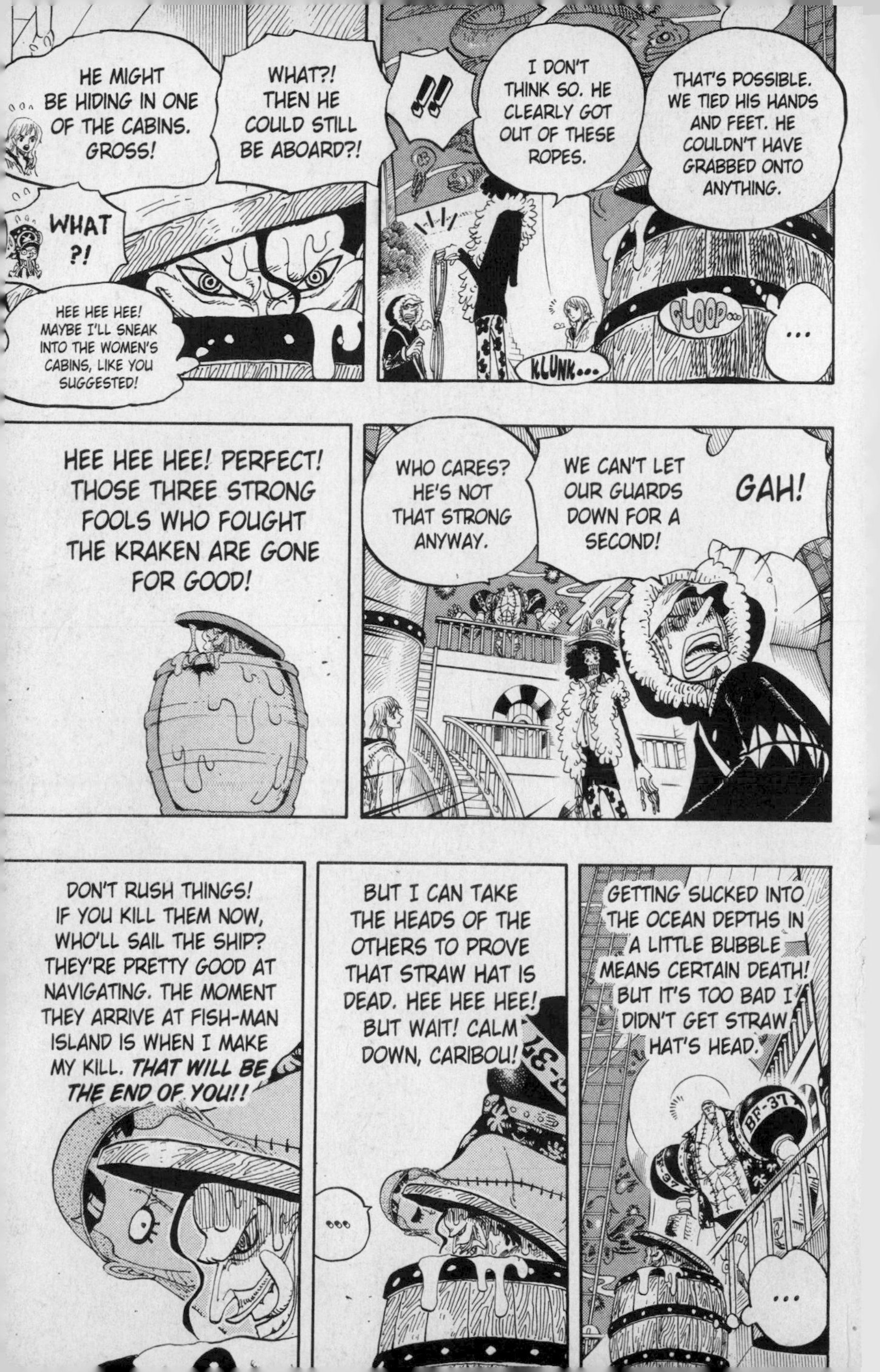
THAT'S POSSIBLE. WE TIED HIS HANDS AND FEET. HE COULDN'T HAVE GRABBED ONTO ANYTHING.
I DON'T THINK SO. HE CLEARLY GOT OUT OF THESE ROPES.
!!
GLOOP...
...
KLUNK...
WHAT?! THEN HE COULD STILL BE ABOARD?!
HE MIGHT BE HIDING IN ONE OF THE CABINS. GROSS!
WHAT ?!
HEE HEE HEE! MAYBE I'LL SNEAK INTO THE WOMEN'S CABINS, LIKE YOU SUGGESTED!
GAH!
WE CAN'T LET OUR GUARDS DOWN FOR A SECOND!
WHO CARES? HE'S NOT THAT STRONG ANYWAY.
HEE HEE HEE! PERFECT! THOSE THREE STRONG FOOLS WHO FOUGHT THE KRAKEN ARE GONE FOR GOOD!
GETTING SUCKED INTO THE OCEAN DEPTHS IN A LITTLE BUBBLE MEANS CERTAIN DEATH! BUT IT'S TOO BAD I DIDN'T GET STRAW HAT'S HEAD.
...
BUT I CAN TAKE THE HEADS OF THE OTHERS TO PROVE THAT STRAW HAT IS DEAD. HEE HEE HEE! BUT WAIT! CALM DOWN, CARIBOU!
...
DON'T RUSH THINGS! IF YOU KILL THEM NOW, WHO'LL SAIL THE SHIP? THEY'RE PRETTY GOOD AT NAVIGATING. THE MOMENT THEY ARRIVE AT FISH-MAN ISLAND IS WHEN I MAKE MY KILL. THAT WILL BE THE END OF YOU!!

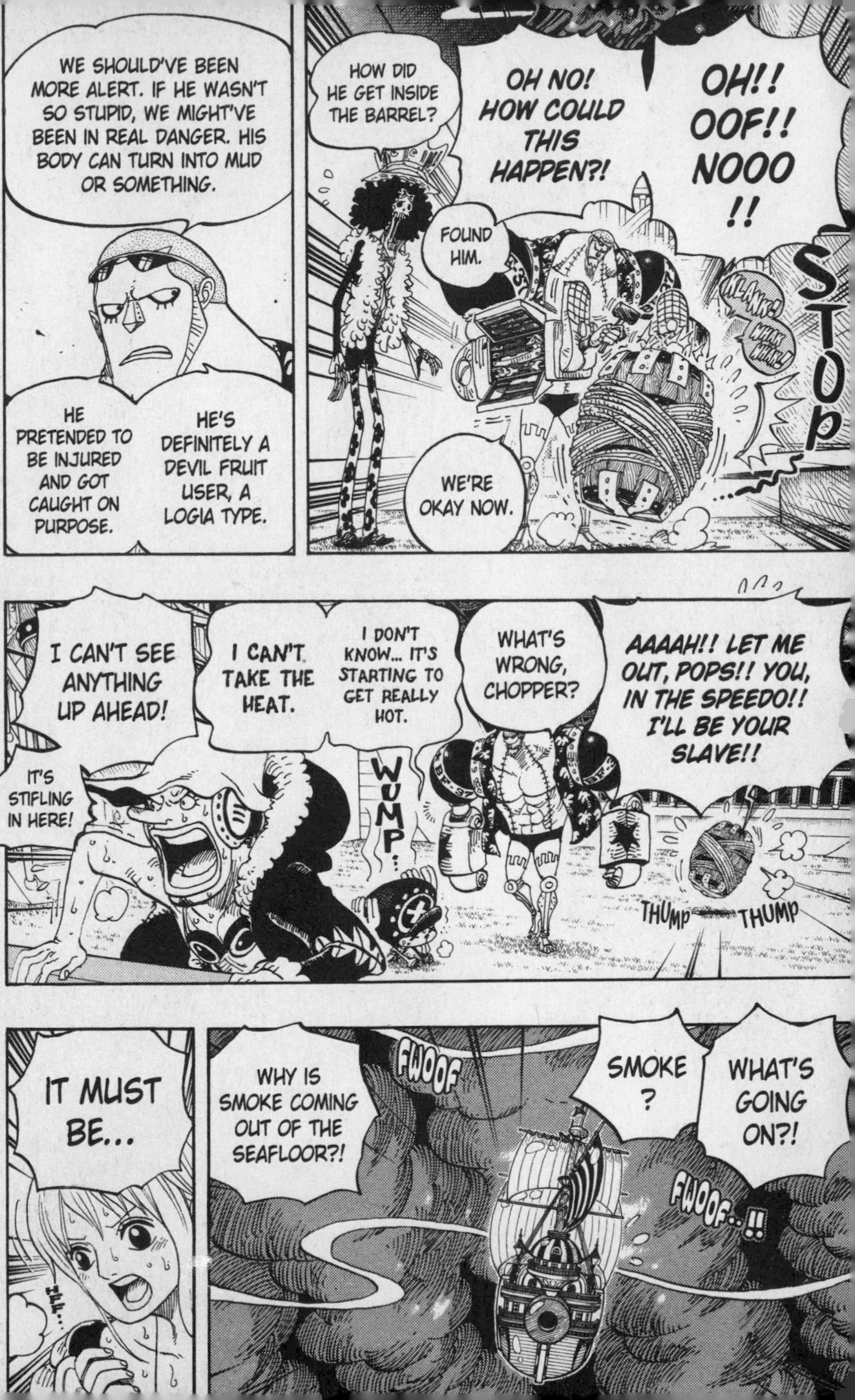
OH!! OOF!! NOOO !!
OH NO! HOW COULD THIS HAPPEN?!
HOW DID HE GET INSIDE THE BARREL?
FOUND HIM.
STOP
WE'RE OKAY NOW.
WE SHOULD'VE BEEN MORE ALERT. IF HE WASN'T SO STUPID, WE MIGHT'VE BEEN IN REAL DANGER. HIS BODY CAN TURN INTO MUD OR SOMETHING.
HE'S DEFINITELY A DEVIL FRUIT USER, A LOGIA TYPE.
HE PRETENDED TO BE INJURED AND GOT CAUGHT ON PURPOSE.
AAAAH!! LET ME OUT, POPS!! YOU, IN THE SPEEDO!! I'LL BE YOUR SLAVE!!
WHAT'S WRONG, CHOPPER?
I DON'T KNOW... IT'S STARTING TO GET REALLY HOT.
I CAN'T TAKE THE HEAT.
WUMP...
I CAN'T SEE ANYTHING UP AHEAD!
IT'S STIFLING IN HERE!
THUMP THUMP
WHAT'S GOING ON?!
SMOKE ?
FWOOF
WHY IS SMOKE COMING OUT OF THE SEAFLOOR?!
FWOOF..!!
IT MUST BE...

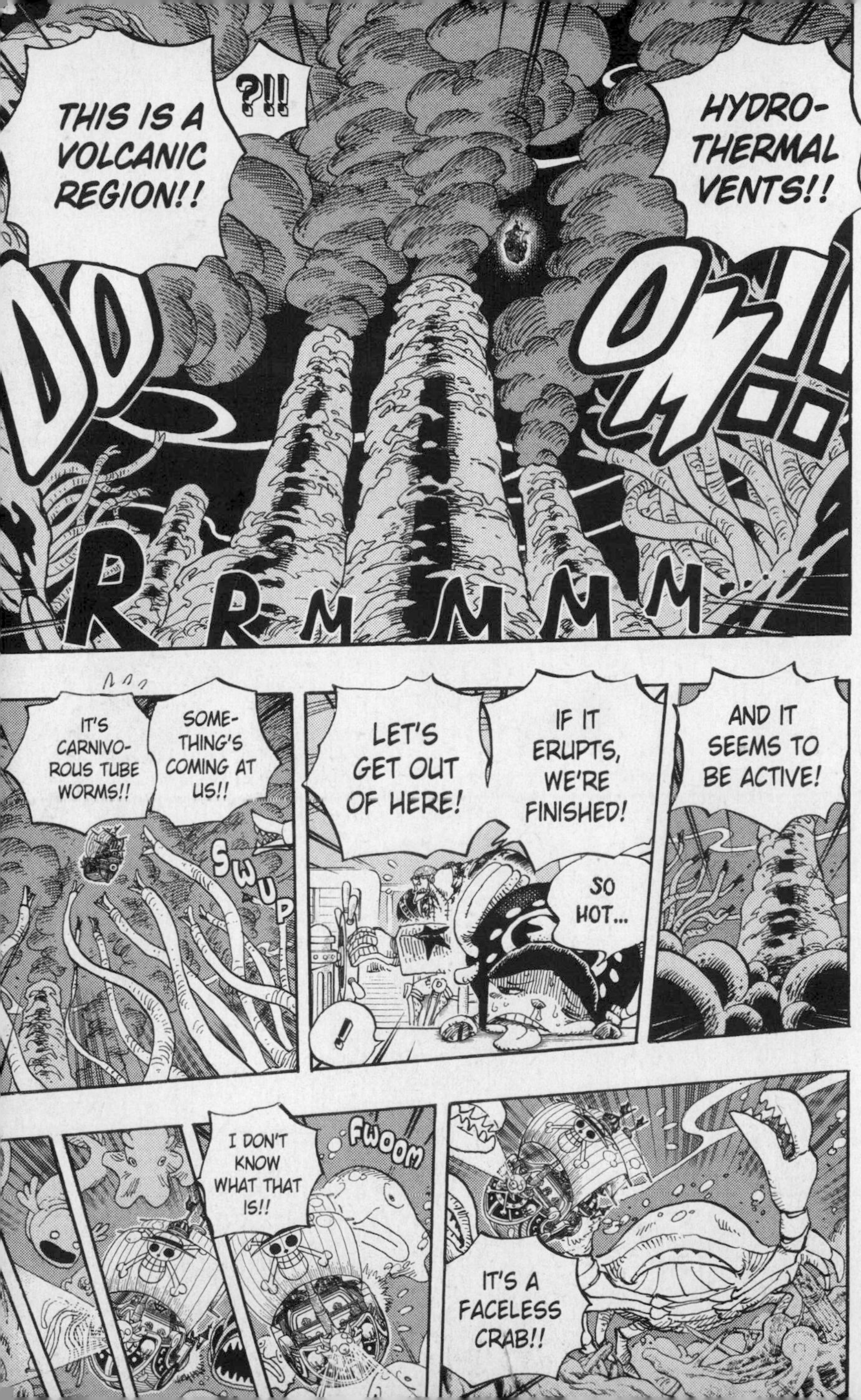
HYDRO-THERMAL VENTS!!
?!!
THIS IS A VOLCANIC REGION!!
DOOM!!...
RRMMMMM
AND IT SEEMS TO BE ACTIVE!
IF IT ERUPTS, WE'RE FINISHED!
LET'S GET OUT OF HERE!
SO HOT...
!
SOME-THING'S COMING AT US!!
IT'S CARNIVO-ROUS TUBE WORMS!!
SWUP
IT'S A FACELESS CRAB!!
FWOOM
I DON'T KNOW WHAT THAT IS!!

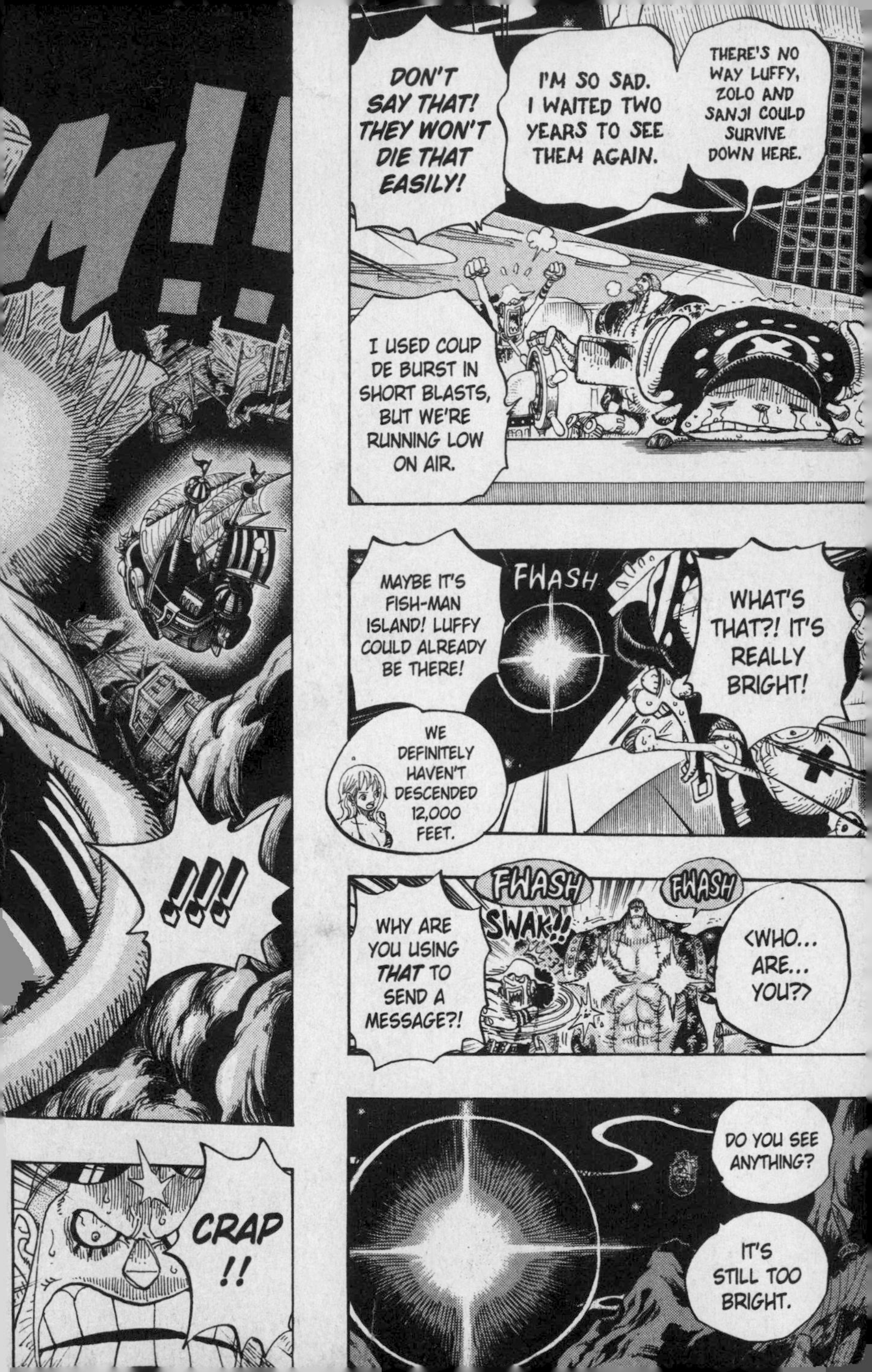
THERE'S NO WAY LUFFY, ZOLO AND SANJI COULD SURVIVE DOWN HERE.
I'M SO SAD. I WAITED TWO YEARS TO SEE THEM AGAIN.
DON'T SAY THAT! THEY WON'T DIE THAT EASILY!
I USED COUP DE BURST IN SHORT BLASTS, BUT WE'RE RUNNING LOW ON AIR.
WHAT'S THAT?! IT'S REALLY BRIGHT!
FWASH
MAYBE IT'S FISH-MAN ISLAND! LUFFY COULD ALREADY BE THERE!
WE DEFINITELY HAVEN'T DESCENDED 12,000 FEET.
<WHO... ARE... YOU?>
FWASH
FWASH
SWAK!!
WHY ARE YOU USING THAT TO SEND A MESSAGE?!
DO YOU SEE ANYTHING?
IT'S STILL TOO BRIGHT.
M!!
!!!
CRAP!!

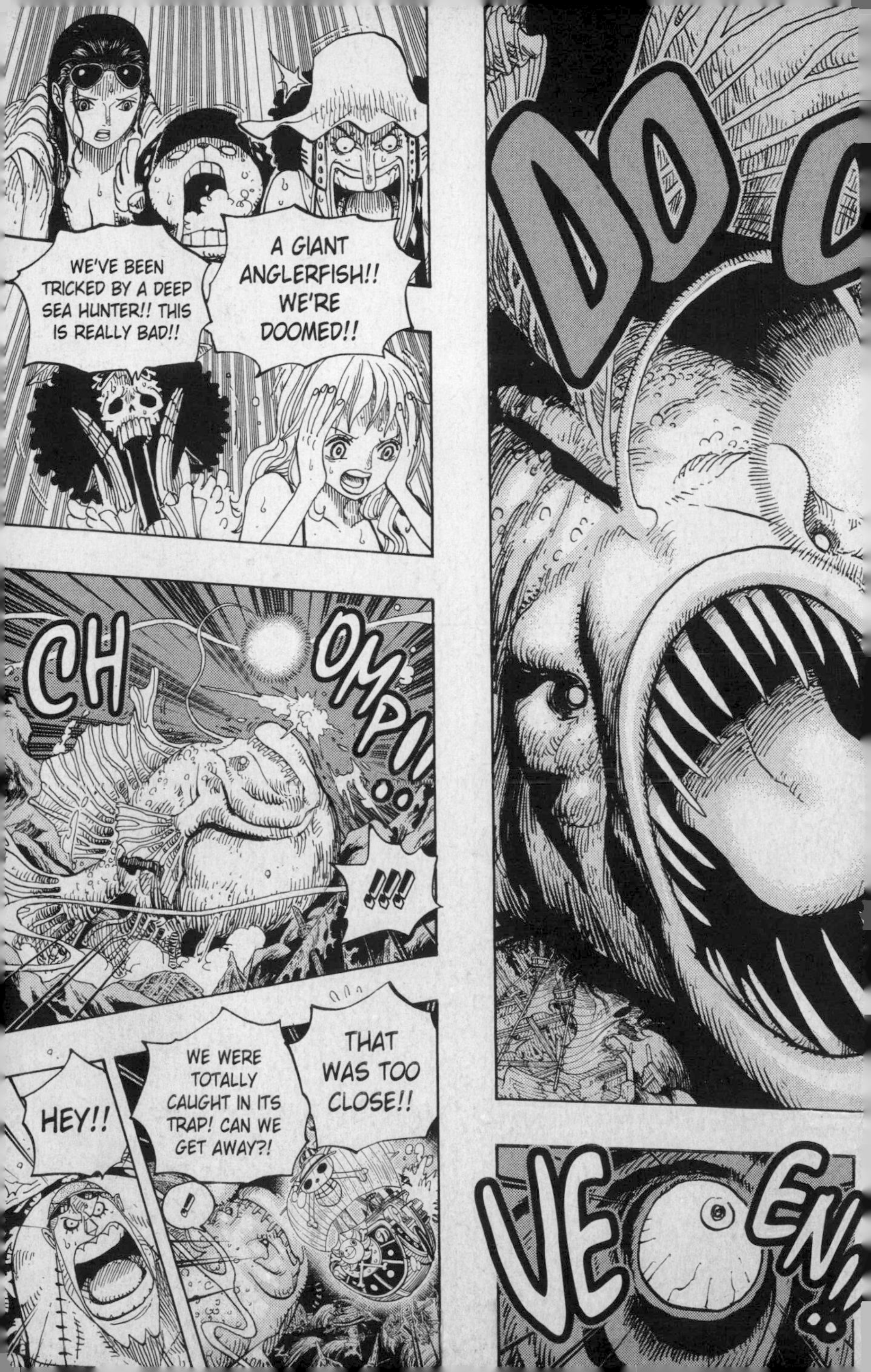
DOO
VE
EN!!
A GIANT ANGLERFISH!! WE'RE DOOMED!!
WE'VE BEEN TRICKED BY A DEEP SEA HUNTER!! THIS IS REALLY BAD!!
CH
OMP!!
!!!
THAT WAS TOO CLOSE!!
WE WERE TOTALLY CAUGHT IN ITS TRAP! CAN WE GET AWAY?!
HEY!!
!

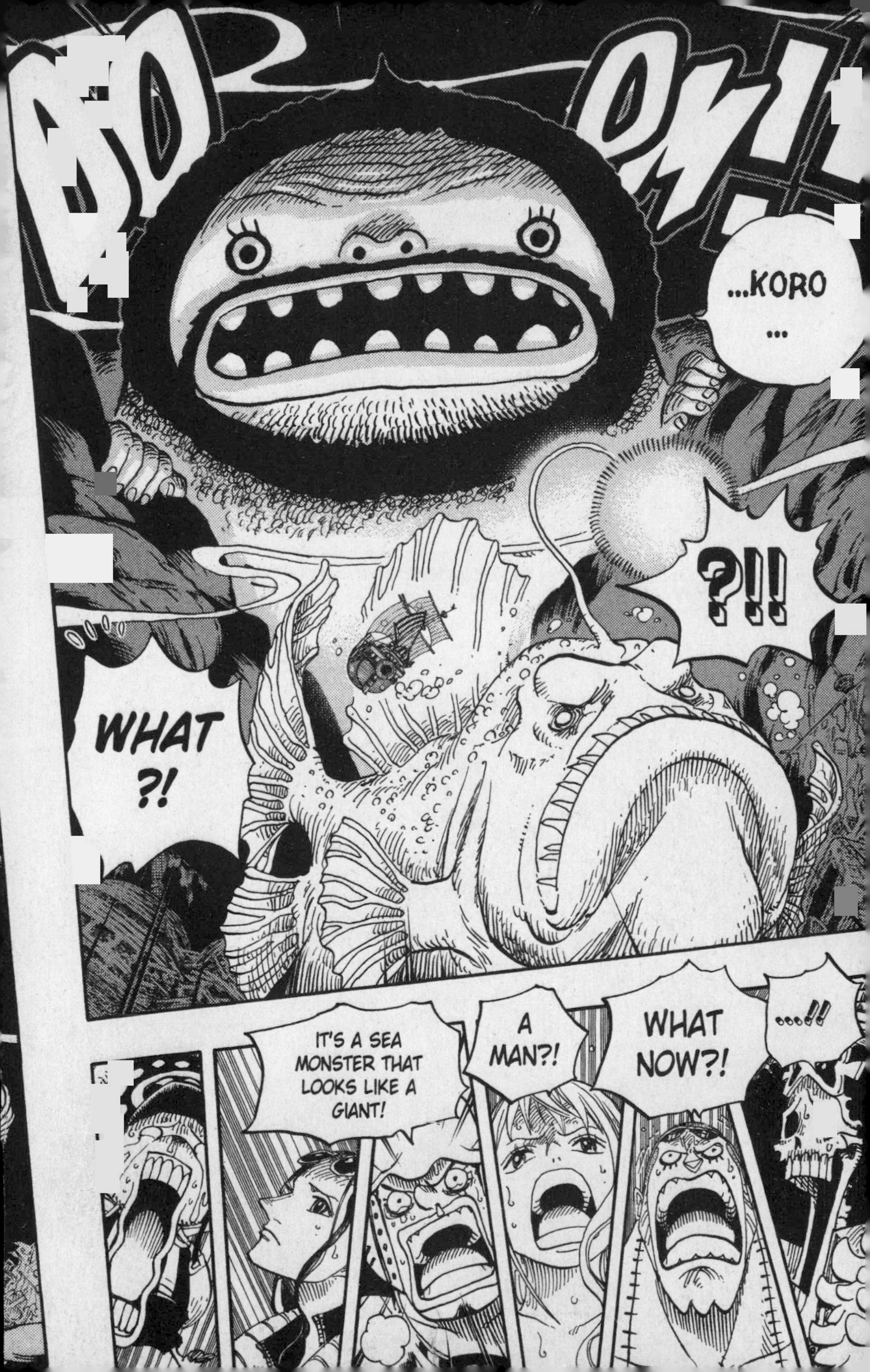
...KORO ...
?!!
WHAT ?!
....!!
WHAT NOW?!
A MAN?!
IT'S A SEA MONSTER THAT LOOKS LIKE A GIANT!

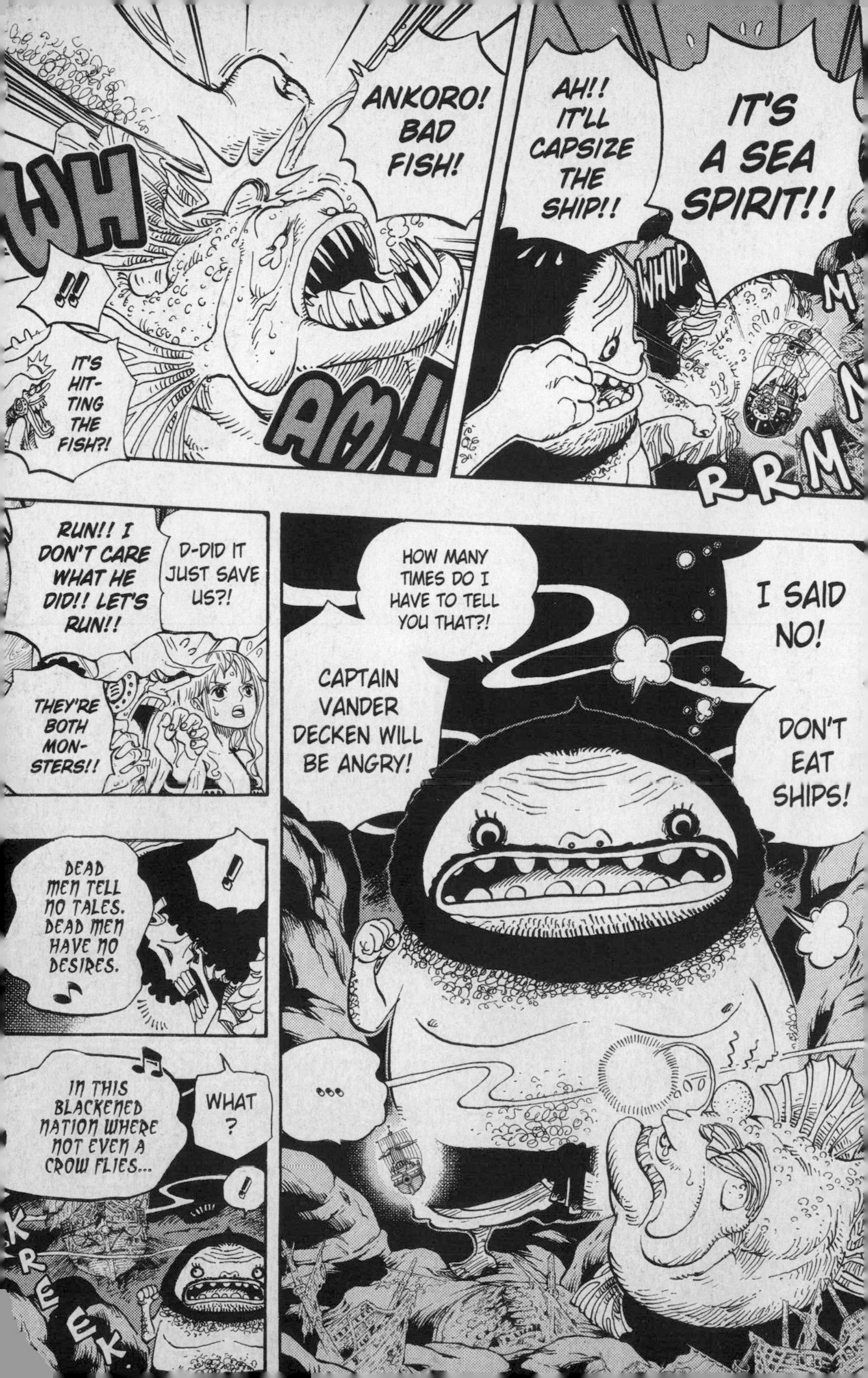
IT'S A SEA SPIRIT!!
AH!! IT'LL CAPSIZE THE SHIP!!
WHUP
ANKORO! BAD FISH!
WH
AM!!
!!
IT'S HIT-TING THE FISH?!
I SAID NO!
DON'T EAT SHIPS!
HOW MANY TIMES DO I HAVE TO TELL YOU THAT?!
CAPTAIN VANDER DECKEN WILL BE ANGRY!
...
D-DID IT JUST SAVE US?!
RUN!! I DON'T CARE WHAT HE DID!! LET'S RUN!!
THEY'RE BOTH MON-STERS!!
!
DEAD MEN TELL NO TALES. DEAD MEN HAVE NO DESIRES.
WHAT?
IN THIS BLACKENED NATION WHERE NOT EVEN A CROW FLIES...
!

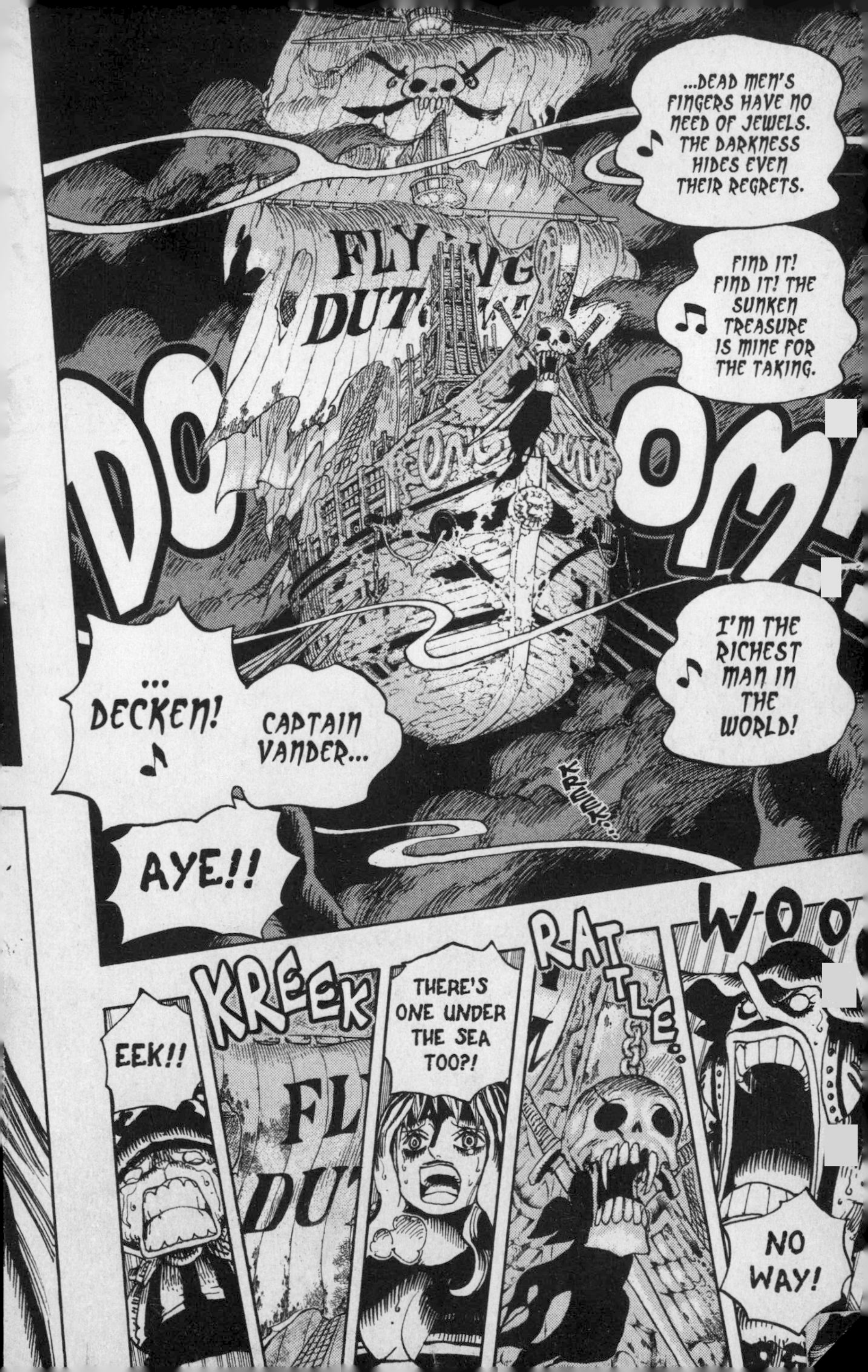
...DEAD MEN'S FINGERS HAVE NO NEED OF JEWELS. THE DARKNESS HIDES EVEN THEIR REGRETS.
FIND IT! FIND IT! THE SUNKEN TREASURE IS MINE FOR THE TAKING.
I'M THE RICHEST MAN IN THE WORLD!
CAPTAIN VANDER...
...DECKEN!
KREEK...
AYE!!
NO WAY!
RATTLE...
THERE'S ONE UNDER THE SEA TOO?!
KREEK
EEK!!

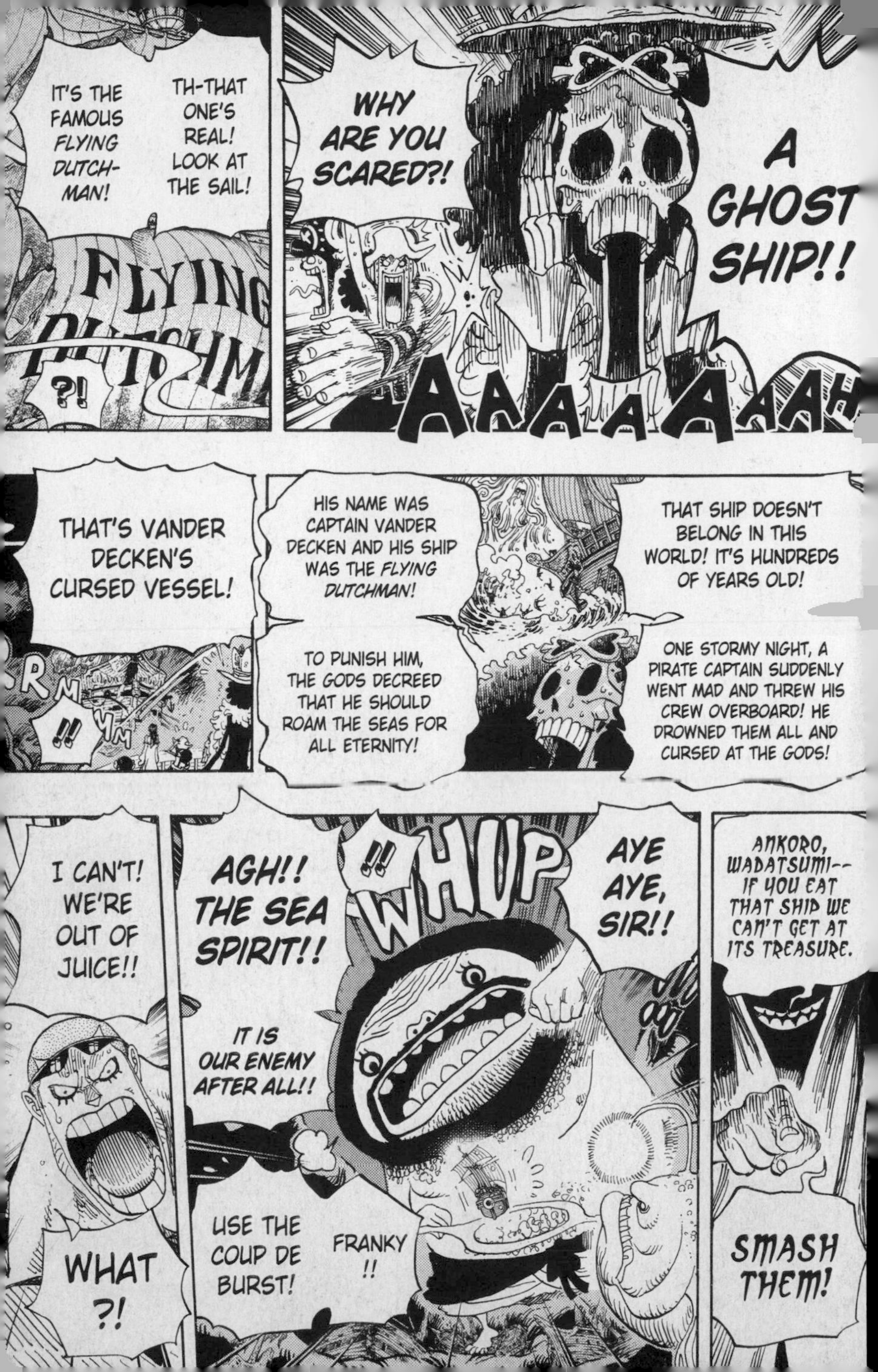
A GHOST SHIP!!
WHY ARE YOU SCARED?!
AAAAAAH
TH-THAT ONE'S REAL! LOOK AT THE SAIL!
IT'S THE FAMOUS FLYING DUTCHMAN!
FLYING DUTCHM
?!
THAT SHIP DOESN'T BELONG IN THIS WORLD! IT'S HUNDREDS OF YEARS OLD!
HIS NAME WAS CAPTAIN VANDER DECKEN AND HIS SHIP WAS THE FLYING DUTCHMAN!
ONE STORMY NIGHT, A PIRATE CAPTAIN SUDDENLY WENT MAD AND THREW HIS CREW OVERBOARD! HE DROWNED THEM ALL AND CURSED AT THE GODS!
TO PUNISH HIM, THE GODS DECREED THAT HE SHOULD ROAM THE SEAS FOR ALL ETERNITY!
THAT'S VANDER DECKEN'S CURSED VESSEL!
RMMM
!!
ANKORO, WADATSUMI-- IF YOU EAT THAT SHIP WE CAN'T GET AT ITS TREASURE.
SMASH THEM!
AYE AYE, SIR!!
WHIP
!!
AGH!! THE SEA SPIRIT!!
IT IS OUR ENEMY AFTER ALL!!
FRANKY !!
USE THE COUP DE BURST!
I CAN'T! WE'RE OUT OF JUICE!!
WHAT ?!

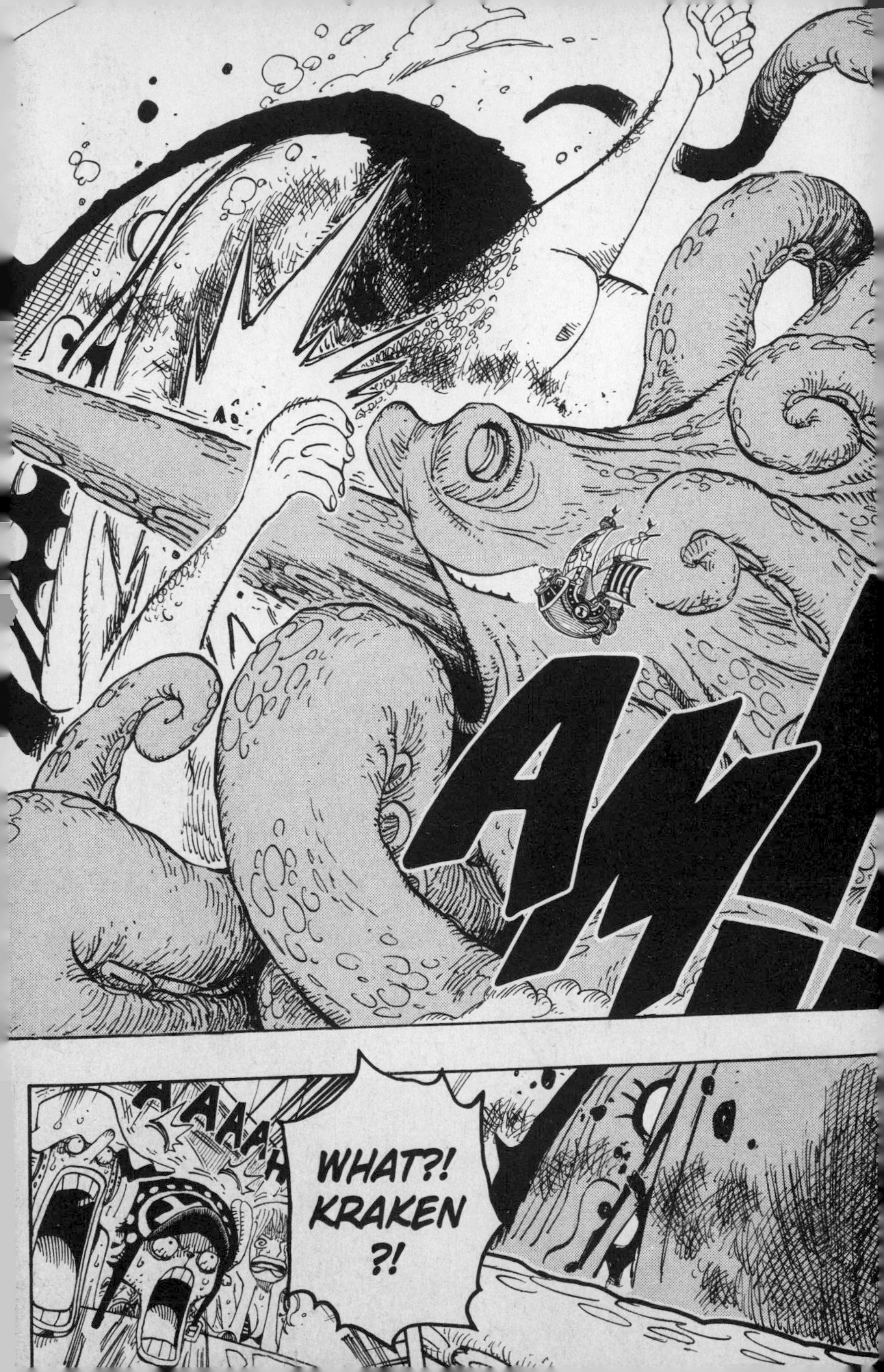
AH!!
AAAAAH
WHAT?! KRAKEN ?!

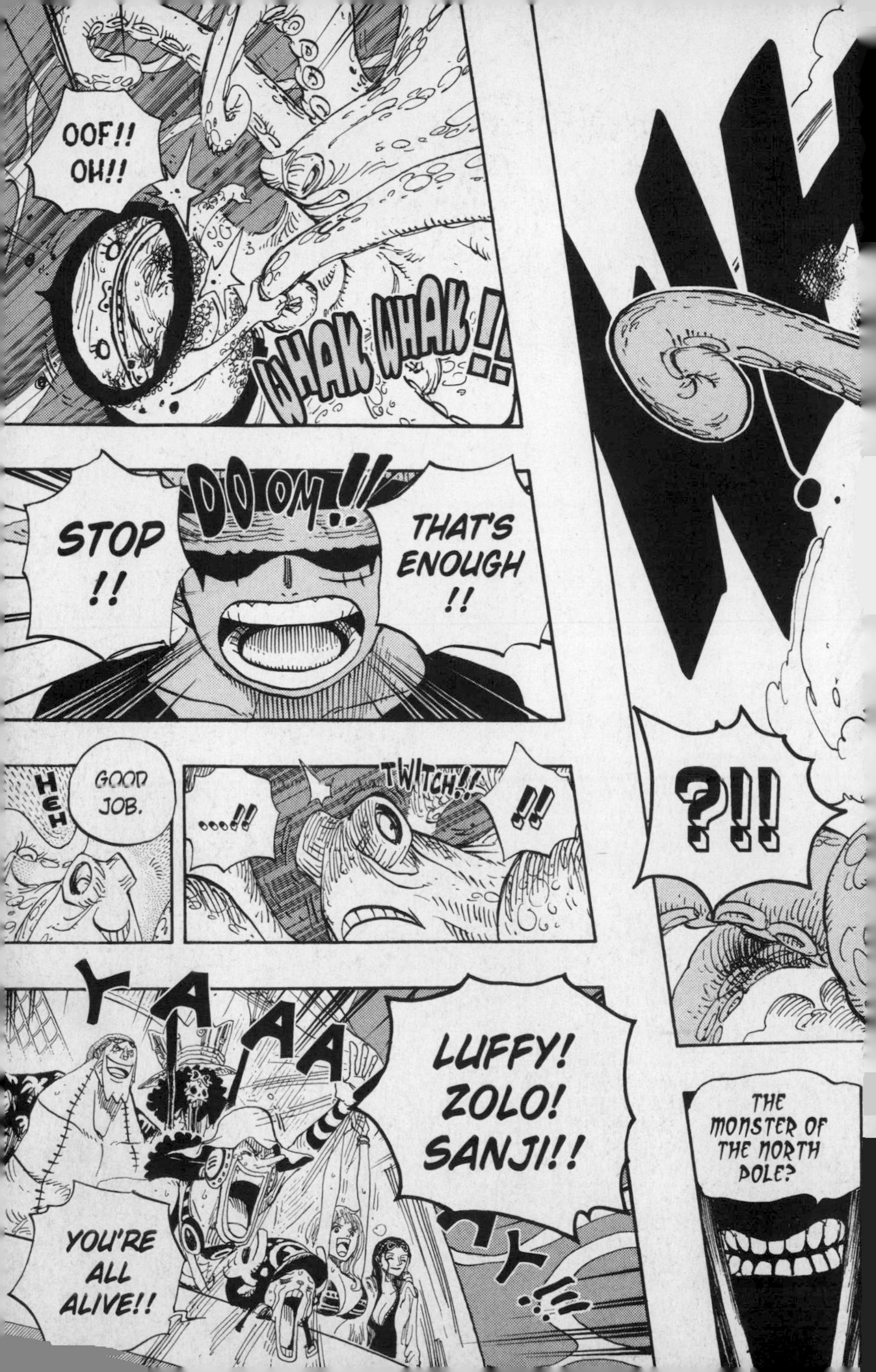
OOF!! OH!!
WHAK WHAK!!
DOOM!!
THAT'S ENOUGH!!
STOP!!
?!!
TWITCH!!
!!
....!!
GOOD JOB.
HEH
LUFFY! ZOLO! SANJI!!
YOU'RE ALL ALIVE!!
YAAAAY!!!
THE MONSTER OF THE NORTH POLE?

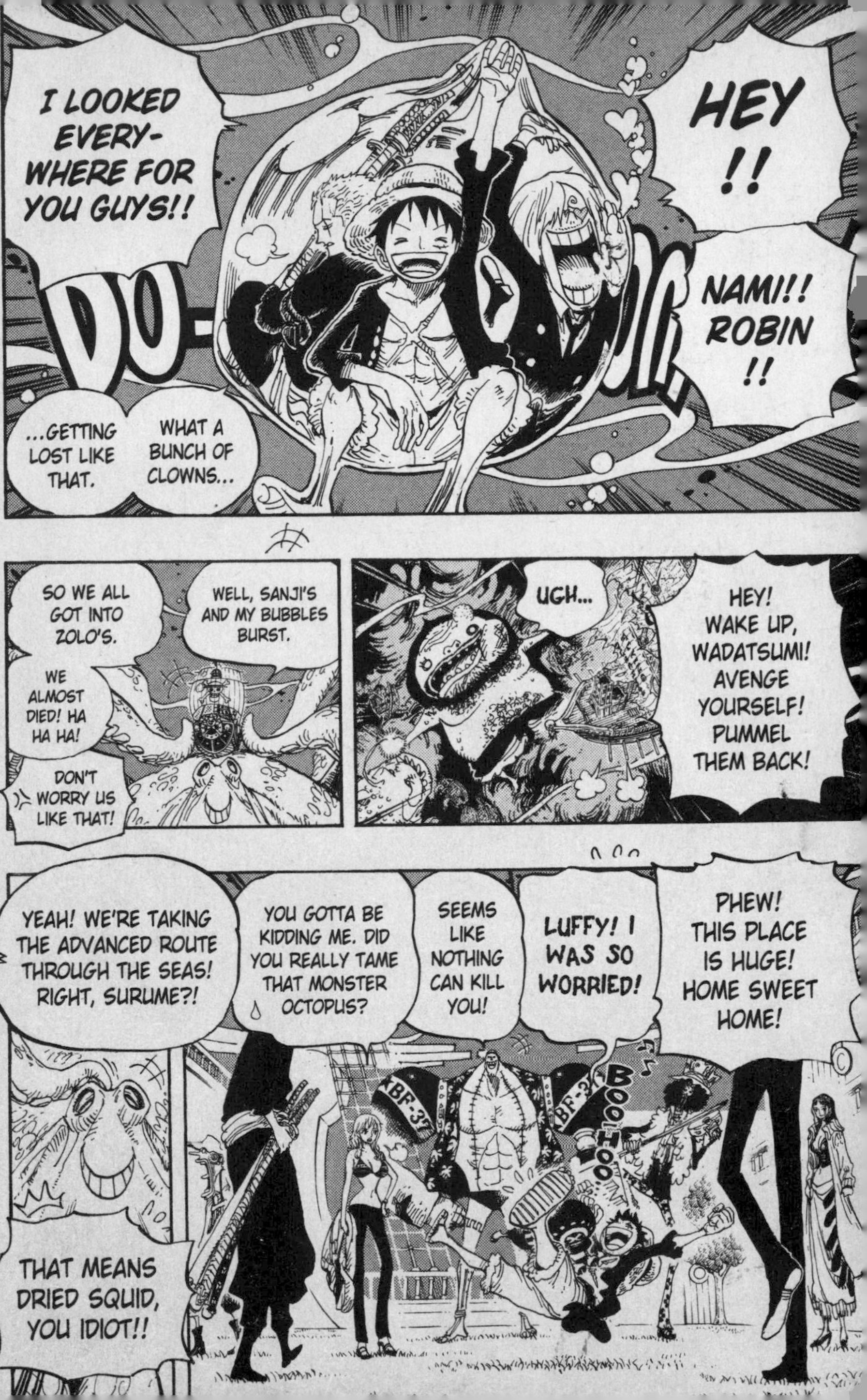
HEY!!
NAMI!! ROBIN!!
I LOOKED EVERY-WHERE FOR YOU GUYS!!
DO-
WHAT A BUNCH OF CLOWNS...
...GETTING LOST LIKE THAT.
HEY! WAKE UP, WADATSUMI! AVENGE YOURSELF! PUMMEL THEM BACK!
UGH...
WELL, SANJI'S AND MY BUBBLES BURST.
SO WE ALL GOT INTO ZOLO'S.
WE ALMOST DIED! HA HA HA!
DON'T WORRY US LIKE THAT!
PHEW! THIS PLACE IS HUGE! HOME SWEET HOME!
LUFFY! I WAS SO WORRIED!
SEEMS LIKE NOTHING CAN KILL YOU!
YOU GOTTA BE KIDDING ME. DID YOU REALLY TAME THAT MONSTER OCTOPUS?
YEAH! WE'RE TAKING THE ADVANCED ROUTE THROUGH THE SEAS! RIGHT, SURUME?!
BOOHOOHOO
THAT MEANS DRIED SQUID, YOU IDIOT!!

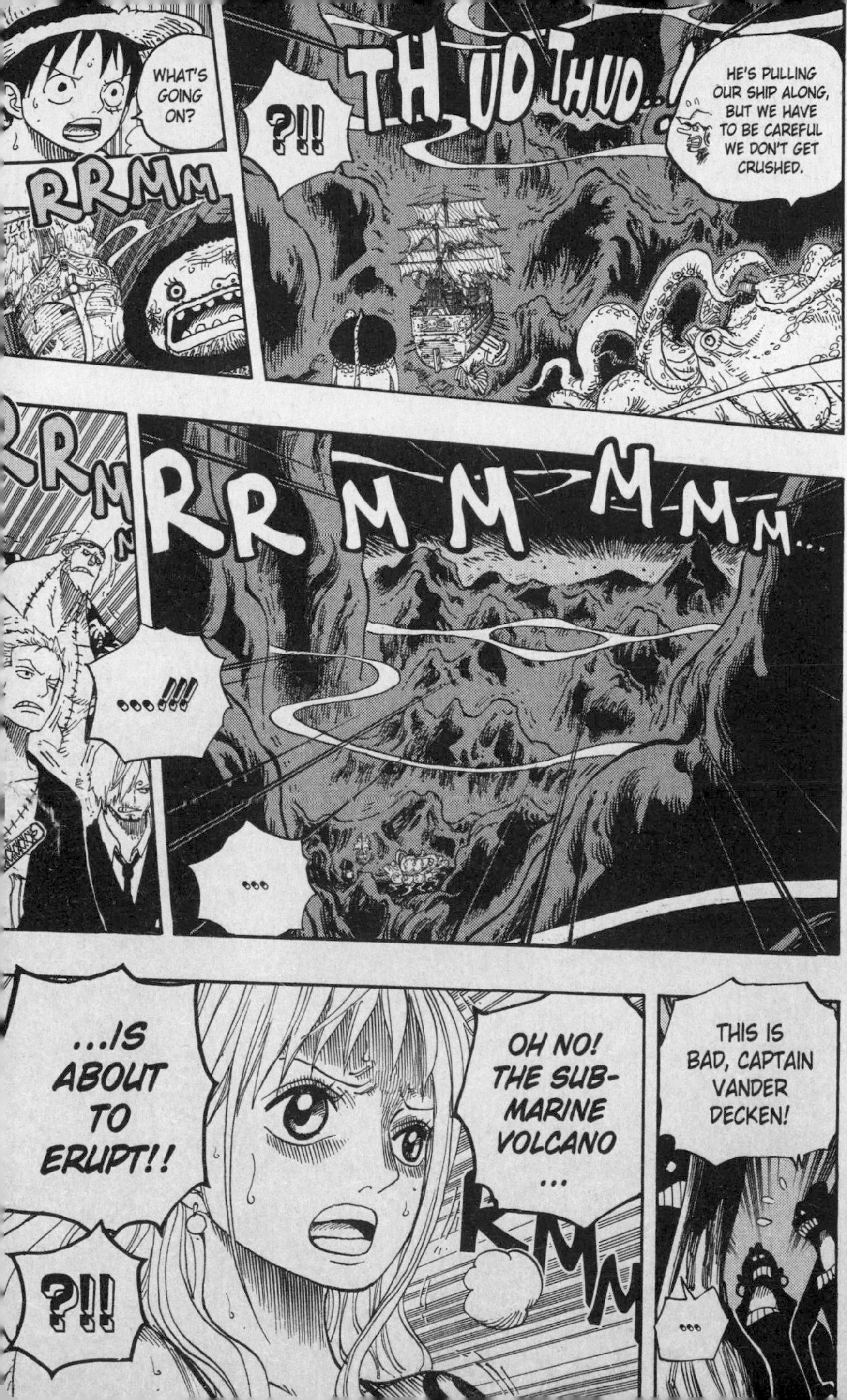
THUD THUD..!!
HE'S PULLING OUR SHIP ALONG, BUT WE HAVE TO BE CAREFUL WE DON'T GET CRUSHED.
?!!
WHAT'S GOING ON?
RRMM
RRMMMMMMM...
...
...!!!
RRMM
THIS IS BAD, CAPTAIN VANDER DECKEN!
...
KMMM
OH NO! THE SUB-MARINE VOLCANO ...
...IS ABOUT TO ERUPT!!
?!!

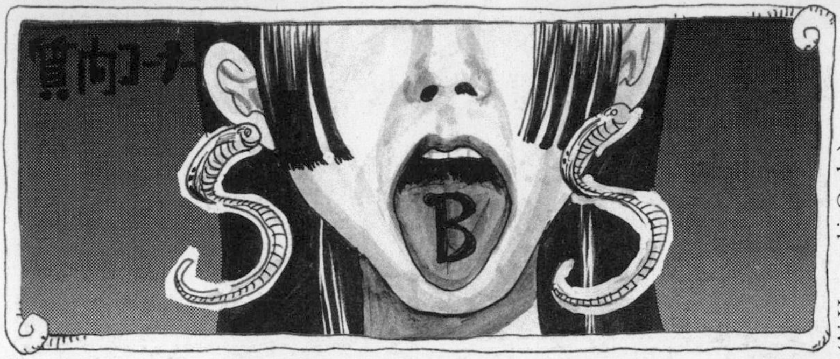
質問コーナー
SBS

(Ai Hamazaki, Osaka)

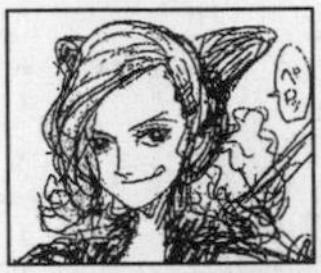

Q: I have a quick question for the Blackbeard Pirates! In the rough designs, I remember seeing a beautiful woman. So why did you end up using Catalina Devon? Vasco Shot also has a long nose. Oh, and Nami is so sexy!

--Midori Mask

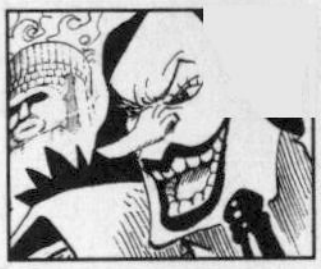

A: The reader is referring to a picture printed in the extra book called One Piece Green. The book has my rough designs and other stuff from my sketchbook. Some characters in that book took years to make it to the public eye while others were put in print right away. Members of the Blackbeard Pirates were the former. Years went by as I continued to make modifications to my design and ended up with what you see in my comics. Some may complain by saying, "It took you years to make that?!" The reason why I decided against having a beautiful woman in there is because the Blackbeard Pirates have a theme where they are the most "pirate-like" band of pirates. They are huge, rough, and exciting. Having a beautiful woman in there would seem to ruin that image (no matter how much I like them). That's why I have her like that!

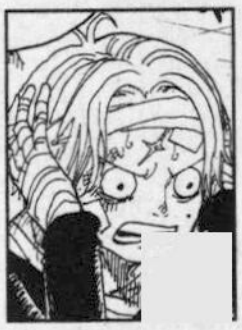

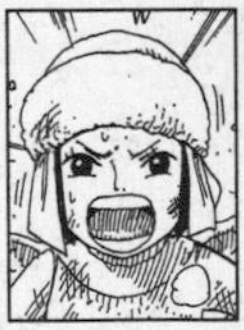

Q: Hello, Mr. Oda.☆ I'm just wondering, but are "Haki" and "Mantra" the same thing? Koby mentioned "feeling the presence of people too strongly" in volume 60, and that made me think about it.

--Black Cat Girl

A: You're absolutely right. Rayleigh said it outright in volume 61. You know how different countries call the same phenomenon different things? It's like that.

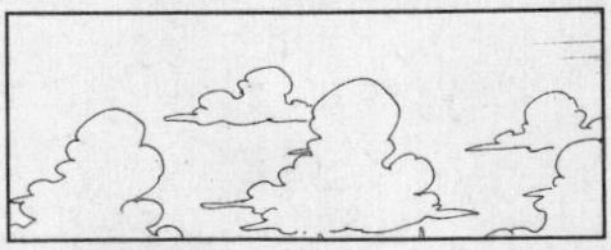

Q: Odacchi, are the clouds you draw cumulonimbus clouds or your farts?

--Seishinrinsho (Wakayama)

A: They're my farts. All clouds you see are my farts.

Chapter 607:
30,000 FEET UNDER THE SEA

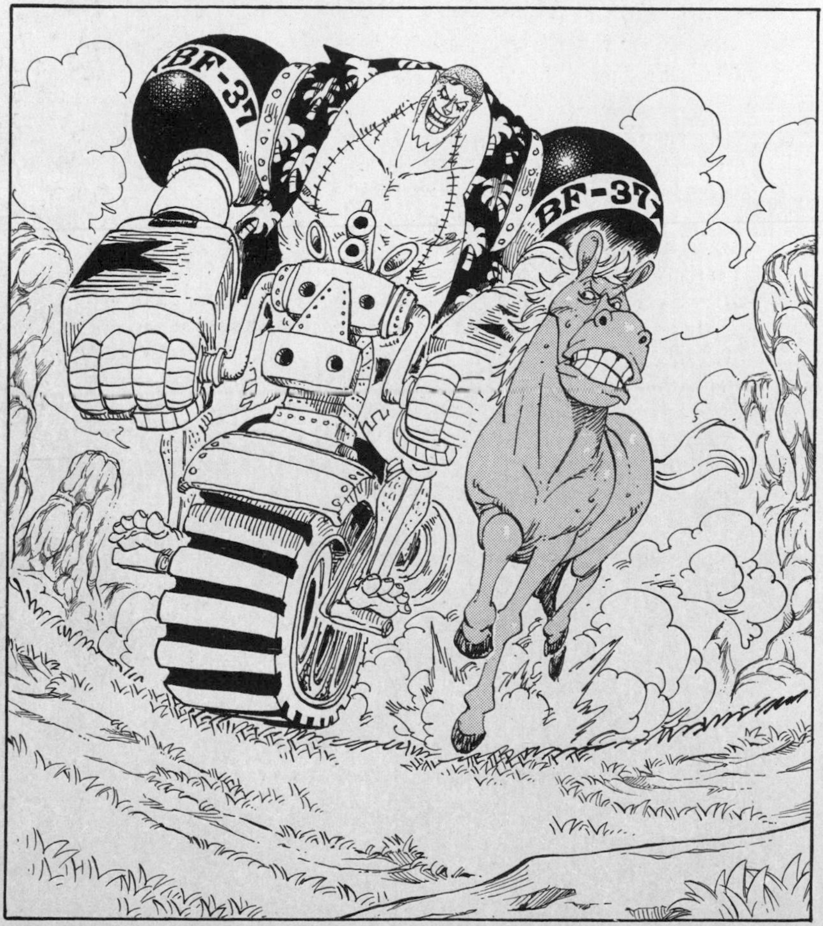

BF-37
BF-37

REQUEST: "FRANKY RACING A MUSTANG ON A MACHINE HE MADE HIMSELF." BY MAGIC MUSHROOM

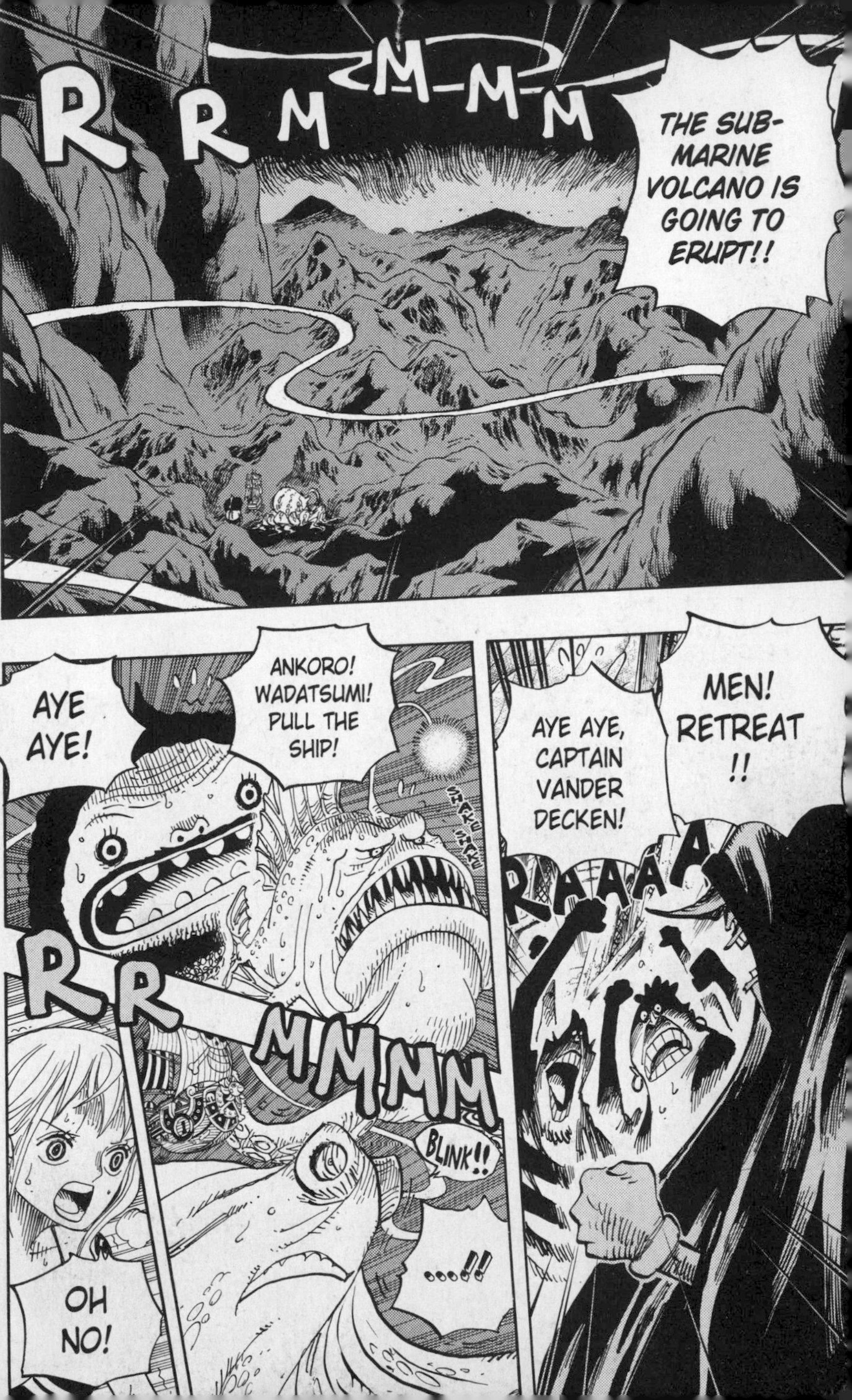
RRRMMMMM
THE SUB-MARINE VOLCANO IS GOING TO ERUPT!!
MEN! RETREAT!!
AYE AYE, CAPTAIN VANDER DECKEN!
RAAAA
ANKORO! WADATSUMI! PULL THE SHIP!
AYE AYE!
SHAKE SHAKE
RRMMMMM
BLINK!!
...!!
OH NO!

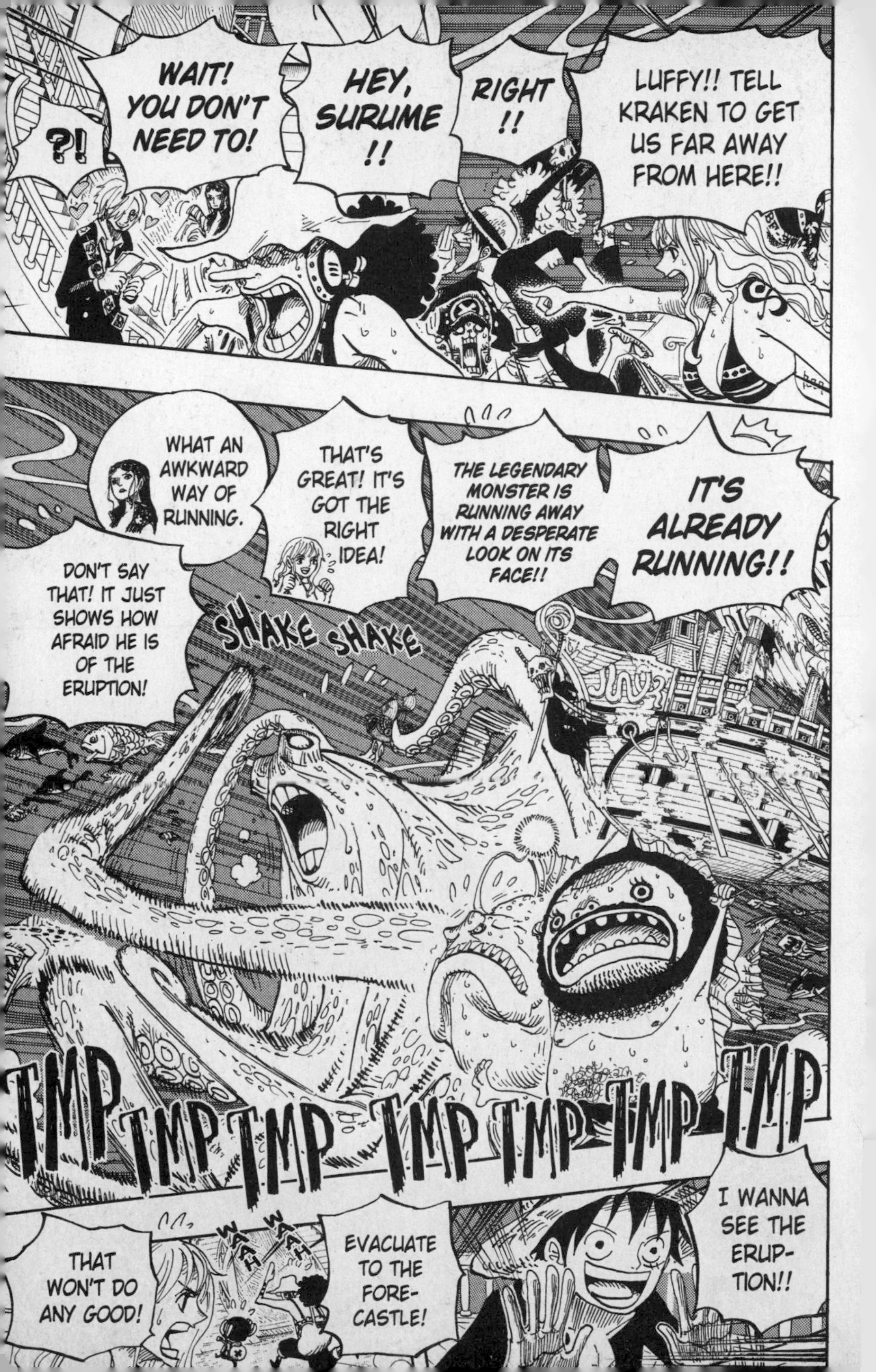
LUFFY!! TELL KRAKEN TO GET US FAR AWAY FROM HERE!!
RIGHT !!
HEY, SURUME !!
WAIT! YOU DON'T NEED TO!
?!
IT'S ALREADY RUNNING!!
THE LEGENDARY MONSTER IS RUNNING AWAY WITH A DESPERATE LOOK ON ITS FACE!!
THAT'S GREAT! IT'S GOT THE RIGHT IDEA!
WHAT AN AWKWARD WAY OF RUNNING.
DON'T SAY THAT! IT JUST SHOWS HOW AFRAID HE IS OF THE ERUPTION!
SHAKE SHAKE
TMP TMP TMP TMP TMP TMP TMP
I WANNA SEE THE ERUP-TION!!
EVACUATE TO THE FORE-CASTLE!
WAH WAH
THAT WON'T DO ANY GOOD!

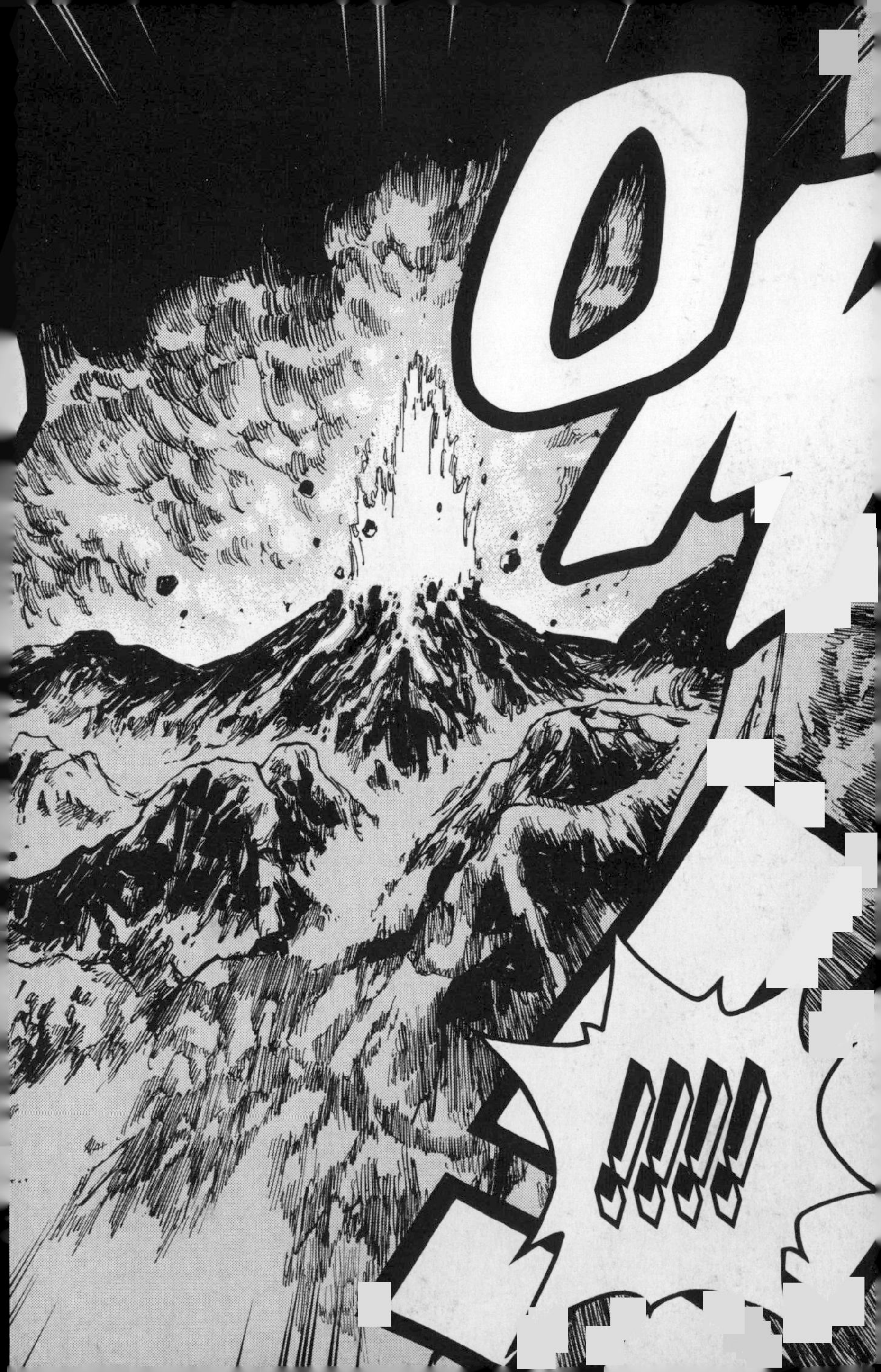
!!!!

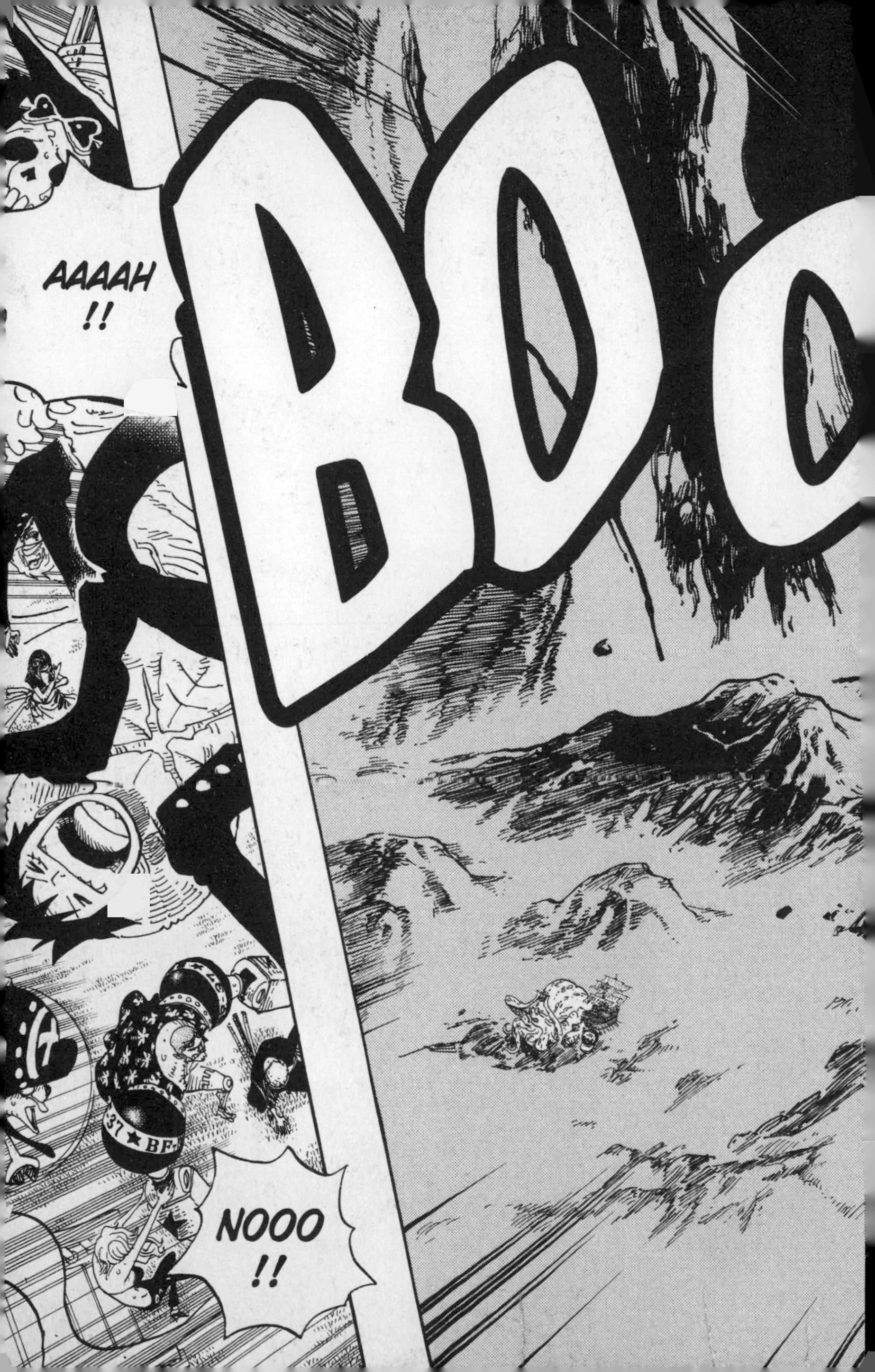
BOO
AAAAH !!
NOOO !!

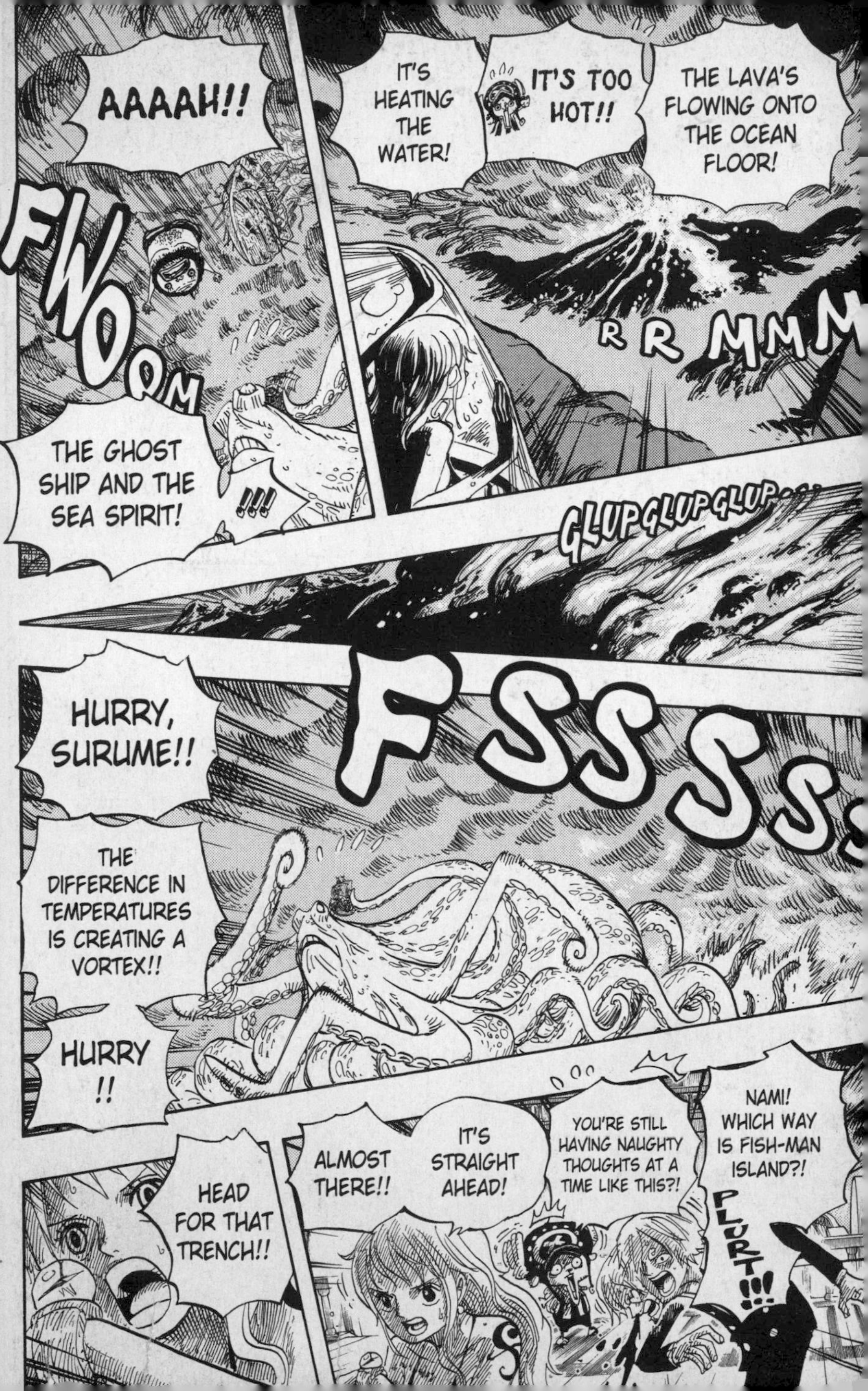
THE LAVA'S FLOWING ONTO THE OCEAN FLOOR!
IT'S TOO HOT!!
IT'S HEATING THE WATER!
RRMMM
AAAAH!!
FWOOM
THE GHOST SHIP AND THE SEA SPIRIT!
!!!
GLUPGLUPGLUP...
FSSSS
HURRY, SURUME!!
THE DIFFERENCE IN TEMPERATURES IS CREATING A VORTEX!!
HURRY!!
NAMI! WHICH WAY IS FISH-MAN ISLAND?!
YOU'RE STILL HAVING NAUGHTY THOUGHTS AT A TIME LIKE THIS?!
PLURT!!!
IT'S STRAIGHT AHEAD!
ALMOST THERE!!
HEAD FOR THAT TRENCH!!

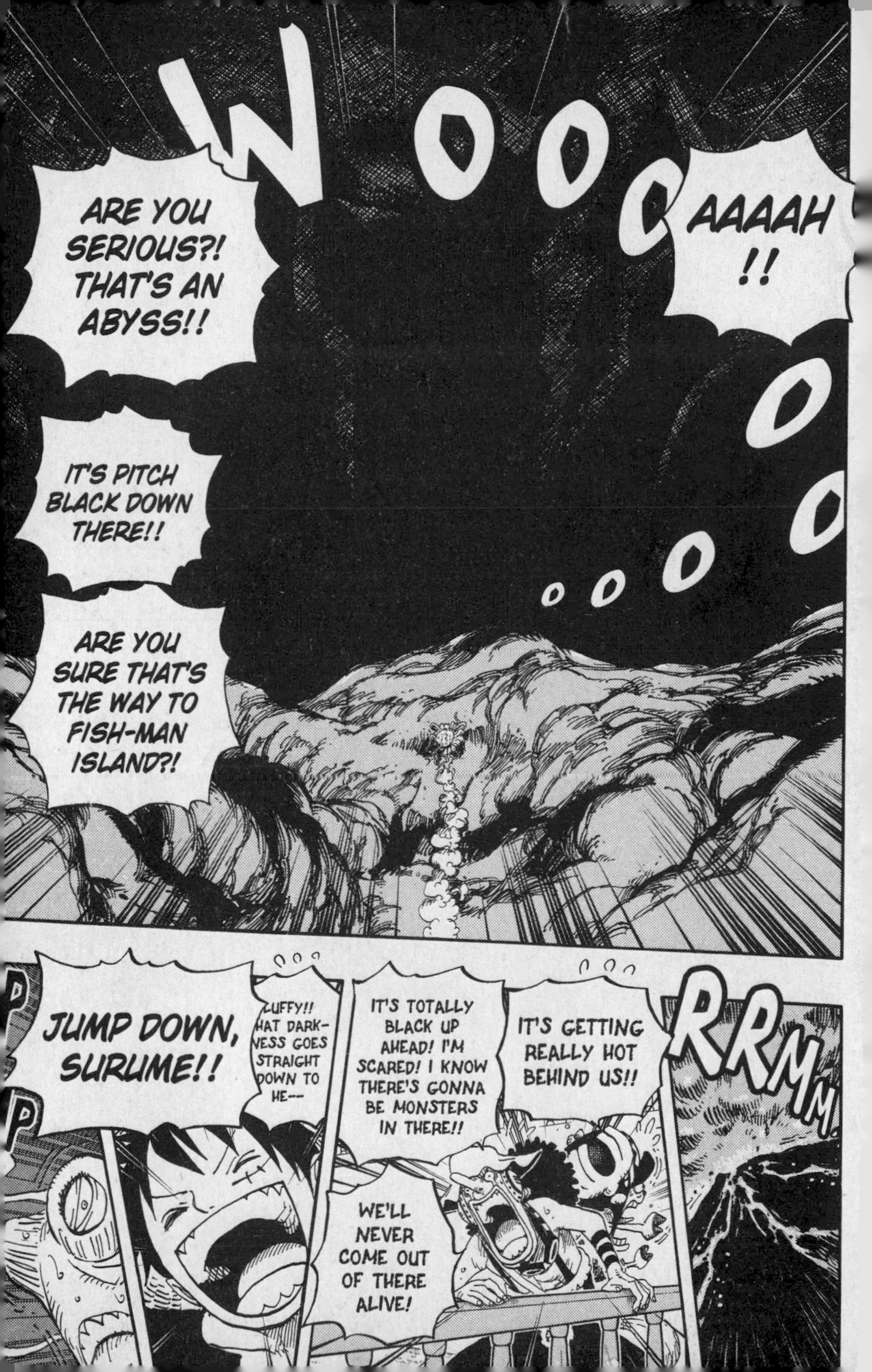
WOOO
AAAAH!!
OOOOO
ARE YOU SERIOUS?! THAT'S AN ABYSS!!
IT'S PITCH BLACK DOWN THERE!!
ARE YOU SURE THAT'S THE WAY TO FISH-MAN ISLAND?!
RRMMM
IT'S GETTING REALLY HOT BEHIND US!!
IT'S TOTALLY BLACK UP AHEAD! I'M SCARED! I KNOW THERE'S GONNA BE MONSTERS IN THERE!!
WE'LL NEVER COME OUT OF THERE ALIVE!
LUFFY!! HAT DARK- NESS GOES STRAIGHT DOWN TO HE--
JUMP DOWN, SURUME!!

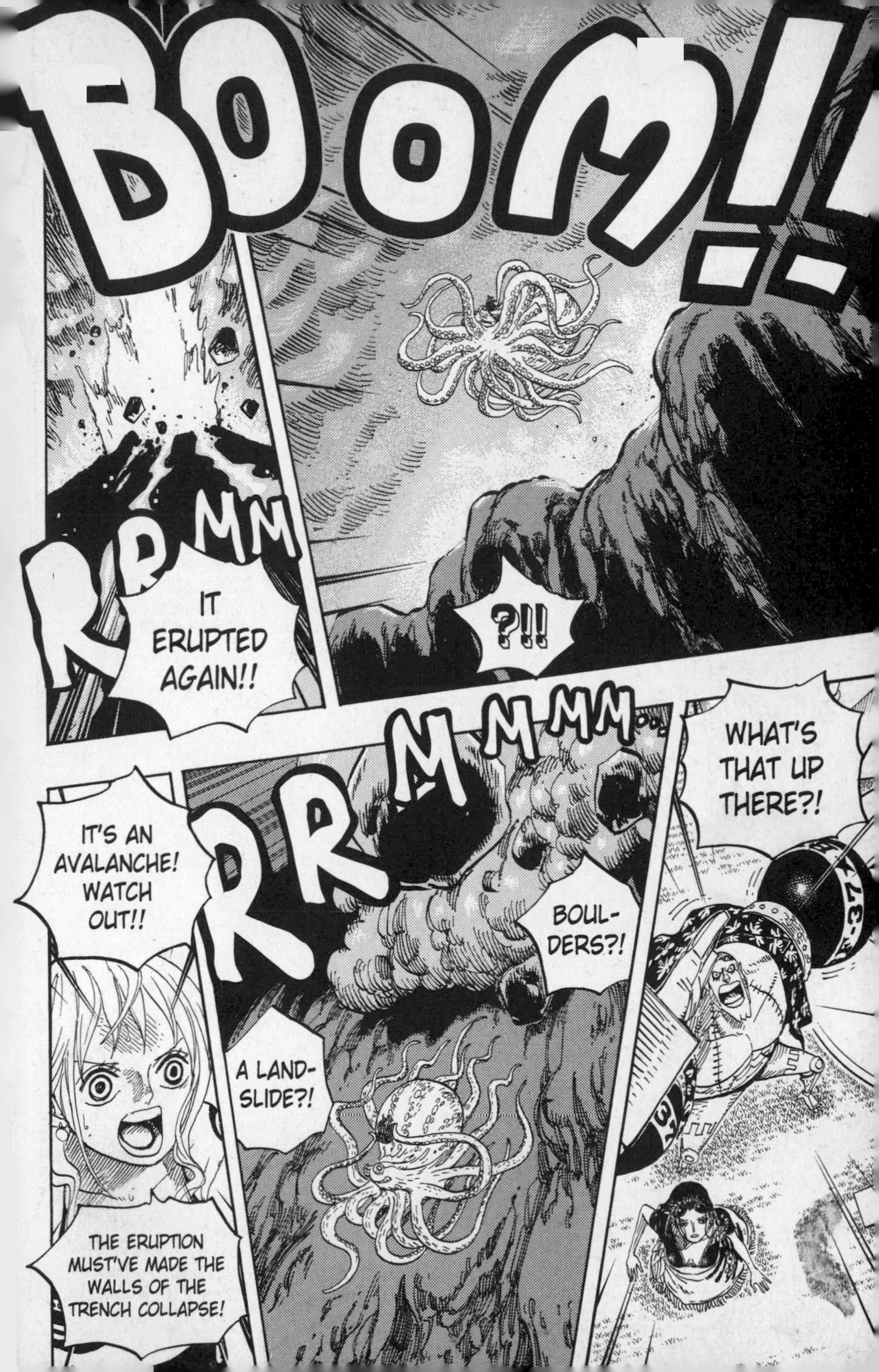
BOOM!!
?!!
RRMM
IT ERUPTED AGAIN!!
WHAT'S THAT UP THERE?!
RRMMMMM
BOUL-DERS?!
A LAND-SLIDE?!
IT'S AN AVALANCHE! WATCH OUT!!
THE ERUPTION MUST'VE MADE THE WALLS OF THE TRENCH COLLAPSE!

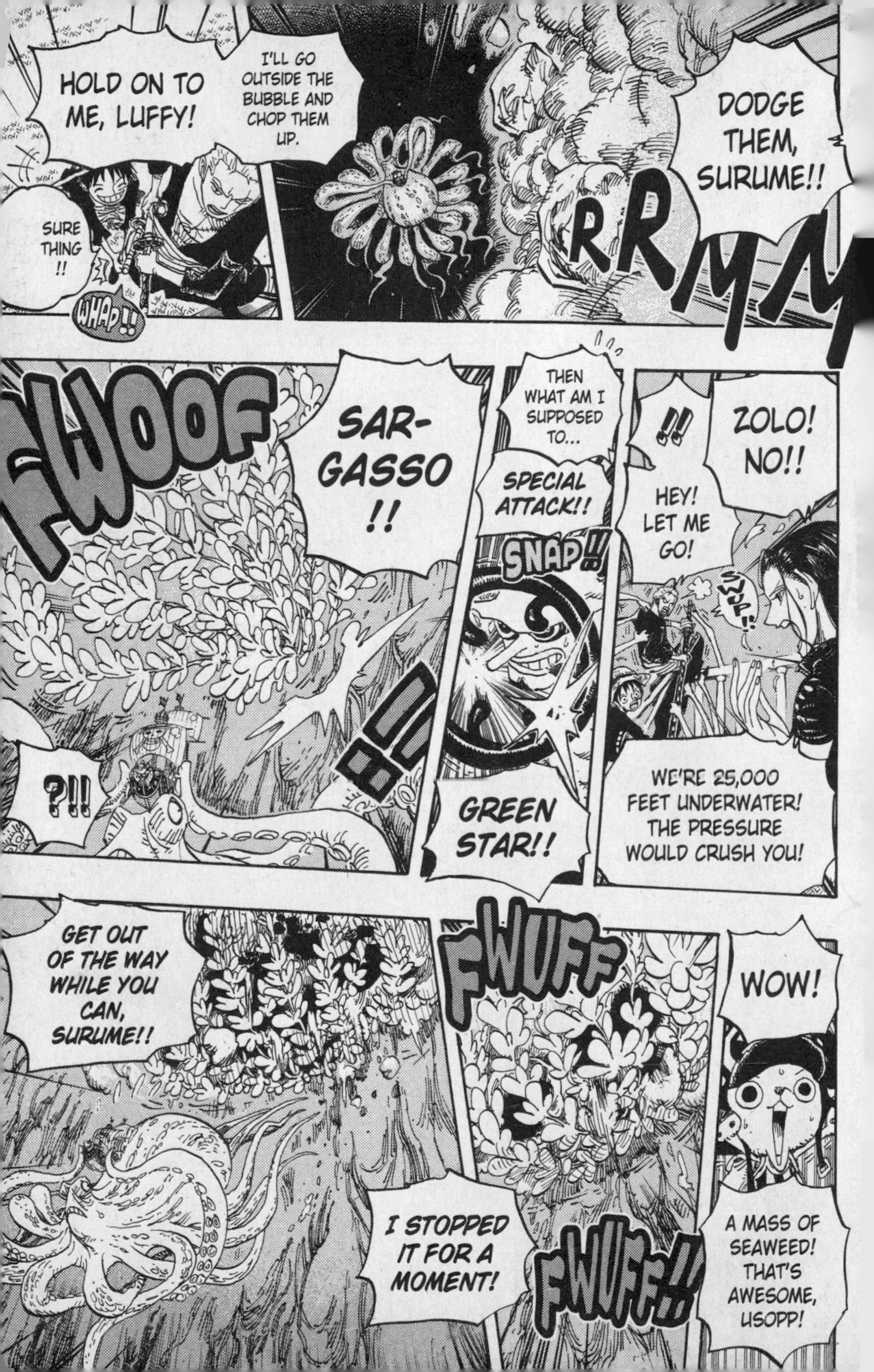
DODGE THEM, SURUME!!
I'LL GO OUTSIDE THE BUBBLE AND CHOP THEM UP.
HOLD ON TO ME, LUFFY!
SURE THING!!
WHAP!!
ZOLO! NO!!
!!
HEY! LET ME GO!
SWUP!!
WE'RE 25,000 FEET UNDERWATER! THE PRESSURE WOULD CRUSH YOU!
THEN WHAT AM I SUPPOSED TO...
SPECIAL ATTACK!!
SNAP!!
GREEN STAR!!
SAR-GASSO!!
FWOOF
!!
?!!
WOW!
A MASS OF SEAWEED! THAT'S AWESOME, USOPP!
FWUFF
I STOPPED IT FOR A MOMENT!
FWUFF!!
GET OUT OF THE WAY WHILE YOU CAN, SURUME!!

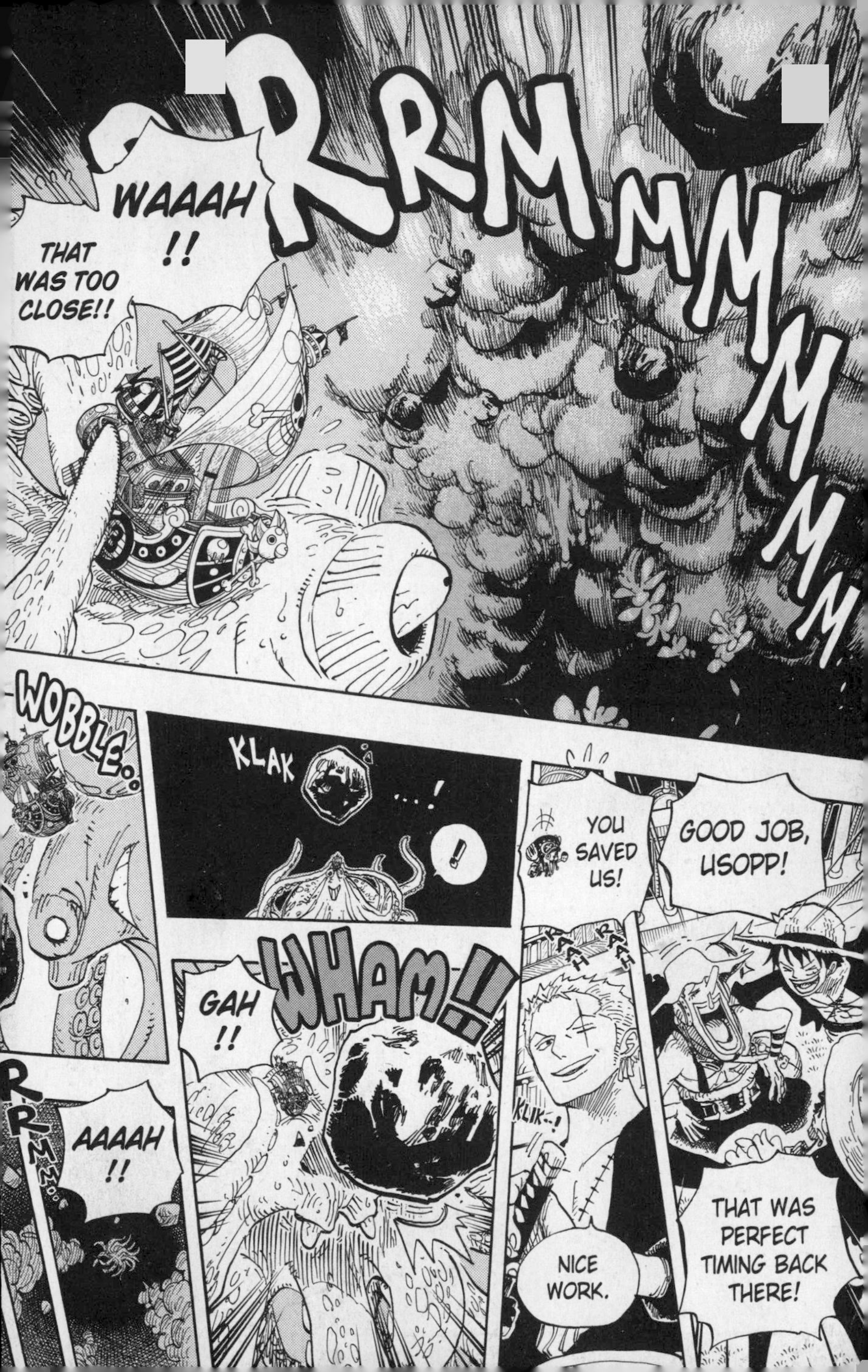
RRMMMMMMMM
WAAAH!!
THAT WAS TOO CLOSE!!
GOOD JOB, USOPP!
YOU SAVED US!
...!
!
KLAK
WOBBLE..
THAT WAS PERFECT TIMING BACK THERE!
RAH RAH
KLIK..!
NICE WORK.
WHAM!!
GAH!!
RRMMM..
AAAAH!!

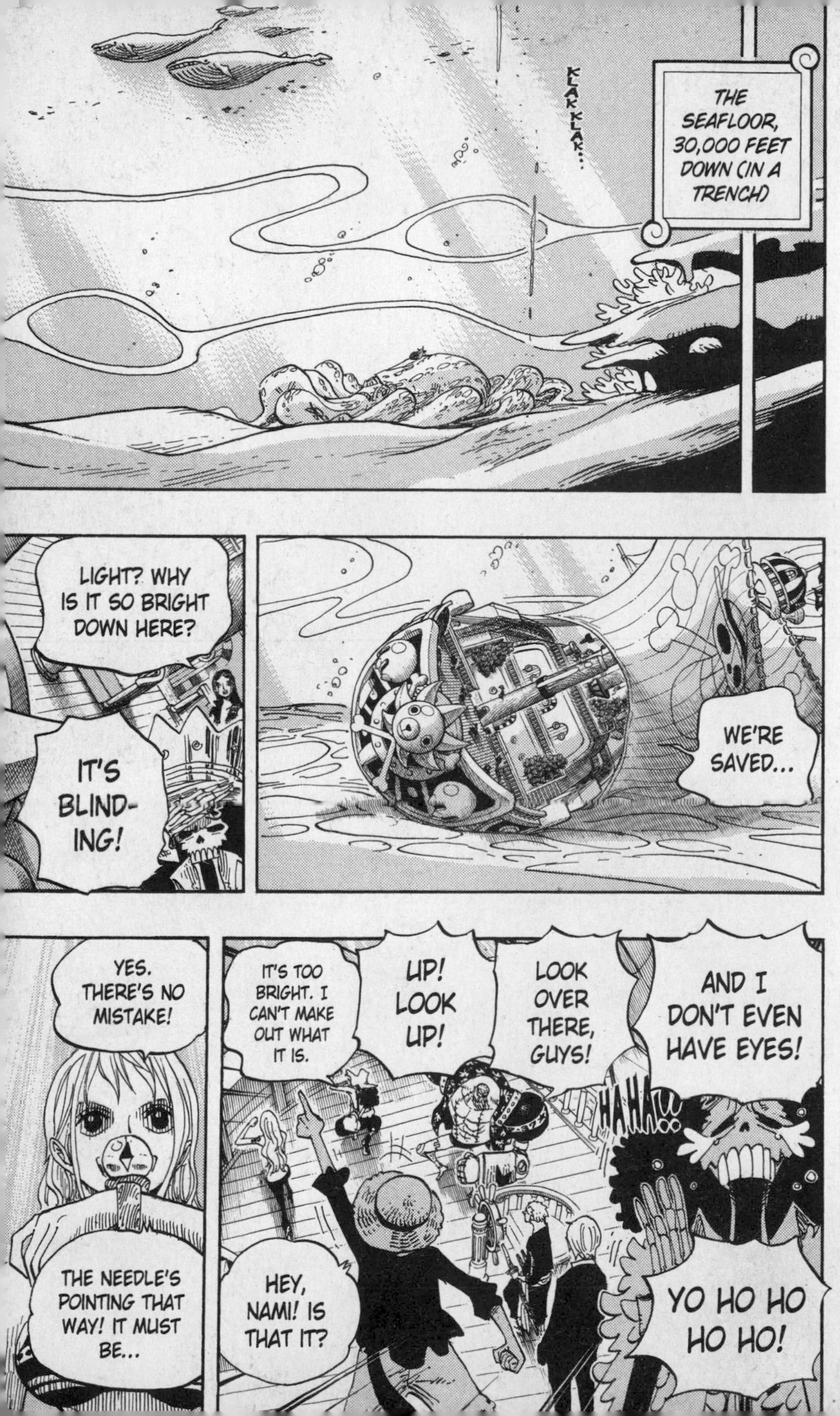
THE SEAFLOOR, 30,000 FEET DOWN (IN A TRENCH)
KLAK KLAK...
WE'RE SAVED...
LIGHT? WHY IS IT SO BRIGHT DOWN HERE?
IT'S BLINDING!
AND I DON'T EVEN HAVE EYES!
HAHA!!
LOOK OVER THERE, GUYS!
UP! LOOK UP!
IT'S TOO BRIGHT. I CAN'T MAKE OUT WHAT IT IS.
YO HO HO HO HO!
HEY, NAMI! IS THAT IT?
YES. THERE'S NO MISTAKE!
THE NEEDLE'S POINTING THAT WAY! IT MUST BE...

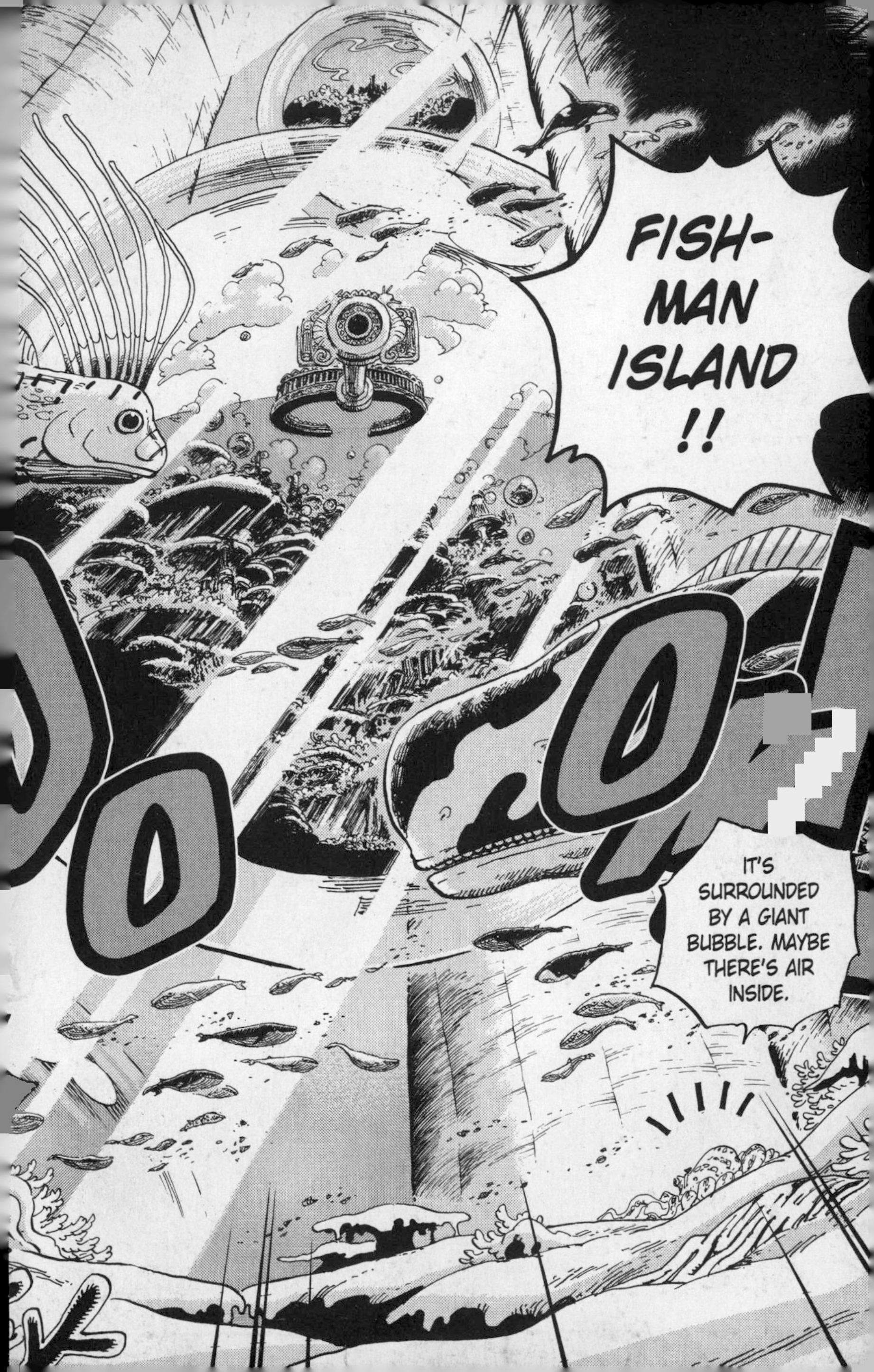
FISH-MAN ISLAND!!
IT'S SURROUNDED BY A GIANT BUBBLE. MAYBE THERE'S AIR INSIDE.

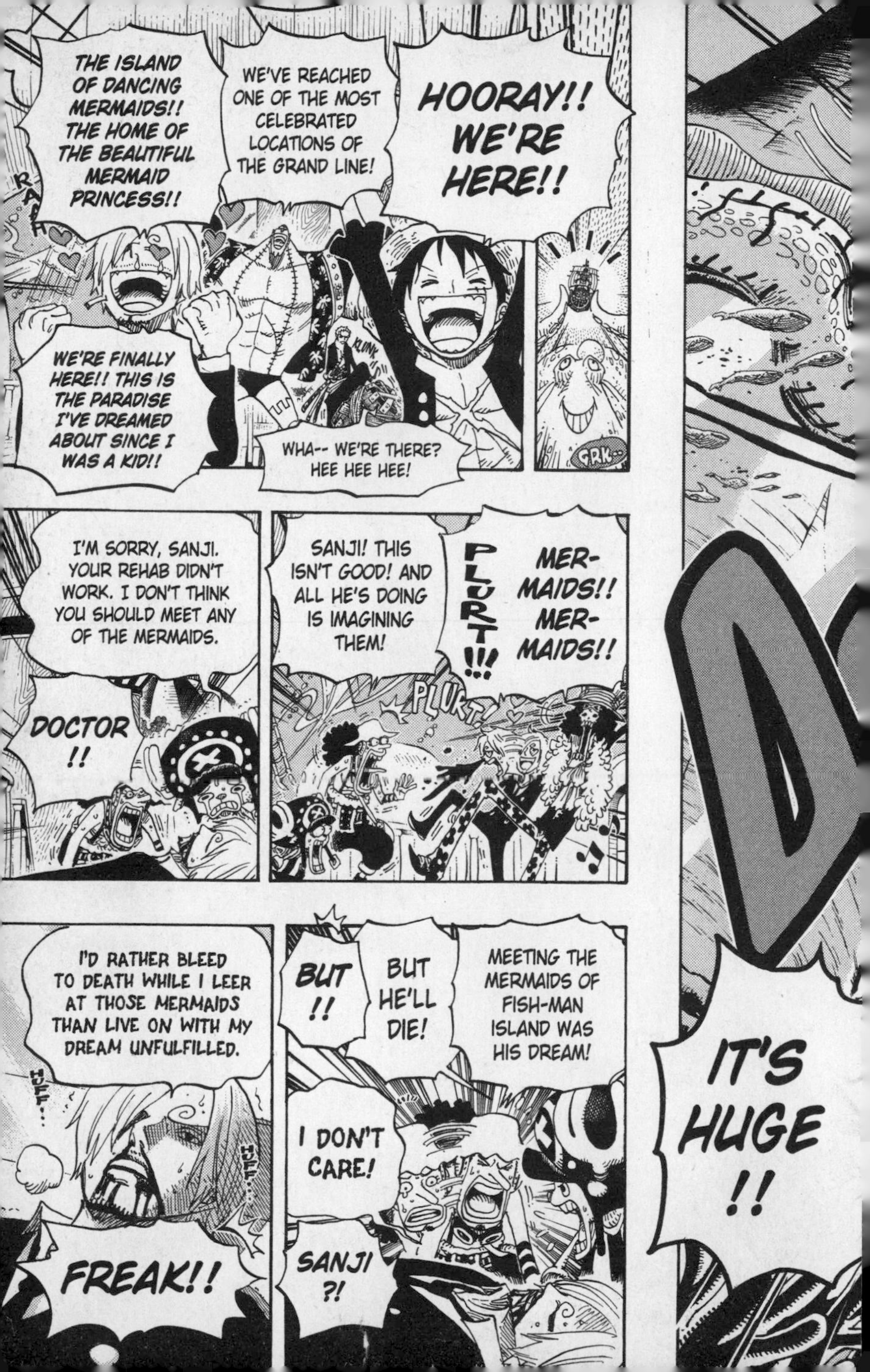
IT'S HUGE!!
GRK...
HOORAY!! WE'RE HERE!!
WE'VE REACHED ONE OF THE MOST CELEBRATED LOCATIONS OF THE GRAND LINE!
THE ISLAND OF DANCING MERMAIDS!! THE HOME OF THE BEAUTIFUL MERMAID PRINCESS!!
KLINK
WHA-- WE'RE THERE? HEE HEE HEE!
WE'RE FINALLY HERE!! THIS IS THE PARADISE I'VE DREAMED ABOUT SINCE I WAS A KID!!
RAH
MER-MAIDS!! MER-MAIDS!!
PLURT!!!
SANJI! THIS ISN'T GOOD! AND ALL HE'S DOING IS IMAGINING THEM!
PLURT!
I'M SORRY, SANJI. YOUR REHAB DIDN'T WORK. I DON'T THINK YOU SHOULD MEET ANY OF THE MERMAIDS.
DOCTOR!!
MEETING THE MERMAIDS OF FISH-MAN ISLAND WAS HIS DREAM!
BUT HE'LL DIE!
BUT!!
I DON'T CARE!
SANJI?!
I'D RATHER BLEED TO DEATH WHILE I LEER AT THOSE MERMAIDS THAN LIVE ON WITH MY DREAM UNFULFILLED.
HUFF...
HUFF...
FREAK!!

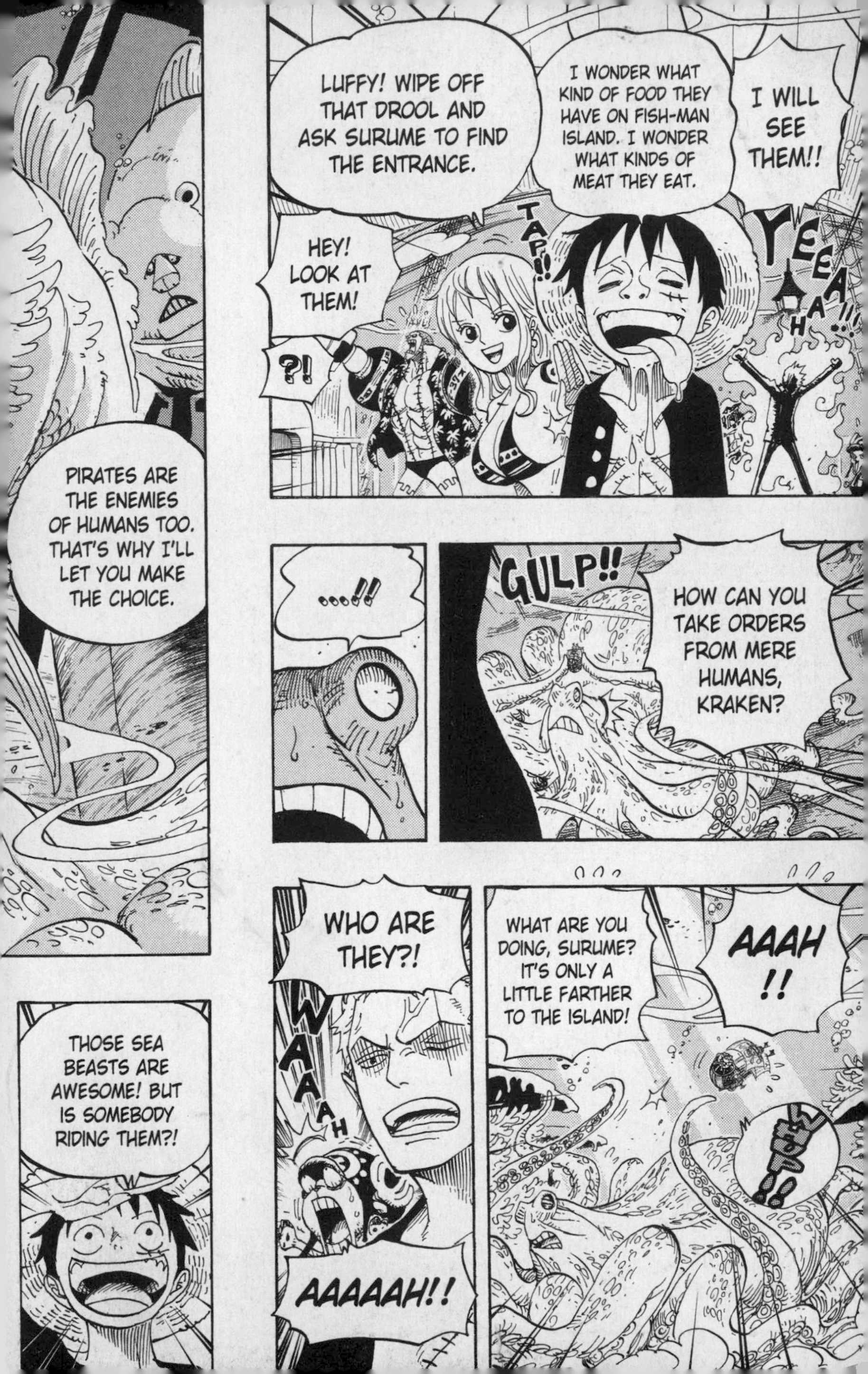
I WILL SEE THEM!!
YEEAAAH!!!
I WONDER WHAT KIND OF FOOD THEY HAVE ON FISH-MAN ISLAND. I WONDER WHAT KINDS OF MEAT THEY EAT.
LUFFY! WIPE OFF THAT DROOL AND ASK SURUME TO FIND THE ENTRANCE.
TAP!!
HEY! LOOK AT THEM!
?!
HOW CAN YOU TAKE ORDERS FROM MERE HUMANS, KRAKEN?
GULP!!
...!!
PIRATES ARE THE ENEMIES OF HUMANS TOO. THAT'S WHY I'LL LET YOU MAKE THE CHOICE.
AAAH!!
WHAT ARE YOU DOING, SURUME? IT'S ONLY A LITTLE FARTHER TO THE ISLAND!
WHO ARE THEY?!
WAAAAH
AAAAAH!!
THOSE SEA BEASTS ARE AWESOME! BUT IS SOMEBODY RIDING THEM?!

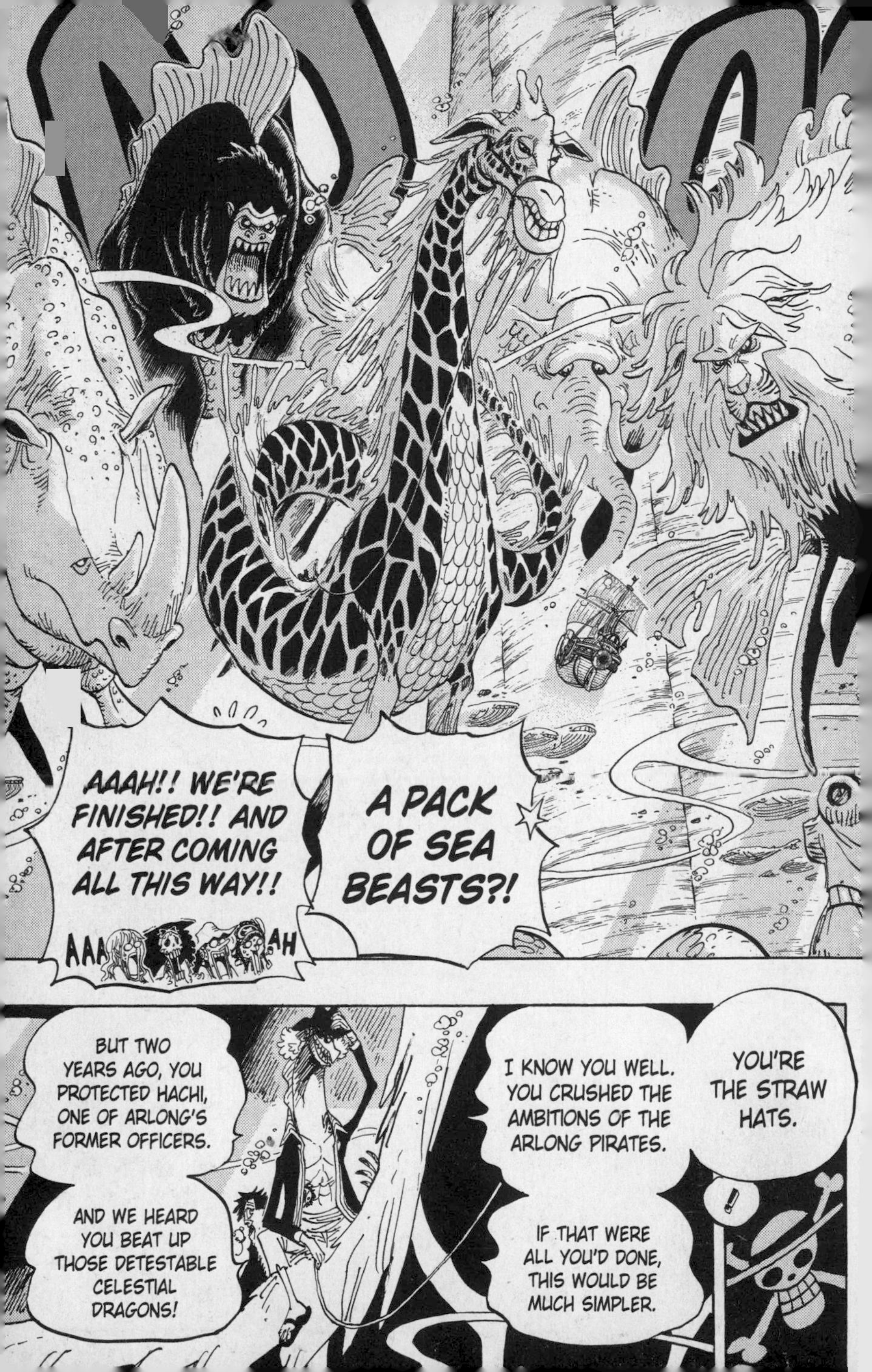
A PACK OF SEA BEASTS?!
AAAH!! WE'RE FINISHED!! AND AFTER COMING ALL THIS WAY!!
AAAAH
!
YOU'RE THE STRAW HATS.
I KNOW YOU WELL. YOU CRUSHED THE AMBITIONS OF THE ARLONG PIRATES.
BUT TWO YEARS AGO, YOU PROTECTED HACHI, ONE OF ARLONG'S FORMER OFFICERS.
AND WE HEARD YOU BEAT UP THOSE DETESTABLE CELESTIAL DRAGONS!
IF THAT WERE ALL YOU'D DONE, THIS WOULD BE MUCH SIMPLER.

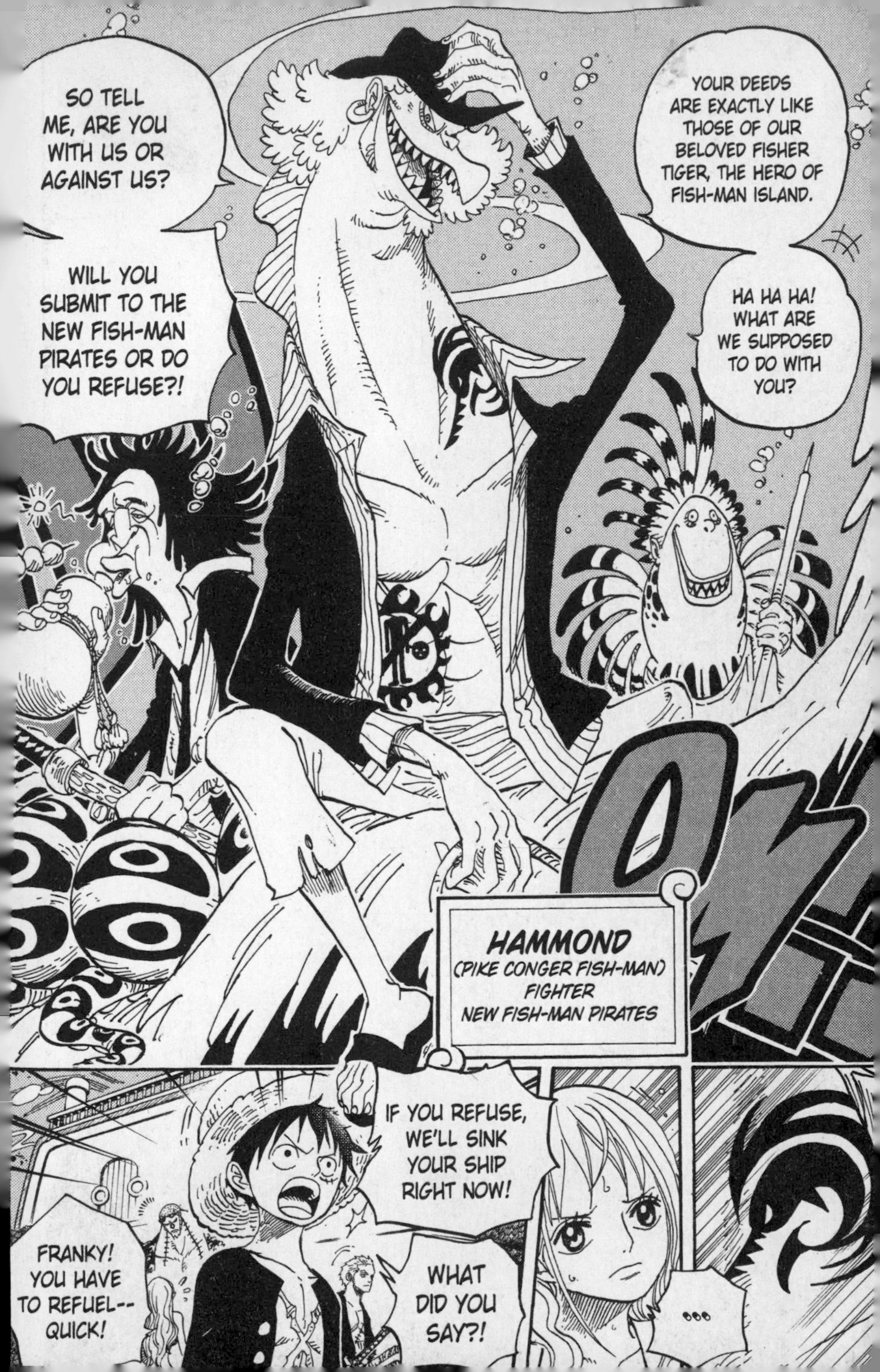
YOUR DEEDS ARE EXACTLY LIKE THOSE OF OUR BELOVED FISHER TIGER, THE HERO OF FISH-MAN ISLAND.
HA HA HA! WHAT ARE WE SUPPOSED TO DO WITH YOU?
SO TELL ME, ARE YOU WITH US OR AGAINST US?
WILL YOU SUBMIT TO THE NEW FISH-MAN PIRATES OR DO YOU REFUSE?!
HAMMOND
(PIKE CONGER FISH-MAN)
FIGHTER
NEW FISH-MAN PIRATES
...
IF YOU REFUSE, WE'LL SINK YOUR SHIP RIGHT NOW!
WHAT DID YOU SAY?!
FRANKY! YOU HAVE TO REFUEL-- QUICK!

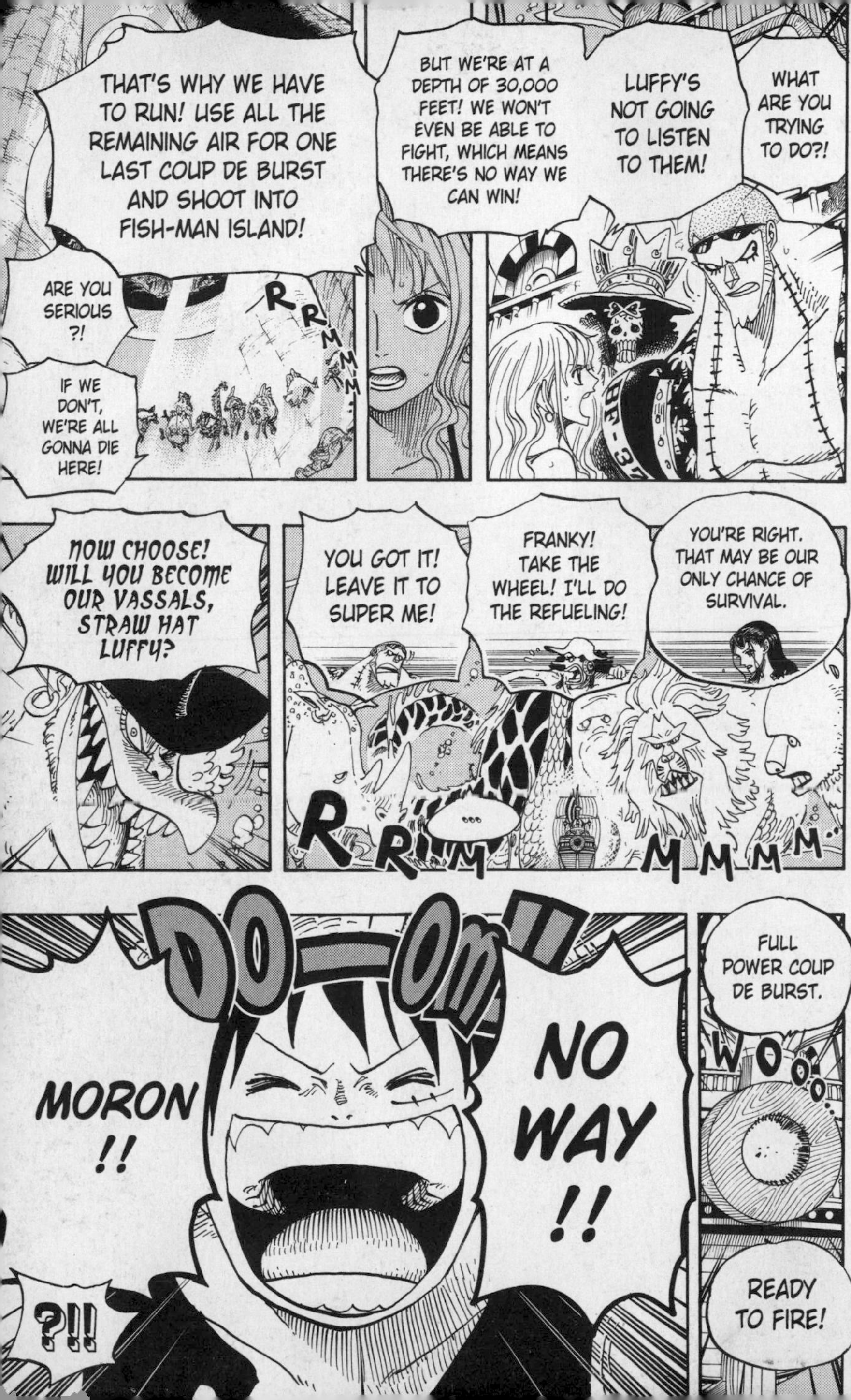
WHAT ARE YOU TRYING TO DO?!
LUFFY'S NOT GOING TO LISTEN TO THEM!
BUT WE'RE AT A DEPTH OF 30,000 FEET! WE WON'T EVEN BE ABLE TO FIGHT, WHICH MEANS THERE'S NO WAY WE CAN WIN!
THAT'S WHY WE HAVE TO RUN! USE ALL THE REMAINING AIR FOR ONE LAST COUP DE BURST AND SHOOT INTO FISH-MAN ISLAND!
RRMMM
ARE YOU SERIOUS?!
IF WE DON'T, WE'RE ALL GONNA DIE HERE!
YOU'RE RIGHT. THAT MAY BE OUR ONLY CHANCE OF SURVIVAL.
FRANKY! TAKE THE WHEEL! I'LL DO THE REFUELING!
YOU GOT IT! LEAVE IT TO SUPER ME!
RRUMMMMM
NOW CHOOSE! WILL YOU BECOME OUR VASSALS, STRAW HAT LUFFY?
FULL POWER COUP DE BURST.
WOOO
READY TO FIRE!
DO-OM
NO WAY!!
MORON!!
?!!

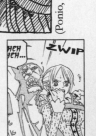

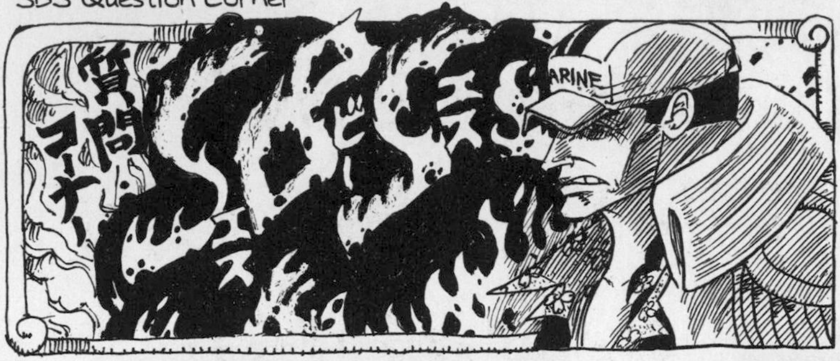

SBS Question Corner

質問コーナー
MARINE

(Ponio, Aichi)

HEH HEH...
ZWIP

Q: Mr. Oda, what kind of Devil Fruit would you like to eat? I'm going to guess it's the Clear-Clear Fruit. I'm sorry I asked.

--Sdd

A: Hey! How dare you assume that! But you're right!

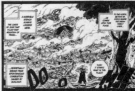

Q: Mr. Oda, hello! I saw something on TV the other day. Is "Gray Terminal" modeled after the slum in the Philippines called "Smokey Mountain"?

--NN Brothers

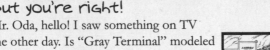

A: Oh, they talked about it on TV? You're right. You know what they say, truth is stranger than fiction. The mountain of trash is burning and constantly has smoke rising. And yet there are actually people who live there. What I talked about in the manga is just scratching the surface. Living in a real mountain of trash makes everyone prone to disease. Corpses can be found at every turn. Even if the people there want to get out, simple motivation isn't enough. No matter how I describe it, I don't think I can do it any justice. If you want to know more about it, I suggest you research it yourself.

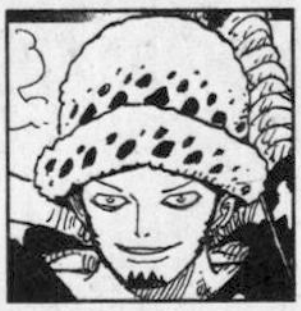

Q: Law calls Luffy "Straw Hat Guy." If there's a person with the first name "Guy," would he call them "Guy Guy"? Tell me, Law!♡

--by Loving Woman

A: Law! They're asking for you! Hm, he's not coming. I guess I can answer for him. It's kind of like saying he's a "football guy." To answer your question, he would probably call anyone "something guy" no matter who it is. Even if it has to be "Guy Guy." Right, Law?

Law: Yeah.

Chapter 608:
UNDERWATER PARADISE

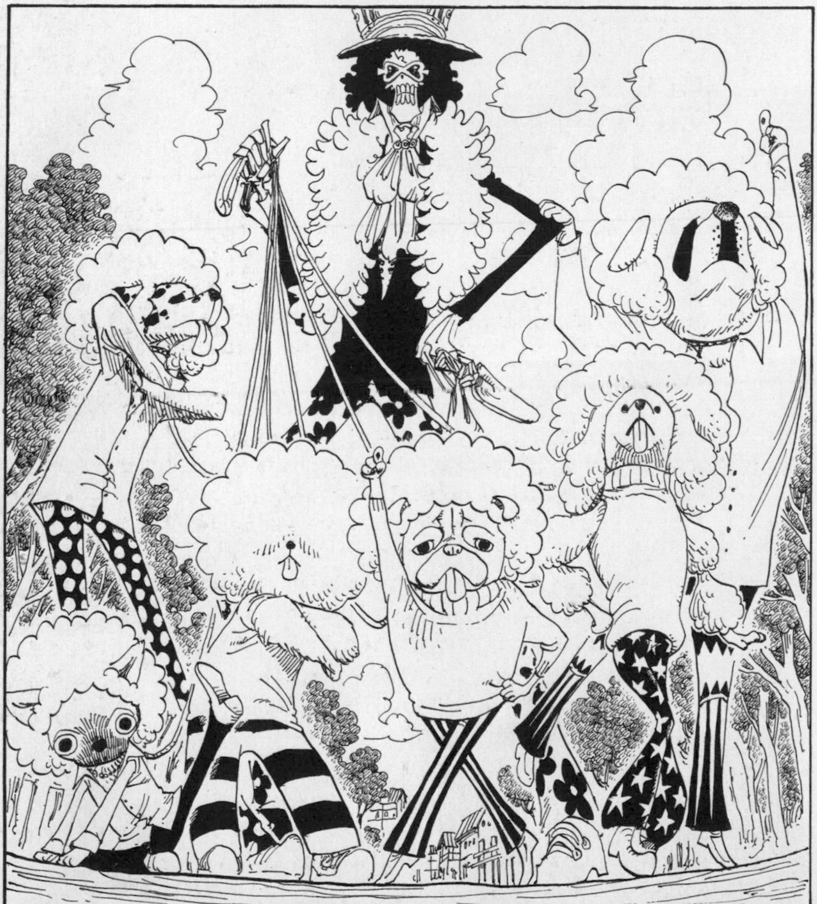

REQUEST: "BROOK WALKING FIVE OR SIX WHITE DOGS WITH AFROS." BY BACHON

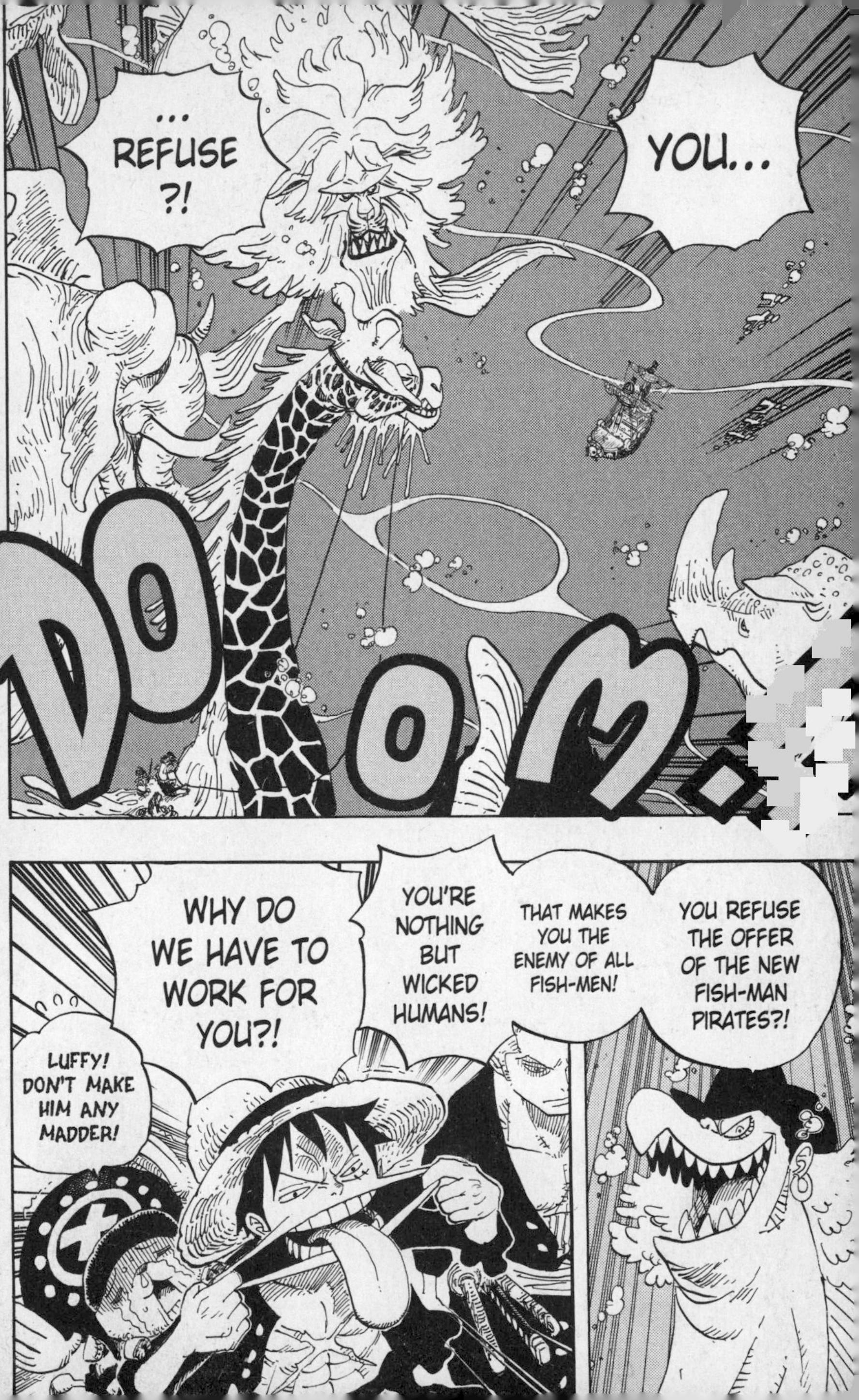
YOU...
...REFUSE ?!
DOOM
YOU REFUSE THE OFFER OF THE NEW FISH-MAN PIRATES?!
THAT MAKES YOU THE ENEMY OF ALL FISH-MEN!
YOU'RE NOTHING BUT WICKED HUMANS!
WHY DO WE HAVE TO WORK FOR YOU?!
LUFFY! DON'T MAKE HIM ANY MADDER!

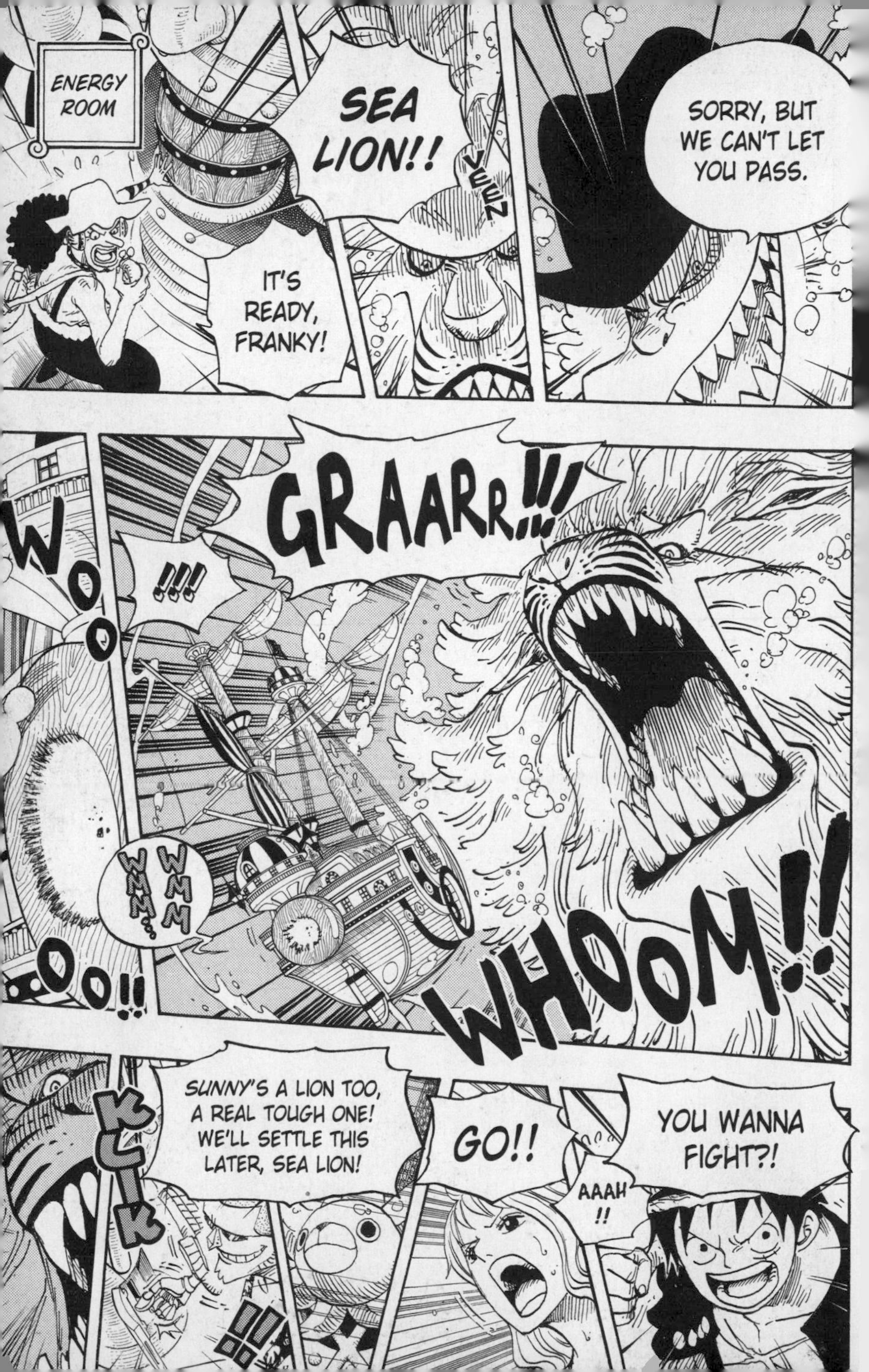
SORRY, BUT WE CAN'T LET YOU PASS.
VEEN
SEA LION!!
ENERGY ROOM
IT'S READY, FRANKY!
GRAARR!!!
WHOOM!!
!!!
WMM WMM...
WOOOO!!
YOU WANNA FIGHT?!
AAAH!!
GO!!
SUNNY'S A LION TOO, A REAL TOUGH ONE! WE'LL SETTLE THIS LATER, SEA LION!
KLIK

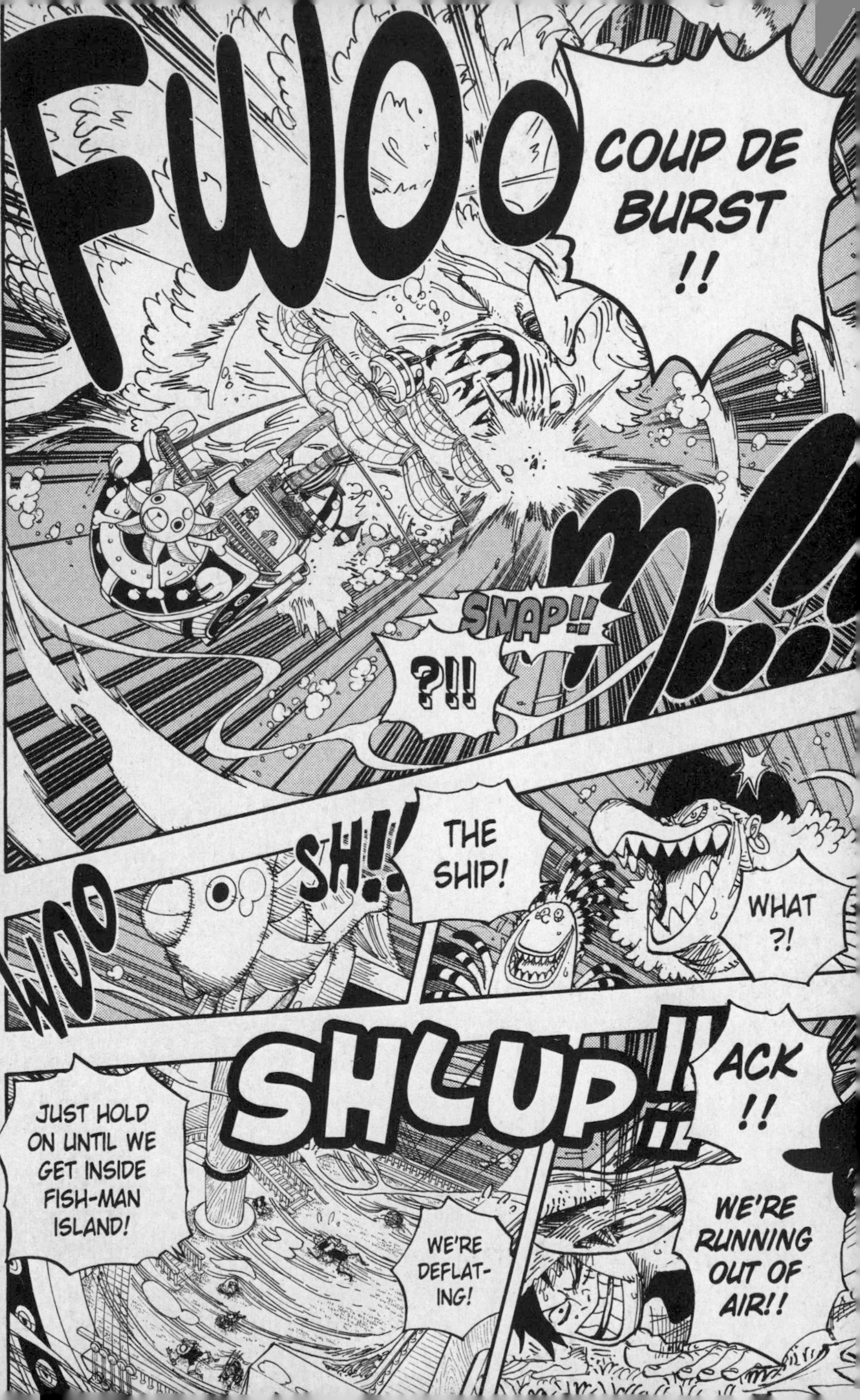
COUP DE BURST !!
FWOOM!!
SNAP!!
?!!
WHAT ?!
THE SHIP!
WOOSH!!
ACK !!
WE'RE RUNNING OUT OF AIR!!
SHLUP!!
WE'RE DEFLAT-ING!
JUST HOLD ON UNTIL WE GET INSIDE FISH-MAN ISLAND!

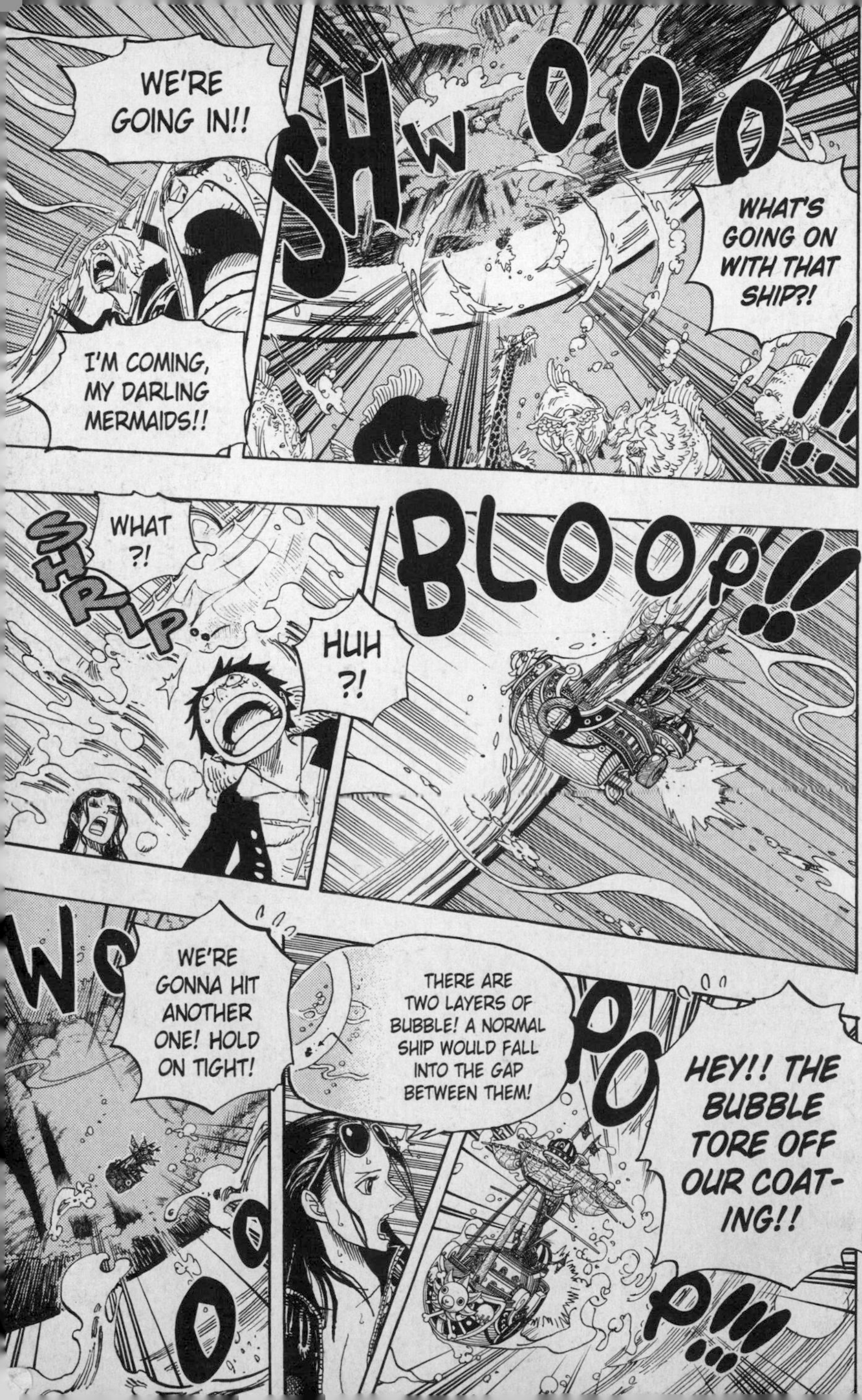
SHWOOOO!!!
WHAT'S GOING ON WITH THAT SHIP?!
WE'RE GOING IN!!
I'M COMING, MY DARLING MERMAIDS!!
BLOOP!!
SHRIP
WHAT ?!
HUH ?!
POP!!!
HEY!! THE BUBBLE TORE OFF OUR COAT-ING!!
THERE ARE TWO LAYERS OF BUBBLE! A NORMAL SHIP WOULD FALL INTO THE GAP BETWEEN THEM!
WOOO
WE'RE GONNA HIT ANOTHER ONE! HOLD ON TIGHT!

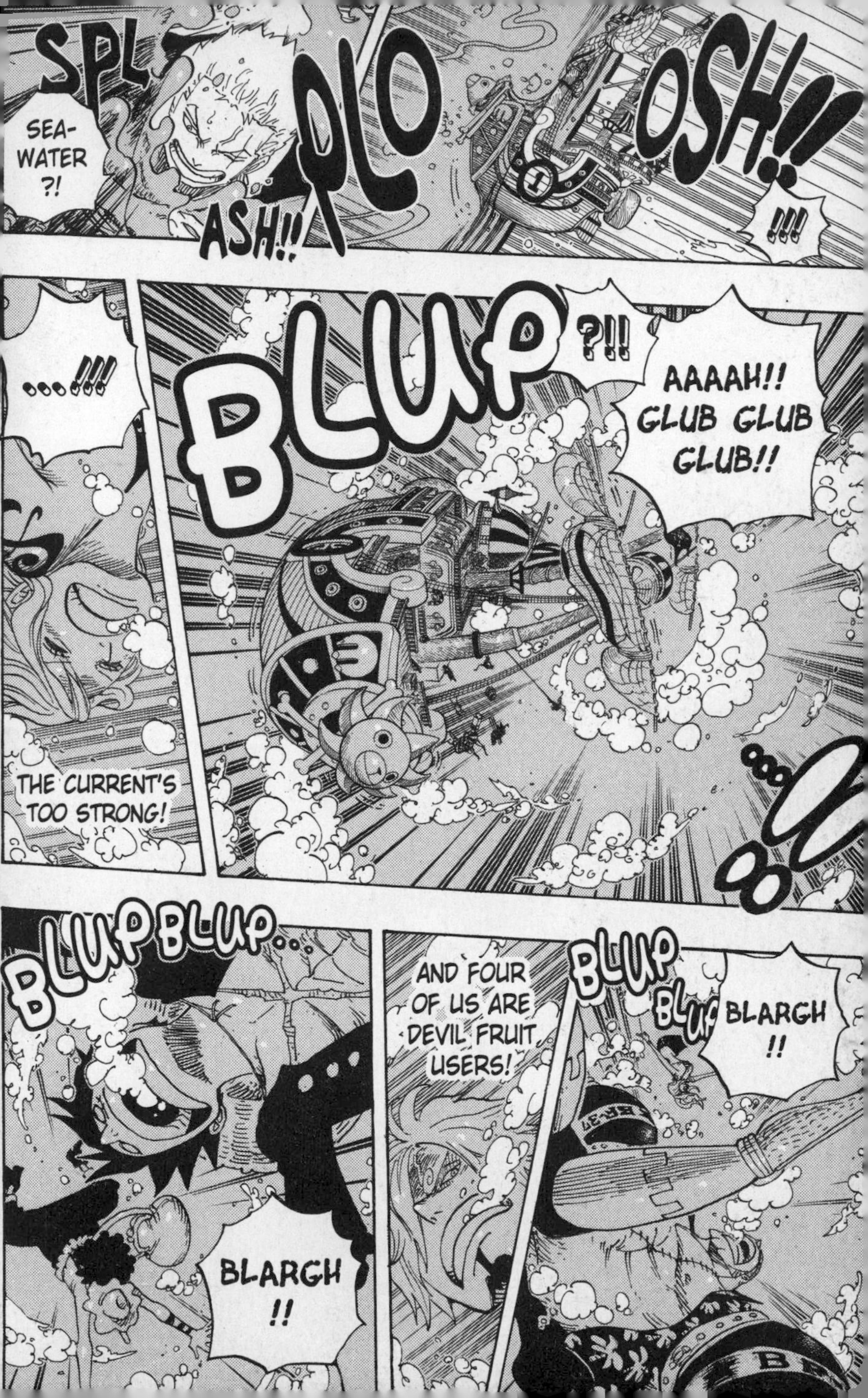
!!!
PLOOSH!!
SEA-WATER ?!
SPLASH!!
?!!
AAAAH!! GLUB GLUB GLUB!!
BLUP
...!!
...!!!
THE CURRENT'S TOO STRONG!
BLUP BLUP
BLARGH !!
AND FOUR OF US ARE DEVIL FRUIT USERS!
BLUP BLUP...
BLARGH !!

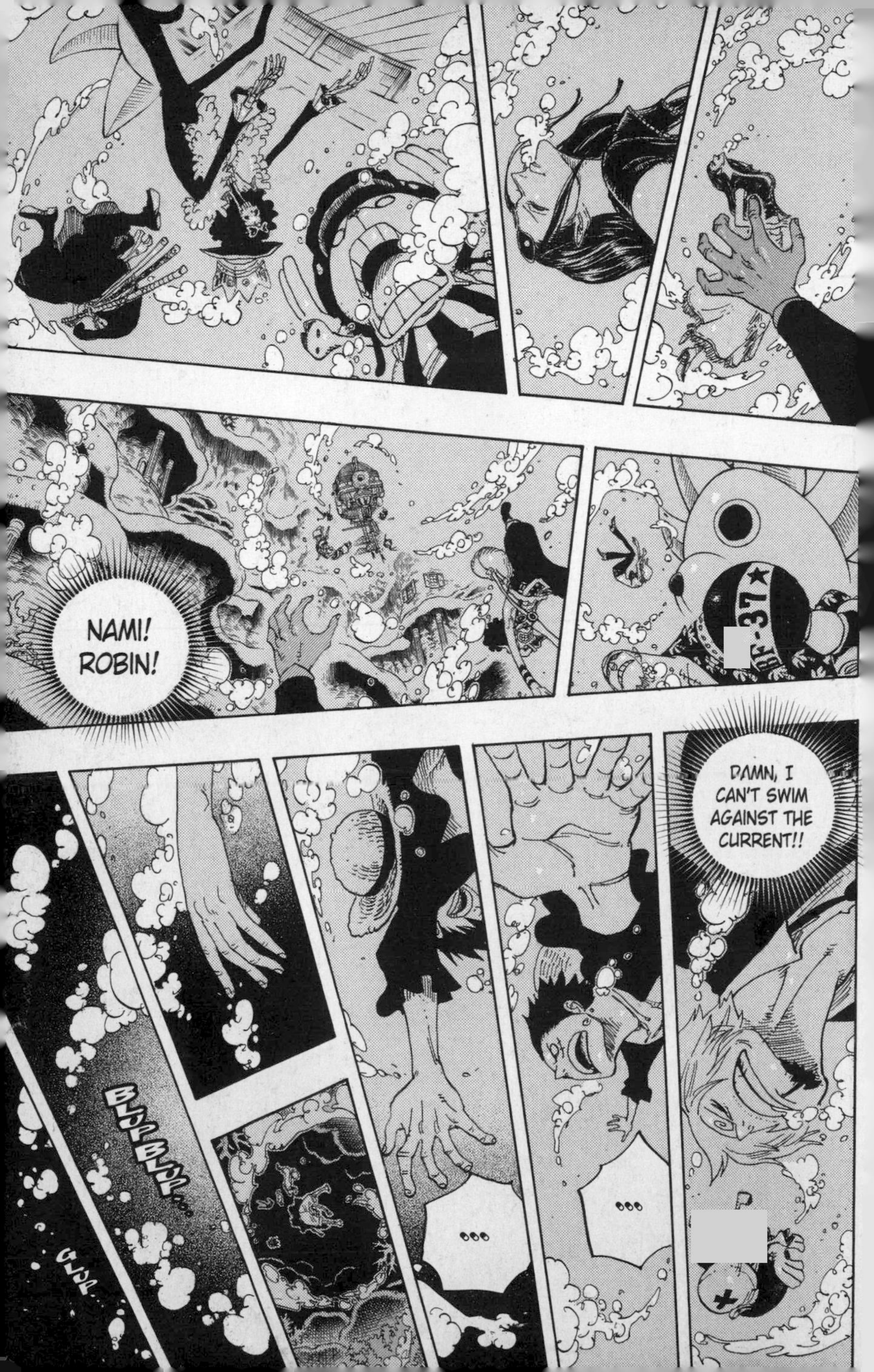
NAMI! ROBIN!
DAMN, I CAN'T SWIM AGAINST THE CURRENT!!
...
...
BLUP BLUP...
GLUP...

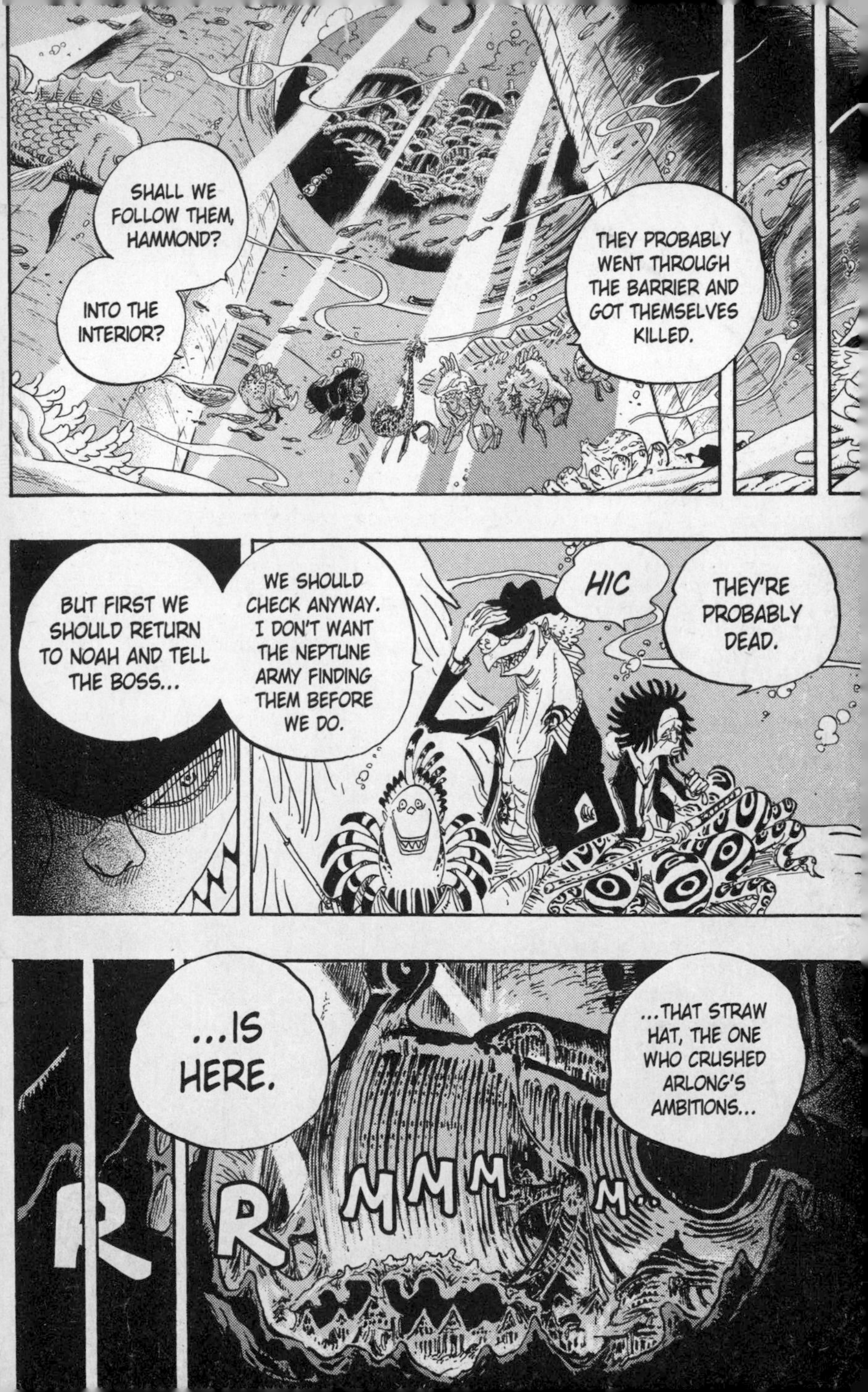
SHALL WE FOLLOW THEM, HAMMOND?
INTO THE INTERIOR?
THEY PROBABLY WENT THROUGH THE BARRIER AND GOT THEMSELVES KILLED.
THEY'RE PROBABLY DEAD.
HIC
WE SHOULD CHECK ANYWAY. I DON'T WANT THE NEPTUNE ARMY FINDING THEM BEFORE WE DO.
BUT FIRST WE SHOULD RETURN TO NOAH AND TELL THE BOSS...
...THAT STRAW HAT, THE ONE WHO CRUSHED ARLONG'S AMBITIONS...
...IS HERE.
RRMMMM...

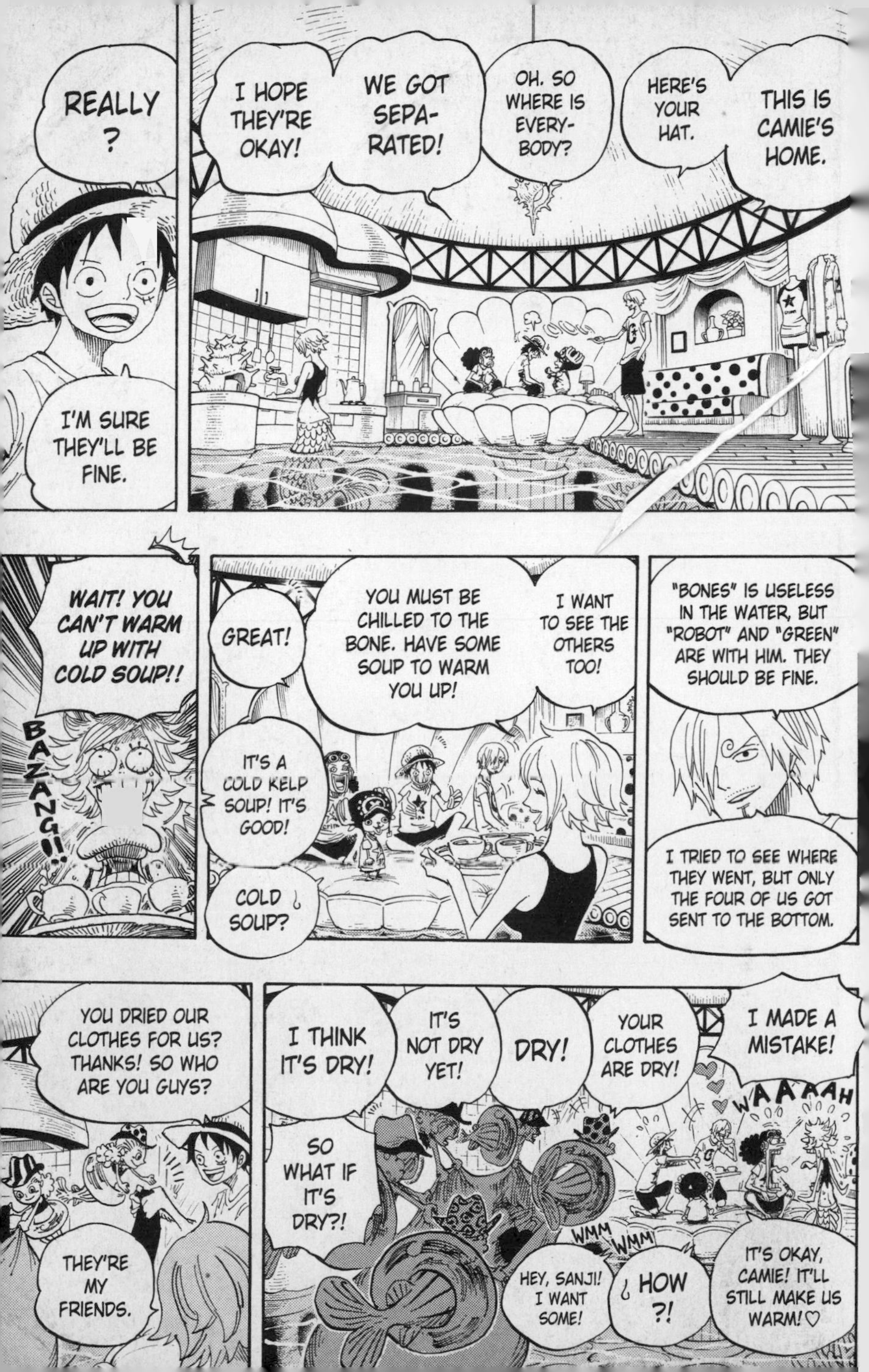
THIS IS CAMIE'S HOME.
HERE'S YOUR HAT.
OH. SO WHERE IS EVERYBODY?
WE GOT SEPARATED!
I HOPE THEY'RE OKAY!
REALLY?
I'M SURE THEY'LL BE FINE.
"BONES" IS USELESS IN THE WATER, BUT "ROBOT" AND "GREEN" ARE WITH HIM. THEY SHOULD BE FINE.
I TRIED TO SEE WHERE THEY WENT, BUT ONLY THE FOUR OF US GOT SENT TO THE BOTTOM.
I WANT TO SEE THE OTHERS TOO!
YOU MUST BE CHILLED TO THE BONE. HAVE SOME SOUP TO WARM YOU UP!
GREAT!
IT'S A COLD KELP SOUP! IT'S GOOD!
COLD SOUP?
WAIT! YOU CAN'T WARM UP WITH COLD SOUP!!
BAZANG!!
I MADE A MISTAKE!
WAAAAH
YOUR CLOTHES ARE DRY!
DRY!
IT'S NOT DRY YET!
I THINK IT'S DRY!
SO WHAT IF IT'S DRY?!
IT'S OKAY, CAMIE! IT'LL STILL MAKE US WARM!♡
HOW?!
WMM WMM
HEY, SANJI! I WANT SOME!
YOU DRIED OUR CLOTHES FOR US? THANKS! SO WHO ARE YOU GUYS?
THEY'RE MY FRIENDS.

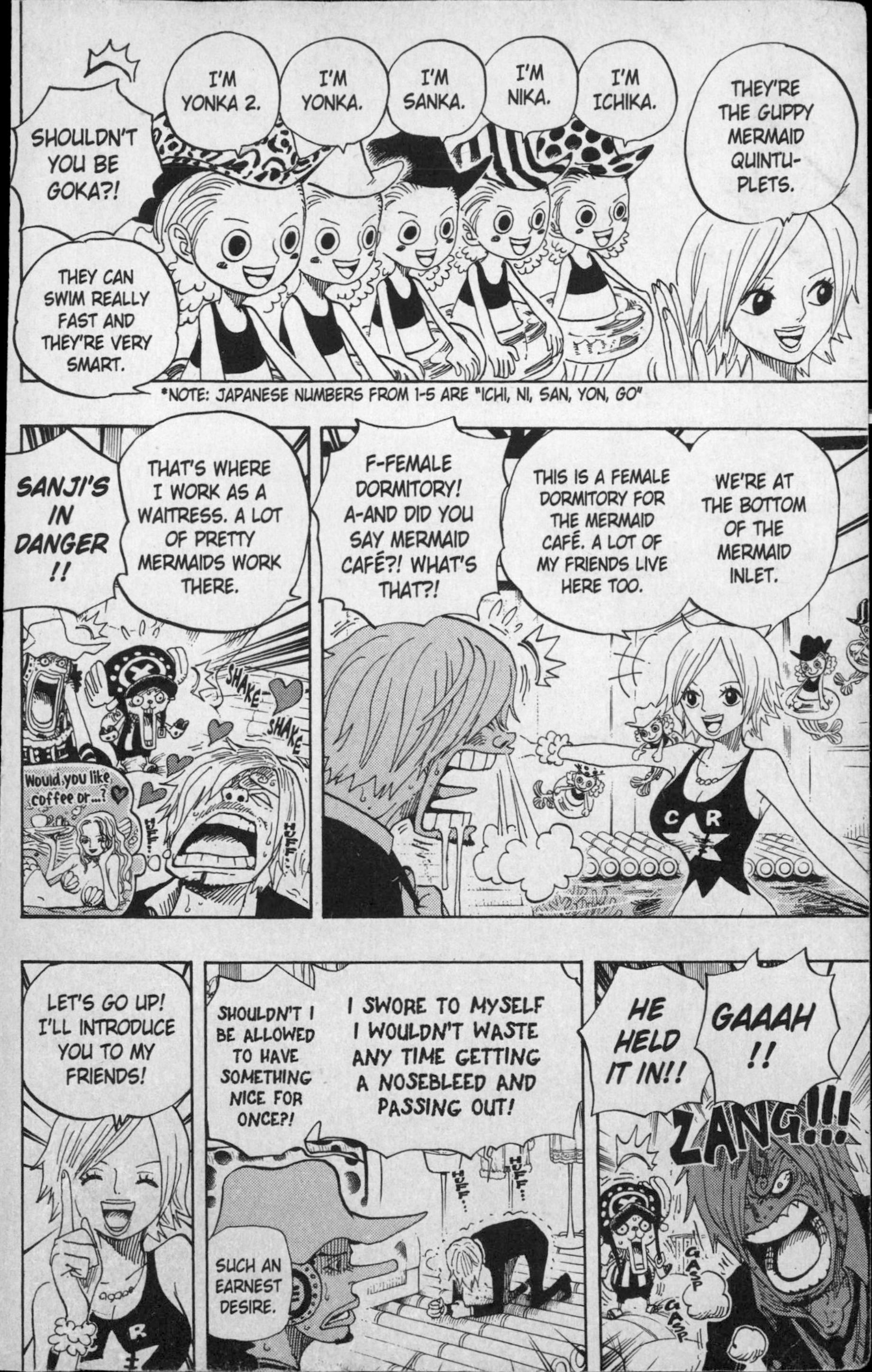
THEY'RE THE GUPPY MERMAID QUINTUPLETS.
I'M ICHIKA.
I'M NIKA.
I'M SANKA.
I'M YONKA.
I'M YONKA 2.
SHOULDN'T YOU BE GOKA?!
THEY CAN SWIM REALLY FAST AND THEY'RE VERY SMART.
WE'RE AT THE BOTTOM OF THE MERMAID INLET.
THIS IS A FEMALE DORMITORY FOR THE MERMAID CAFÉ. A LOT OF MY FRIENDS LIVE HERE TOO.
F-FEMALE DORMITORY! A-AND DID YOU SAY MERMAID CAFÉ?! WHAT'S THAT?!
THAT'S WHERE I WORK AS A WAITRESS. A LOT OF PRETTY MERMAIDS WORK THERE.
SANJI'S IN DANGER!!
SHAKE
SHAKE
Would you like coffee or...?
HUFF...
HUFF...
GAAAH!!
HE HELD IT IN!!
ZANG!!!
GASP
GASP
I SWORE TO MYSELF I WOULDN'T WASTE ANY TIME GETTING A NOSEBLEED AND PASSING OUT!
SHOULDN'T I BE ALLOWED TO HAVE SOMETHING NICE FOR ONCE?!
HUFF...
HUFF...
SUCH AN EARNEST DESIRE.
LET'S GO UP! I'LL INTRODUCE YOU TO MY FRIENDS!
*NOTE: JAPANESE NUMBERS FROM 1-5 ARE "ICHI, NI, SAN, YON, GO"

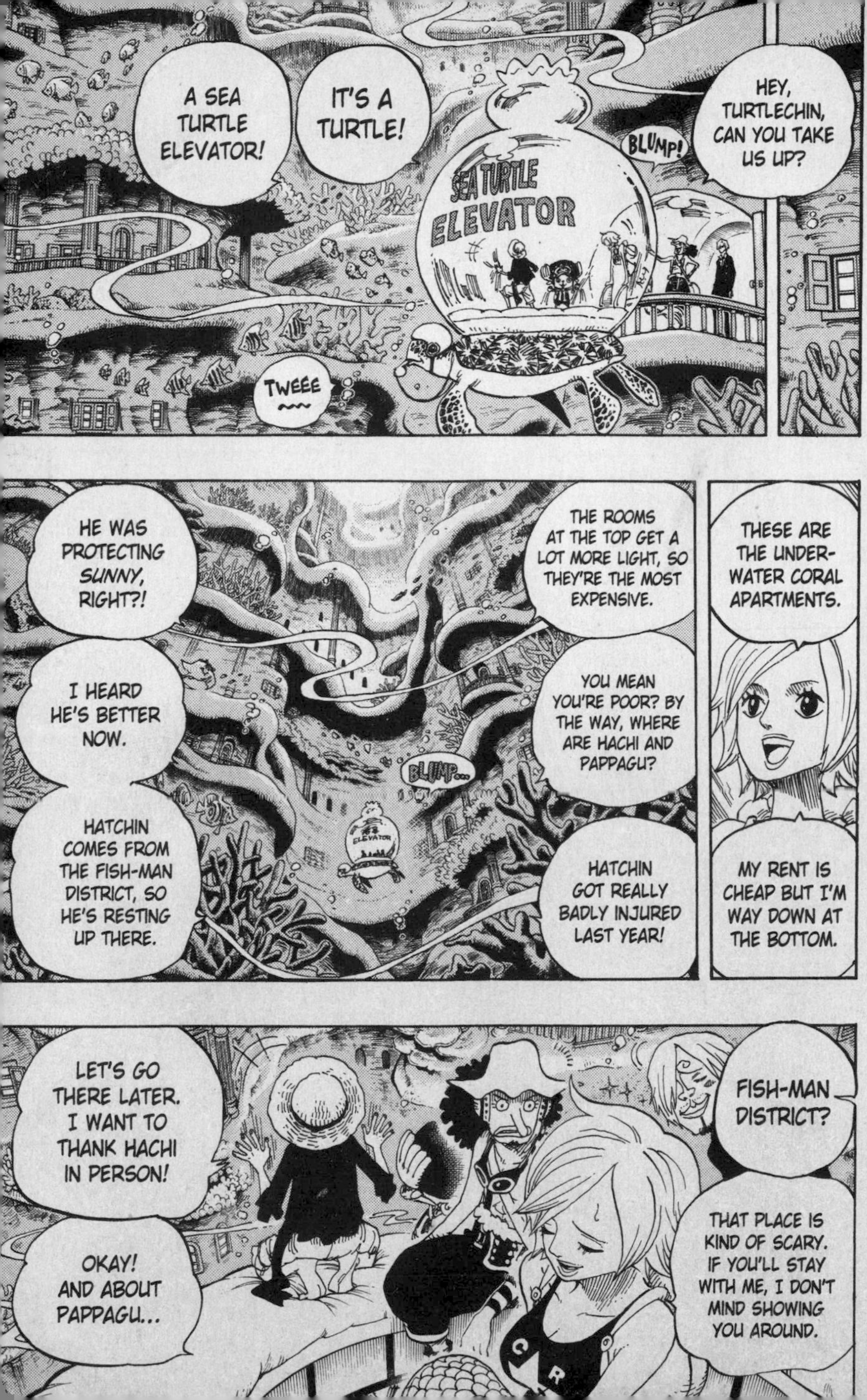
HEY, TURTLECHIN, CAN YOU TAKE US UP?
BLUMP!
SEA TURTLE ELEVATOR
IT'S A TURTLE!
A SEA TURTLE ELEVATOR!
TWEEE ~~~
THESE ARE THE UNDER-WATER CORAL APARTMENTS.
MY RENT IS CHEAP BUT I'M WAY DOWN AT THE BOTTOM.
THE ROOMS AT THE TOP GET A LOT MORE LIGHT, SO THEY'RE THE MOST EXPENSIVE.
YOU MEAN YOU'RE POOR? BY THE WAY, WHERE ARE HACHI AND PAPPAGU?
HATCHIN GOT REALLY BADLY INJURED LAST YEAR!
BLUMP...
HE WAS PROTECTING SUNNY, RIGHT?!
I HEARD HE'S BETTER NOW.
HATCHIN COMES FROM THE FISH-MAN DISTRICT, SO HE'S RESTING UP THERE.
FISH-MAN DISTRICT?
THAT PLACE IS KIND OF SCARY. IF YOU'LL STAY WITH ME, I DON'T MIND SHOWING YOU AROUND.
LET'S GO THERE LATER. I WANT TO THANK HACHI IN PERSON!
OKAY! AND ABOUT PAPPAGU...

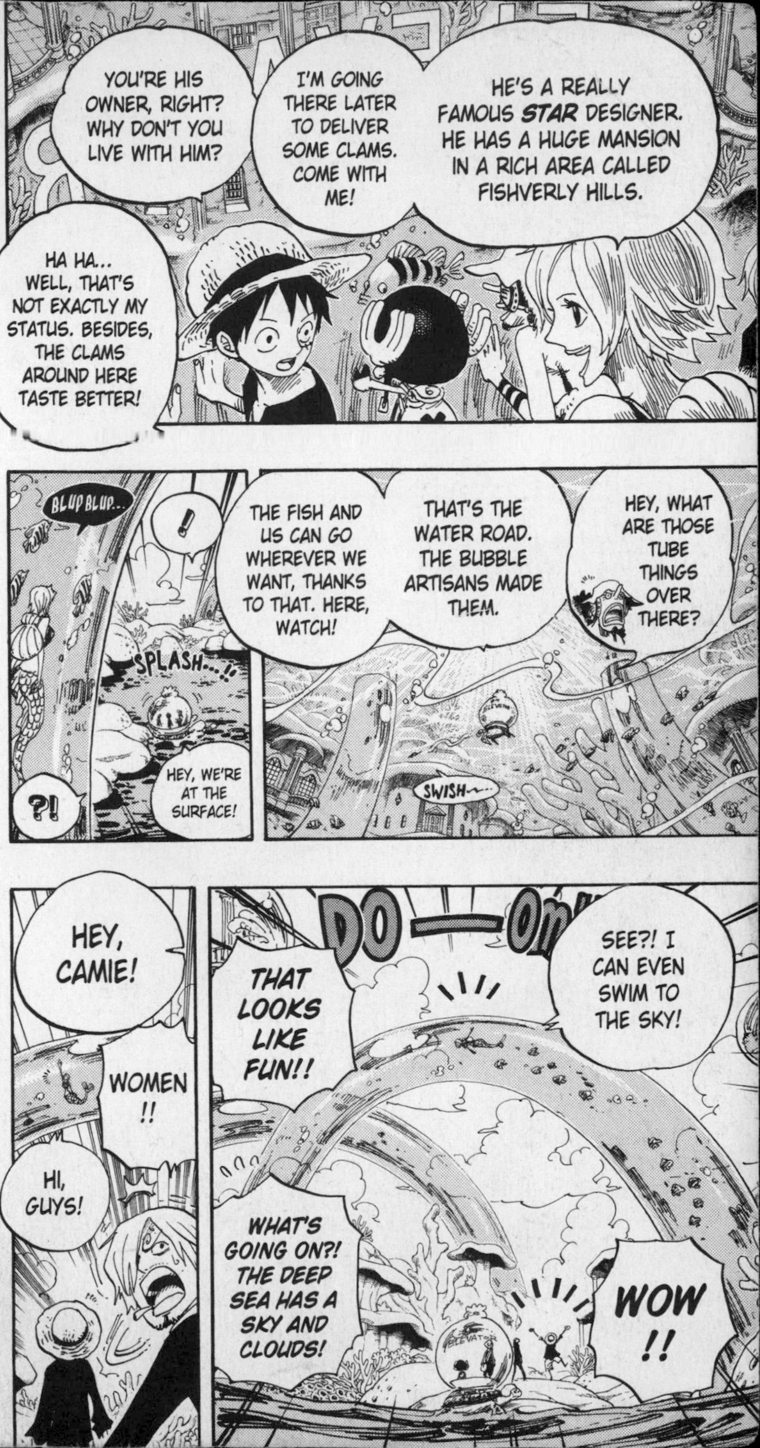
HE'S A REALLY FAMOUS STAR DESIGNER. HE HAS A HUGE MANSION IN A RICH AREA CALLED FISHVERLY HILLS.
I'M GOING THERE LATER TO DELIVER SOME CLAMS. COME WITH ME!
YOU'RE HIS OWNER, RIGHT? WHY DON'T YOU LIVE WITH HIM?
HA HA... WELL, THAT'S NOT EXACTLY MY STATUS. BESIDES, THE CLAMS AROUND HERE TASTE BETTER!
HEY, WHAT ARE THOSE TUBE THINGS OVER THERE?
THAT'S THE WATER ROAD. THE BUBBLE ARTISANS MADE THEM.
THE FISH AND US CAN GO WHEREVER WE WANT, THANKS TO THAT. HERE, WATCH!
SWISH
BLUP BLUP...
!
SPLASH...!!
HEY, WE'RE AT THE SURFACE!
?!
DO—ON
SEE?! I CAN EVEN SWIM TO THE SKY!
THAT LOOKS LIKE FUN!!
WOW!!
WHAT'S GOING ON?! THE DEEP SEA HAS A SKY AND CLOUDS!
HEY, CAMIE!
WOMEN!!
HI, GUYS!

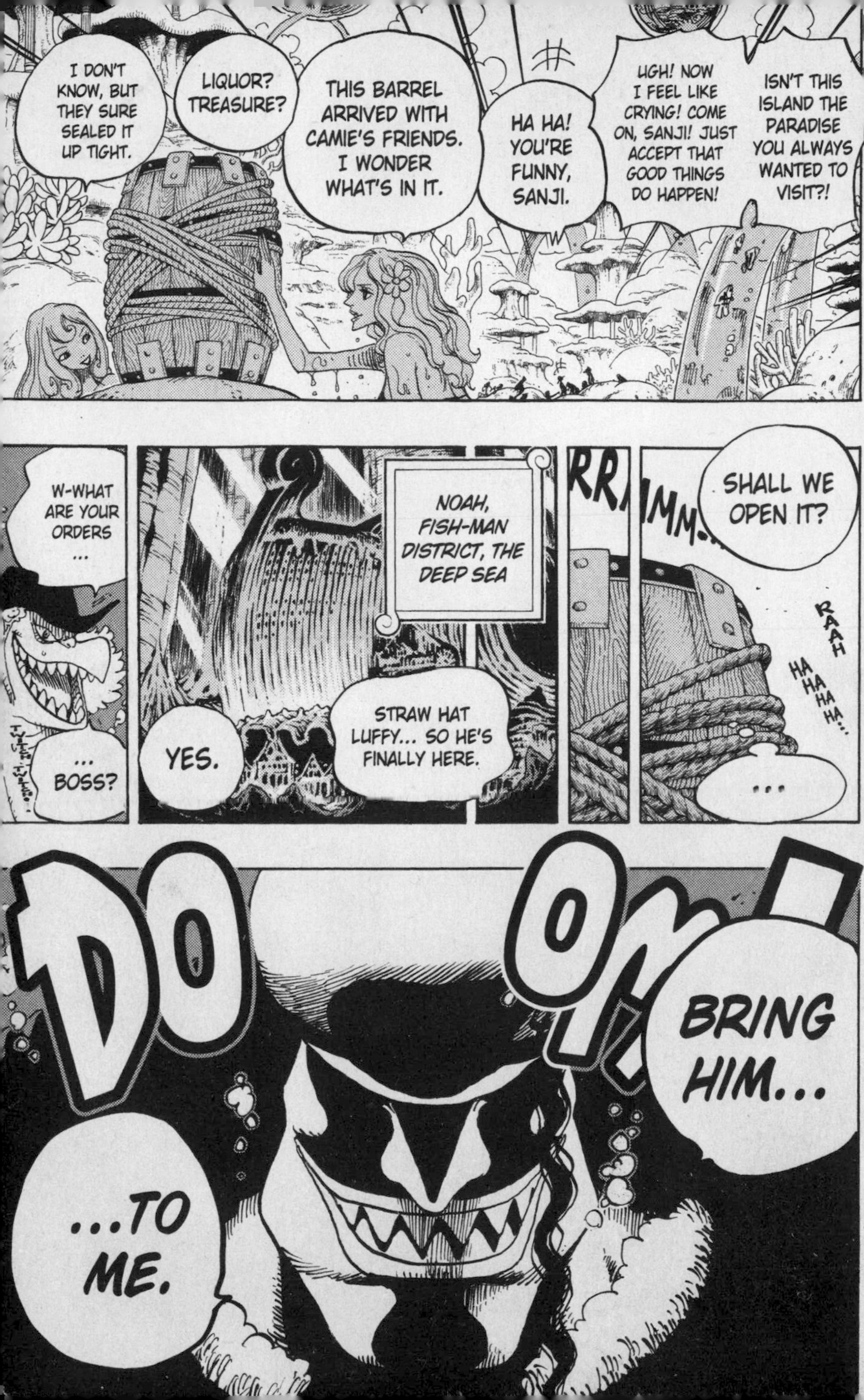
ISN'T THIS ISLAND THE PARADISE YOU ALWAYS WANTED TO VISIT?!
UGH! NOW I FEEL LIKE CRYING! COME ON, SANJI! JUST ACCEPT THAT GOOD THINGS DO HAPPEN!
HA HA! YOU'RE FUNNY, SANJI.
THIS BARREL ARRIVED WITH CAMIE'S FRIENDS. I WONDER WHAT'S IN IT.
LIQUOR? TREASURE?
I DON'T KNOW, BUT THEY SURE SEALED IT UP TIGHT.
SHALL WE OPEN IT?
RAAH HA HA HA HA...
...
RRRMMM...
NOAH, FISH-MAN DISTRICT, THE DEEP SEA
STRAW HAT LUFFY... SO HE'S FINALLY HERE.
YES.
W-WHAT ARE YOUR ORDERS ...
... BOSS?
DOOOM!
BRING HIM...
...TO ME.

ON FISH-MAN ISLAND

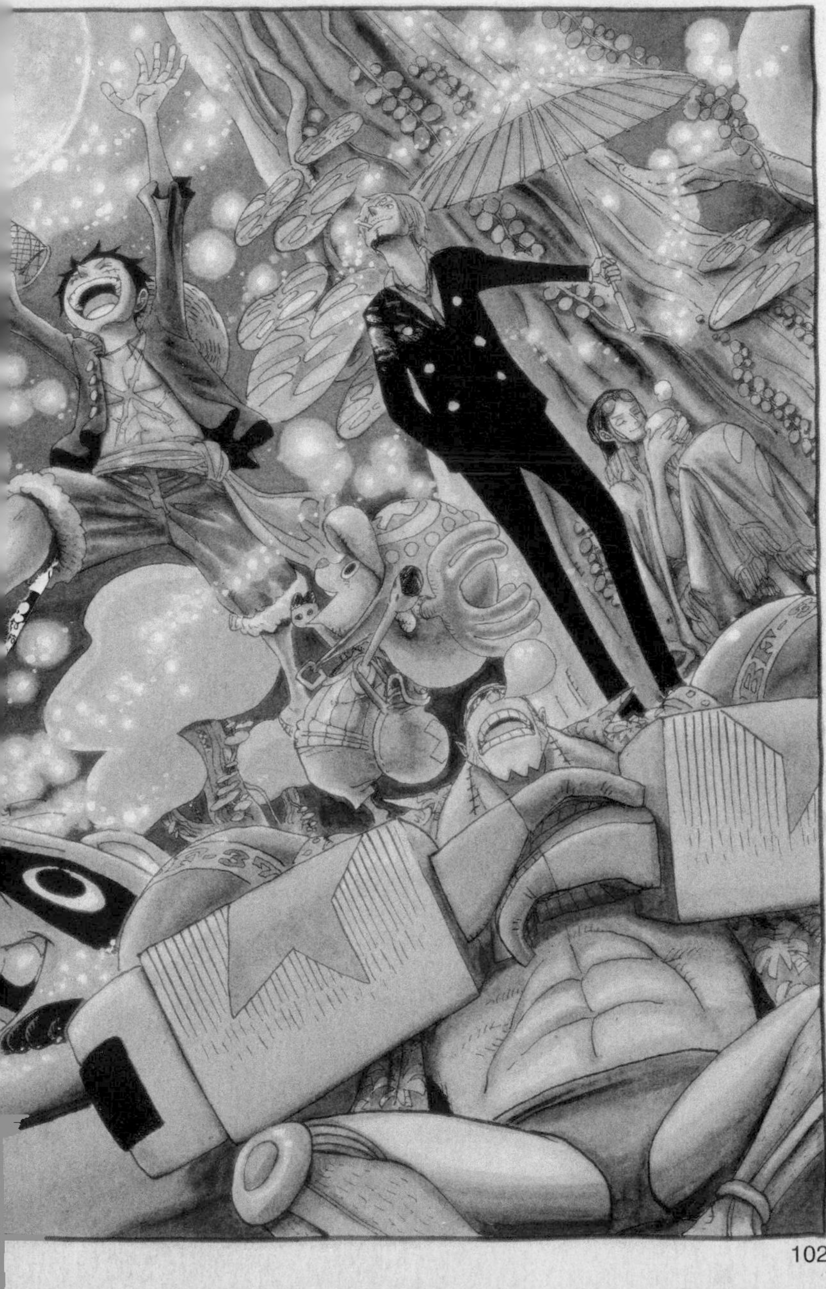

Chapter 609: ADVENTURE

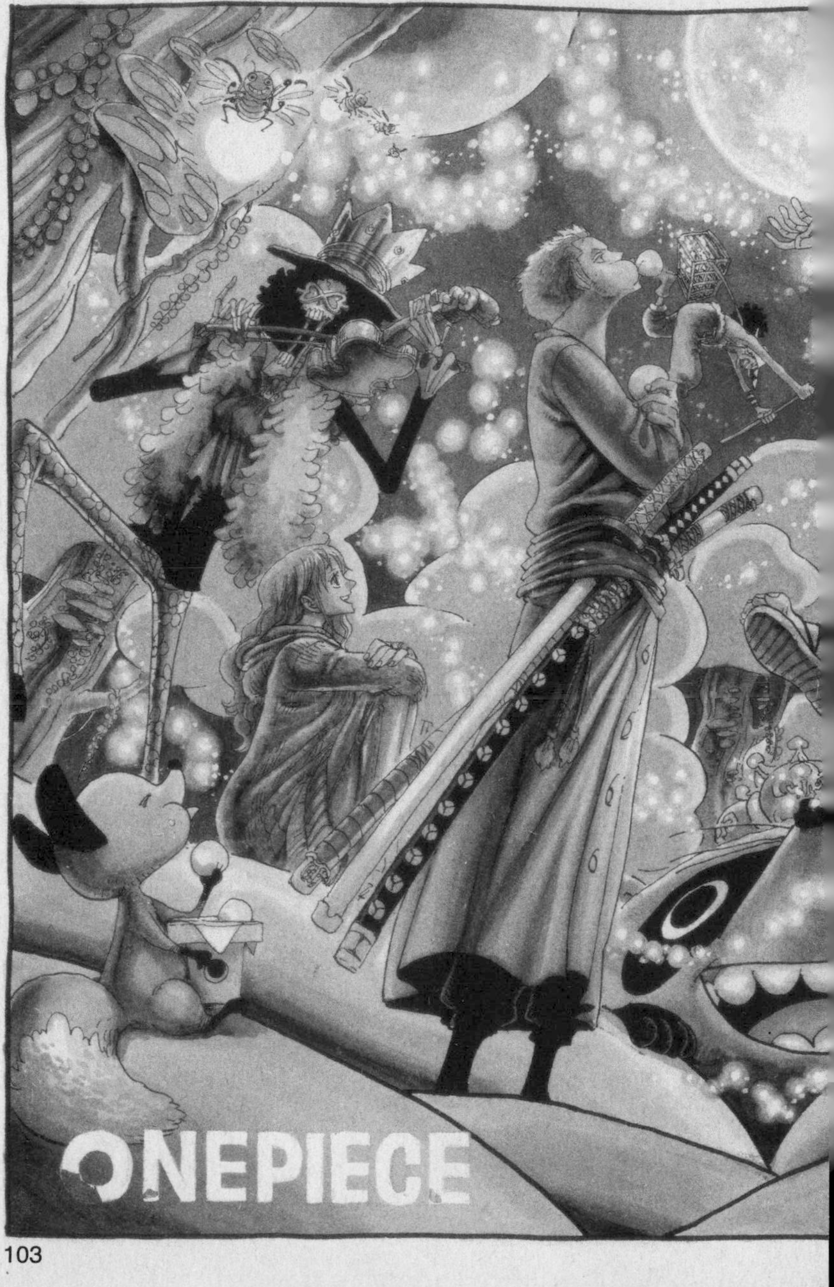
ONEPIECE

vol.62
ONE PIECE

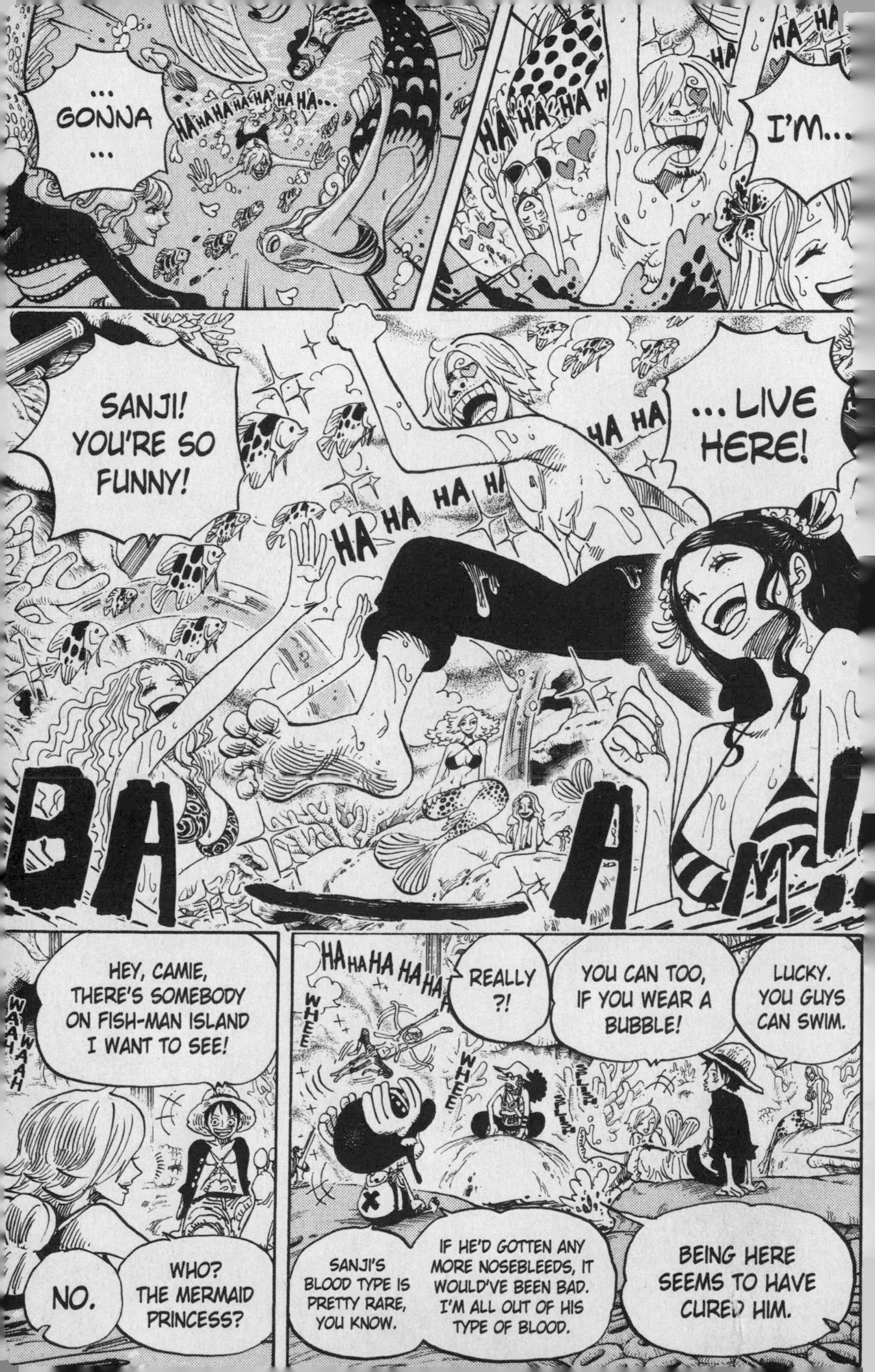
HA HA
I'M...
... GONNA ...
HA HA HA HA HA HA HA...
... LIVE HERE!
HA HA
SANJI! YOU'RE SO FUNNY!
HA HA HA HA
BA A M!!
LUCKY. YOU GUYS CAN SWIM.
YOU CAN TOO, IF YOU WEAR A BUBBLE!
REALLY ?!
HA HA HA HA HA HA
WHEE
WHEE
BEING HERE SEEMS TO HAVE CURED HIM.
IF HE'D GOTTEN ANY MORE NOSEBLEEDS, IT WOULD'VE BEEN BAD. I'M ALL OUT OF HIS TYPE OF BLOOD.
SANJI'S BLOOD TYPE IS PRETTY RARE, YOU KNOW.
HEY, CAMIE, THERE'S SOMEBODY ON FISH-MAN ISLAND I WANT TO SEE!
WAAAH WAAAH
WHO? THE MERMAID PRINCESS?
NO.

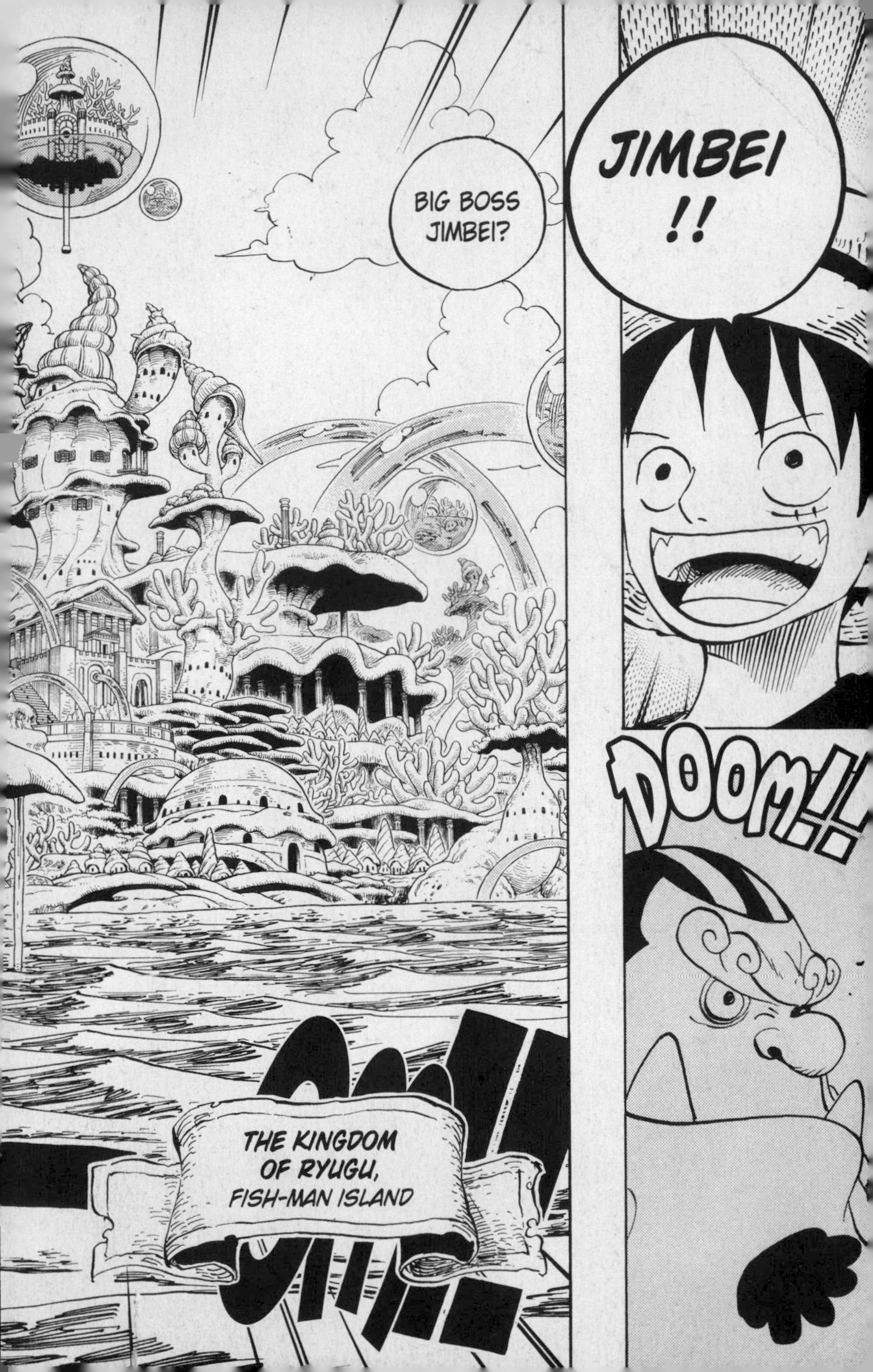
JIMBEI !!
DOOM!!
BIG BOSS JIMBEI?
THE KINGDOM OF RYUGU, FISH-MAN ISLAND

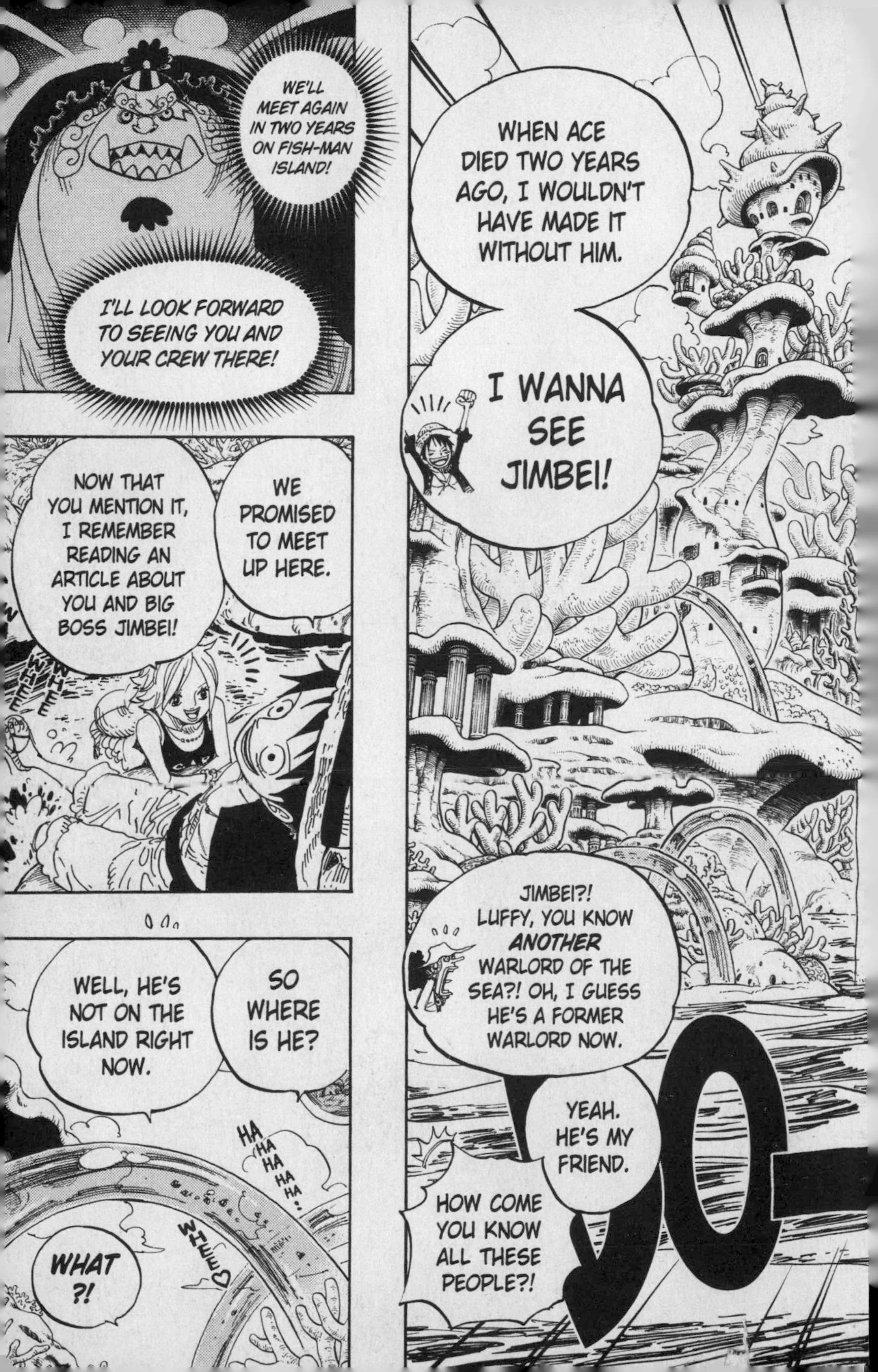
WHEN ACE DIED TWO YEARS AGO, I WOULDN'T HAVE MADE IT WITHOUT HIM.
I WANNA SEE JIMBEI!
JIMBEI?! LUFFY, YOU KNOW ANOTHER WARLORD OF THE SEA?! OH, I GUESS HE'S A FORMER WARLORD NOW.
YEAH. HE'S MY FRIEND.
HOW COME YOU KNOW ALL THESE PEOPLE?!
WE'LL MEET AGAIN IN TWO YEARS ON FISH-MAN ISLAND!
I'LL LOOK FORWARD TO SEEING YOU AND YOUR CREW THERE!
WE PROMISED TO MEET UP HERE.
NOW THAT YOU MENTION IT, I REMEMBER READING AN ARTICLE ABOUT YOU AND BIG BOSS JIMBEI!
WHEE
SO WHERE IS HE?
WELL, HE'S NOT ON THE ISLAND RIGHT NOW.
HA HA HA HA HA!
WHEE♡
WHAT ?!

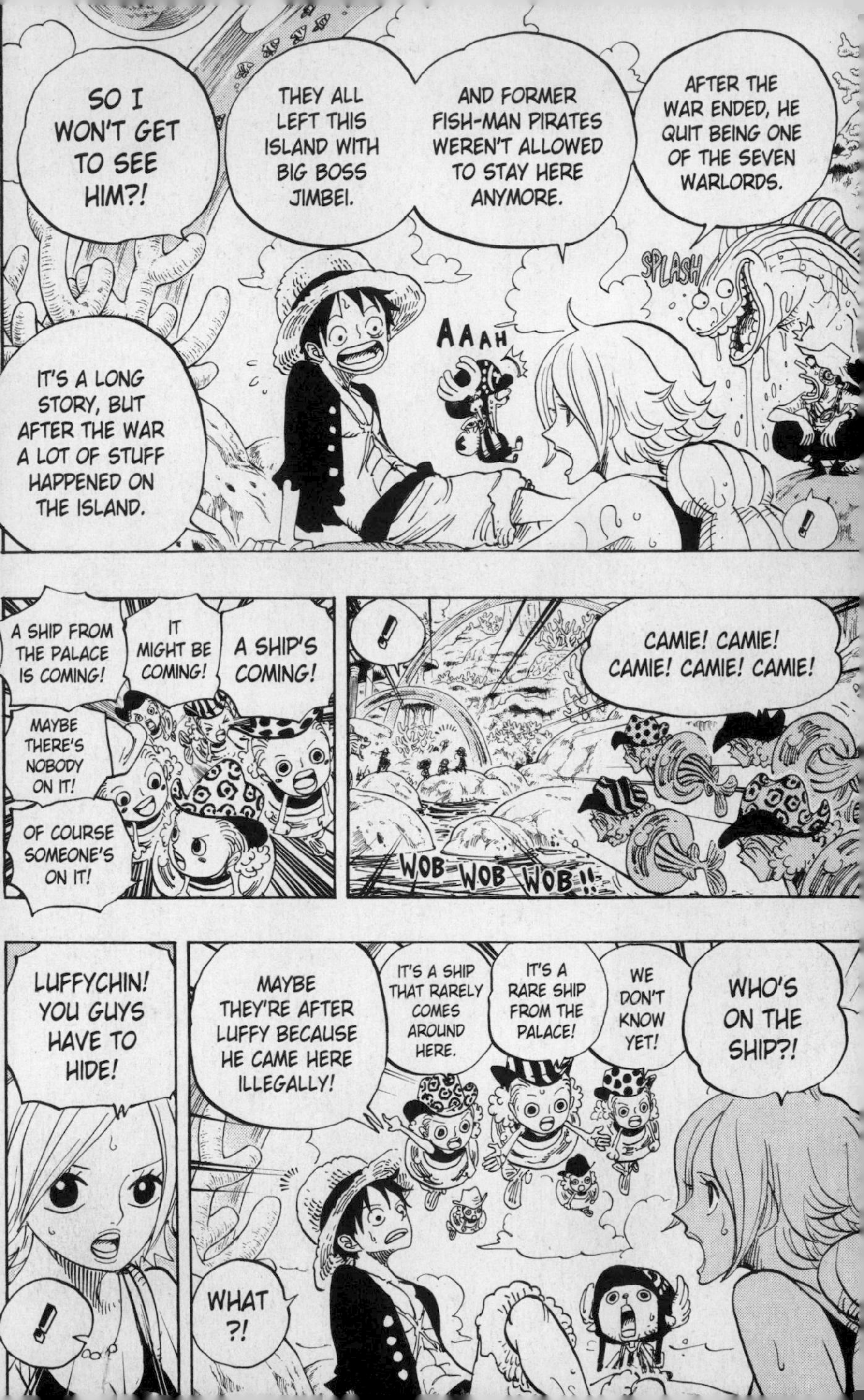
AFTER THE WAR ENDED, HE QUIT BEING ONE OF THE SEVEN WARLORDS.
AND FORMER FISH-MAN PIRATES WEREN'T ALLOWED TO STAY HERE ANYMORE.
THEY ALL LEFT THIS ISLAND WITH BIG BOSS JIMBEI.
SO I WON'T GET TO SEE HIM?!
SPLASH
AAAH
IT'S A LONG STORY, BUT AFTER THE WAR A LOT OF STUFF HAPPENED ON THE ISLAND.
!
!
CAMIE! CAMIE! CAMIE! CAMIE! CAMIE!
WOB WOB WOB!!
A SHIP'S COMING!
IT MIGHT BE COMING!
A SHIP FROM THE PALACE IS COMING!
MAYBE THERE'S NOBODY ON IT!
OF COURSE SOMEONE'S ON IT!
WHO'S ON THE SHIP?!
WE DON'T KNOW YET!
IT'S A RARE SHIP FROM THE PALACE!
IT'S A SHIP THAT RARELY COMES AROUND HERE.
MAYBE THEY'RE AFTER LUFFY BECAUSE HE CAME HERE ILLEGALLY!
WHAT?!
LUFFYCHIN! YOU GUYS HAVE TO HIDE!
!

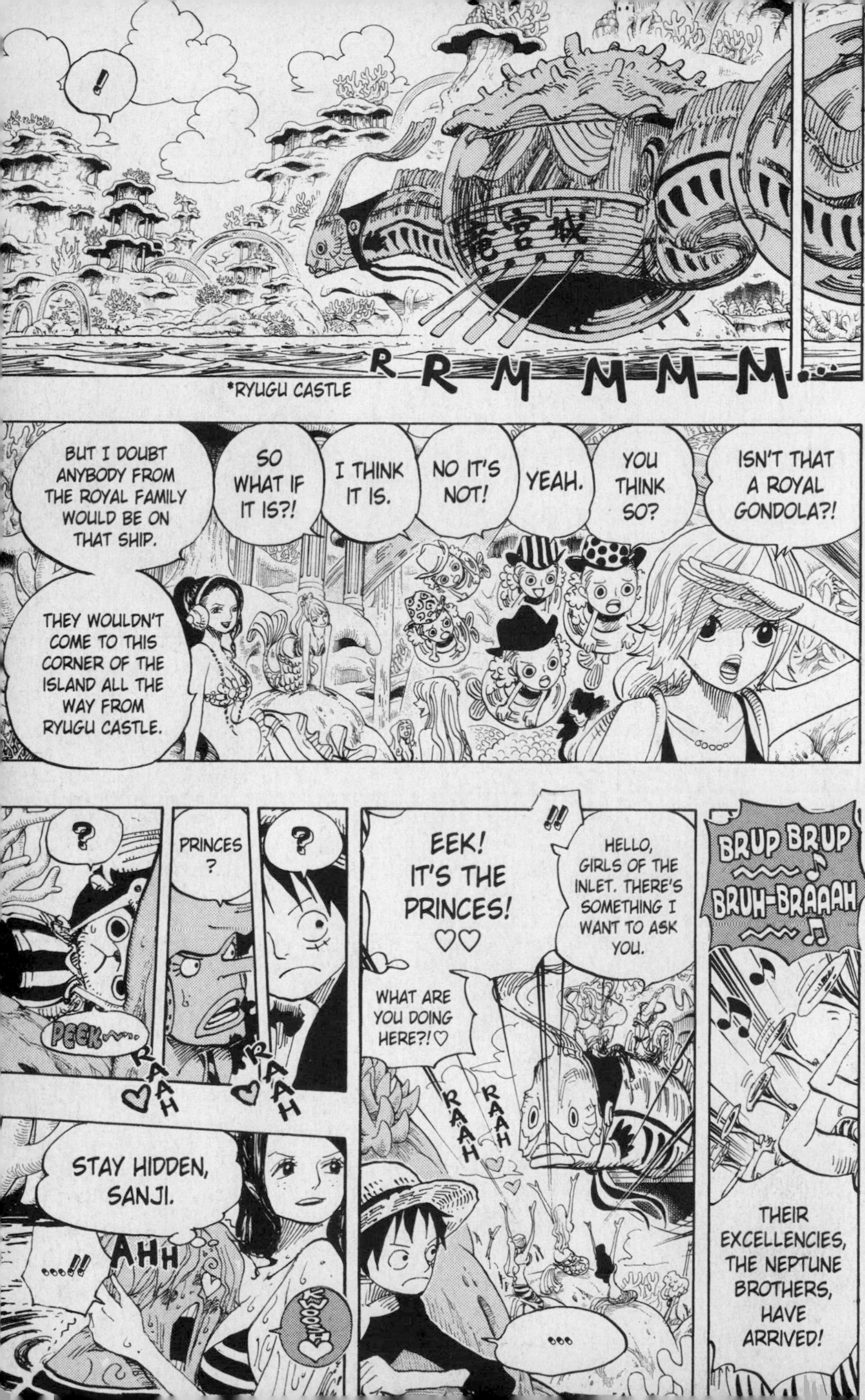
!
竜宮城
RRMMMMM...
*RYUGU CASTLE
ISN'T THAT A ROYAL GONDOLA?!
YOU THINK SO?
YEAH.
NO IT'S NOT!
I THINK IT IS.
SO WHAT IF IT IS?!
BUT I DOUBT ANYBODY FROM THE ROYAL FAMILY WOULD BE ON THAT SHIP.
THEY WOULDN'T COME TO THIS CORNER OF THE ISLAND ALL THE WAY FROM RYUGU CASTLE.
BRUP BRUP ~~~ ♪ BRUH-BRAAAH ~~~ ♪
THEIR EXCELLENCIES, THE NEPTUNE BROTHERS, HAVE ARRIVED!
!!
HELLO, GIRLS OF THE INLET. THERE'S SOMETHING I WANT TO ASK YOU.
EEK! IT'S THE PRINCES! ♡♡
WHAT ARE YOU DOING HERE?!♡
RAAH
RAAH
SWOON♡
...
?
PRINCES?
?
PEEK...
RAAH♡
RAAH♡
STAY HIDDEN, SANJI.
...!!
AHH

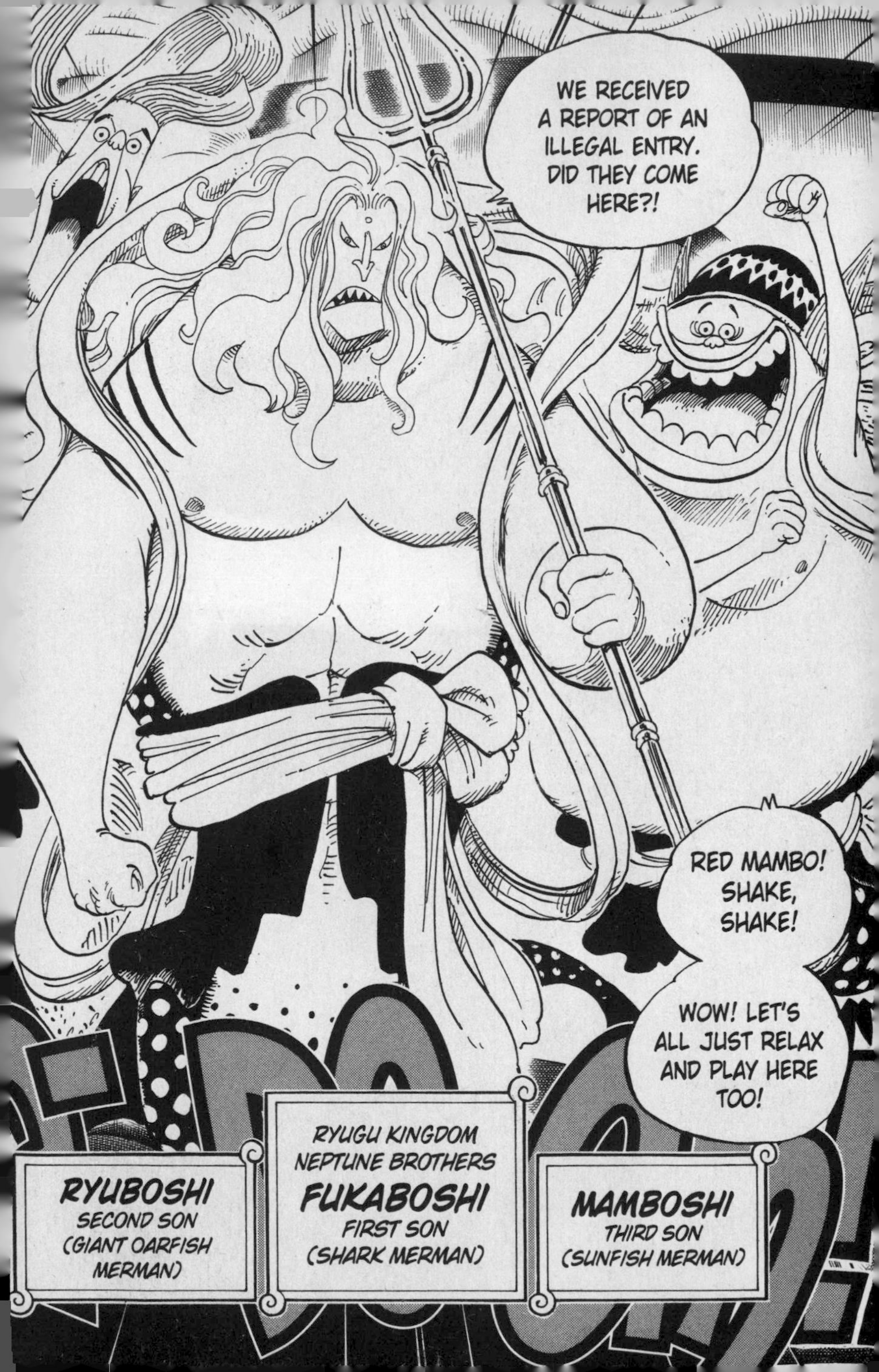
WE RECEIVED A REPORT OF AN ILLEGAL ENTRY. DID THEY COME HERE?!
RED MAMBO! SHAKE, SHAKE!
WOW! LET'S ALL JUST RELAX AND PLAY HERE TOO!
MAMBOSHI THIRD SON (SUNFISH MERMAN)
RYUGU KINGDOM NEPTUNE BROTHERS
FUKABOSHI FIRST SON (SHARK MERMAN)
RYUBOSHI SECOND SON (GIANT OARFISH MERMAN)

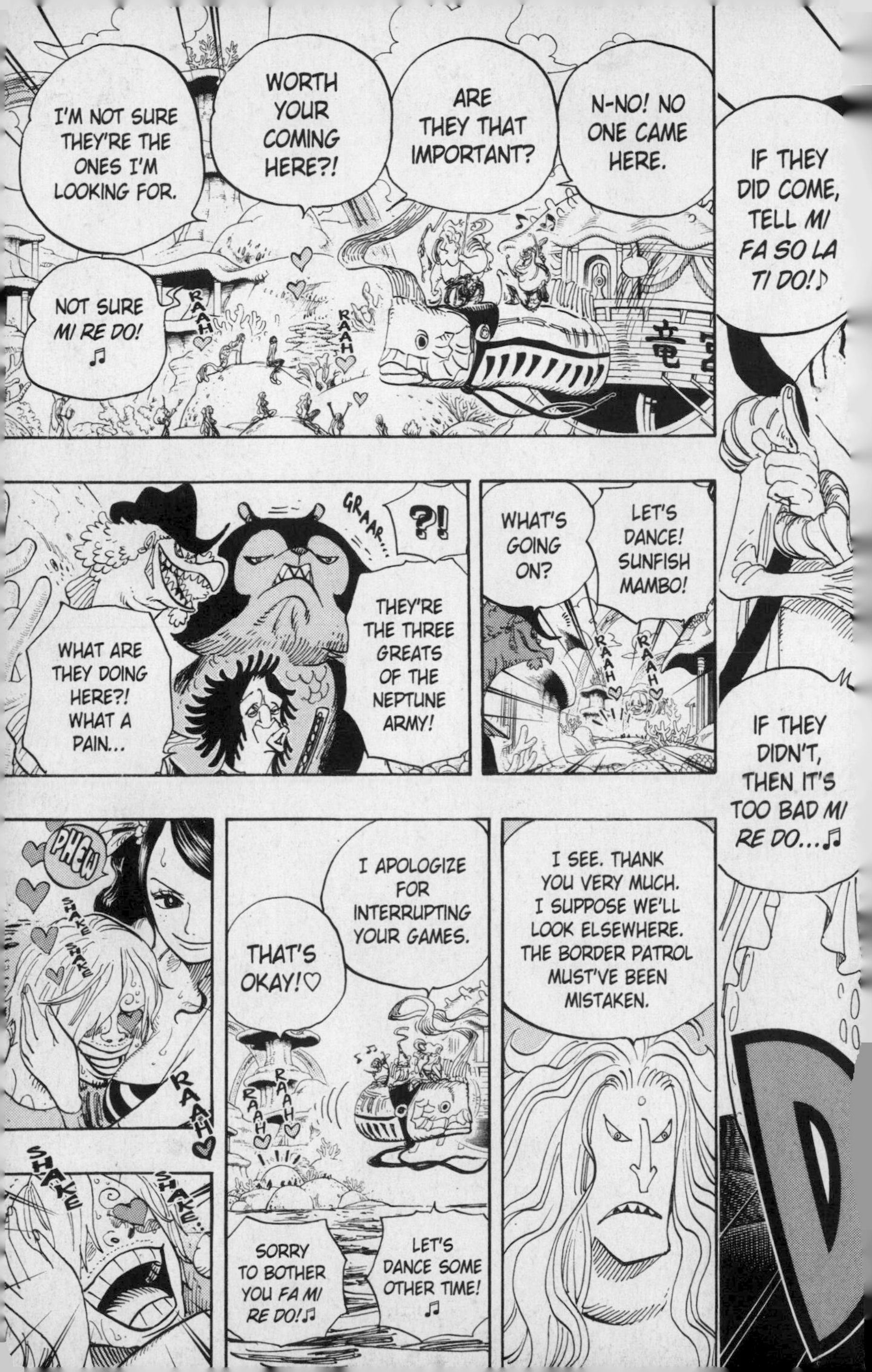
IF THEY DID COME, TELL MI FA SO LA TI DO!♪
IF THEY DIDN'T, THEN IT'S TOO BAD MI RE DO...♫
N-NO! NO ONE CAME HERE.
ARE THEY THAT IMPORTANT?
WORTH YOUR COMING HERE?!
I'M NOT SURE THEY'RE THE ONES I'M LOOKING FOR.
RAAH♡
RAAH♡
NOT SURE MI RE DO! ♫
竜宮
LET'S DANCE! SUNFISH MAMBO!
WHAT'S GOING ON?
RAAH♡
RAAH♡
?!
GRAAAR...
THEY'RE THE THREE GREATS OF THE NEPTUNE ARMY!
WHAT ARE THEY DOING HERE?! WHAT A PAIN...
I SEE. THANK YOU VERY MUCH. I SUPPOSE WE'LL LOOK ELSEWHERE. THE BORDER PATROL MUST'VE BEEN MISTAKEN.
I APOLOGIZE FOR INTERRUPTING YOUR GAMES.
THAT'S OKAY!♡
RAAH♡
RAAH♡
LET'S DANCE SOME OTHER TIME! ♫
SORRY TO BOTHER YOU FA MI RE DO!♫
PHEW
SHAKE
SHAKE
RAAH♡
SHAKE
SHAKE...

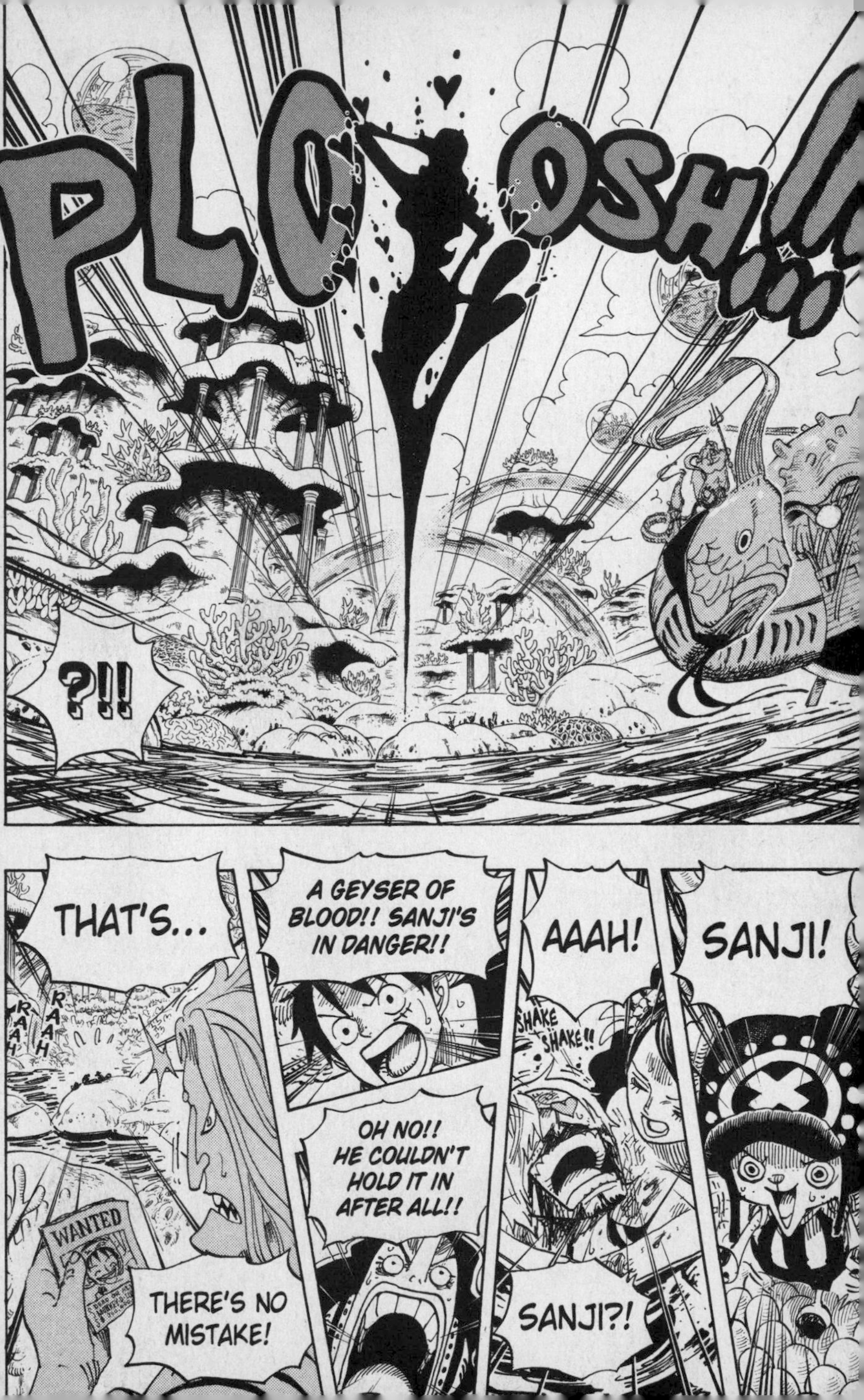
PLOOSH!!
?!!
SANJI!
AAAH!
SHAKE SHAKE!!
SANJI?!
A GEYSER OF BLOOD!! SANJI'S IN DANGER!!
OH NO!! HE COULDN'T HOLD IT IN AFTER ALL!!
THAT'S...
RAAH RAAH
WANTED
THERE'S NO MISTAKE!

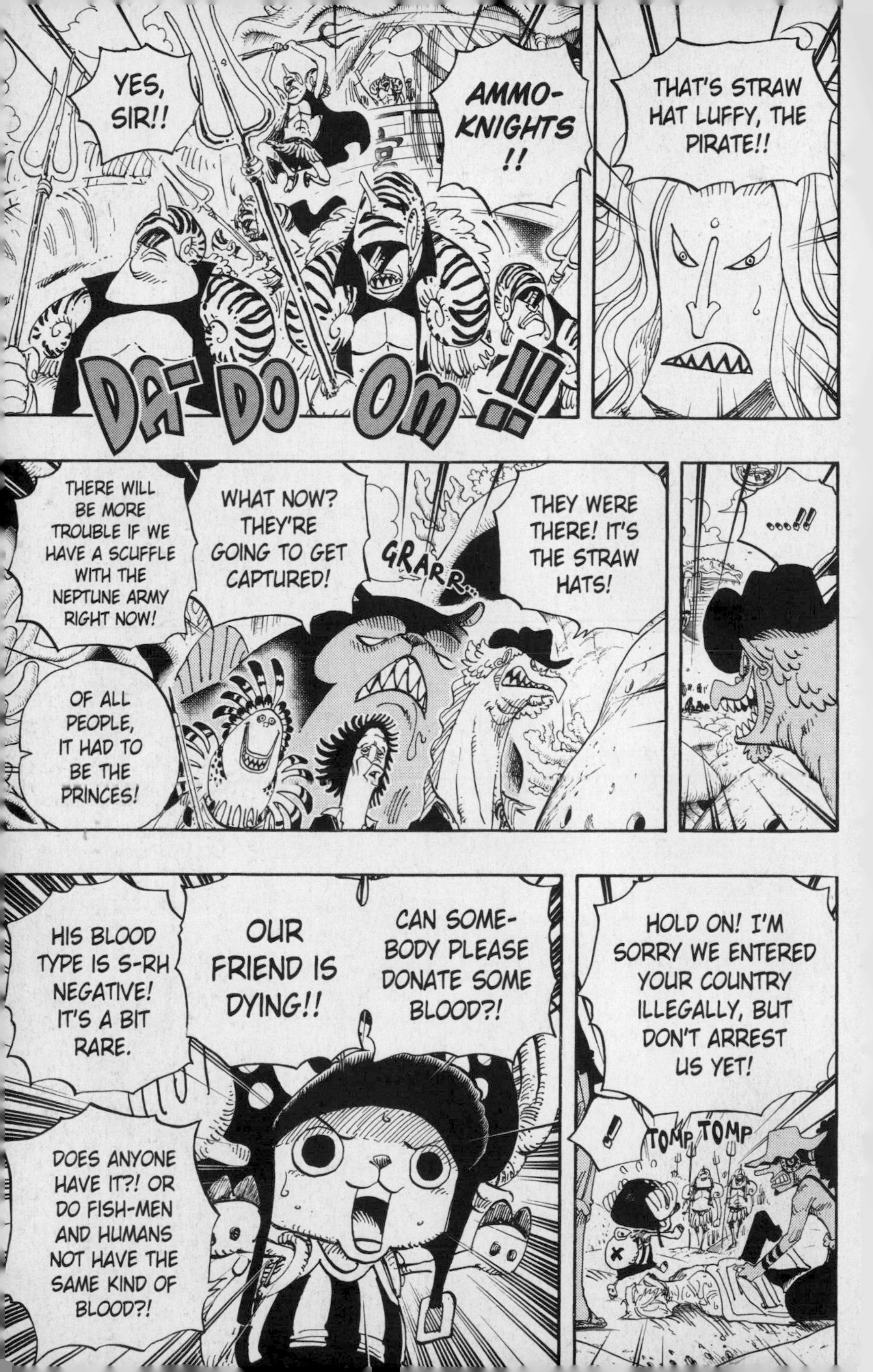
THAT'S STRAW HAT LUFFY, THE PIRATE!!
AMMO-KNIGHTS!!
YES, SIR!!
DA-DO-OM!!
...!!
THEY WERE THERE! IT'S THE STRAW HATS!
GRARR...
WHAT NOW? THEY'RE GOING TO GET CAPTURED!
THERE WILL BE MORE TROUBLE IF WE HAVE A SCUFFLE WITH THE NEPTUNE ARMY RIGHT NOW!
OF ALL PEOPLE, IT HAD TO BE THE PRINCES!
HOLD ON! I'M SORRY WE ENTERED YOUR COUNTRY ILLEGALLY, BUT DON'T ARREST US YET!
!
TOMP TOMP
CAN SOME-BODY PLEASE DONATE SOME BLOOD?!
OUR FRIEND IS DYING!!
HIS BLOOD TYPE IS S-RH NEGATIVE! IT'S A BIT RARE.
DOES ANYONE HAVE IT?! OR DO FISH-MEN AND HUMANS NOT HAVE THE SAME KIND OF BLOOD?!

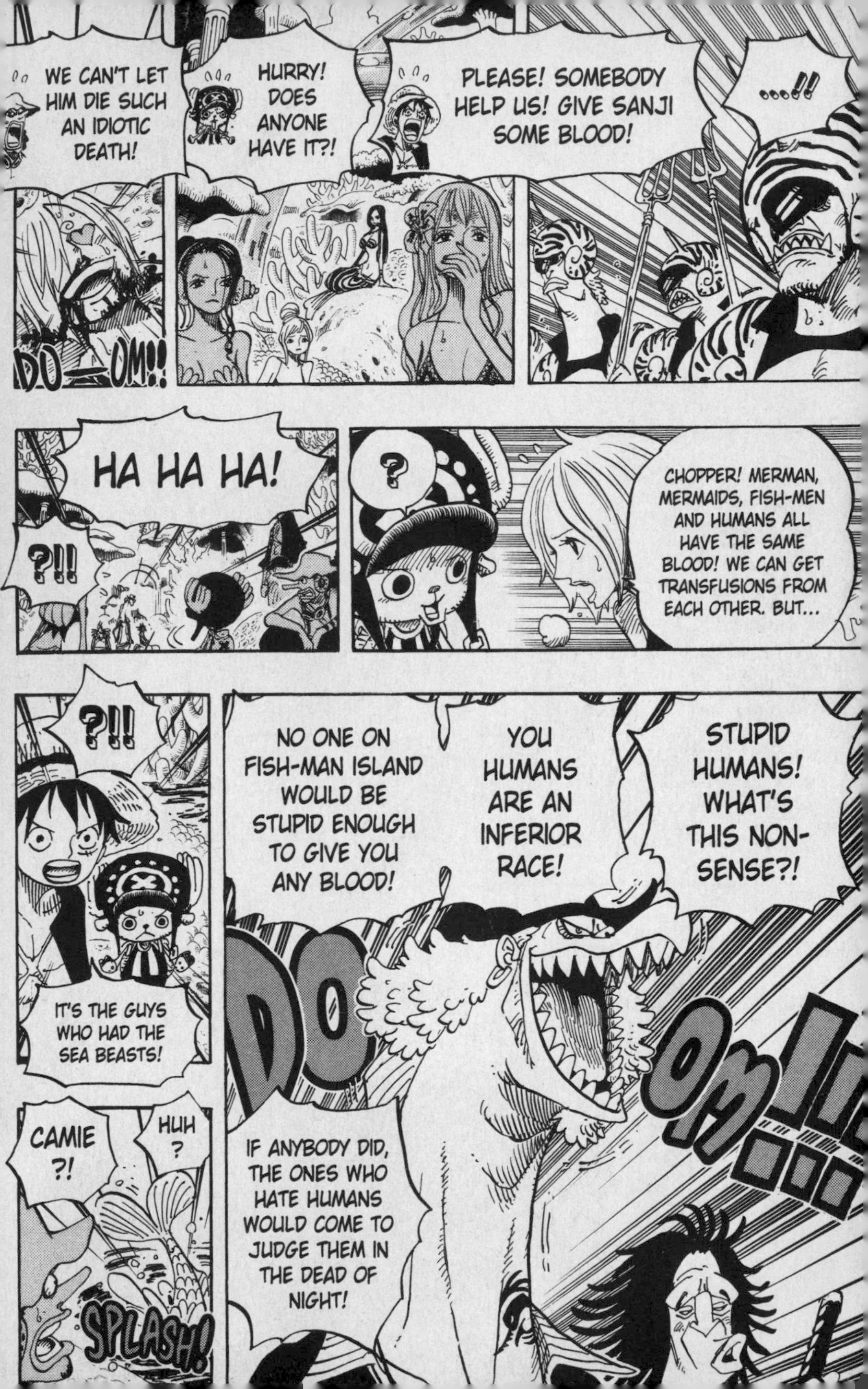
...!!
PLEASE! SOMEBODY HELP US! GIVE SANJI SOME BLOOD!
HURRY! DOES ANYONE HAVE IT?!
WE CAN'T LET HIM DIE SUCH AN IDIOTIC DEATH!
DO—OM!!
CHOPPER! MERMAN, MERMAIDS, FISH-MEN AND HUMANS ALL HAVE THE SAME BLOOD! WE CAN GET TRANSFUSIONS FROM EACH OTHER. BUT...
?
HA HA HA!
?!!
STUPID HUMANS! WHAT'S THIS NON-SENSE?!
YOU HUMANS ARE AN INFERIOR RACE!
NO ONE ON FISH-MAN ISLAND WOULD BE STUPID ENOUGH TO GIVE YOU ANY BLOOD!
DO—OM!!
IF ANYBODY DID, THE ONES WHO HATE HUMANS WOULD COME TO JUDGE THEM IN THE DEAD OF NIGHT!
?!!
IT'S THE GUYS WHO HAD THE SEA BEASTS!
HUH ?
CAMIE ?!
SPLASH!

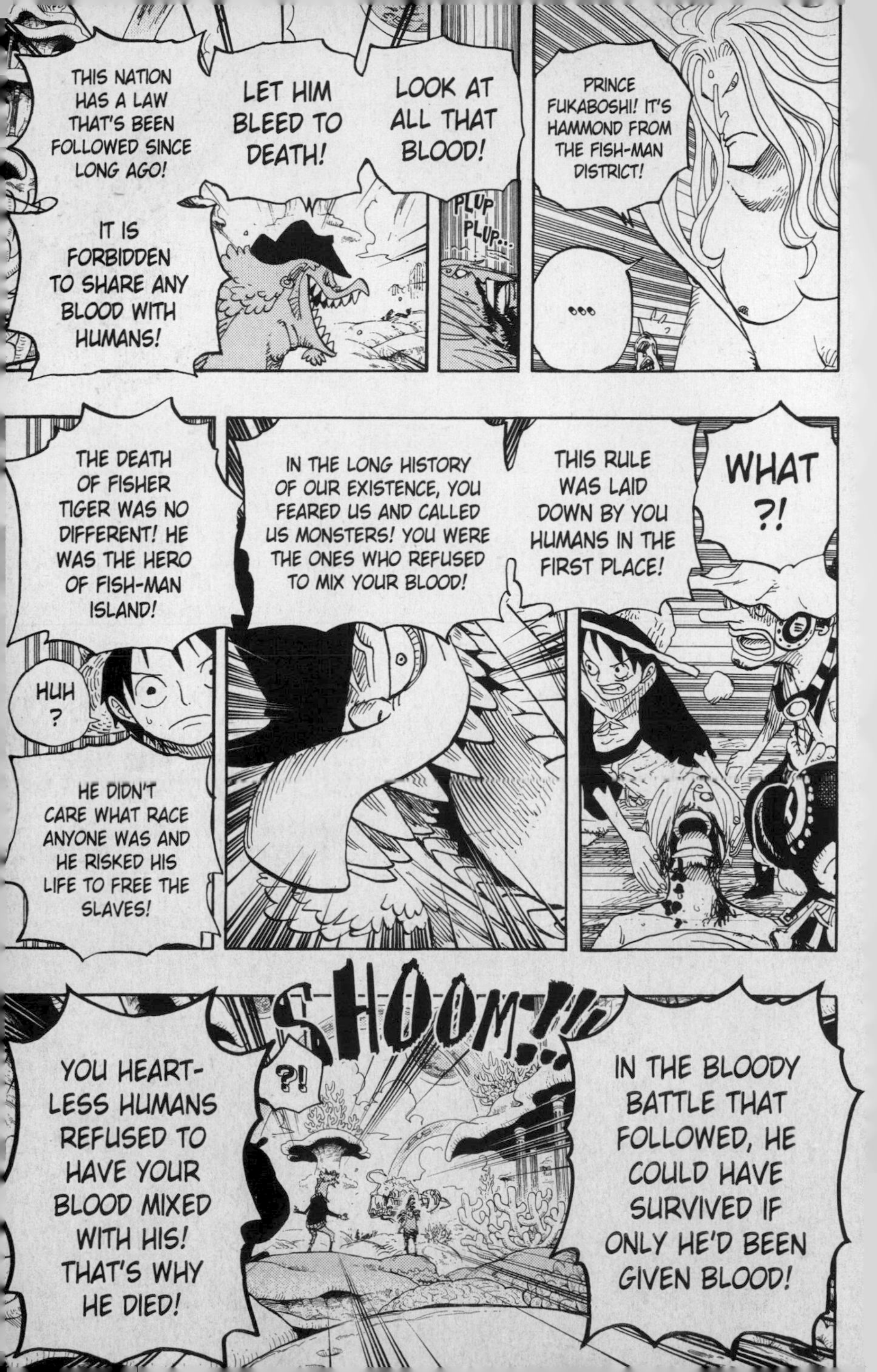
PRINCE FUKABOSHI! IT'S HAMMOND FROM THE FISH-MAN DISTRICT!
...
LOOK AT ALL THAT BLOOD!
PLUP PLUP...
LET HIM BLEED TO DEATH!
THIS NATION HAS A LAW THAT'S BEEN FOLLOWED SINCE LONG AGO!
IT IS FORBIDDEN TO SHARE ANY BLOOD WITH HUMANS!
WHAT ?!
THIS RULE WAS LAID DOWN BY YOU HUMANS IN THE FIRST PLACE!
IN THE LONG HISTORY OF OUR EXISTENCE, YOU FEARED US AND CALLED US MONSTERS! YOU WERE THE ONES WHO REFUSED TO MIX YOUR BLOOD!
THE DEATH OF FISHER TIGER WAS NO DIFFERENT! HE WAS THE HERO OF FISH-MAN ISLAND!
HUH ?
HE DIDN'T CARE WHAT RACE ANYONE WAS AND HE RISKED HIS LIFE TO FREE THE SLAVES!
IN THE BLOODY BATTLE THAT FOLLOWED, HE COULD HAVE SURVIVED IF ONLY HE'D BEEN GIVEN BLOOD!
SHOOM!!
?!
YOU HEART-LESS HUMANS REFUSED TO HAVE YOUR BLOOD MIXED WITH HIS! THAT'S WHY HE DIED!

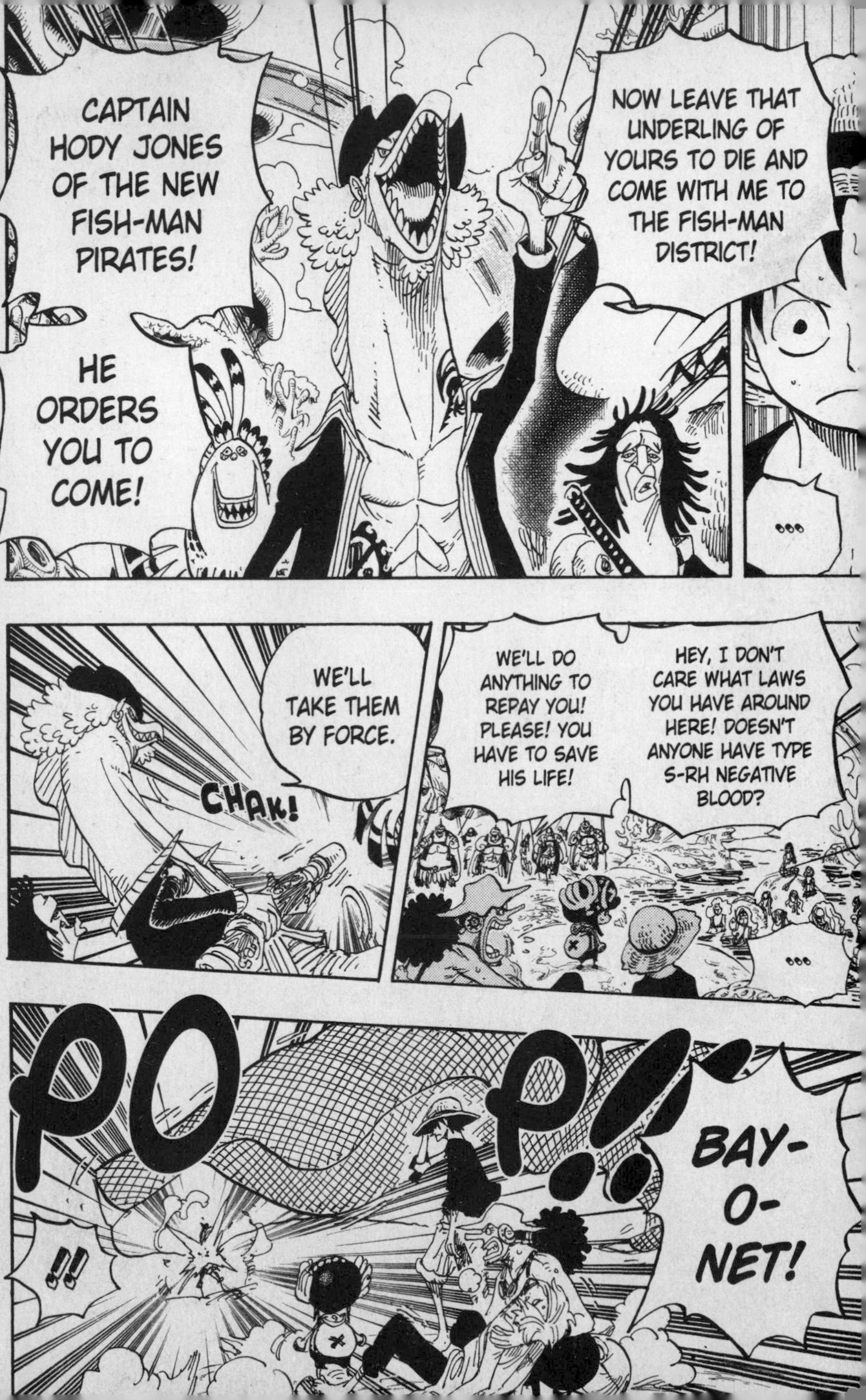
NOW LEAVE THAT UNDERLING OF YOURS TO DIE AND COME WITH ME TO THE FISH-MAN DISTRICT!
CAPTAIN HODY JONES OF THE NEW FISH-MAN PIRATES!
HE ORDERS YOU TO COME!
...
HEY, I DON'T CARE WHAT LAWS YOU HAVE AROUND HERE! DOESN'T ANYONE HAVE TYPE S-RH NEGATIVE BLOOD?
WE'LL DO ANYTHING TO REPAY YOU! PLEASE! YOU HAVE TO SAVE HIS LIFE!
...
WE'LL TAKE THEM BY FORCE.
CHAK!
BAY-O-NET!
POP!!
!!

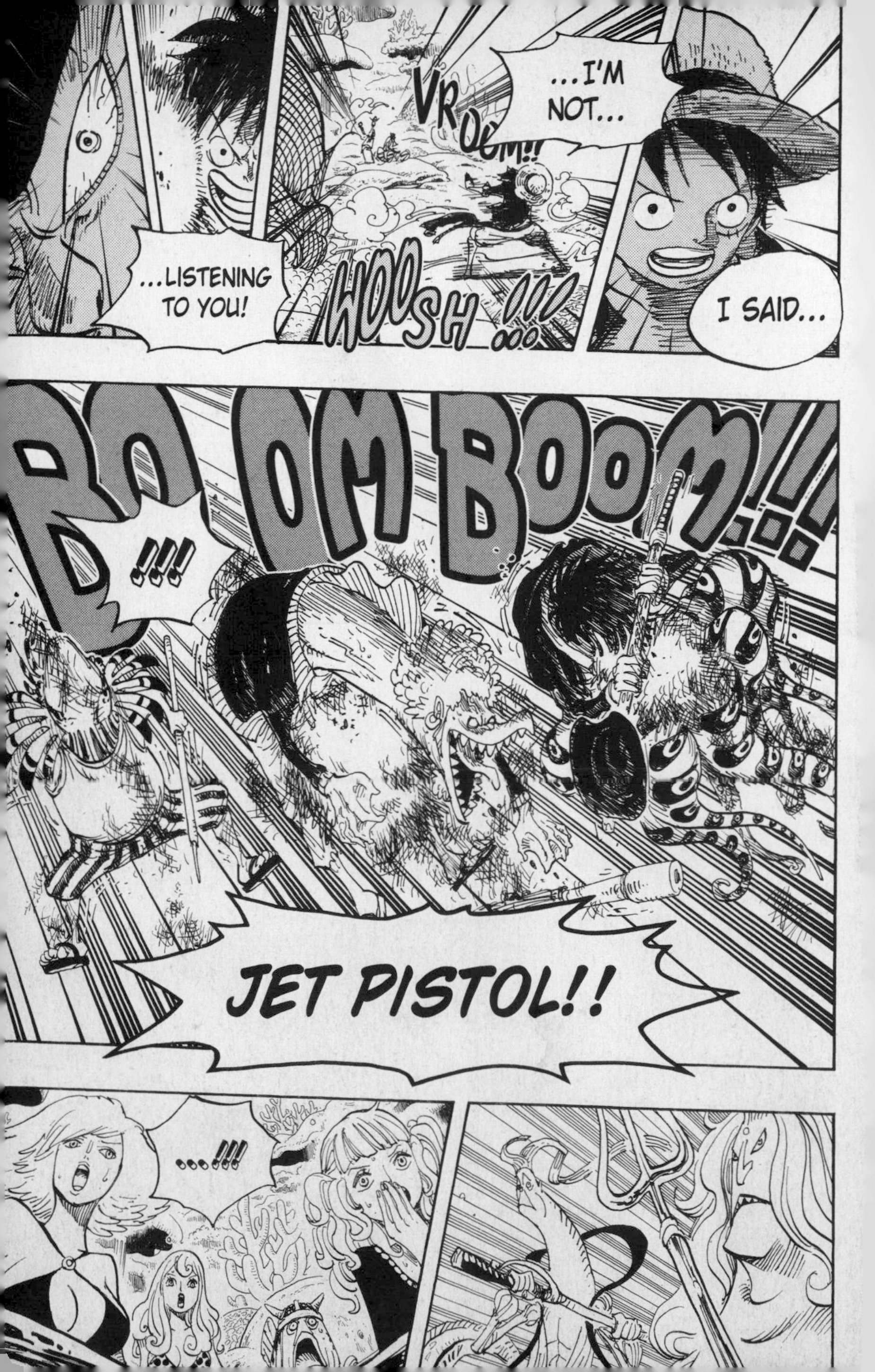
I SAID...
...I'M NOT...
VROOOM!!
WHOOSH!!!
...LISTENING TO YOU!
BOOM BOOM!!!
JET PISTOL!!
...!!!

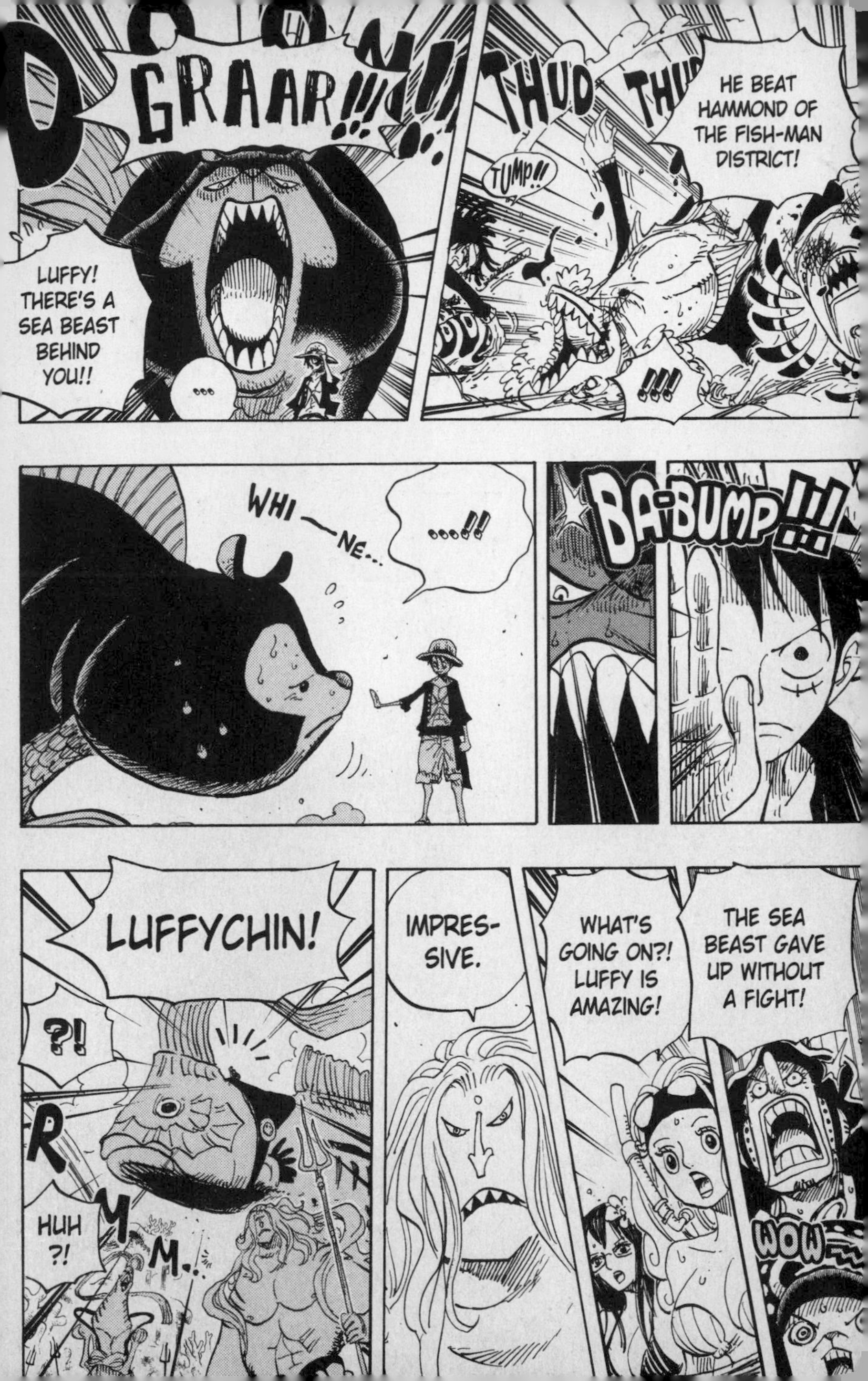

THUD
THU
HE BEAT HAMMOND OF THE FISH-MAN DISTRICT!
TUMP!!
!!!
GRAAR!!!
LUFFY! THERE'S A SEA BEAST BEHIND YOU!!
...
BA-BUMP!!!
....!!
WHI—NE...
THE SEA BEAST GAVE UP WITHOUT A FIGHT!
WOW
WHAT'S GOING ON?! LUFFY IS AMAZING!
IMPRES-SIVE.
LUFFYCHIN!
?!
HUH ?!
R M M...

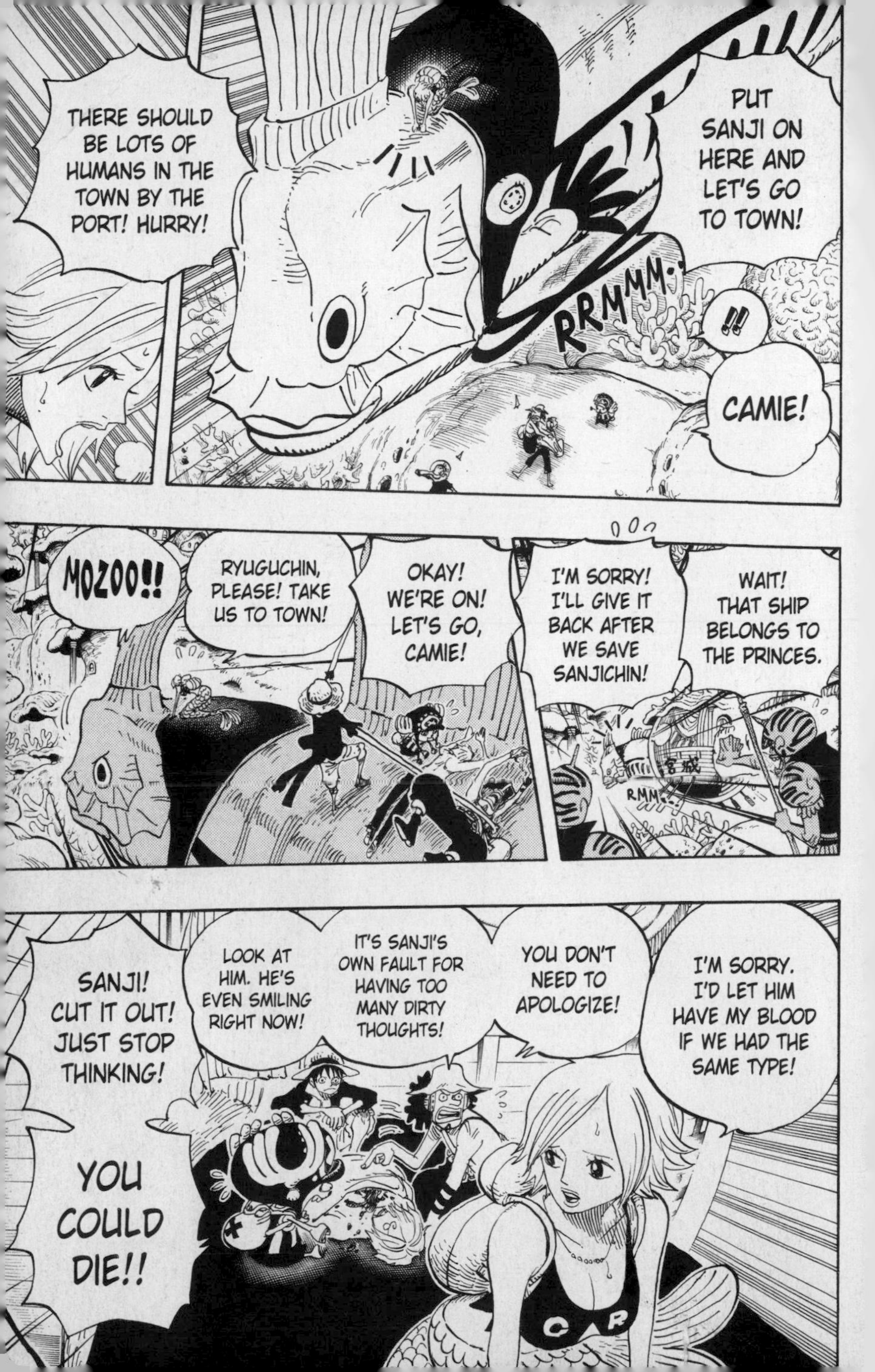
PUT SANJI ON HERE AND LET'S GO TO TOWN!
THERE SHOULD BE LOTS OF HUMANS IN THE TOWN BY THE PORT! HURRY!
RRMMM
!!
CAMIE!
WAIT! THAT SHIP BELONGS TO THE PRINCES.
I'M SORRY! I'LL GIVE IT BACK AFTER WE SAVE SANJICHIN!
RMM
OKAY! WE'RE ON! LET'S GO, CAMIE!
RYUGUCHIN, PLEASE! TAKE US TO TOWN!
MOZOO!!
I'M SORRY. I'D LET HIM HAVE MY BLOOD IF WE HAD THE SAME TYPE!
YOU DON'T NEED TO APOLOGIZE!
IT'S SANJI'S OWN FAULT FOR HAVING TOO MANY DIRTY THOUGHTS!
LOOK AT HIM. HE'S EVEN SMILING RIGHT NOW!
SANJI! CUT IT OUT! JUST STOP THINKING!
YOU COULD DIE!!

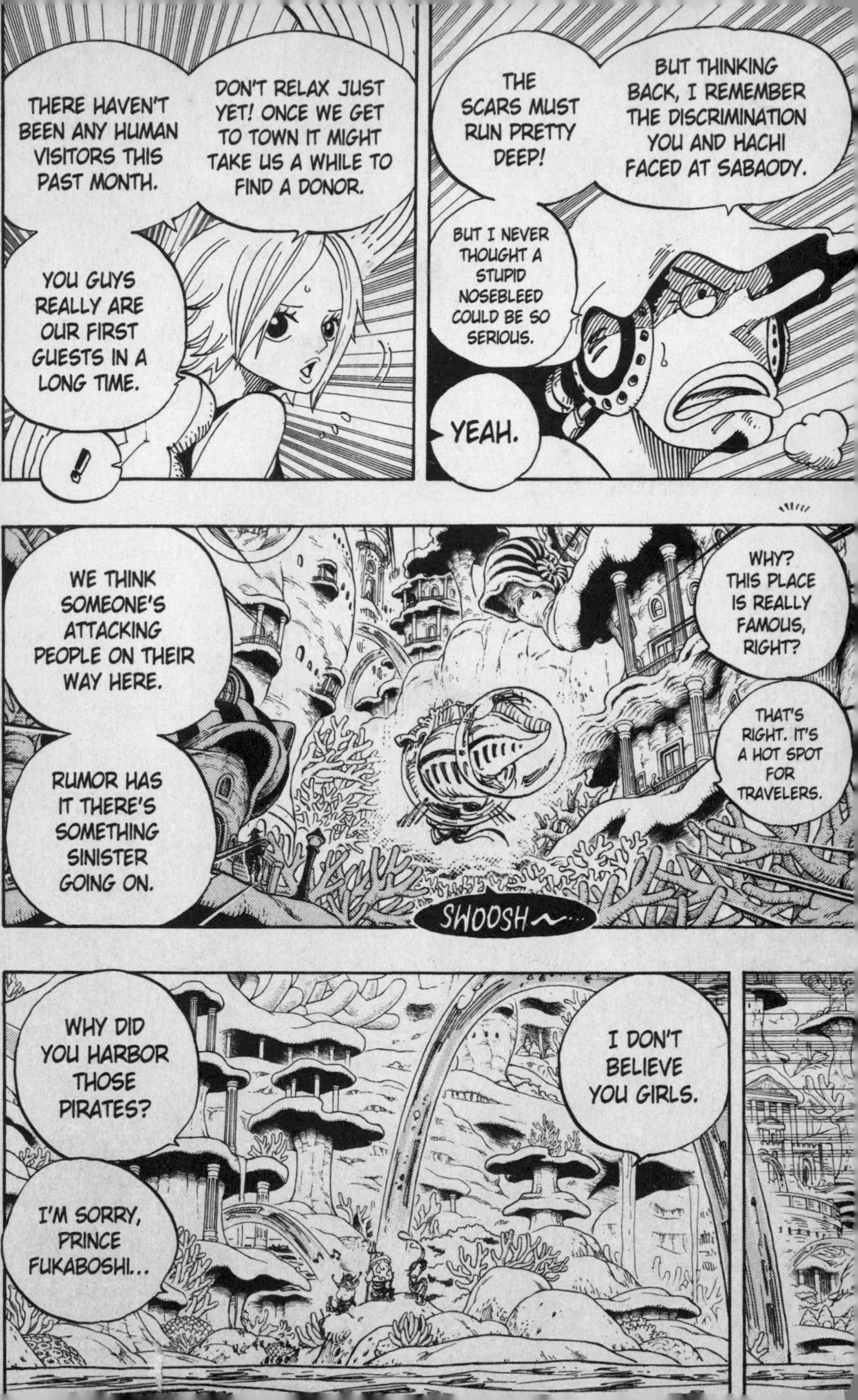
BUT THINKING BACK, I REMEMBER THE DISCRIMINATION YOU AND HACHI FACED AT SABAODY.
THE SCARS MUST RUN PRETTY DEEP!
BUT I NEVER THOUGHT A STUPID NOSEBLEED COULD BE SO SERIOUS.
YEAH.
DON'T RELAX JUST YET! ONCE WE GET TO TOWN IT MIGHT TAKE US A WHILE TO FIND A DONOR.
THERE HAVEN'T BEEN ANY HUMAN VISITORS THIS PAST MONTH.
YOU GUYS REALLY ARE OUR FIRST GUESTS IN A LONG TIME.
!
WHY? THIS PLACE IS REALLY FAMOUS, RIGHT?
THAT'S RIGHT. IT'S A HOT SPOT FOR TRAVELERS.
WE THINK SOMEONE'S ATTACKING PEOPLE ON THEIR WAY HERE.
RUMOR HAS IT THERE'S SOMETHING SINISTER GOING ON.
SWOOSH~...
I DON'T BELIEVE YOU GIRLS.
WHY DID YOU HARBOR THOSE PIRATES?
I'M SORRY, PRINCE FUKABOSHI...

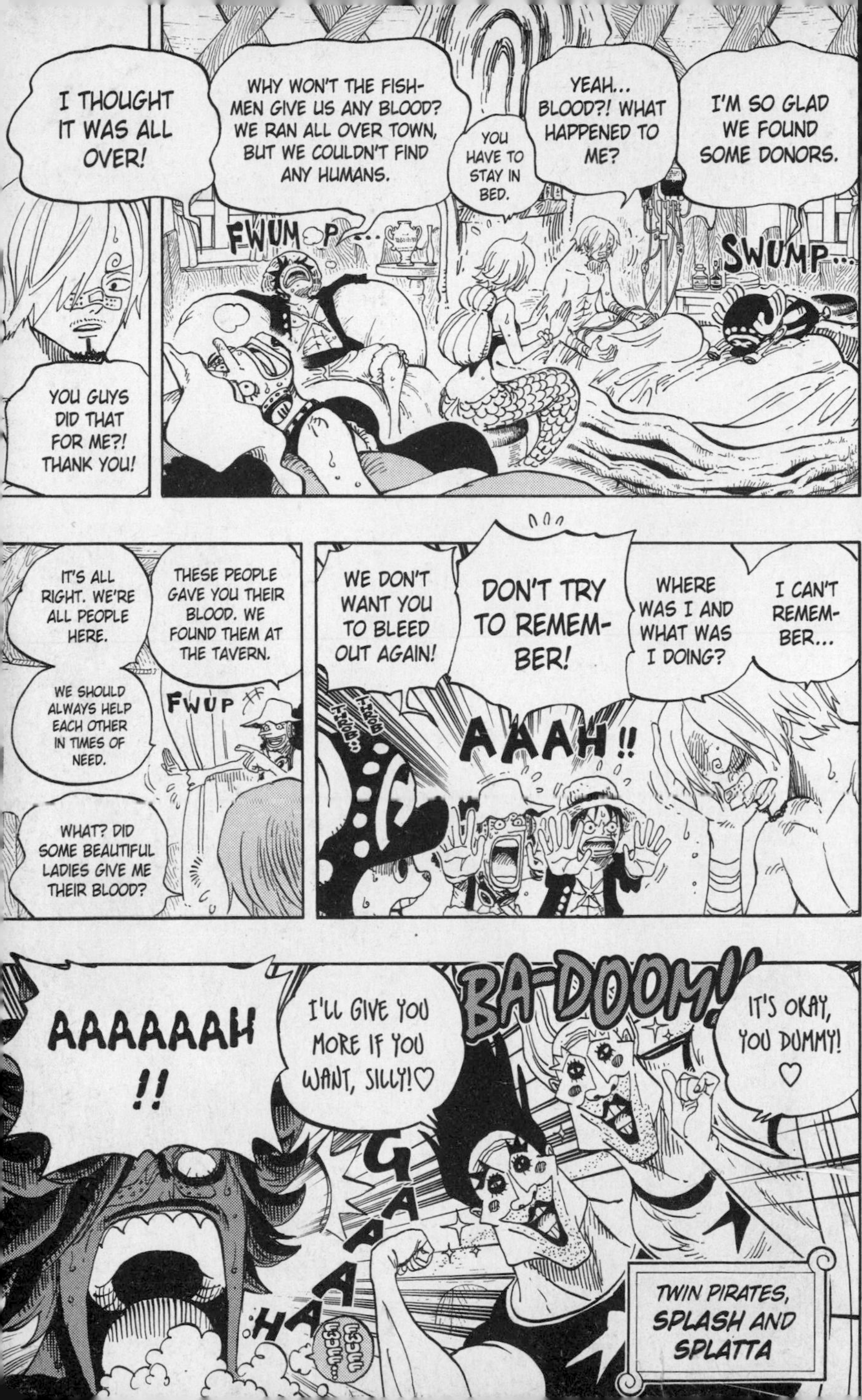
I'M SO GLAD WE FOUND SOME DONORS.
YEAH... BLOOD?! WHAT HAPPENED TO ME?
YOU HAVE TO STAY IN BED.
WHY WON'T THE FISH-MEN GIVE US ANY BLOOD? WE RAN ALL OVER TOWN, BUT WE COULDN'T FIND ANY HUMANS.
SWUMP...
FWUMP...
I THOUGHT IT WAS ALL OVER!
YOU GUYS DID THAT FOR ME?! THANK YOU!
I CAN'T REMEMBER...
WHERE WAS I AND WHAT WAS I DOING?
DON'T TRY TO REMEMBER!
WE DON'T WANT YOU TO BLEED OUT AGAIN!
THROB THROB
AAAH!!
THESE PEOPLE GAVE YOU THEIR BLOOD. WE FOUND THEM AT THE TAVERN.
IT'S ALL RIGHT. WE'RE ALL PEOPLE HERE.
WE SHOULD ALWAYS HELP EACH OTHER IN TIMES OF NEED.
FWUP
WHAT? DID SOME BEAUTIFUL LADIES GIVE ME THEIR BLOOD?
IT'S OKAY, YOU DUMMY! ♡
BA-DOOM!!
I'LL GIVE YOU MORE IF YOU WANT, SILLY!♡
AAAAAAH!!
GAAAAHA
TWIN PIRATES, SPLASH AND SPLATTA

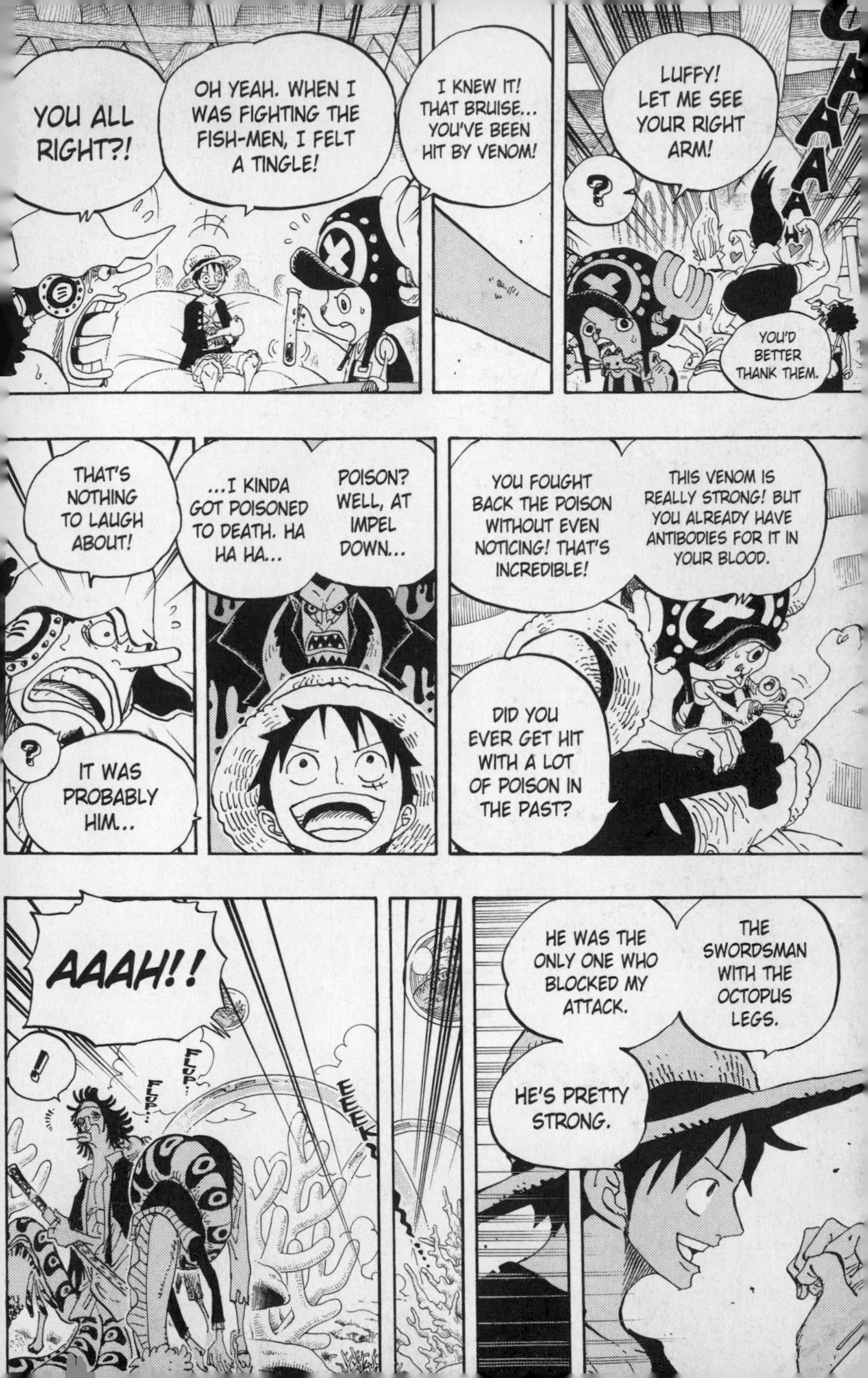

LUFFY! LET ME SEE YOUR RIGHT ARM!
?
YOU'D BETTER THANK THEM.
I KNEW IT! THAT BRUISE... YOU'VE BEEN HIT BY VENOM!
OH YEAH. WHEN I WAS FIGHTING THE FISH-MEN, I FELT A TINGLE!
YOU ALL RIGHT?!
THIS VENOM IS REALLY STRONG! BUT YOU ALREADY HAVE ANTIBODIES FOR IT IN YOUR BLOOD.
YOU FOUGHT BACK THE POISON WITHOUT EVEN NOTICING! THAT'S INCREDIBLE!
DID YOU EVER GET HIT WITH A LOT OF POISON IN THE PAST?
POISON? WELL, AT IMPEL DOWN...
...I KINDA GOT POISONED TO DEATH. HA HA HA...
THAT'S NOTHING TO LAUGH ABOUT!
?
IT WAS PROBABLY HIM...
THE SWORDSMAN WITH THE OCTOPUS LEGS.
HE WAS THE ONLY ONE WHO BLOCKED MY ATTACK.
HE'S PRETTY STRONG.
EEEK
AAAH!!
!
FLUP...
FLUP...

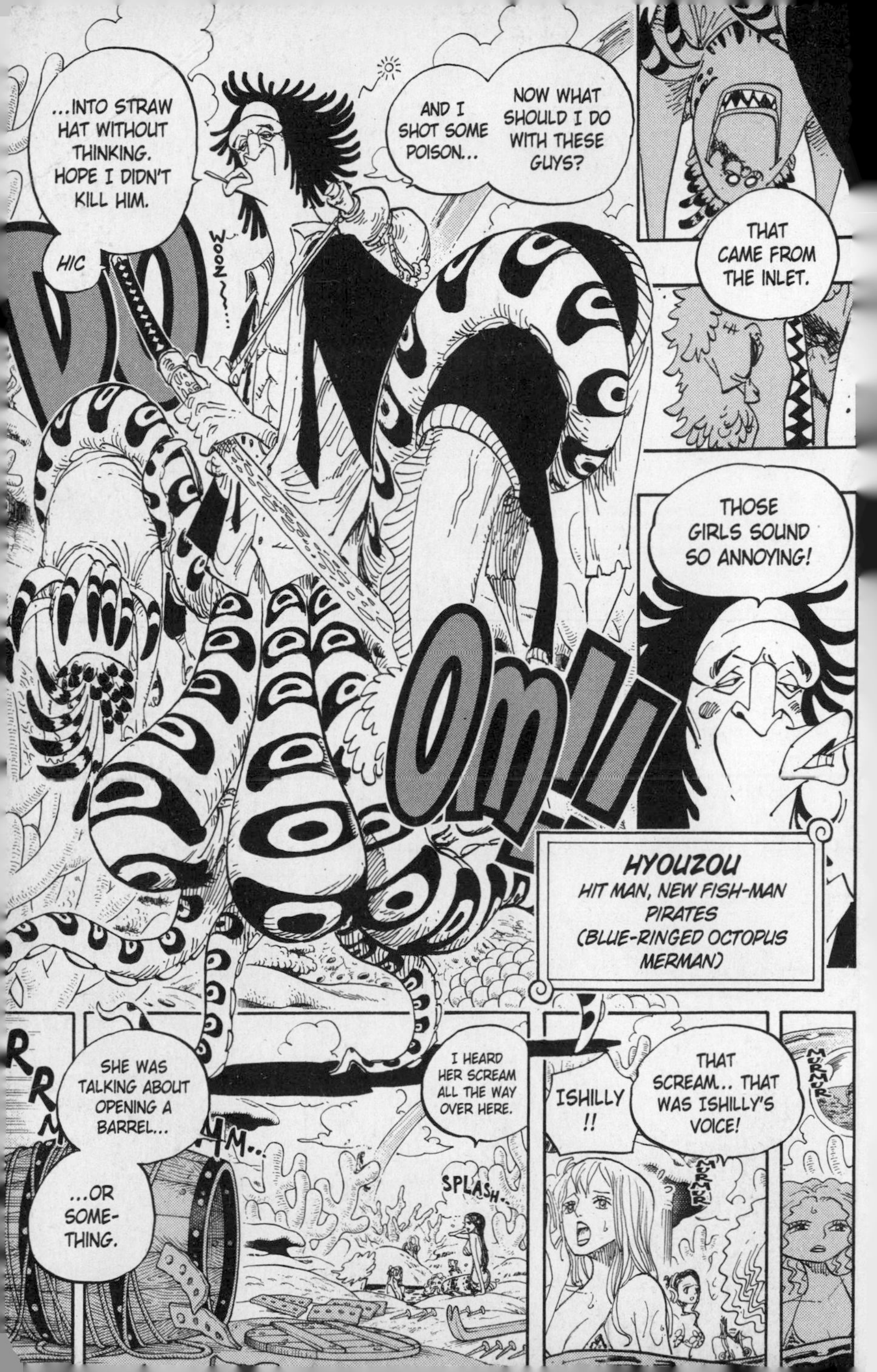
THAT CAME FROM THE INLET.
THOSE GIRLS SOUND SO ANNOYING!
HYOUZOU
HIT MAN, NEW FISH-MAN PIRATES
(BLUE-RINGED OCTOPUS MERMAN)
NOW WHAT SHOULD I DO WITH THESE GUYS?
AND I SHOT SOME POISON...
...INTO STRAW HAT WITHOUT THINKING. HOPE I DIDN'T KILL HIM.
WOOZ~...
HIC
OM!!
MURMUR
THAT SCREAM... THAT WAS ISHILLY'S VOICE!
ISHILLY!!
MURMUR
I HEARD HER SCREAM ALL THE WAY OVER HERE.
SPLASH...
SHE WAS TALKING ABOUT OPENING A BARREL...
...OR SOMETHING.

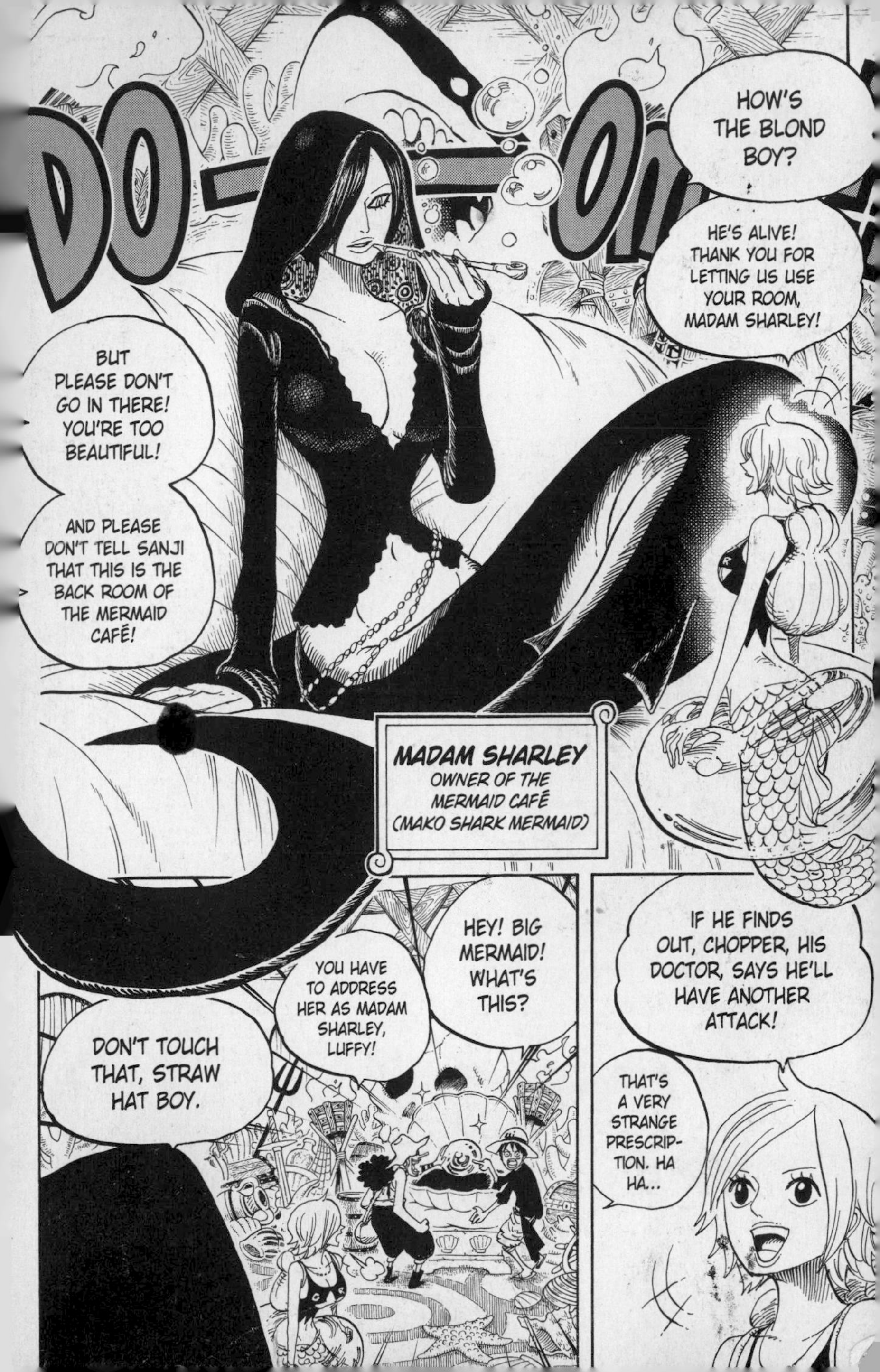
DO-OM
HOW'S THE BLOND BOY?
HE'S ALIVE! THANK YOU FOR LETTING US USE YOUR ROOM, MADAM SHARLEY!
BUT PLEASE DON'T GO IN THERE! YOU'RE TOO BEAUTIFUL!
AND PLEASE DON'T TELL SANJI THAT THIS IS THE BACK ROOM OF THE MERMAID CAFÉ!
MADAM SHARLEY
OWNER OF THE MERMAID CAFÉ
(MAKO SHARK MERMAID)
IF HE FINDS OUT, CHOPPER, HIS DOCTOR, SAYS HE'LL HAVE ANOTHER ATTACK!
THAT'S A VERY STRANGE PRESCRIP-TION. HA HA...
HEY! BIG MERMAID! WHAT'S THIS?
YOU HAVE TO ADDRESS HER AS MADAM SHARLEY, LUFFY!
DON'T TOUCH THAT, STRAW HAT BOY.

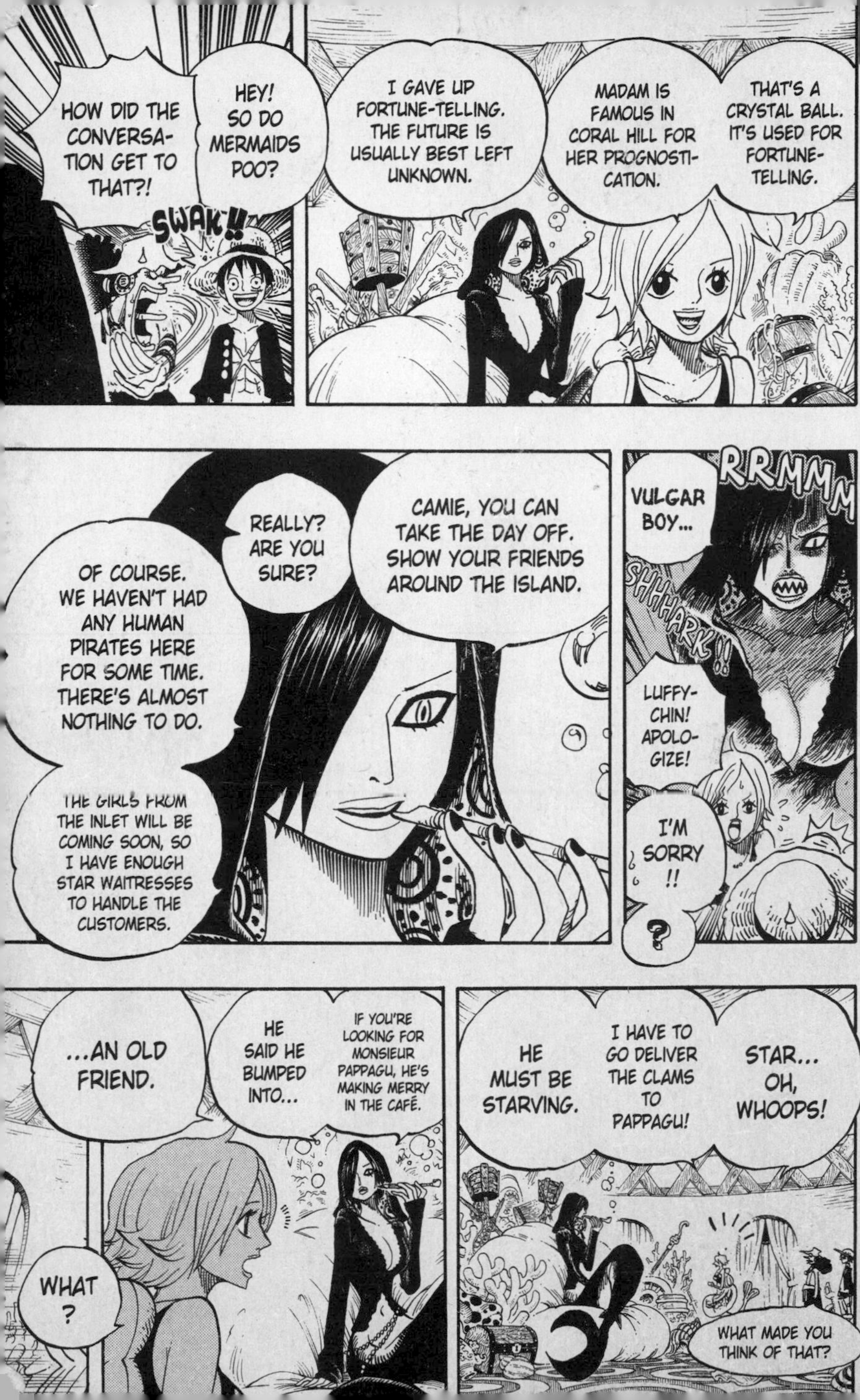
THAT'S A CRYSTAL BALL. IT'S USED FOR FORTUNE-TELLING.
MADAM IS FAMOUS IN CORAL HILL FOR HER PROGNOSTICATION.
I GAVE UP FORTUNE-TELLING. THE FUTURE IS USUALLY BEST LEFT UNKNOWN.
HEY! SO DO MERMAIDS POO?
HOW DID THE CONVERSATION GET TO THAT?!
SWAK!!
RRMMMM
VULGAR BOY...
SHHHARK!!
LUFFY-CHIN! APOLOGIZE!
I'M SORRY!!
?
CAMIE, YOU CAN TAKE THE DAY OFF. SHOW YOUR FRIENDS AROUND THE ISLAND.
REALLY? ARE YOU SURE?
OF COURSE. WE HAVEN'T HAD ANY HUMAN PIRATES HERE FOR SOME TIME. THERE'S ALMOST NOTHING TO DO.
THE GIRLS FROM THE INLET WILL BE COMING SOON, SO I HAVE ENOUGH STAR WAITRESSES TO HANDLE THE CUSTOMERS.
STAR... OH, WHOOPS!
I HAVE TO GO DELIVER THE CLAMS TO PAPPAGU!
HE MUST BE STARVING.
WHAT MADE YOU THINK OF THAT?
IF YOU'RE LOOKING FOR MONSIEUR PAPPAGU, HE'S MAKING MERRY IN THE CAFÉ.
HE SAID HE BUMPED INTO...
...AN OLD FRIEND.
WHAT ?

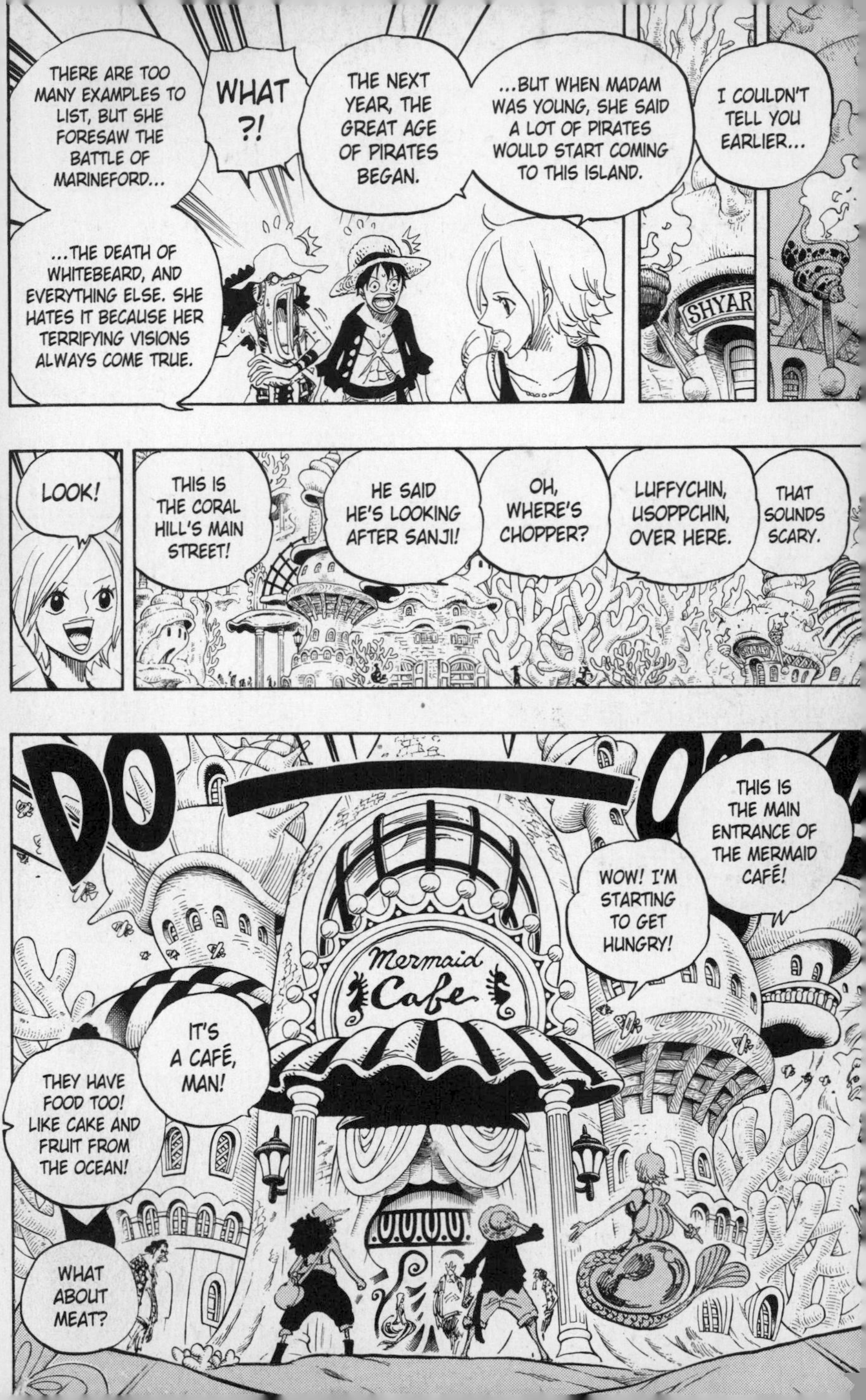
I COULDN'T TELL YOU EARLIER...
SHYAR
...BUT WHEN MADAM WAS YOUNG, SHE SAID A LOT OF PIRATES WOULD START COMING TO THIS ISLAND.
THE NEXT YEAR, THE GREAT AGE OF PIRATES BEGAN.
WHAT ?!
THERE ARE TOO MANY EXAMPLES TO LIST, BUT SHE FORESAW THE BATTLE OF MARINEFORD...
...THE DEATH OF WHITEBEARD, AND EVERYTHING ELSE. SHE HATES IT BECAUSE HER TERRIFYING VISIONS ALWAYS COME TRUE.
THAT SOUNDS SCARY.
LUFFYCHIN, USOPPCHIN, OVER HERE.
OH, WHERE'S CHOPPER?
HE SAID HE'S LOOKING AFTER SANJI!
THIS IS THE CORAL HILL'S MAIN STREET!
LOOK!
DO
THIS IS THE MAIN ENTRANCE OF THE MERMAID CAFÉ!
WOW! I'M STARTING TO GET HUNGRY!
Mermaid Cafe
IT'S A CAFÉ, MAN!
THEY HAVE FOOD TOO! LIKE CAKE AND FRUIT FROM THE OCEAN!
WHAT ABOUT MEAT?

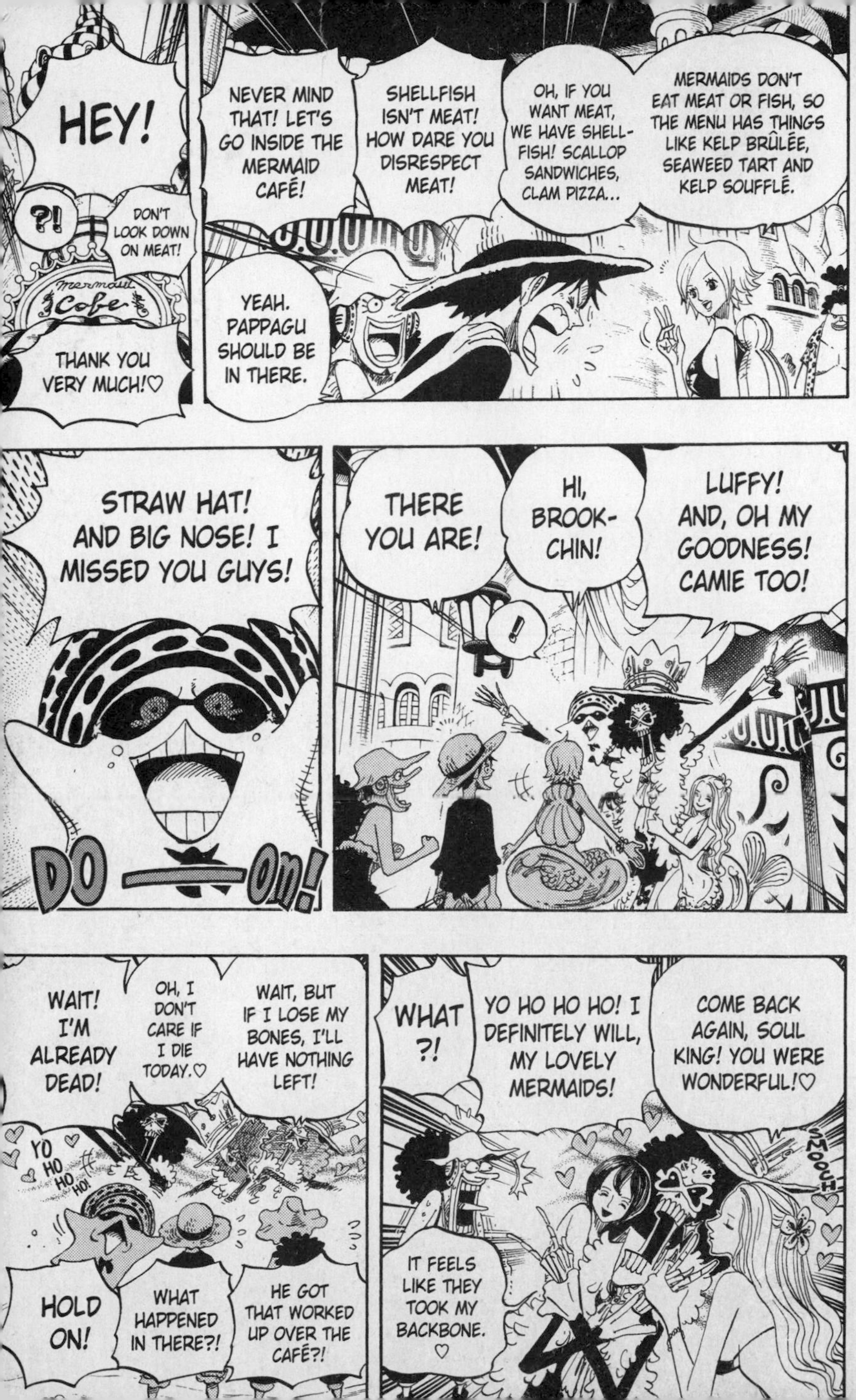

MERMAIDS DON'T EAT MEAT OR FISH, SO THE MENU HAS THINGS LIKE KELP BRÛLÉE, SEAWEED TART AND KELP SOUFFLÉ.
OH, IF YOU WANT MEAT, WE HAVE SHELLFISH! SCALLOP SANDWICHES, CLAM PIZZA...
SHELLFISH ISN'T MEAT! HOW DARE YOU DISRESPECT MEAT!
NEVER MIND THAT! LET'S GO INSIDE THE MERMAID CAFÉ!
YEAH. PAPPAGU SHOULD BE IN THERE.
HEY!
DON'T LOOK DOWN ON MEAT!
?!
THANK YOU VERY MUCH!♡
LUFFY! AND, OH MY GOODNESS! CAMIE TOO!
HI, BROOK-CHIN!
THERE YOU ARE!
!
STRAW HAT! AND BIG NOSE! I MISSED YOU GUYS!
DO—ON!
COME BACK AGAIN, SOUL KING! YOU WERE WONDERFUL!♡
SMOOCH
YO HO HO HO! I DEFINITELY WILL, MY LOVELY MERMAIDS!
WHAT?!
IT FEELS LIKE THEY TOOK MY BACKBONE. ♡
WAIT, BUT IF I LOSE MY BONES, I'LL HAVE NOTHING LEFT!
OH, I DON'T CARE IF I DIE TODAY.♡
WAIT! I'M ALREADY DEAD!
YO HO HO HO!
HE GOT THAT WORKED UP OVER THE CAFÉ?!
WHAT HAPPENED IN THERE?!
HOLD ON!

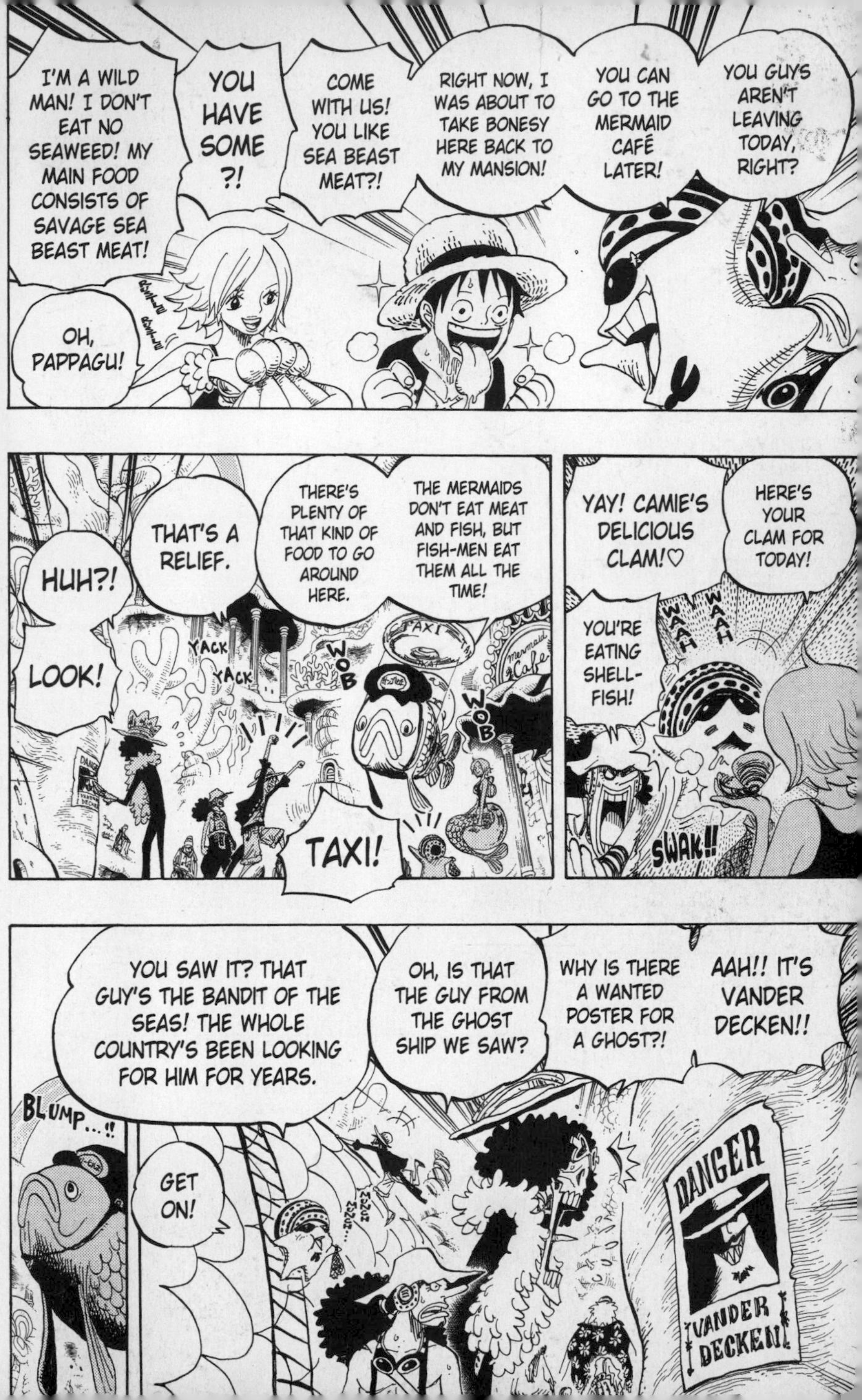
YOU GUYS AREN'T LEAVING TODAY, RIGHT?
YOU CAN GO TO THE MERMAID CAFÉ LATER!
RIGHT NOW, I WAS ABOUT TO TAKE BONESY HERE BACK TO MY MANSION!
COME WITH US! YOU LIKE SEA BEAST MEAT?!
YOU HAVE SOME ?!
I'M A WILD MAN! I DON'T EAT NO SEAWEED! MY MAIN FOOD CONSISTS OF SAVAGE SEA BEAST MEAT!
OH, PAPPAGU!
HERE'S YOUR CLAM FOR TODAY!
YAY! CAMIE'S DELICIOUS CLAM!♡
WAAH WAAH
YOU'RE EATING SHELL-FISH!
SWAK!!
THE MERMAIDS DON'T EAT MEAT AND FISH, BUT FISH-MEN EAT THEM ALL THE TIME!
THERE'S PLENTY OF THAT KIND OF FOOD TO GO AROUND HERE.
THAT'S A RELIEF.
HUH?!
LOOK!
TAXI
Mermaid Cafe
WOB
WOB
YACK
YACK
TAXI!
AAH!! IT'S VANDER DECKEN!!
WHY IS THERE A WANTED POSTER FOR A GHOST?!
OH, IS THAT THE GUY FROM THE GHOST SHIP WE SAW?
YOU SAW IT? THAT GUY'S THE BANDIT OF THE SEAS! THE WHOLE COUNTRY'S BEEN LOOKING FOR HIM FOR YEARS.
DANGER
VANDER DECKEN
MUNCH MUNCH
GET ON!
BLUMP...!!

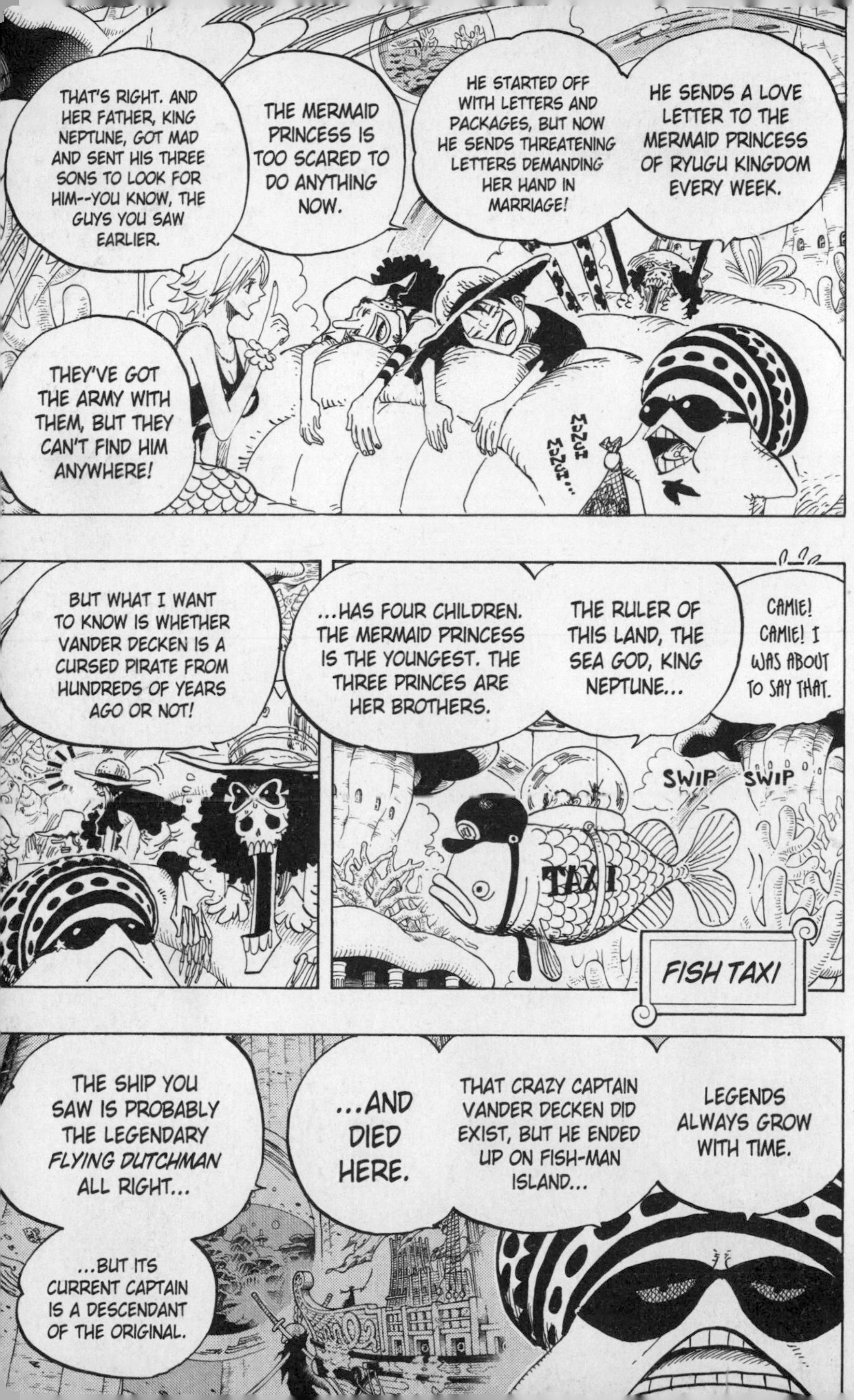
HE SENDS A LOVE LETTER TO THE MERMAID PRINCESS OF RYUGU KINGDOM EVERY WEEK.
HE STARTED OFF WITH LETTERS AND PACKAGES, BUT NOW HE SENDS THREATENING LETTERS DEMANDING HER HAND IN MARRIAGE!
THE MERMAID PRINCESS IS TOO SCARED TO DO ANYTHING NOW.
THAT'S RIGHT. AND HER FATHER, KING NEPTUNE, GOT MAD AND SENT HIS THREE SONS TO LOOK FOR HIM--YOU KNOW, THE GUYS YOU SAW EARLIER.
THEY'VE GOT THE ARMY WITH THEM, BUT THEY CAN'T FIND HIM ANYWHERE!
MUNCH MUNCH...
CAMIE! CAMIE! I WAS ABOUT TO SAY THAT.
THE RULER OF THIS LAND, THE SEA GOD, KING NEPTUNE...
...HAS FOUR CHILDREN. THE MERMAID PRINCESS IS THE YOUNGEST. THE THREE PRINCES ARE HER BROTHERS.
SWIP SWIP
TAXI
FISH TAXI
BUT WHAT I WANT TO KNOW IS WHETHER VANDER DECKEN IS A CURSED PIRATE FROM HUNDREDS OF YEARS AGO OR NOT!
LEGENDS ALWAYS GROW WITH TIME.
THAT CRAZY CAPTAIN VANDER DECKEN DID EXIST, BUT HE ENDED UP ON FISH-MAN ISLAND...
...AND DIED HERE.
THE SHIP YOU SAW IS PROBABLY THE LEGENDARY *FLYING DUTCHMAN* ALL RIGHT...
...BUT ITS CURRENT CAPTAIN IS A DESCENDANT OF THE ORIGINAL.

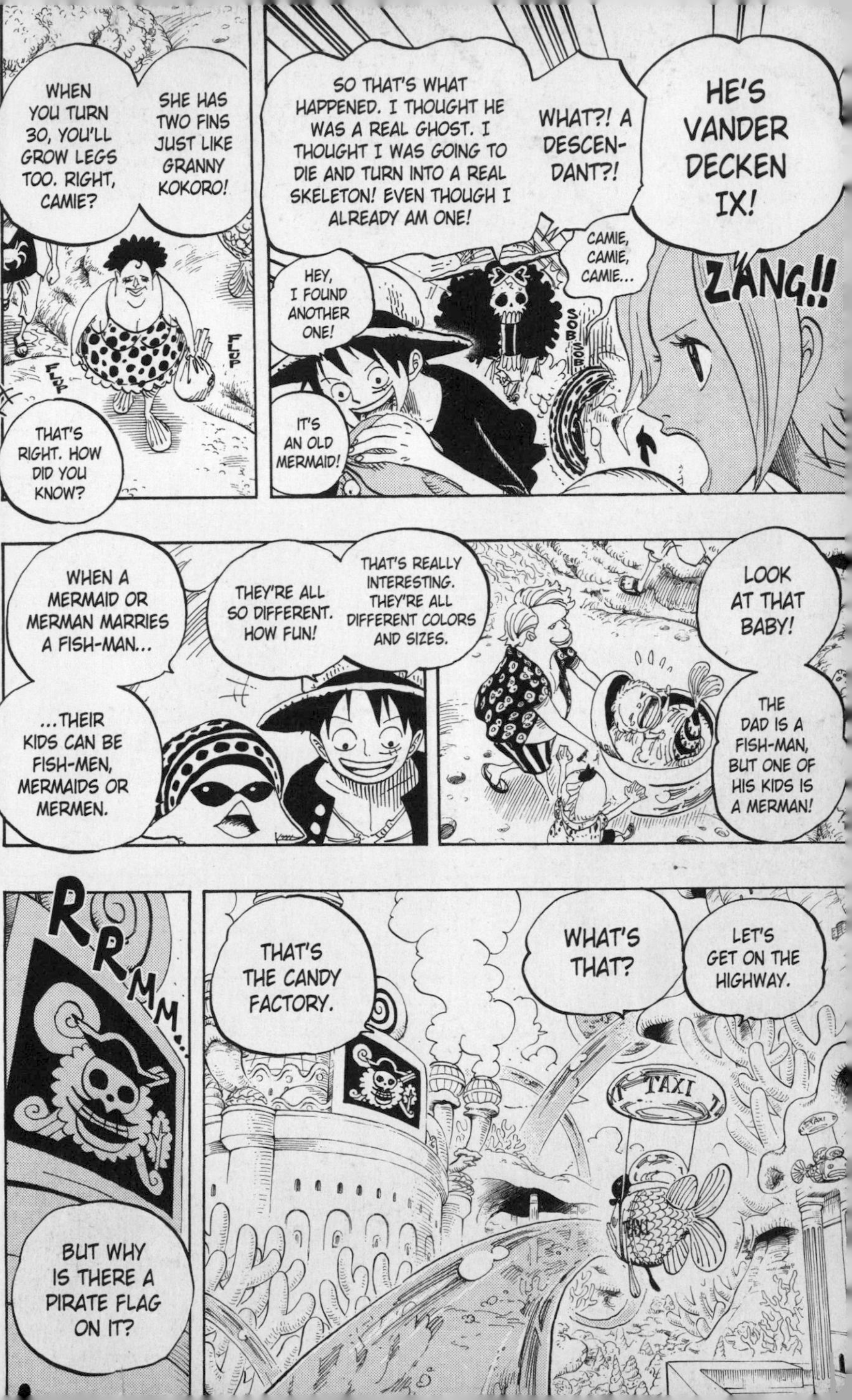
HE'S VANDER DECKEN IX!
ZANG!!
WHAT?! A DESCEN-DANT?!
SO THAT'S WHAT HAPPENED. I THOUGHT HE WAS A REAL GHOST. I THOUGHT I WAS GOING TO DIE AND TURN INTO A REAL SKELETON! EVEN THOUGH I ALREADY AM ONE!
CAMIE, CAMIE, CAMIE...
SOB SOB
HEY, I FOUND ANOTHER ONE!
IT'S AN OLD MERMAID!
SHE HAS TWO FINS JUST LIKE GRANNY KOKORO!
WHEN YOU TURN 30, YOU'LL GROW LEGS TOO. RIGHT, CAMIE?
FLUP
FLUP
THAT'S RIGHT. HOW DID YOU KNOW?
LOOK AT THAT BABY!
THE DAD IS A FISH-MAN, BUT ONE OF HIS KIDS IS A MERMAN!
THAT'S REALLY INTERESTING. THEY'RE ALL DIFFERENT COLORS AND SIZES.
THEY'RE ALL SO DIFFERENT. HOW FUN!
WHEN A MERMAID OR MERMAN MARRIES A FISH-MAN...
...THEIR KIDS CAN BE FISH-MEN, MERMAIDS OR MERMEN.
LET'S GET ON THE HIGHWAY.
WHAT'S THAT?
THAT'S THE CANDY FACTORY.
TAXI
RRMMM..
BUT WHY IS THERE A PIRATE FLAG ON IT?

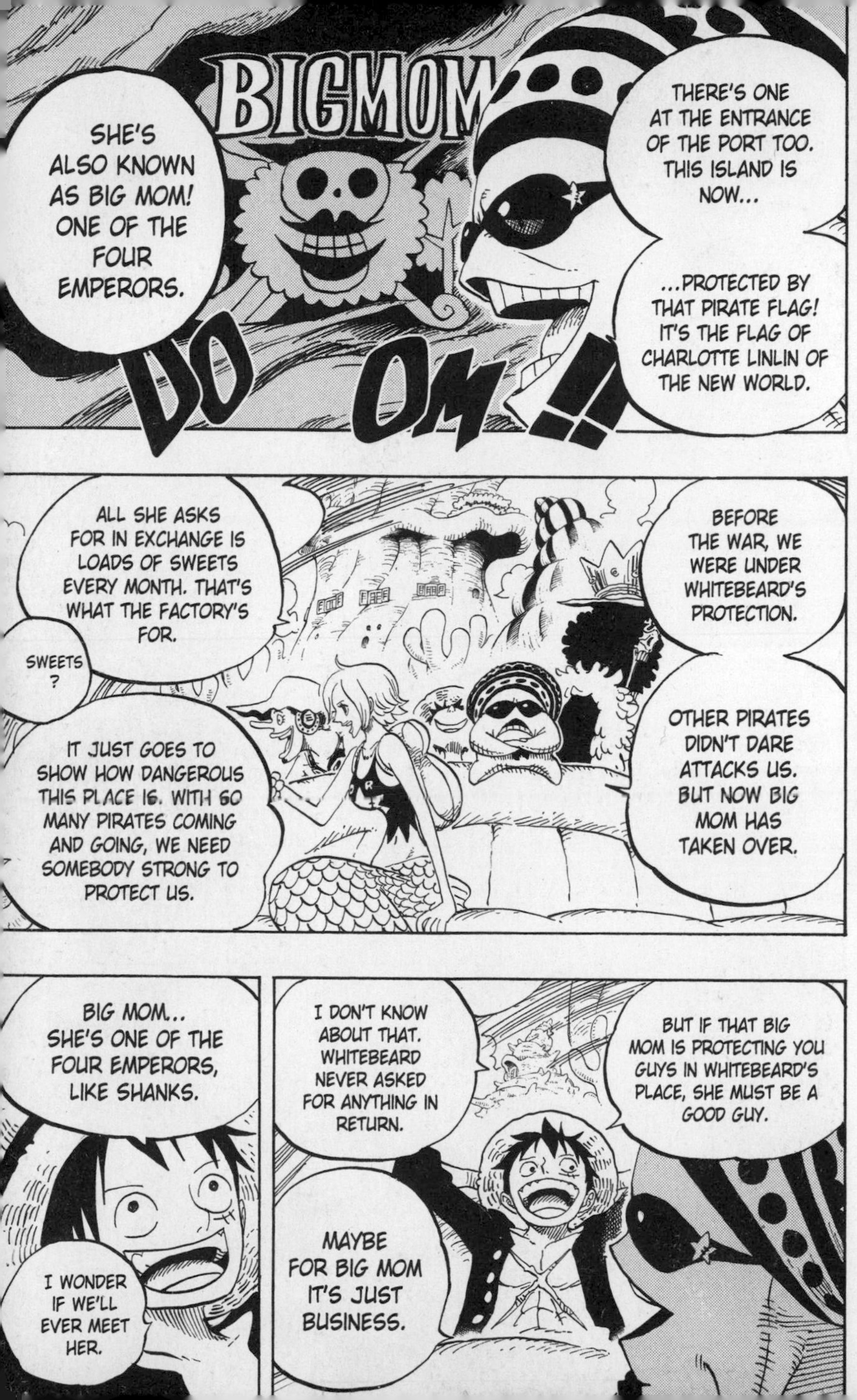
THERE'S ONE AT THE ENTRANCE OF THE PORT TOO. THIS ISLAND IS NOW...
...PROTECTED BY THAT PIRATE FLAG! IT'S THE FLAG OF CHARLOTTE LINLIN OF THE NEW WORLD.
BIGMOM
SHE'S ALSO KNOWN AS BIG MOM! ONE OF THE FOUR EMPERORS.
DO OM!!
BEFORE THE WAR, WE WERE UNDER WHITEBEARD'S PROTECTION.
OTHER PIRATES DIDN'T DARE ATTACKS US. BUT NOW BIG MOM HAS TAKEN OVER.
ALL SHE ASKS FOR IN EXCHANGE IS LOADS OF SWEETS EVERY MONTH. THAT'S WHAT THE FACTORY'S FOR.
SWEETS ?
IT JUST GOES TO SHOW HOW DANGEROUS THIS PLACE IS. WITH SO MANY PIRATES COMING AND GOING, WE NEED SOMEBODY STRONG TO PROTECT US.
BUT IF THAT BIG MOM IS PROTECTING YOU GUYS IN WHITEBEARD'S PLACE, SHE MUST BE A GOOD GUY.
I DON'T KNOW ABOUT THAT. WHITEBEARD NEVER ASKED FOR ANYTHING IN RETURN.
MAYBE FOR BIG MOM IT'S JUST BUSINESS.
BIG MOM... SHE'S ONE OF THE FOUR EMPERORS, LIKE SHANKS.
I WONDER IF WE'LL EVER MEET HER.

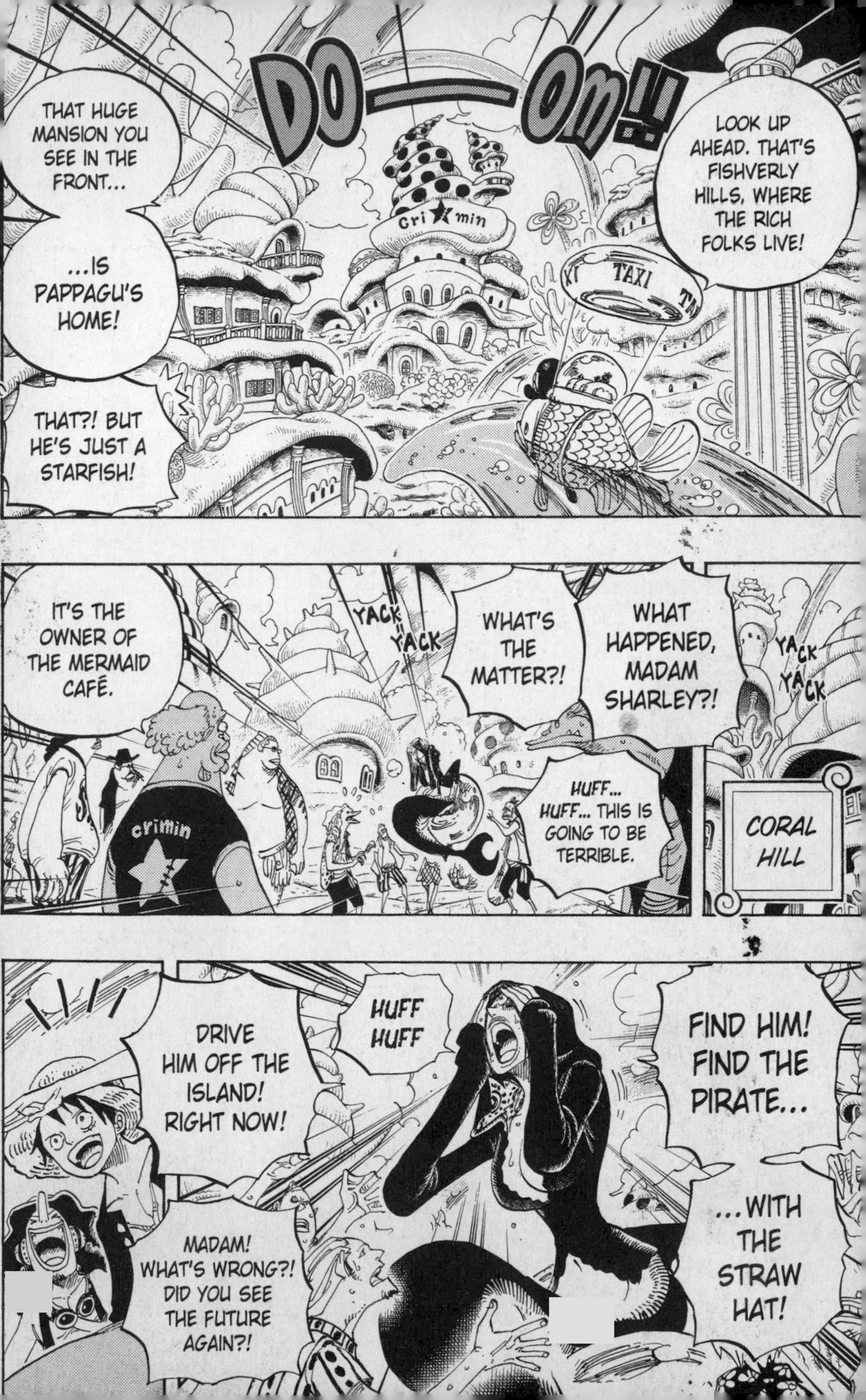
LOOK UP AHEAD. THAT'S FISHVERLY HILLS, WHERE THE RICH FOLKS LIVE!
TAXI
DO—OM!!
Cri★min
THAT HUGE MANSION YOU SEE IN THE FRONT...
...IS PAPPAGU'S HOME!
THAT?! BUT HE'S JUST A STARFISH!
CORAL HILL
YACK YACK
WHAT HAPPENED, MADAM SHARLEY?!
WHAT'S THE MATTER?!
YACK YACK
IT'S THE OWNER OF THE MERMAID CAFÉ.
crimin
HUFF... HUFF... THIS IS GOING TO BE TERRIBLE.
FIND HIM! FIND THE PIRATE...
...WITH THE STRAW HAT!
HUFF HUFF
DRIVE HIM OFF THE ISLAND! RIGHT NOW!
MADAM! WHAT'S WRONG?! DID YOU SEE THE FUTURE AGAIN?!

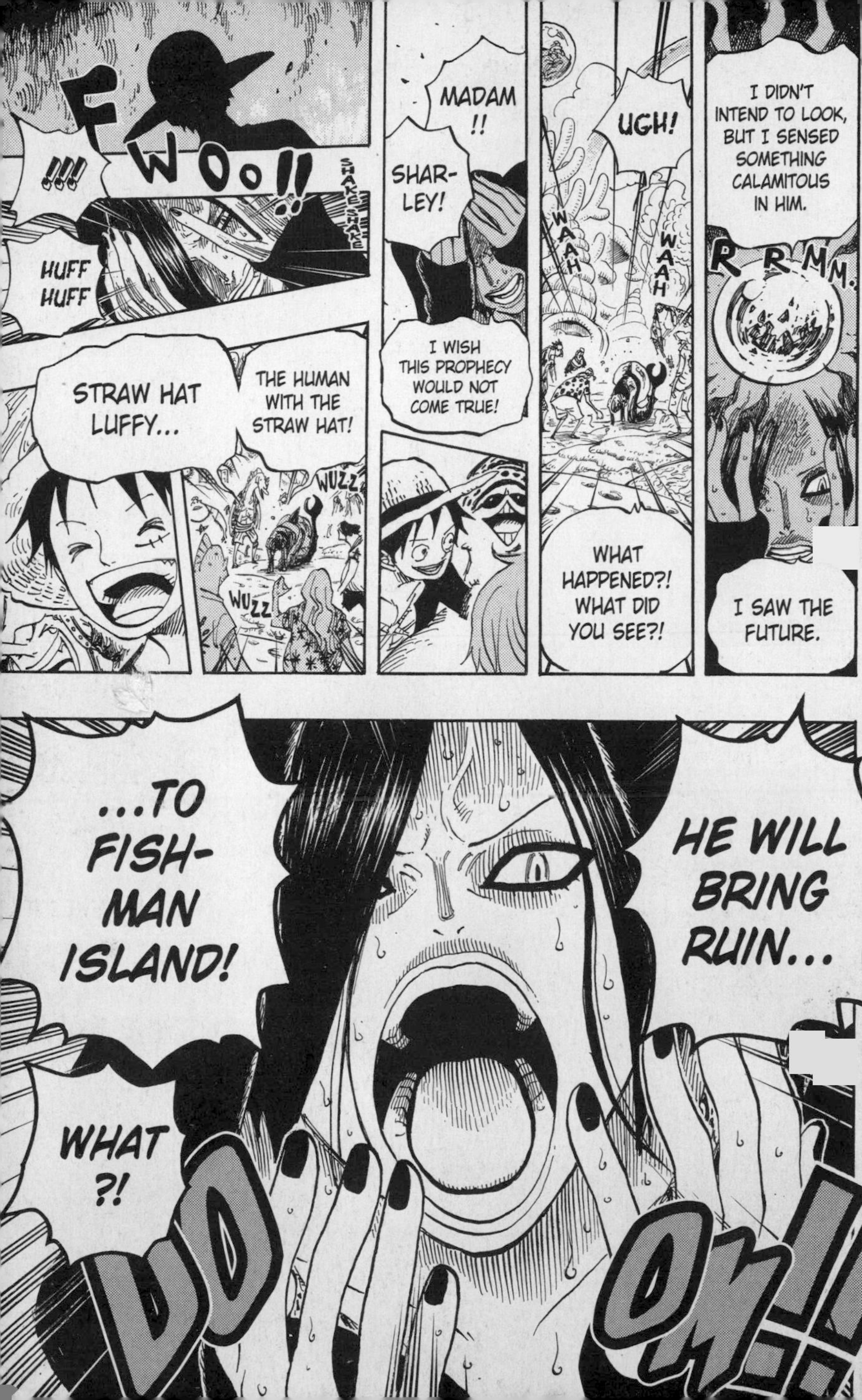
I DIDN'T INTEND TO LOOK, BUT I SENSED SOMETHING CALAMITOUS IN HIM.
RRMM.
I SAW THE FUTURE.
UGH!
WAAH
WAAH
WHAT HAPPENED?! WHAT DID YOU SEE?!
MADAM !!
SHAR-LEY!
I WISH THIS PROPHECY WOULD NOT COME TRUE!
FWOO!!
!!!
SHAKE SHAKE
HUFF HUFF
THE HUMAN WITH THE STRAW HAT!
WUZZ
WUZZ
STRAW HAT LUFFY...
HE WILL BRING RUIN...
...TO FISH-MAN ISLAND!
WHAT ?!
DOON!!

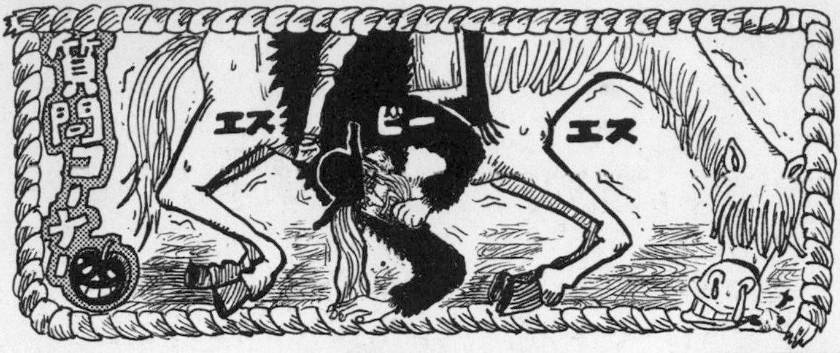
質問コーナー
エス
ピー
エス

(Ponio, Aichi)

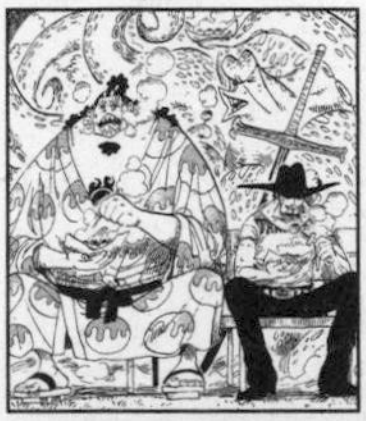

Q: Nice to meet you, Mr. Odacchi! I want to go to Gloom Island to meet Mihawk. Should I bring some takoyaki as a gift? Oh, by the way, I'm coming from Osaka.

--Appi I

A: Bring some roasted squid. It's one of my faves. Oh, you didn't ask?

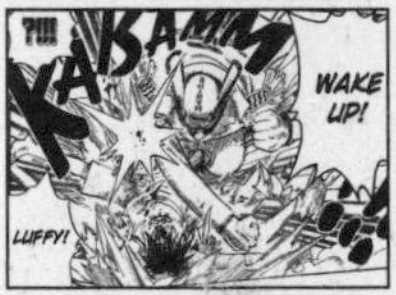
?!!
KABAMM
WAKE UP!
LUFFY!

Q: In volume 45, why did Garp's punch hurt Luffy? Was it Haki? Or was it "love"?

--Mori

A: In this instance, it was "love."

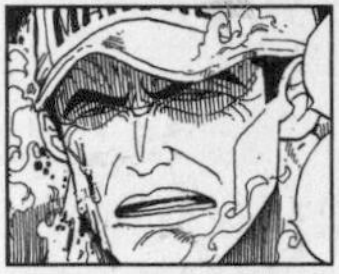

Q: I love Akainu's powers. Did he eat the Bubble-Bubble Fruit? Or is it the Mag-Mag Fruit? There are so many potential names, I don't know which is which! Please tell me!

--Isshi 414

A: Didn't I officially write it down somewhere? I've been receiving questions about the three admirals, so I'll put it down below. ⬇

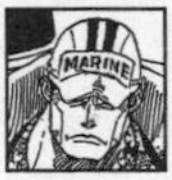

Mag-Mag Fruit
Magma Human

Akainu

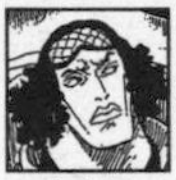

Chilly-Chilly Fruit
Ice Human

Aokiji

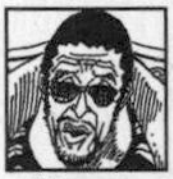

Glint-Glint Fruit
Light Human

Kizaru

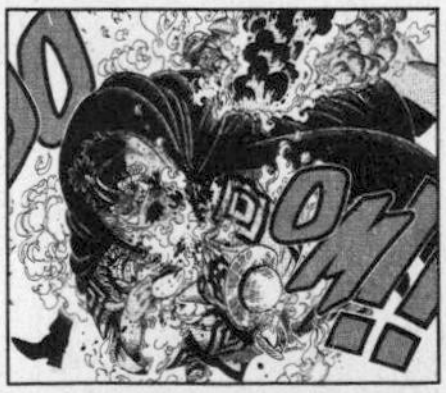

Q: I have a question. Is the scar on Luffy's chest from the Paramount War two years ago? You know, when Akainu attacked Jimbei and Luffy at the same time. I thought about it when I saw it on TV the other day...

--Princess Shirasuboshi

A: You're right. Akainu punched through Jimbei's left shoulder and into Luffy's chest!
Anyway, this marks the end of this SBS Question Corner. We had some technical difficulties, so the SBS with Brook's voice actor that was supposed to be in this volume will be moved to the next. This will be the very last Voice Actor SBS so make sure you have no regrets! See you next volume!

Chapter 611:
HODY JONES

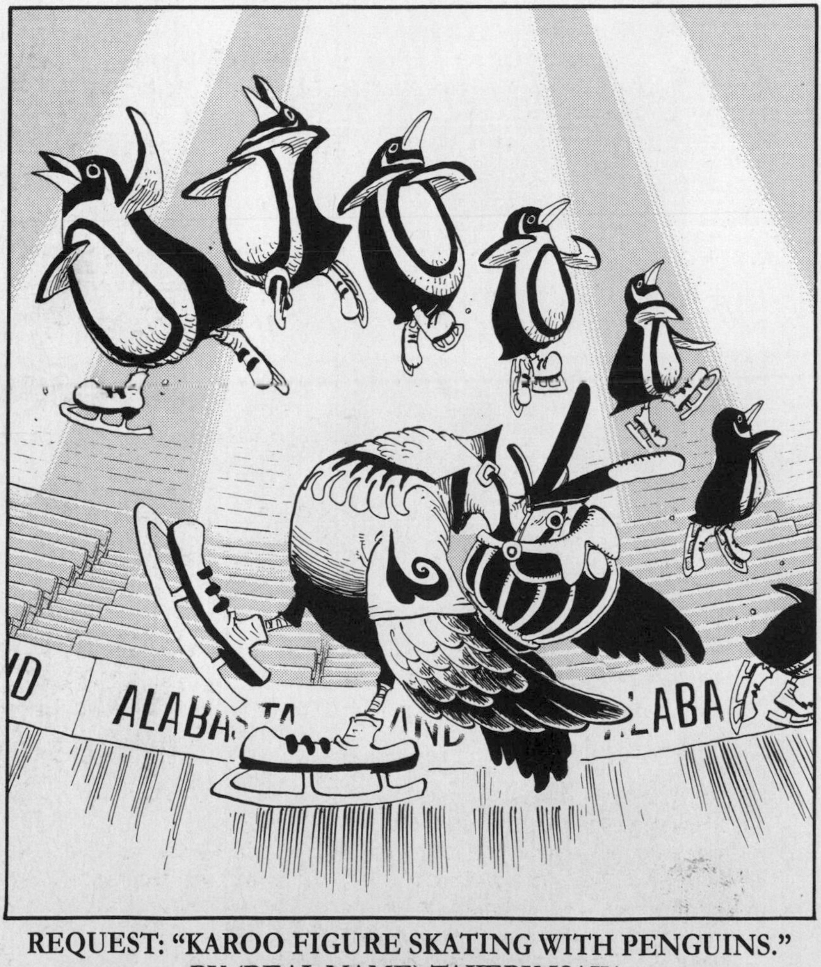
ALABASTA
ALABA

REQUEST: "KAROO FIGURE SKATING WITH PENGUINS."
BY (REAL NAME) TAKERU ISAKA

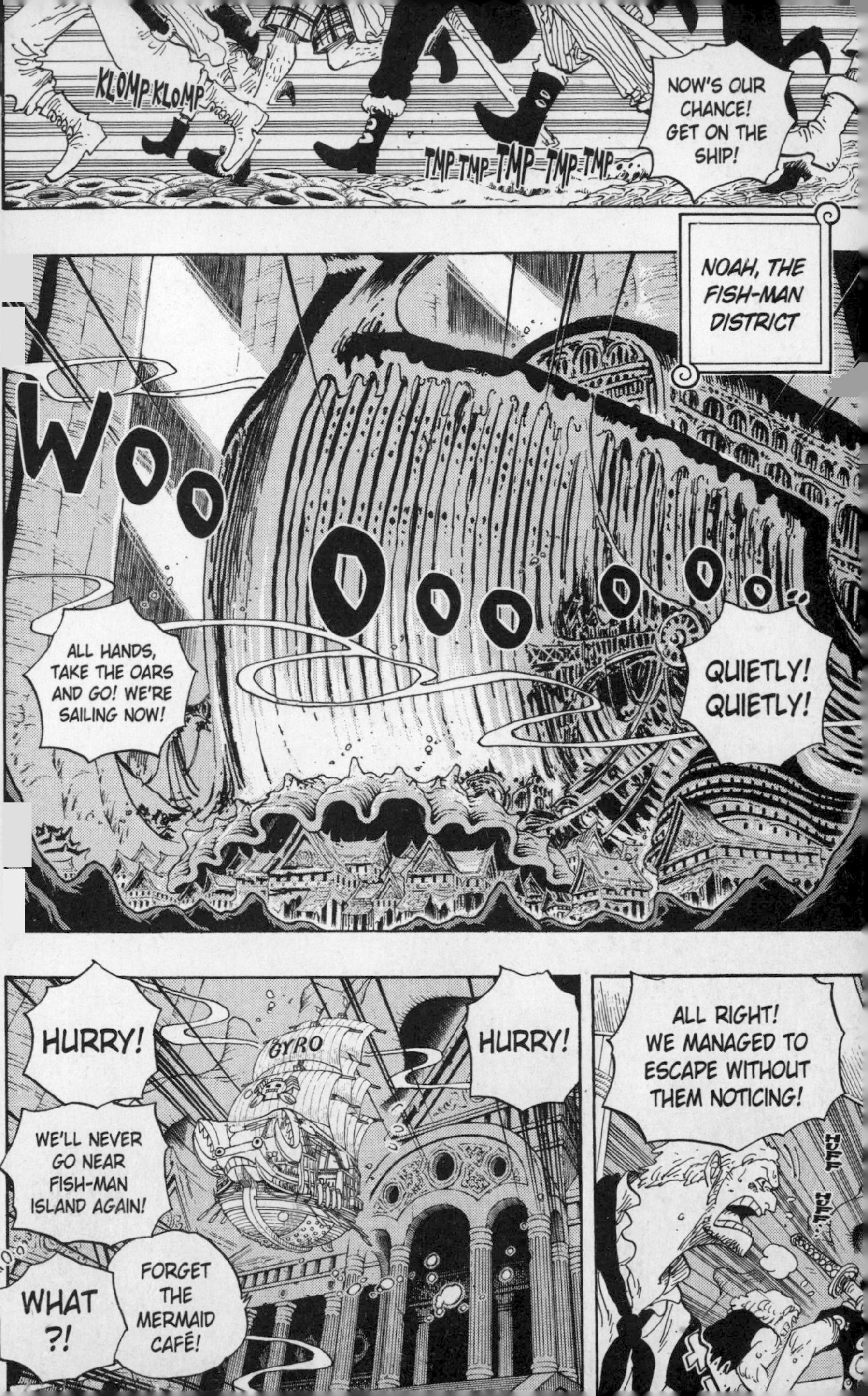
NOW'S OUR CHANCE! GET ON THE SHIP!
TMP TMP TMP TMP TMP
KLOMP KLOMP
NOAH, THE FISH-MAN DISTRICT
QUIETLY! QUIETLY!
WOOOOOOOO..
ALL HANDS, TAKE THE OARS AND GO! WE'RE SAILING NOW!
ALL RIGHT! WE MANAGED TO ESCAPE WITHOUT THEM NOTICING!
HUFF
HUFF...
HURRY!
HURRY!
GYRO
WE'LL NEVER GO NEAR FISH-MAN ISLAND AGAIN!
FORGET THE MERMAID CAFÉ!
WHAT ?!

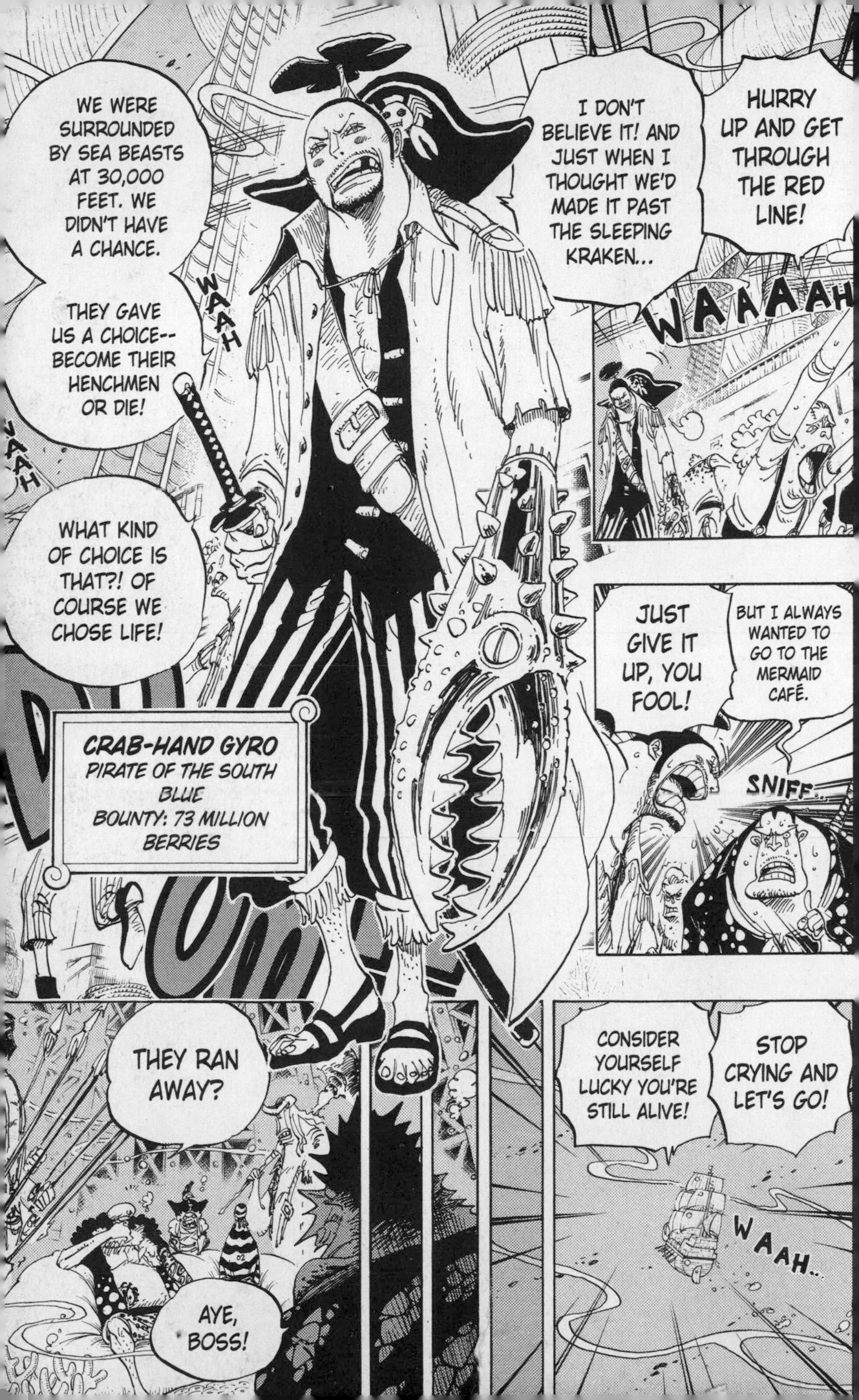
HURRY UP AND GET THROUGH THE RED LINE!
I DON'T BELIEVE IT! AND JUST WHEN I THOUGHT WE'D MADE IT PAST THE SLEEPING KRAKEN...
WAAAAAH
BUT I ALWAYS WANTED TO GO TO THE MERMAID CAFÉ.
JUST GIVE IT UP, YOU FOOL!
SNIFF...
WE WERE SURROUNDED BY SEA BEASTS AT 30,000 FEET. WE DIDN'T HAVE A CHANCE.
WAAH
THEY GAVE US A CHOICE-- BECOME THEIR HENCHMEN OR DIE!
WAAH
WHAT KIND OF CHOICE IS THAT?! OF COURSE WE CHOSE LIFE!
CRAB-HAND GYRO
PIRATE OF THE SOUTH BLUE
BOUNTY: 73 MILLION BERRIES
STOP CRYING AND LET'S GO!
CONSIDER YOURSELF LUCKY YOU'RE STILL ALIVE!
WAAH..
THEY RAN AWAY?
AYE, BOSS!

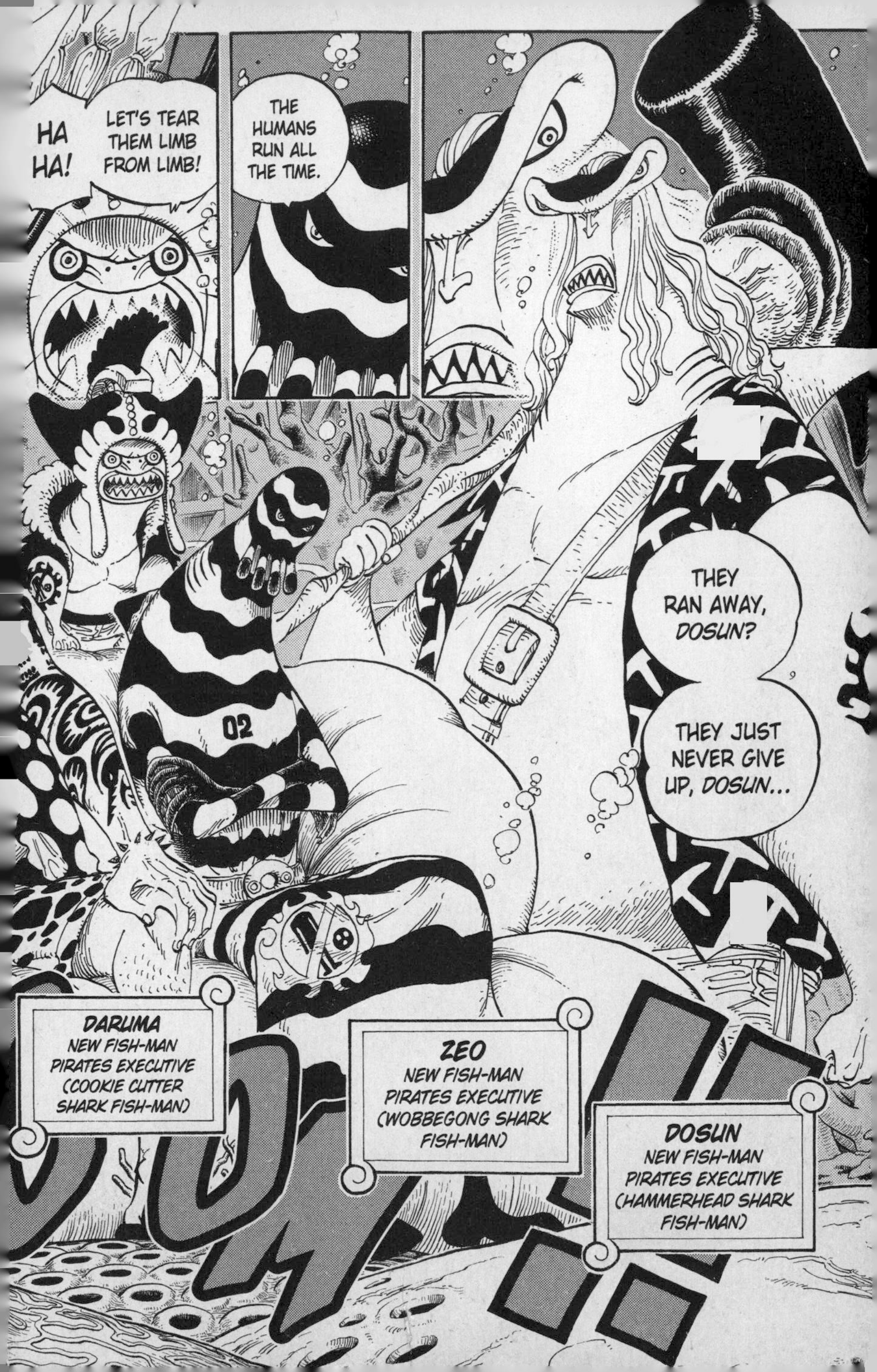
THE HUMANS RUN ALL THE TIME.
HA HA!
LET'S TEAR THEM LIMB FROM LIMB!
THEY RAN AWAY, DOSUN?
THEY JUST NEVER GIVE UP, DOSUN...
DOSUN
NEW FISH-MAN PIRATES EXECUTIVE (HAMMERHEAD SHARK FISH-MAN)
ZEO
NEW FISH-MAN PIRATES EXECUTIVE (WOBBEGONG SHARK FISH-MAN)
DARUMA
NEW FISH-MAN PIRATES EXECUTIVE (COOKIE CUTTER SHARK FISH-MAN)

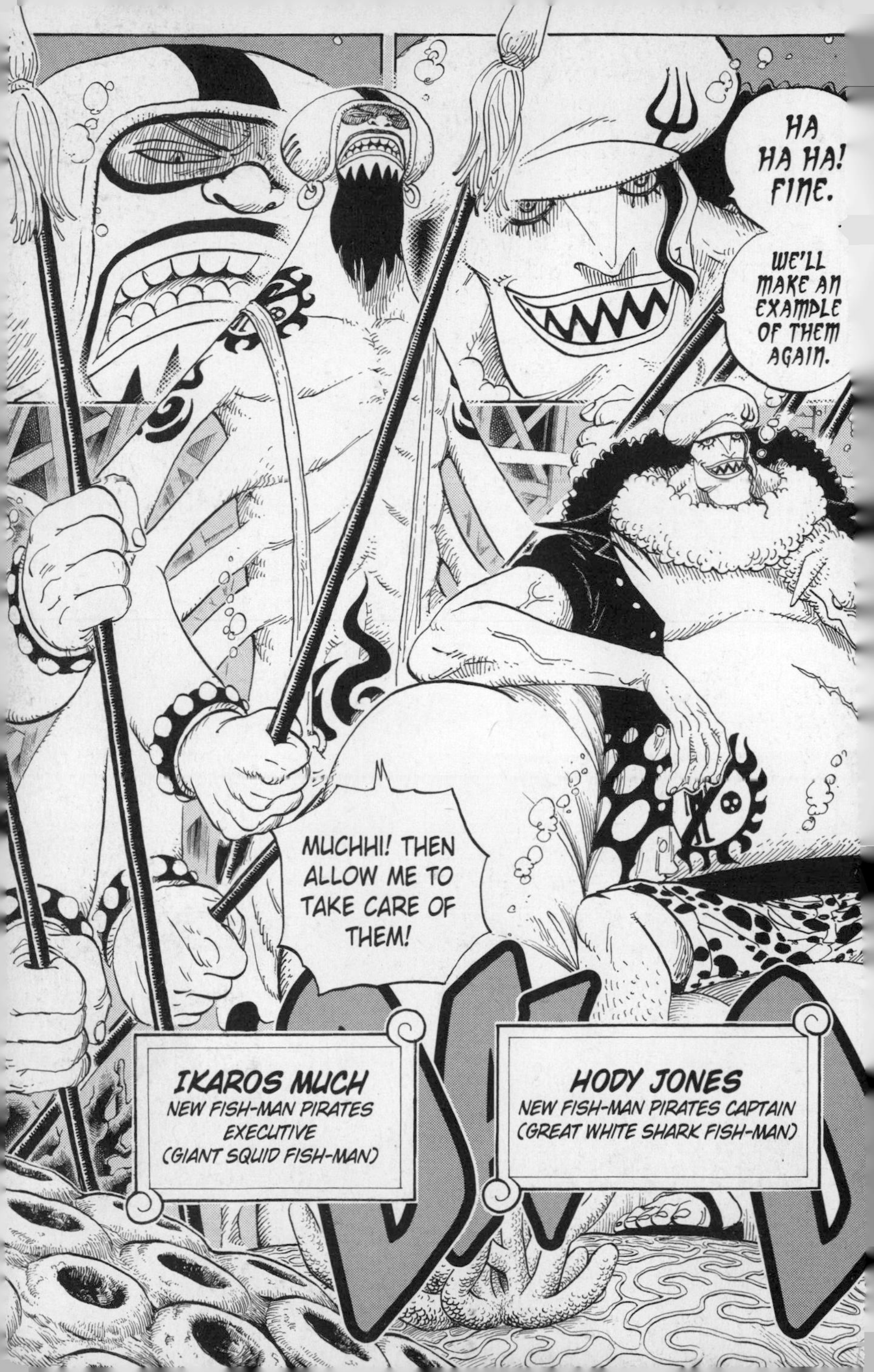
HA HA HA! FINE.
WE'LL MAKE AN EXAMPLE OF THEM AGAIN.
MUCHHI! THEN ALLOW ME TO TAKE CARE OF THEM!
HODY JONES
NEW FISH-MAN PIRATES CAPTAIN
(GREAT WHITE SHARK FISH-MAN)
IKAROS MUCH
NEW FISH-MAN PIRATES EXECUTIVE
(GIANT SQUID FISH-MAN)

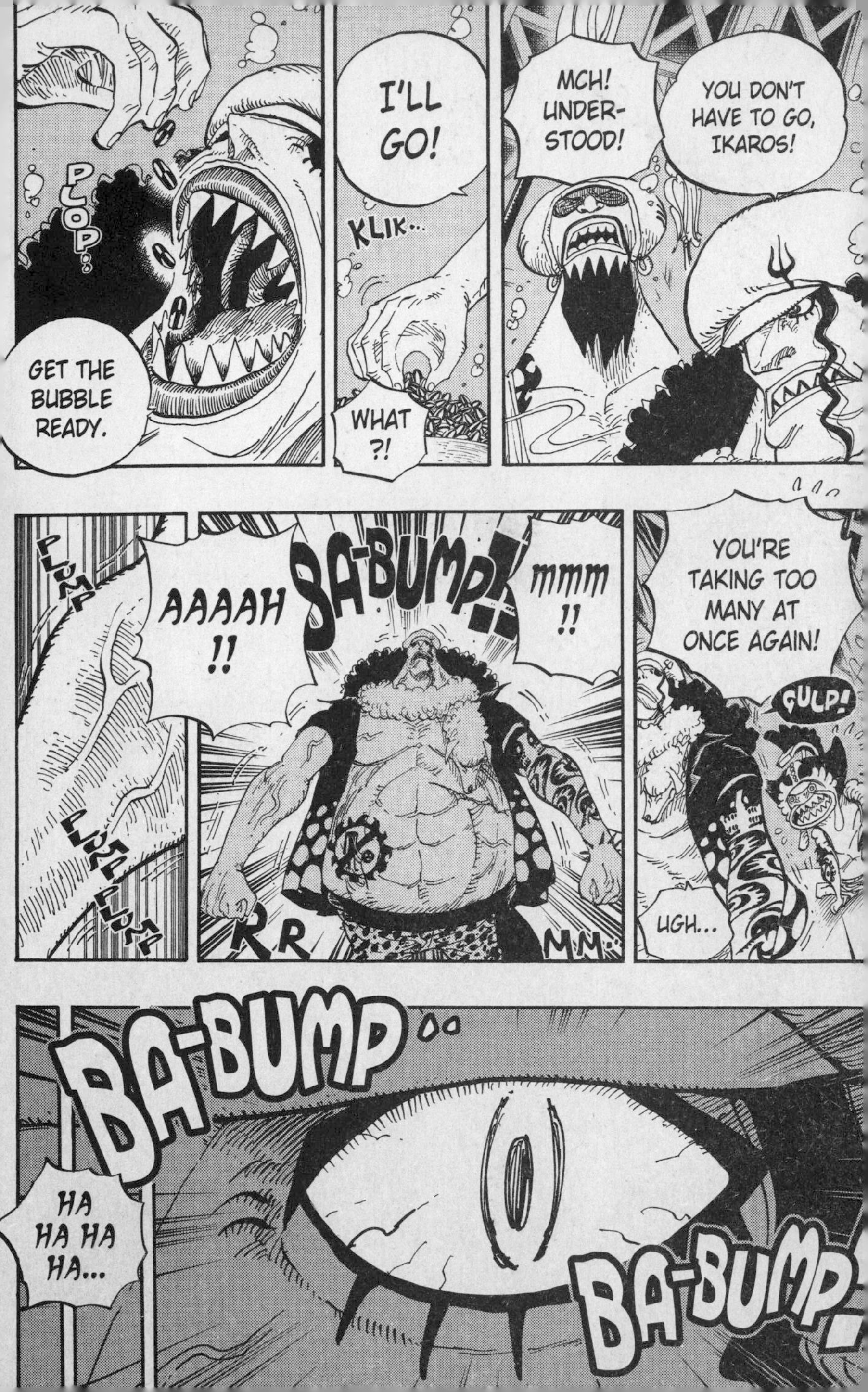
YOU DON'T HAVE TO GO, IKAROS!
MCH! UNDER-STOOD!
I'LL GO!
KLIK...
WHAT ?!
PLOP...
GET THE BUBBLE READY.
YOU'RE TAKING TOO MANY AT ONCE AGAIN!
GULP!
UGH...
BA-BUMP!!
mmm !!
AAAAH !!
RR
MM
PLUMP
PLUMP PLUMP PLUMP
BA-BUMP
BA-BUMP
HA HA HA HA HA...

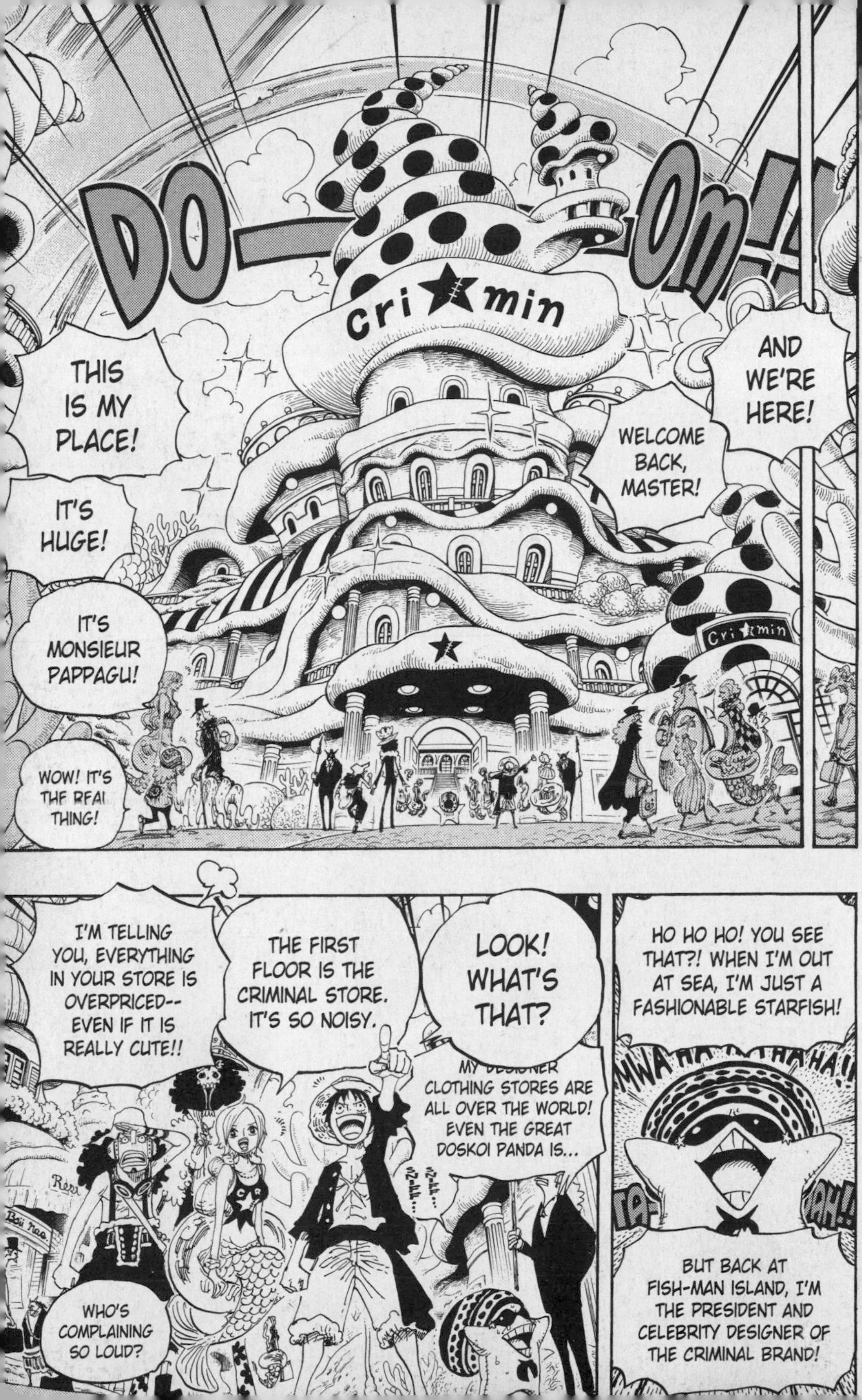
DO—OM!!
Cri min
AND WE'RE HERE!
WELCOME BACK, MASTER!
THIS IS MY PLACE!
IT'S HUGE!
IT'S MONSIEUR PAPPAGU!
WOW! IT'S THE REAL THING!
HO HO HO! YOU SEE THAT?! WHEN I'M OUT AT SEA, I'M JUST A FASHIONABLE STARFISH!
MWA HA HA HA HA HA!!
TA-DAH!!
BUT BACK AT FISH-MAN ISLAND, I'M THE PRESIDENT AND CELEBRITY DESIGNER OF THE CRIMINAL BRAND!
LOOK! WHAT'S THAT?
MY DESIGNER CLOTHING STORES ARE ALL OVER THE WORLD! EVEN THE GREAT DOSKOI PANDA IS...
THE FIRST FLOOR IS THE CRIMINAL STORE. IT'S SO NOISY.
I'M TELLING YOU, EVERYTHING IN YOUR STORE IS OVERPRICED-- EVEN IF IT IS REALLY CUTE!!
SNIFF... SNIFF...
WHO'S COMPLAINING SO LOUD?

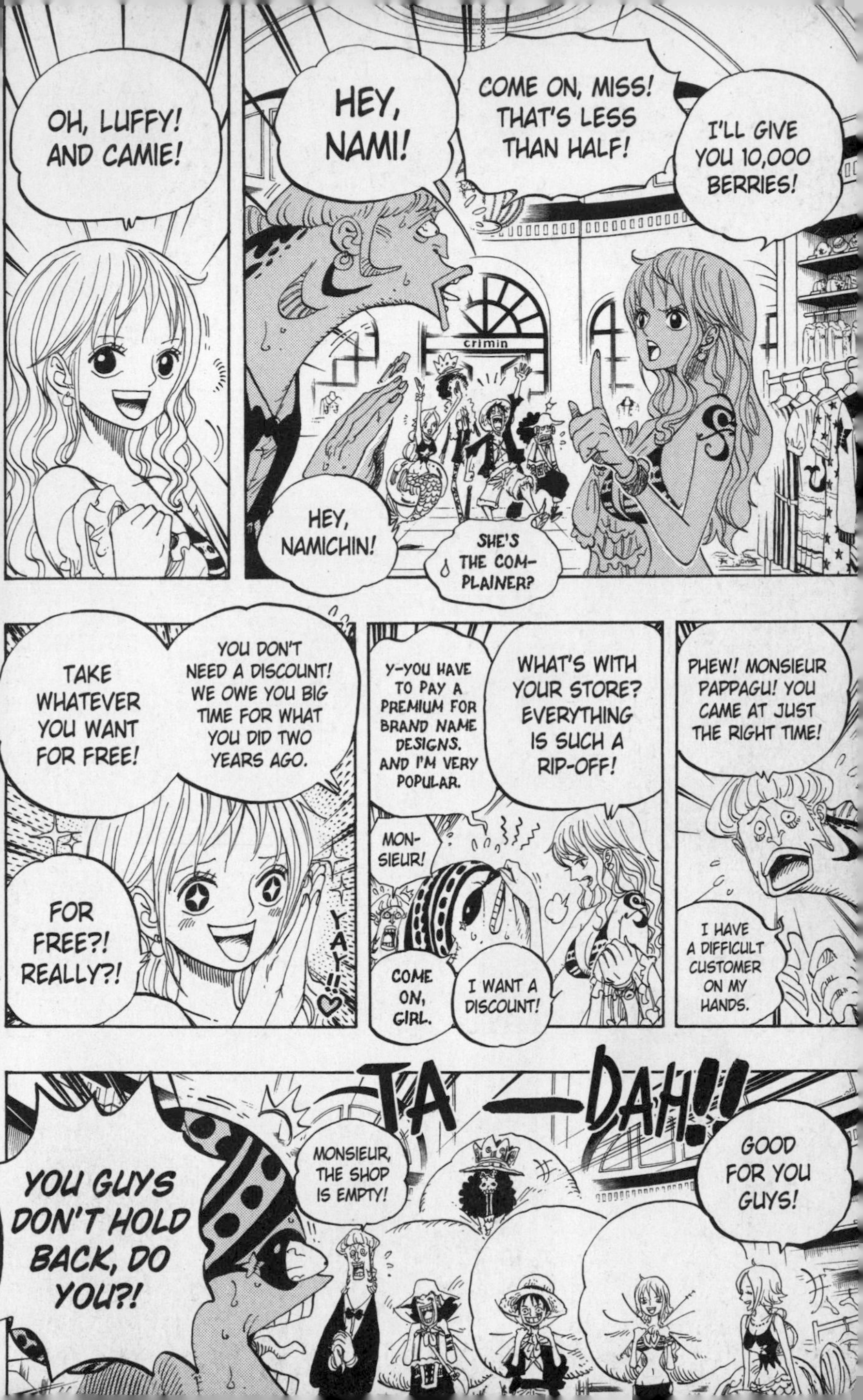
I'LL GIVE YOU 10,000 BERRIES!
COME ON, MISS! THAT'S LESS THAN HALF!
HEY, NAMI!
crimin
SHE'S THE COM-PLAINER?
HEY, NAMICHIN!
OH, LUFFY! AND CAMIE!
PHEW! MONSIEUR PAPPAGU! YOU CAME AT JUST THE RIGHT TIME!
I HAVE A DIFFICULT CUSTOMER ON MY HANDS.
WHAT'S WITH YOUR STORE? EVERYTHING IS SUCH A RIP-OFF!
Y-YOU HAVE TO PAY A PREMIUM FOR BRAND NAME DESIGNS. AND I'M VERY POPULAR.
MON-SIEUR!
I WANT A DISCOUNT!
COME ON, GIRL.
YOU DON'T NEED A DISCOUNT! WE OWE YOU BIG TIME FOR WHAT YOU DID TWO YEARS AGO.
TAKE WHATEVER YOU WANT FOR FREE!
YAY!!
FOR FREE?! REALLY?!
GOOD FOR YOU GUYS!
TA—DAH!!
MONSIEUR, THE SHOP IS EMPTY!
YOU GUYS DON'T HOLD BACK, DO YOU?!

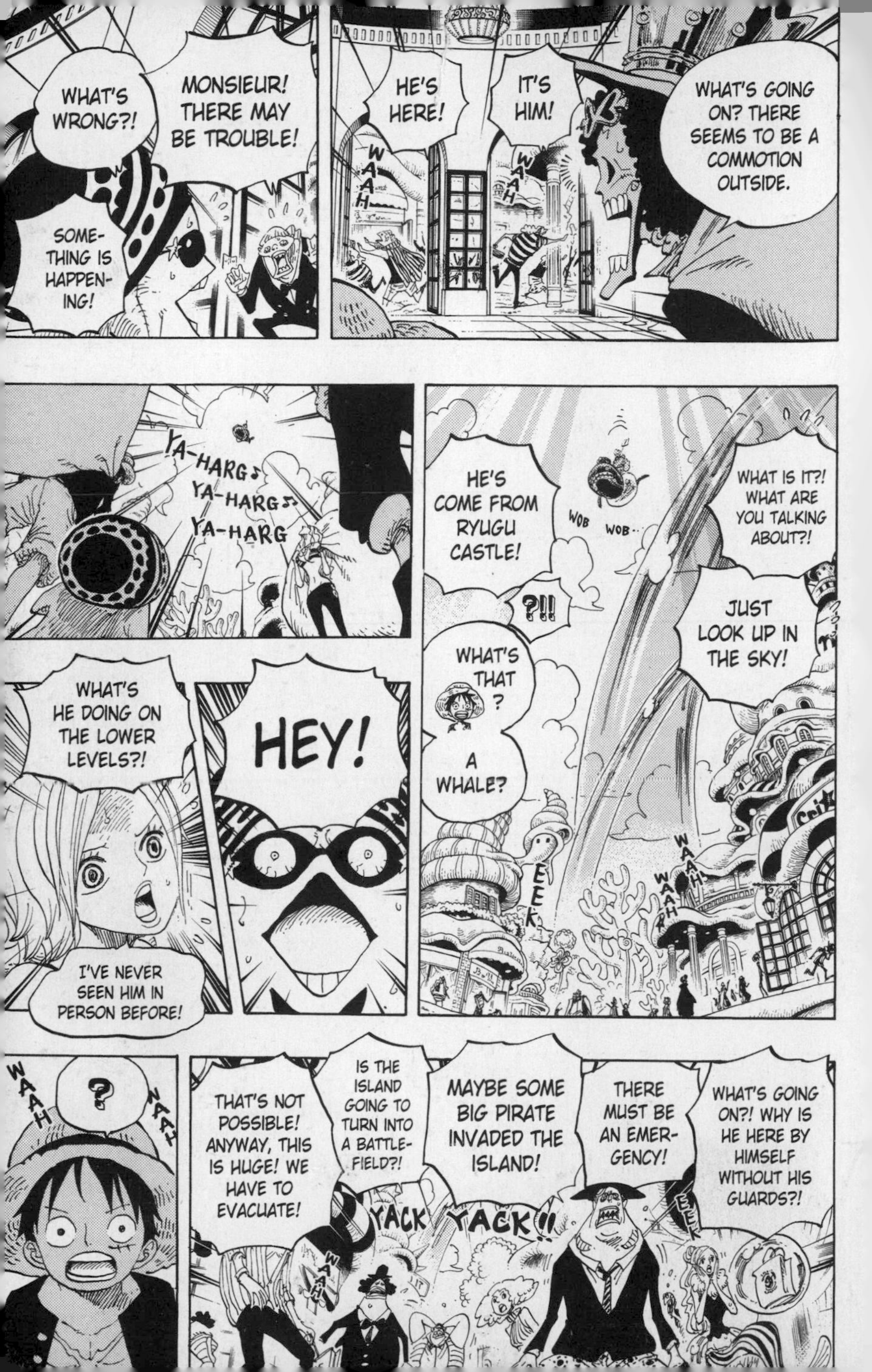
WHAT'S GOING ON? THERE SEEMS TO BE A COMMOTION OUTSIDE.
IT'S HIM!
WAAH
HE'S HERE!
WAAH
MONSIEUR! THERE MAY BE TROUBLE!
WHAT'S WRONG?!
SOMETHING IS HAPPENING!
WHAT IS IT?! WHAT ARE YOU TALKING ABOUT?!
HE'S COME FROM RYUGU CASTLE!
WOB WOB...
?!!
JUST LOOK UP IN THE SKY!
WHAT'S THAT?
A WHALE?
EEEK
WAAAH
WAAAH
YA-HARG♪
YA-HARG♪
YA-HARG
HEY!
WHAT'S HE DOING ON THE LOWER LEVELS?!
I'VE NEVER SEEN HIM IN PERSON BEFORE!
WHAT'S GOING ON?! WHY IS HE HERE BY HIMSELF WITHOUT HIS GUARDS?!
THERE MUST BE AN EMERGENCY!
MAYBE SOME BIG PIRATE INVADED THE ISLAND!
IS THE ISLAND GOING TO TURN INTO A BATTLE-FIELD?!
THAT'S NOT POSSIBLE! ANYWAY, THIS IS HUGE! WE HAVE TO EVACUATE!
EEEK
YACK YACK!!
WAAH
WAAH
?
WAAH

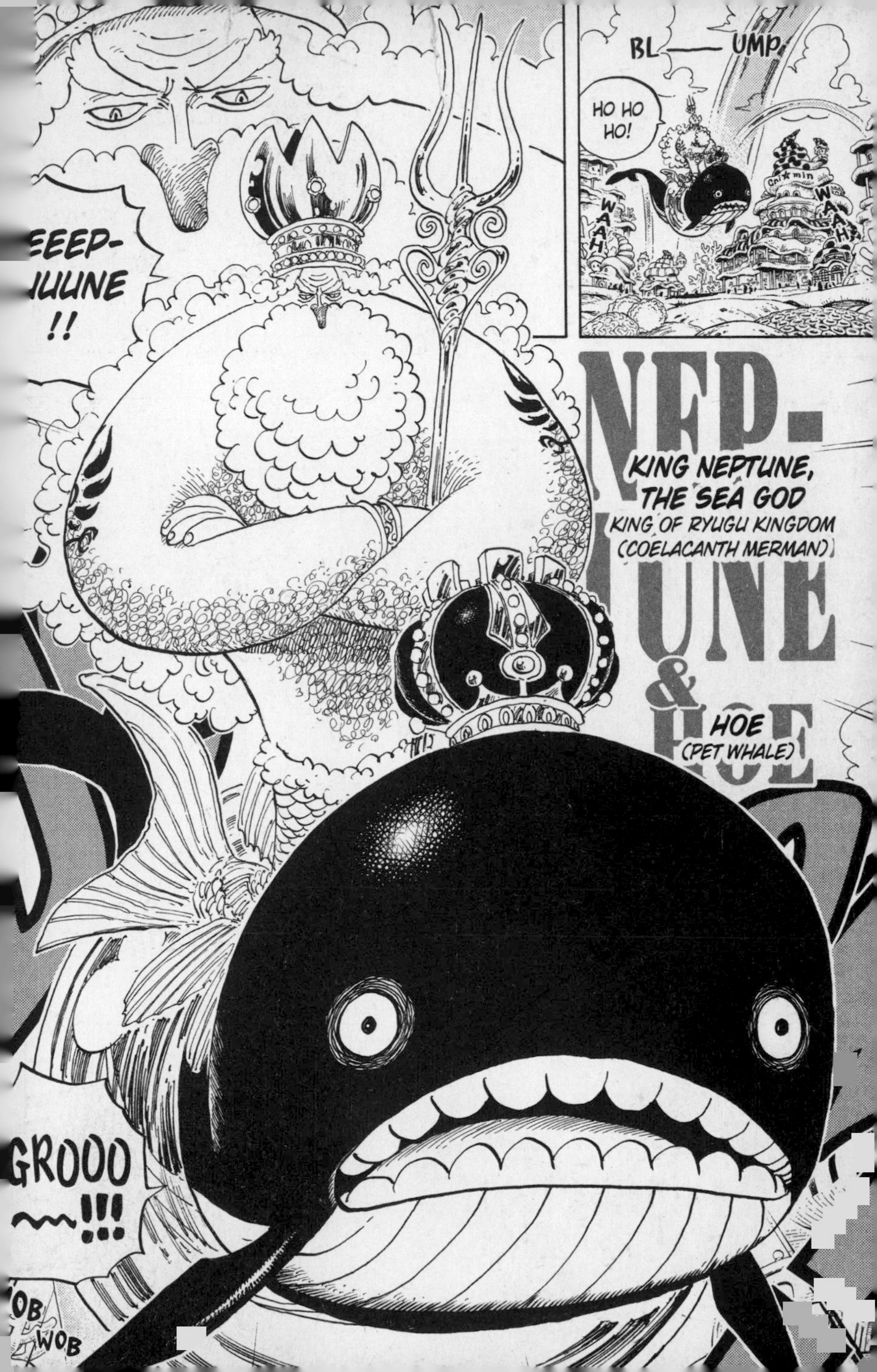
BL—UMP
HO HO HO!
WAAH
WAAH
NEP-TUNE & HOE
KING NEPTUNE, THE SEA GOD
KING OF RYUGU KINGDOM (COELACANTH MERMAN)
HOE (PET WHALE)
EEEP-UUNE !!
GROOO ~~!!!
OB WOB

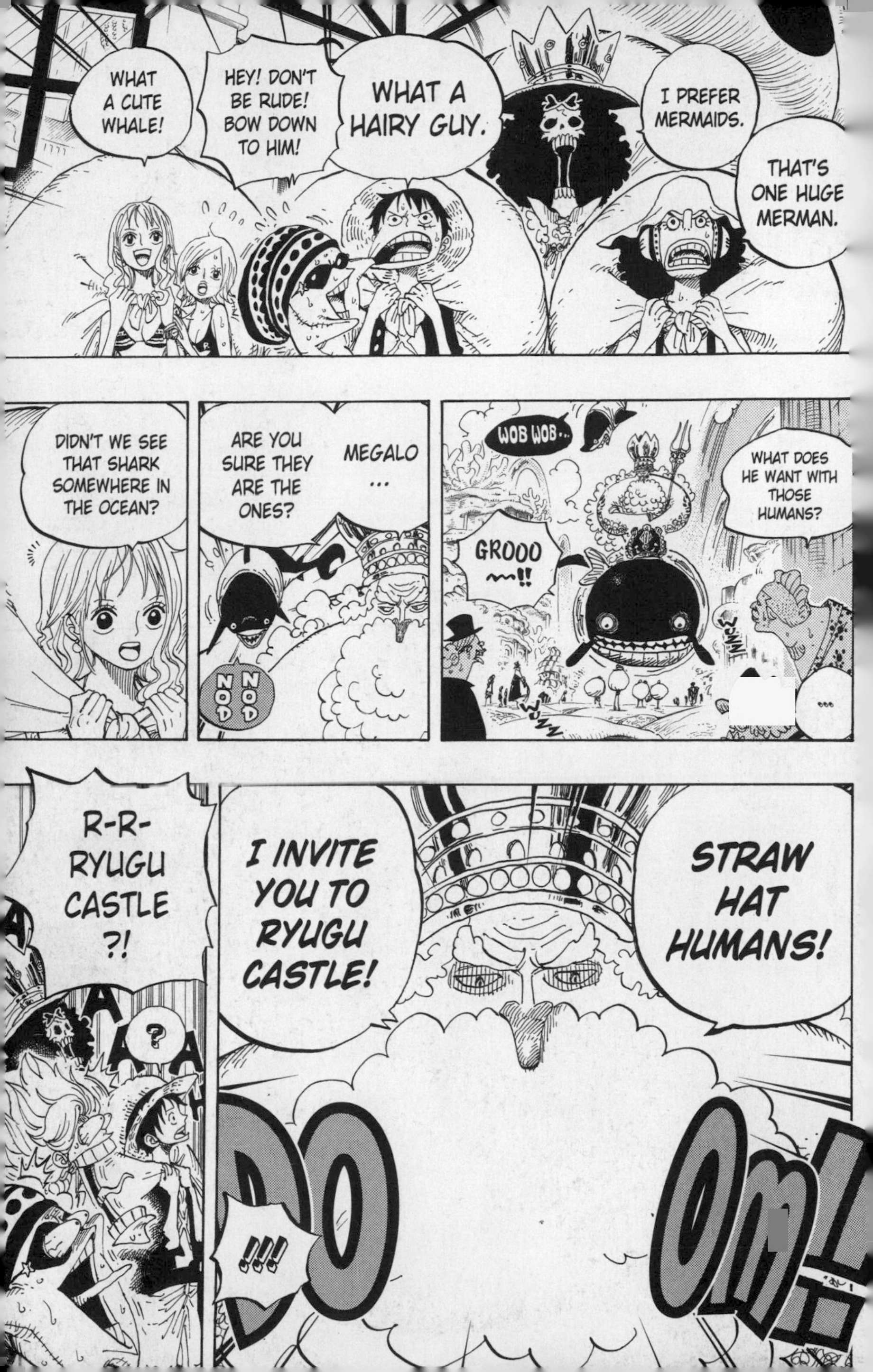
THAT'S ONE HUGE MERMAN.
I PREFER MERMAIDS.
WHAT A HAIRY GUY.
HEY! DON'T BE RUDE! BOW DOWN TO HIM!
WHAT A CUTE WHALE!
WHAT DOES HE WANT WITH THOSE HUMANS?
WOB WOB...
GROOO ~!!
...
MEGALO ...
ARE YOU SURE THEY ARE THE ONES?
NOD NOD
DIDN'T WE SEE THAT SHARK SOMEWHERE IN THE OCEAN?
STRAW HAT HUMANS!
I INVITE YOU TO RYUGU CASTLE!
DOOM!!
!!!
R-R-RYUGU CASTLE ?!
?

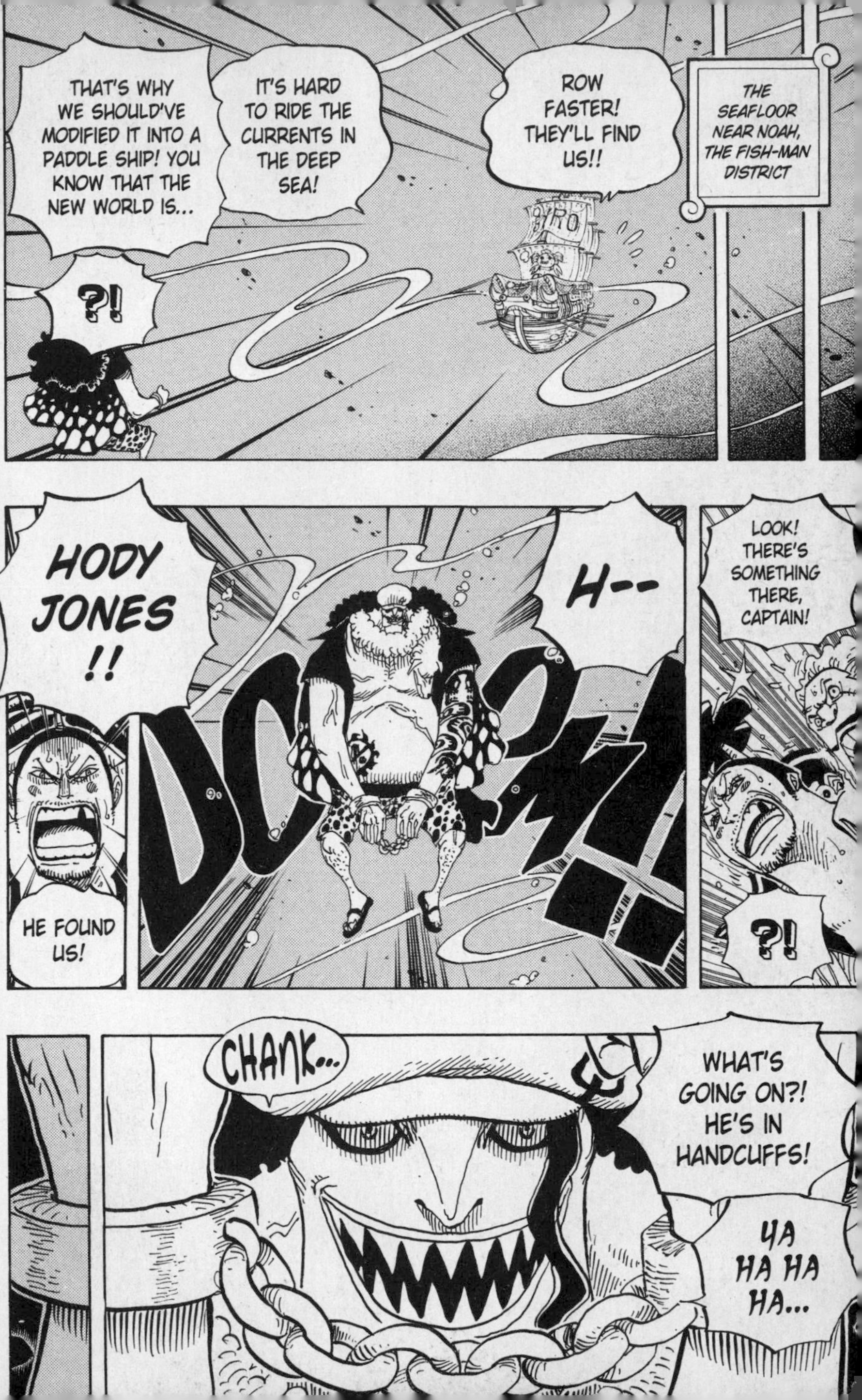
THE SEAFLOOR NEAR NOAH, THE FISH-MAN DISTRICT
ROW FASTER! THEY'LL FIND US!!
IT'S HARD TO RIDE THE CURRENTS IN THE DEEP SEA!
THAT'S WHY WE SHOULD'VE MODIFIED IT INTO A PADDLE SHIP! YOU KNOW THAT THE NEW WORLD IS...
?!
LOOK! THERE'S SOMETHING THERE, CAPTAIN!
?!
H--
HODY JONES!!
HE FOUND US!
WHAT'S GOING ON?! HE'S IN HANDCUFFS!
YA HA HA HA...
CHANK...

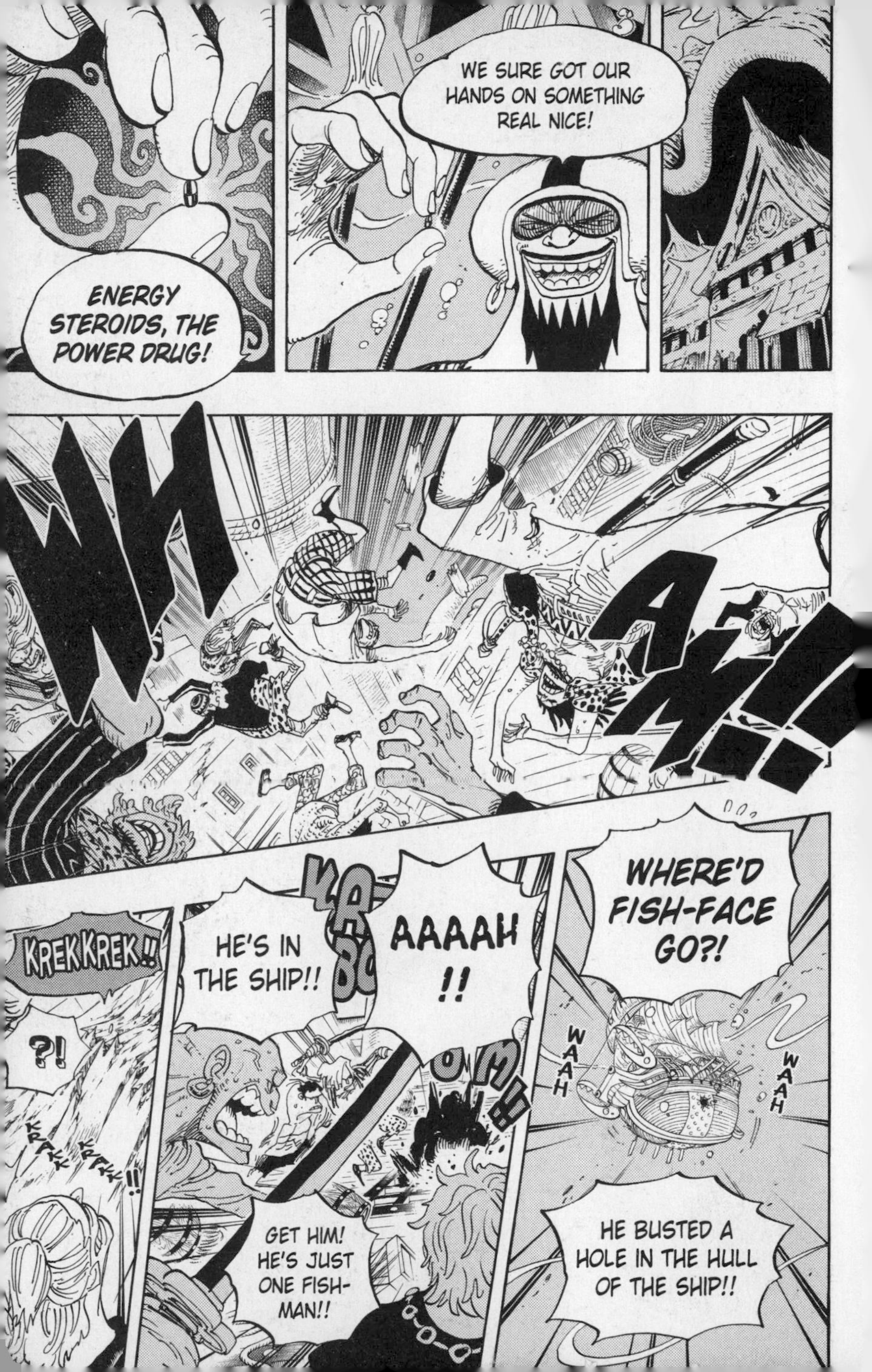

WE SURE GOT OUR HANDS ON SOMETHING REAL NICE!
ENERGY STEROIDS, THE POWER DRUG!
WHERE'D FISH-FACE GO?!
WAAH
WAAH
HE BUSTED A HOLE IN THE HULL OF THE SHIP!!
AAAAH !!
HE'S IN THE SHIP!!
GET HIM! HE'S JUST ONE FISH-MAN!!
KREK KREK!!
?!
KRAKK KRAKK!!

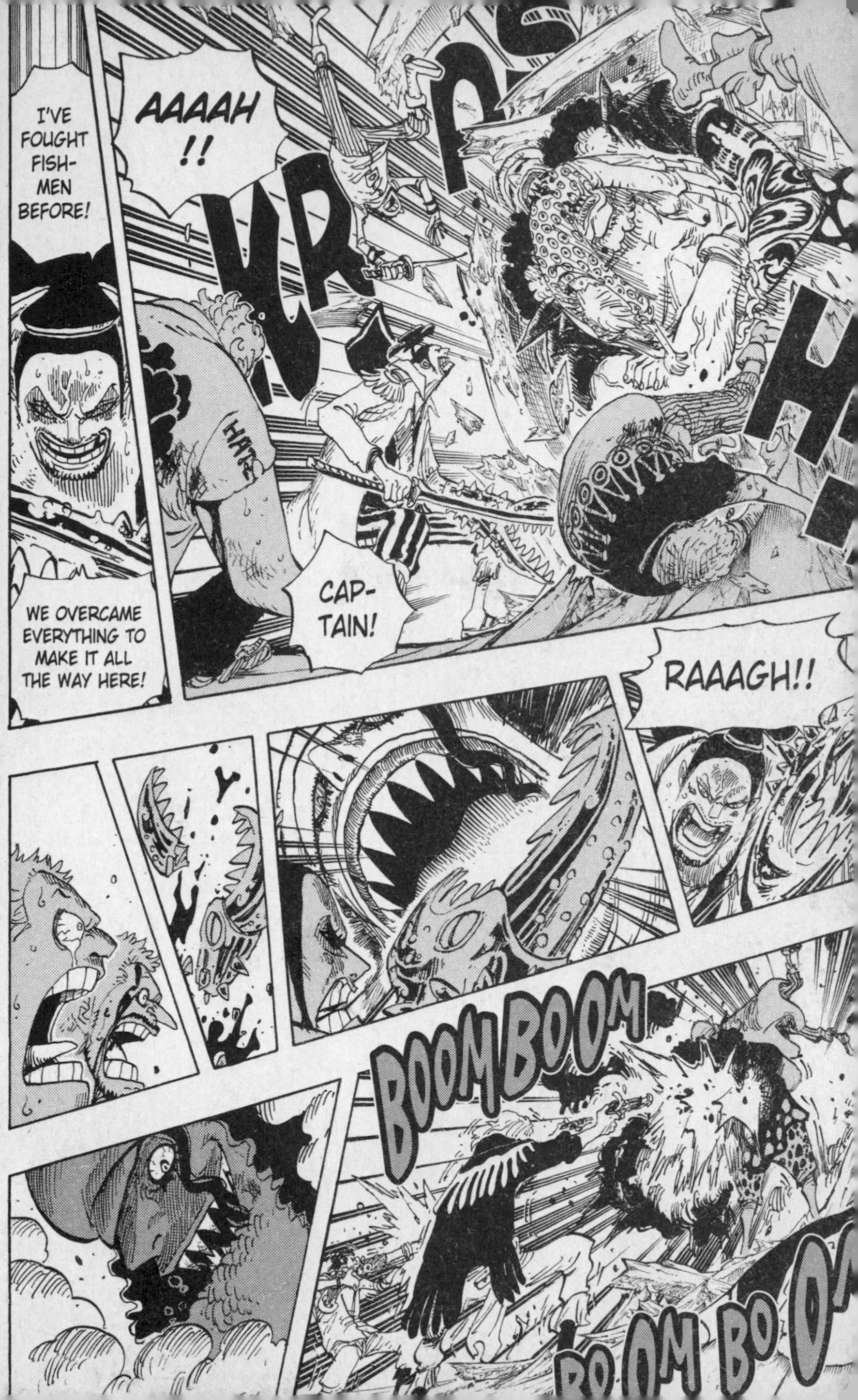
AAAAH!!
CAP-TAIN!
I'VE FOUGHT FISH-MEN BEFORE!
WE OVERCAME EVERYTHING TO MAKE IT ALL THE WAY HERE!
RAAAGH!!
BOOM BOOM

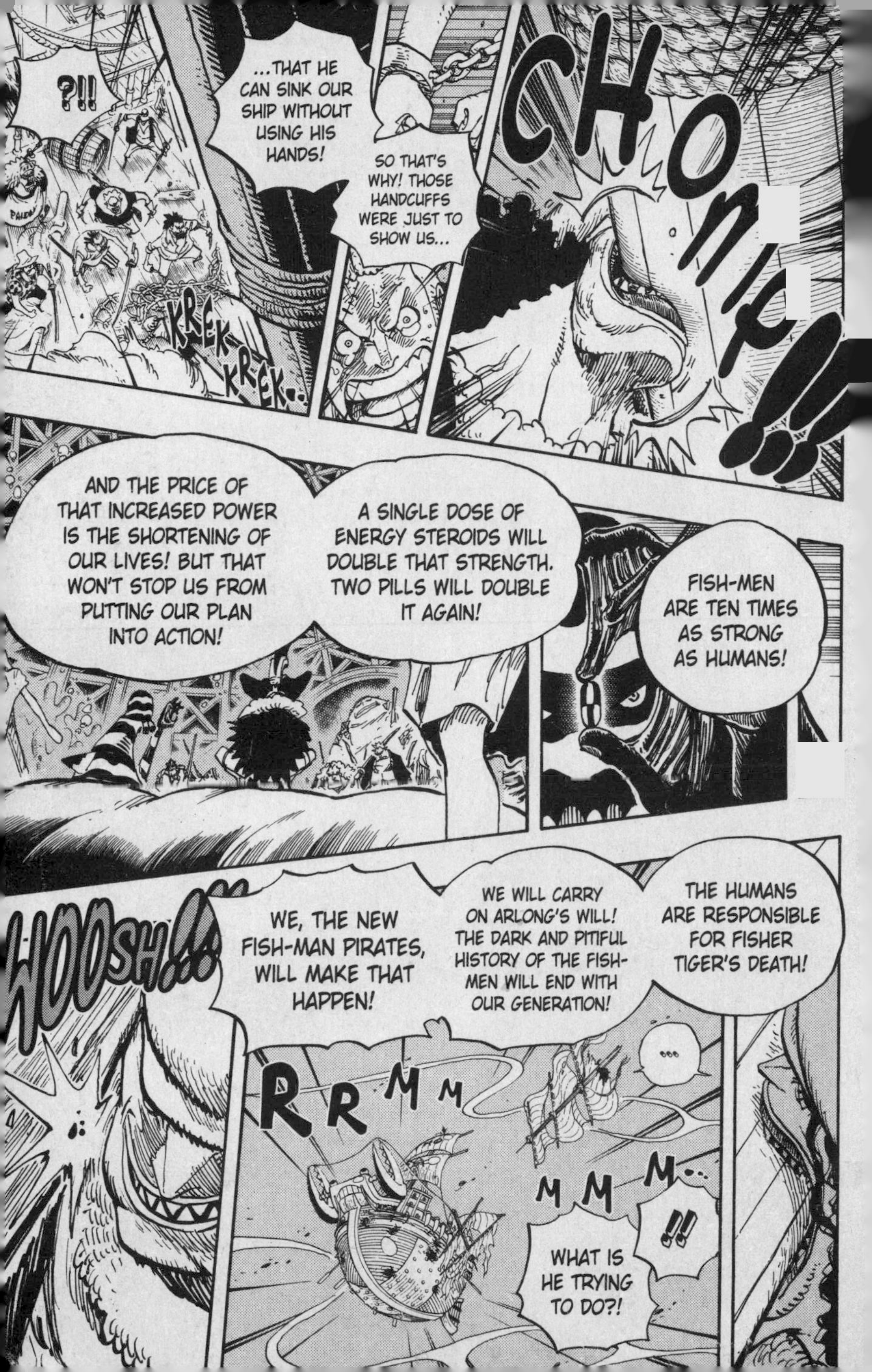
CHOMP!!!
...THAT HE CAN SINK OUR SHIP WITHOUT USING HIS HANDS!
SO THAT'S WHY! THOSE HANDCUFFS WERE JUST TO SHOW US...
?!!
KREK KREK..
FISH-MEN ARE TEN TIMES AS STRONG AS HUMANS!
A SINGLE DOSE OF ENERGY STEROIDS WILL DOUBLE THAT STRENGTH. TWO PILLS WILL DOUBLE IT AGAIN!
AND THE PRICE OF THAT INCREASED POWER IS THE SHORTENING OF OUR LIVES! BUT THAT WON'T STOP US FROM PUTTING OUR PLAN INTO ACTION!
THE HUMANS ARE RESPONSIBLE FOR FISHER TIGER'S DEATH!
WE WILL CARRY ON ARLONG'S WILL! THE DARK AND PITIFUL HISTORY OF THE FISH-MEN WILL END WITH OUR GENERATION!
WE, THE NEW FISH-MAN PIRATES, WILL MAKE THAT HAPPEN!
...
RRMMMMMM...!!
WHAT IS HE TRYING TO DO?!
WHOOSH...

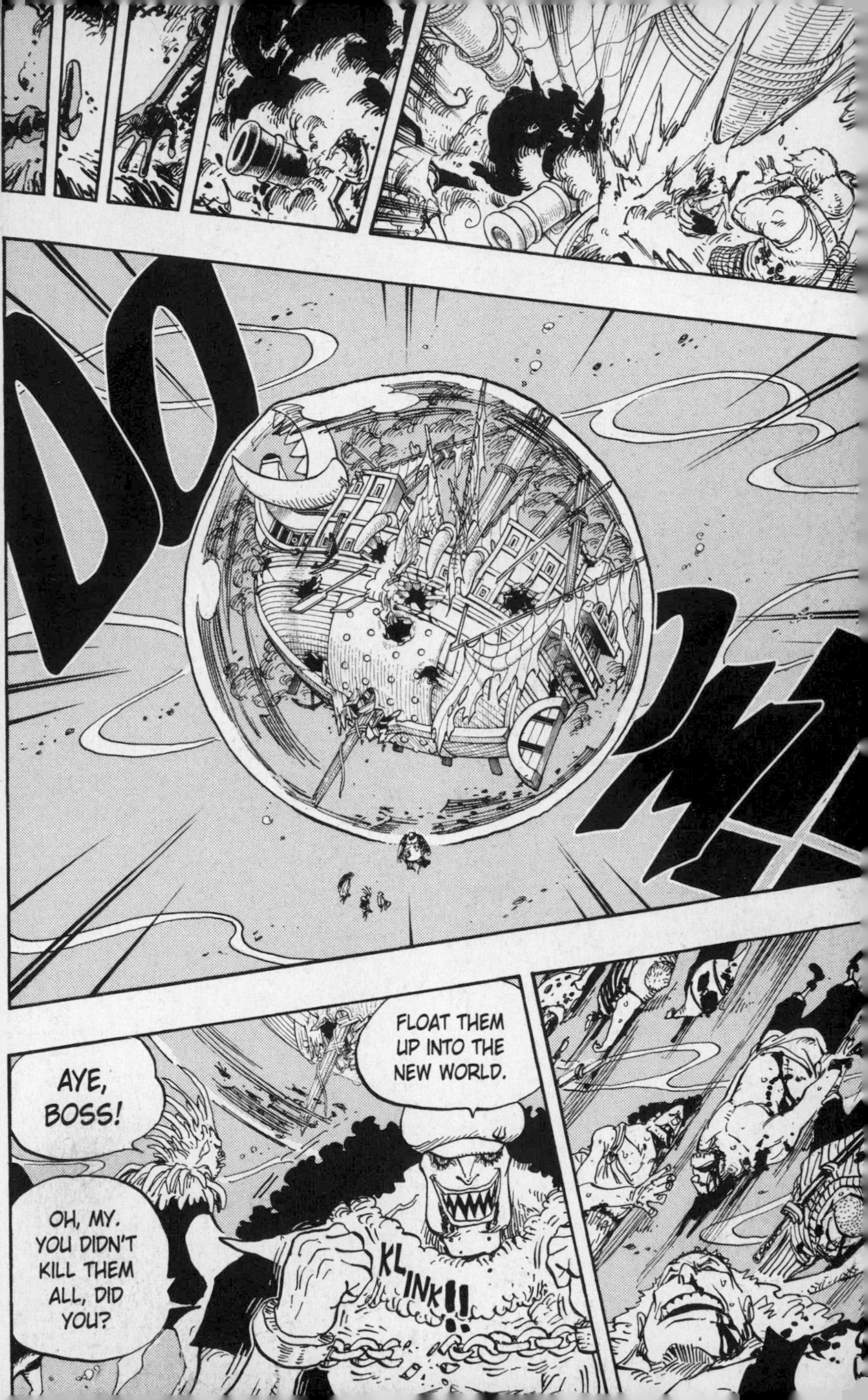
DOOM
FLOAT THEM UP INTO THE NEW WORLD.
AYE, BOSS!
KLINK!!
OH, MY. YOU DIDN'T KILL THEM ALL, DID YOU?

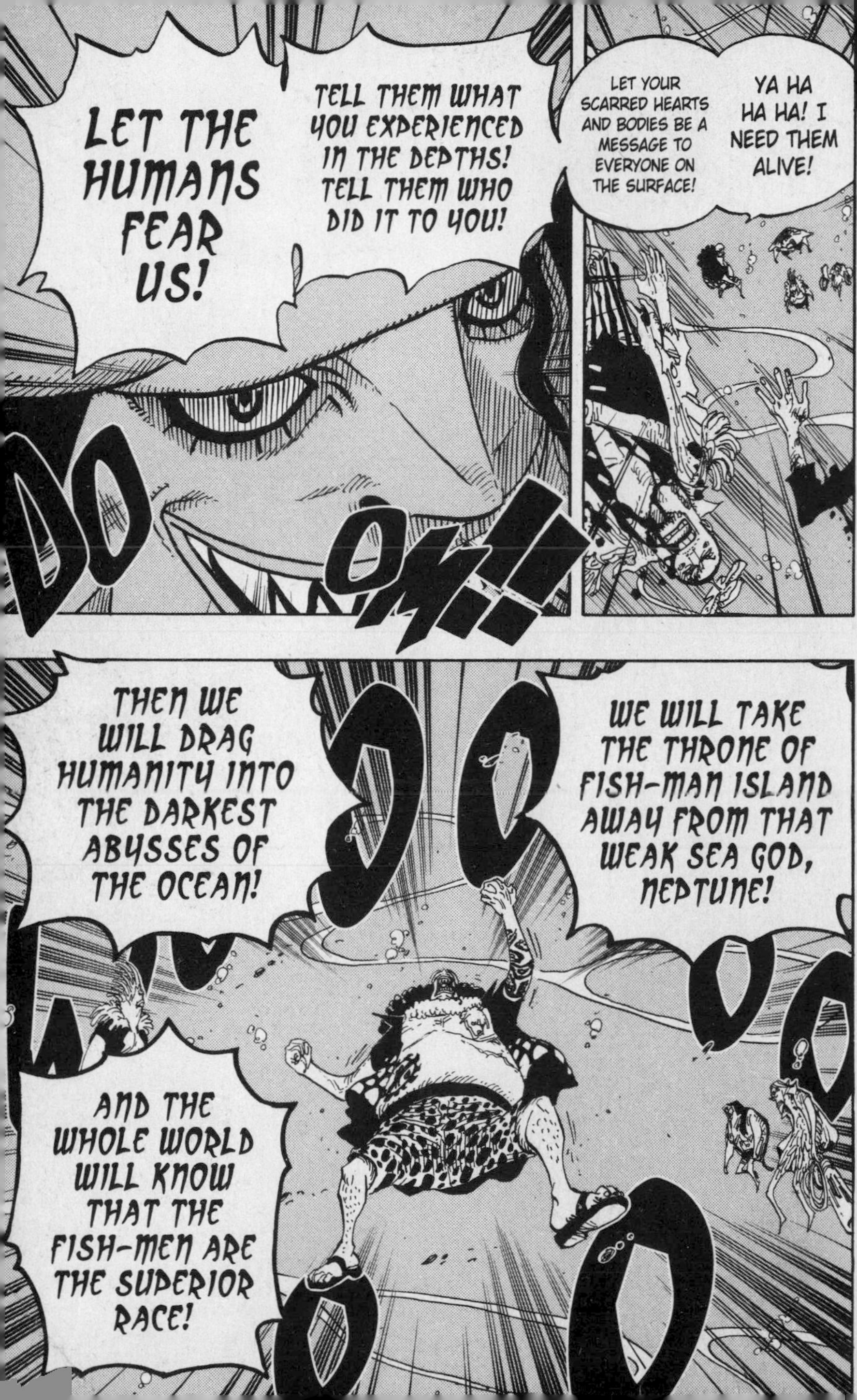
YA HA HA HA! I NEED THEM ALIVE!
LET YOUR SCARRED HEARTS AND BODIES BE A MESSAGE TO EVERYONE ON THE SURFACE!
TELL THEM WHAT YOU EXPERIENCED IN THE DEPTHS! TELL THEM WHO DID IT TO YOU!
LET THE HUMANS FEAR US!
DOOM!!
WE WILL TAKE THE THRONE OF FISH-MAN ISLAND AWAY FROM THAT WEAK SEA GOD, NEPTUNE!
THEN WE WILL DRAG HUMANITY INTO THE DARKEST ABYSSES OF THE OCEAN!
AND THE WHOLE WORLD WILL KNOW THAT THE FISH-MEN ARE THE SUPERIOR RACE!

THE SHARK THEY SAVED

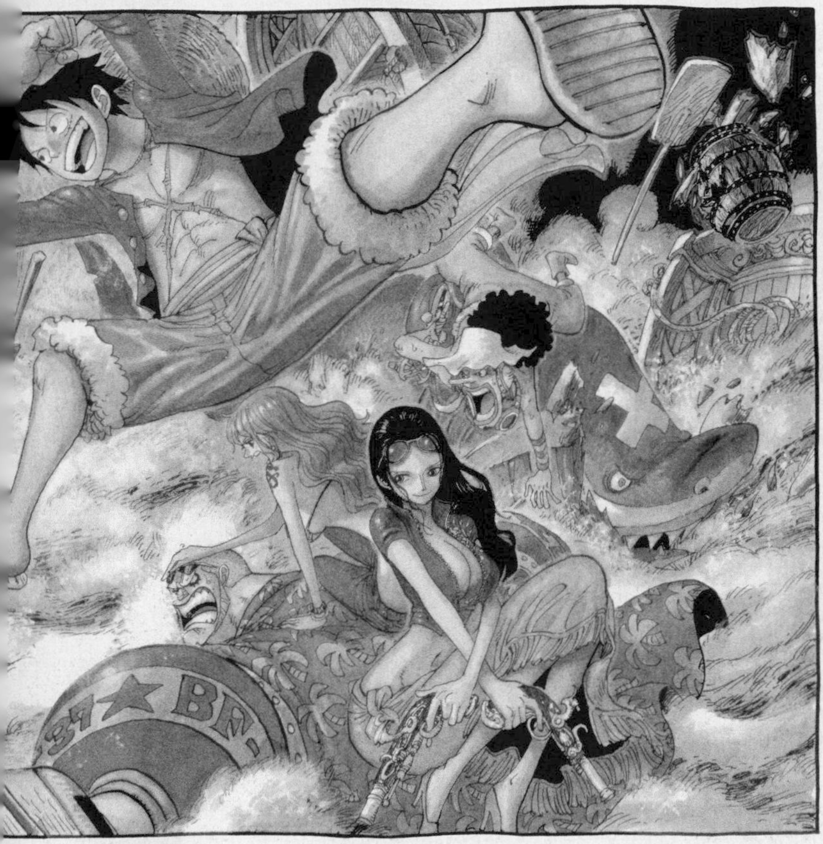

Chapter 612: TAKEN BY

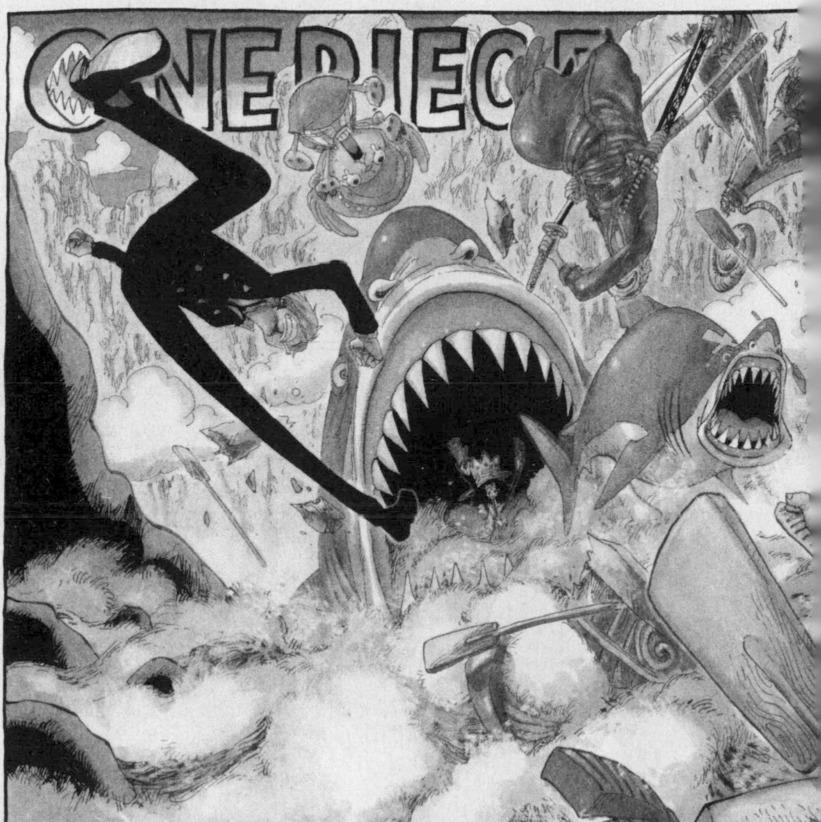

ONE PIECE vol.62

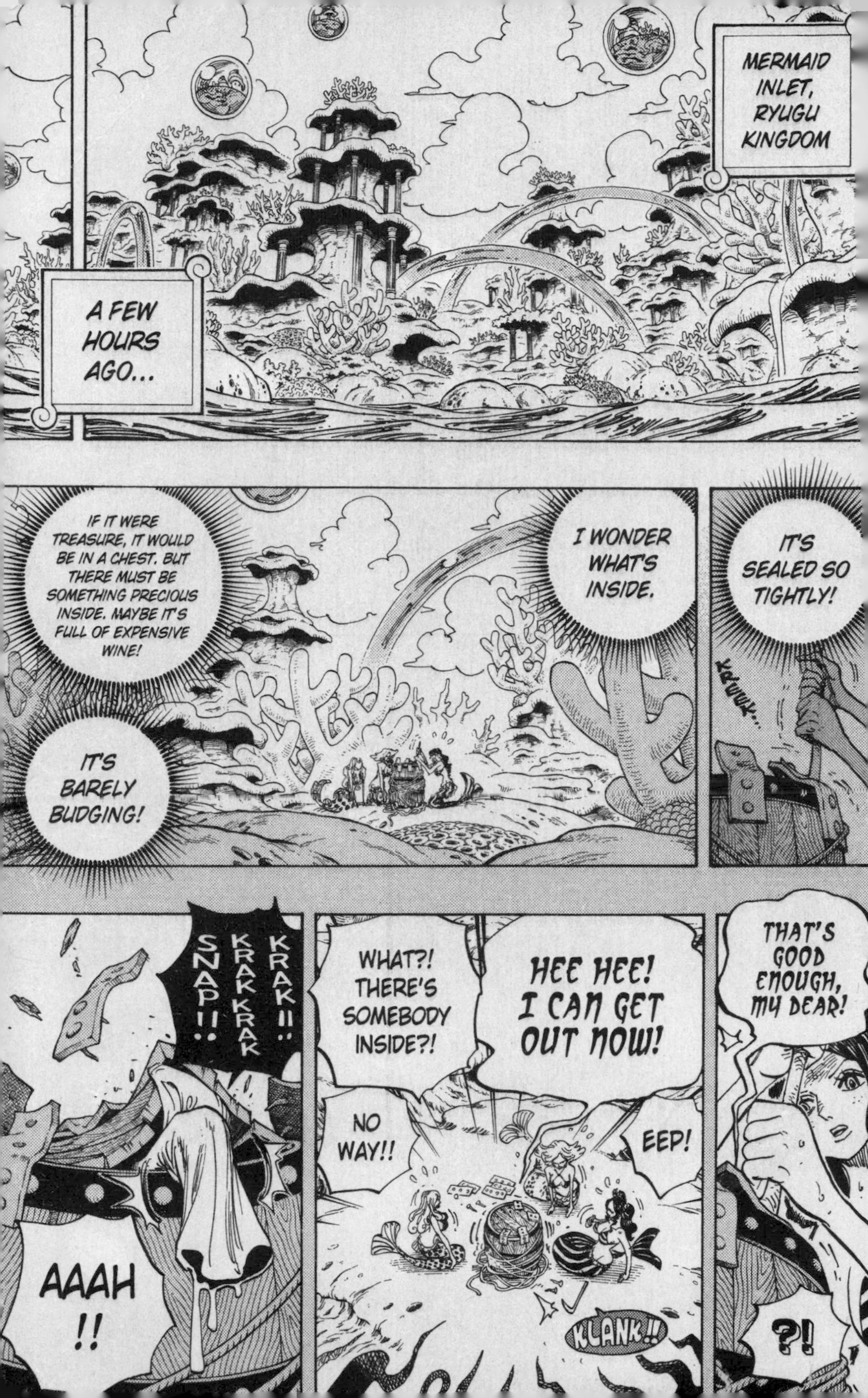
MERMAID INLET, RYUGU KINGDOM
A FEW HOURS AGO...
IT'S SEALED SO TIGHTLY!
KRUNK...
I WONDER WHAT'S INSIDE.
IF IT WERE TREASURE, IT WOULD BE IN A CHEST. BUT THERE MUST BE SOMETHING PRECIOUS INSIDE. MAYBE IT'S FULL OF EXPENSIVE WINE!
IT'S BARELY BUDGING!
THAT'S GOOD ENOUGH, MY DEAR!
?!
HEE HEE! I CAN GET OUT NOW!
WHAT?! THERE'S SOMEBODY INSIDE?!
EEP!
NO WAY!!
KLANK!!
KRAK!! KRAK KRAK SNAP!!
AAAH!!

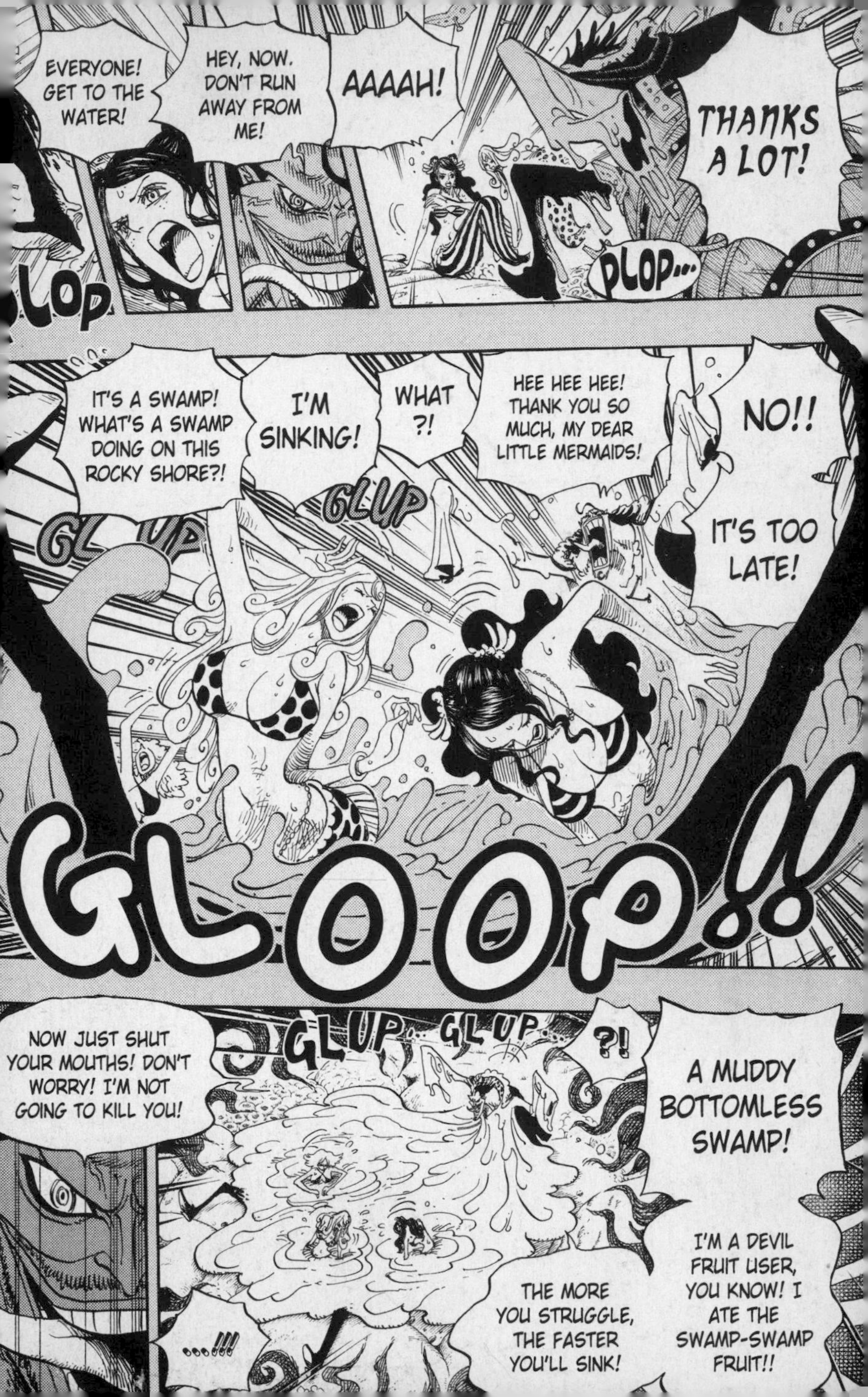
THANKS A LOT!
PLOP...
AAAAH!
HEY, NOW. DON'T RUN AWAY FROM ME!
EVERYONE! GET TO THE WATER!
SLOP
NO!!
IT'S TOO LATE!
HEE HEE HEE! THANK YOU SO MUCH, MY DEAR LITTLE MERMAIDS!
WHAT?!
I'M SINKING!
IT'S A SWAMP! WHAT'S A SWAMP DOING ON THIS ROCKY SHORE?!
GLUP
GL UP
GLOOP!!
A MUDDY BOTTOMLESS SWAMP!
?!
GLUP... GLUP...
NOW JUST SHUT YOUR MOUTHS! DON'T WORRY! I'M NOT GOING TO KILL YOU!
I'M A DEVIL FRUIT USER, YOU KNOW! I ATE THE SWAMP-SWAMP FRUIT!!
THE MORE YOU STRUGGLE, THE FASTER YOU'LL SINK!
...!!!

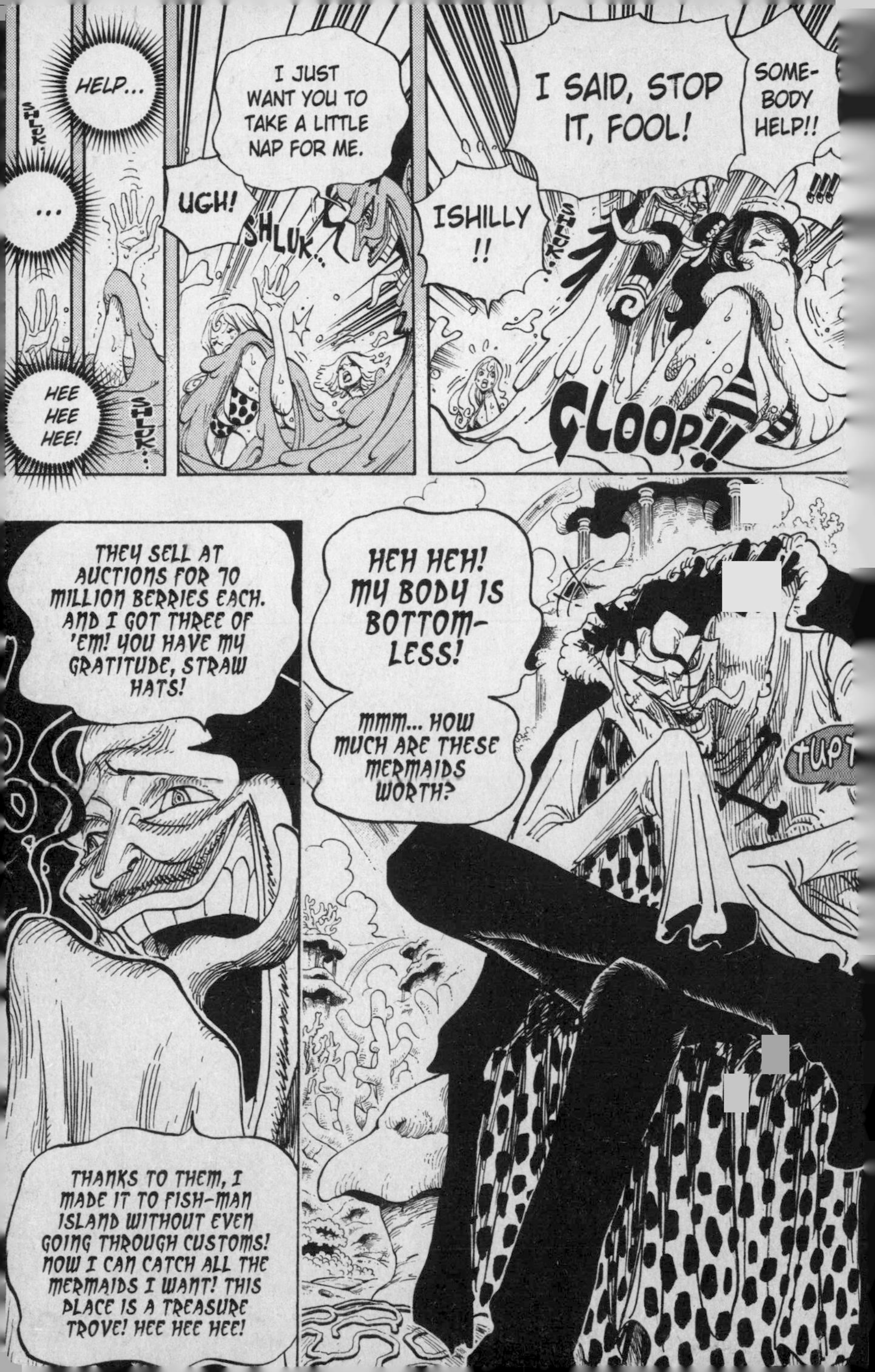
SOME-BODY HELP!!
I SAID, STOP IT, FOOL!
!!!
SHLUK...
ISHILLY !!
GLOOP!!
I JUST WANT YOU TO TAKE A LITTLE NAP FOR ME.
UGH!
SHLUK...
HELP...
SHLUK...
...
HEE HEE HEE!
SHLUK...
HEH HEH! MY BODY IS BOTTOM-LESS!
MMM... HOW MUCH ARE THESE MERMAIDS WORTH?
THEY SELL AT AUCTIONS FOR 70 MILLION BERRIES EACH. AND I GOT THREE OF 'EM! YOU HAVE MY GRATITUDE, STRAW HATS!
THANKS TO THEM, I MADE IT TO FISH-MAN ISLAND WITHOUT EVEN GOING THROUGH CUSTOMS! NOW I CAN CATCH ALL THE MERMAIDS I WANT! THIS PLACE IS A TREASURE TROVE! HEE HEE HEE!

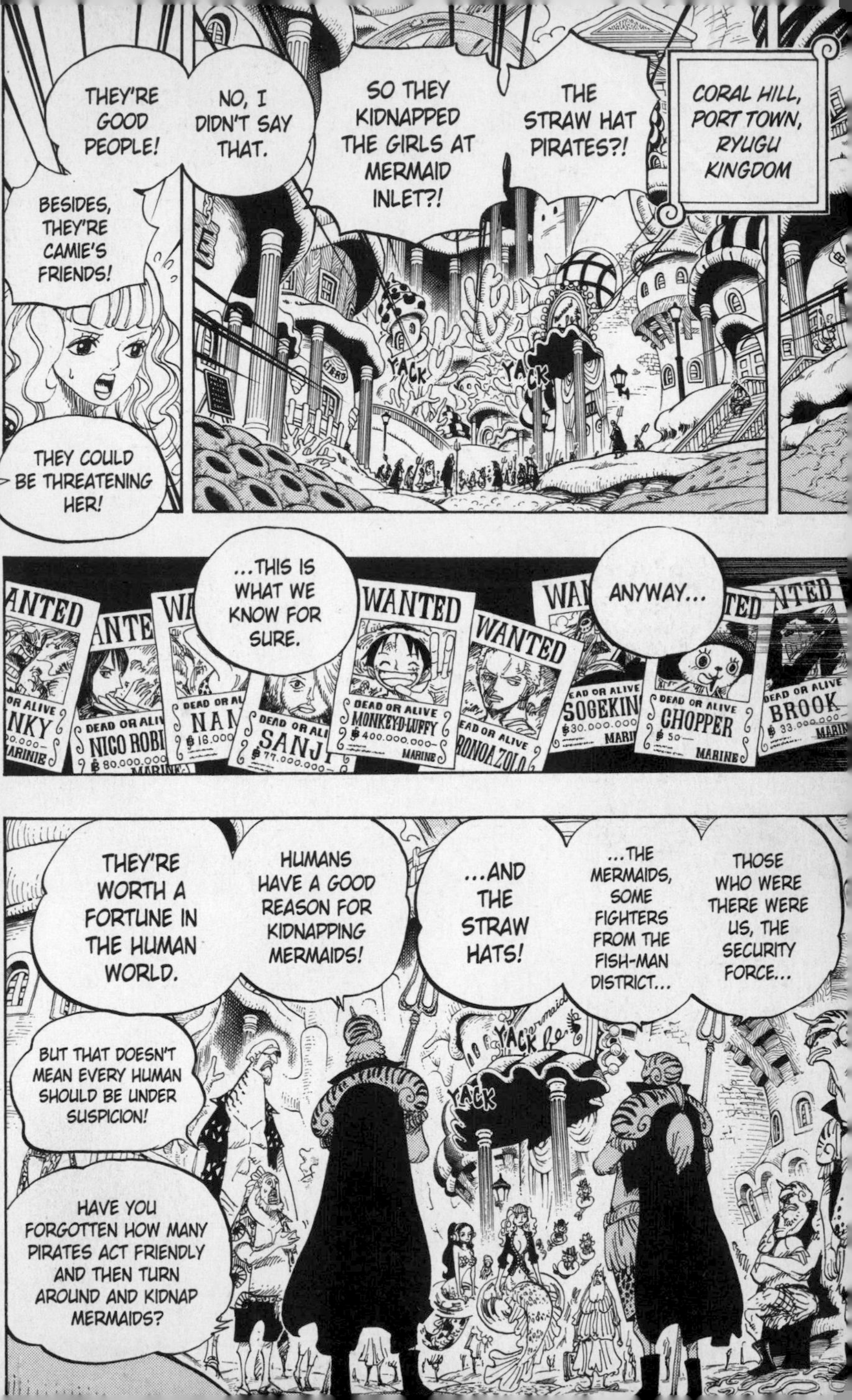
CORAL HILL, PORT TOWN, RYUGU KINGDOM
THE STRAW HAT PIRATES?!
SO THEY KIDNAPPED THE GIRLS AT MERMAID INLET?!
YACK
YACK
NO, I DIDN'T SAY THAT.
THEY'RE GOOD PEOPLE!
BESIDES, THEY'RE CAMIE'S FRIENDS!
THEY COULD BE THREATENING HER!
ANYWAY...
...THIS IS WHAT WE KNOW FOR SURE.
DEAD OR ALIVE
BROOK
DEAD OR ALIVE
CHOPPER
฿50—
MARINE
WANTED
WANTED
DEAD OR ALIVE
MONKEY·D·LUFFY
฿400,000,000—
MARINE
THOSE WHO WERE THERE WERE US, THE SECURITY FORCE...
...THE MERMAIDS, SOME FIGHTERS FROM THE FISH-MAN DISTRICT...
...AND THE STRAW HATS!
HUMANS HAVE A GOOD REASON FOR KIDNAPPING MERMAIDS!
THEY'RE WORTH A FORTUNE IN THE HUMAN WORLD.
YACK
YACK
BUT THAT DOESN'T MEAN EVERY HUMAN SHOULD BE UNDER SUSPICION!
HAVE YOU FORGOTTEN HOW MANY PIRATES ACT FRIENDLY AND THEN TURN AROUND AND KIDNAP MERMAIDS?

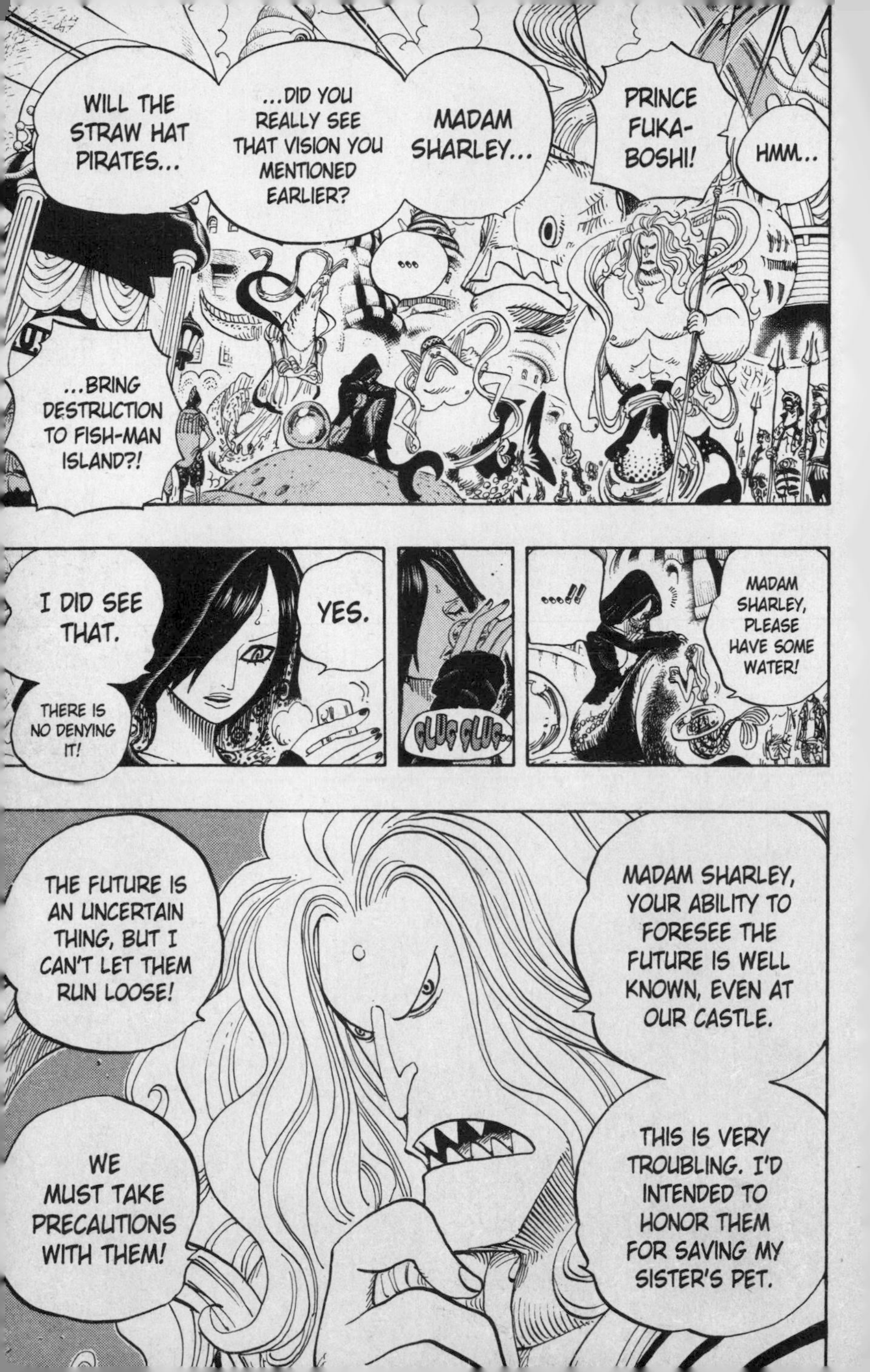
HMM...
PRINCE FUKA-BOSHI!
MADAM SHARLEY...
...DID YOU REALLY SEE THAT VISION YOU MENTIONED EARLIER?
WILL THE STRAW HAT PIRATES...
...
...BRING DESTRUCTION TO FISH-MAN ISLAND?!
MADAM SHARLEY, PLEASE HAVE SOME WATER!
....!!
GLUG GLUG...
YES.
I DID SEE THAT.
THERE IS NO DENYING IT!
MADAM SHARLEY, YOUR ABILITY TO FORESEE THE FUTURE IS WELL KNOWN, EVEN AT OUR CASTLE.
THE FUTURE IS AN UNCERTAIN THING, BUT I CAN'T LET THEM RUN LOOSE!
THIS IS VERY TROUBLING. I'D INTENDED TO HONOR THEM FOR SAVING MY SISTER'S PET.
WE MUST TAKE PRECAUTIONS WITH THEM!

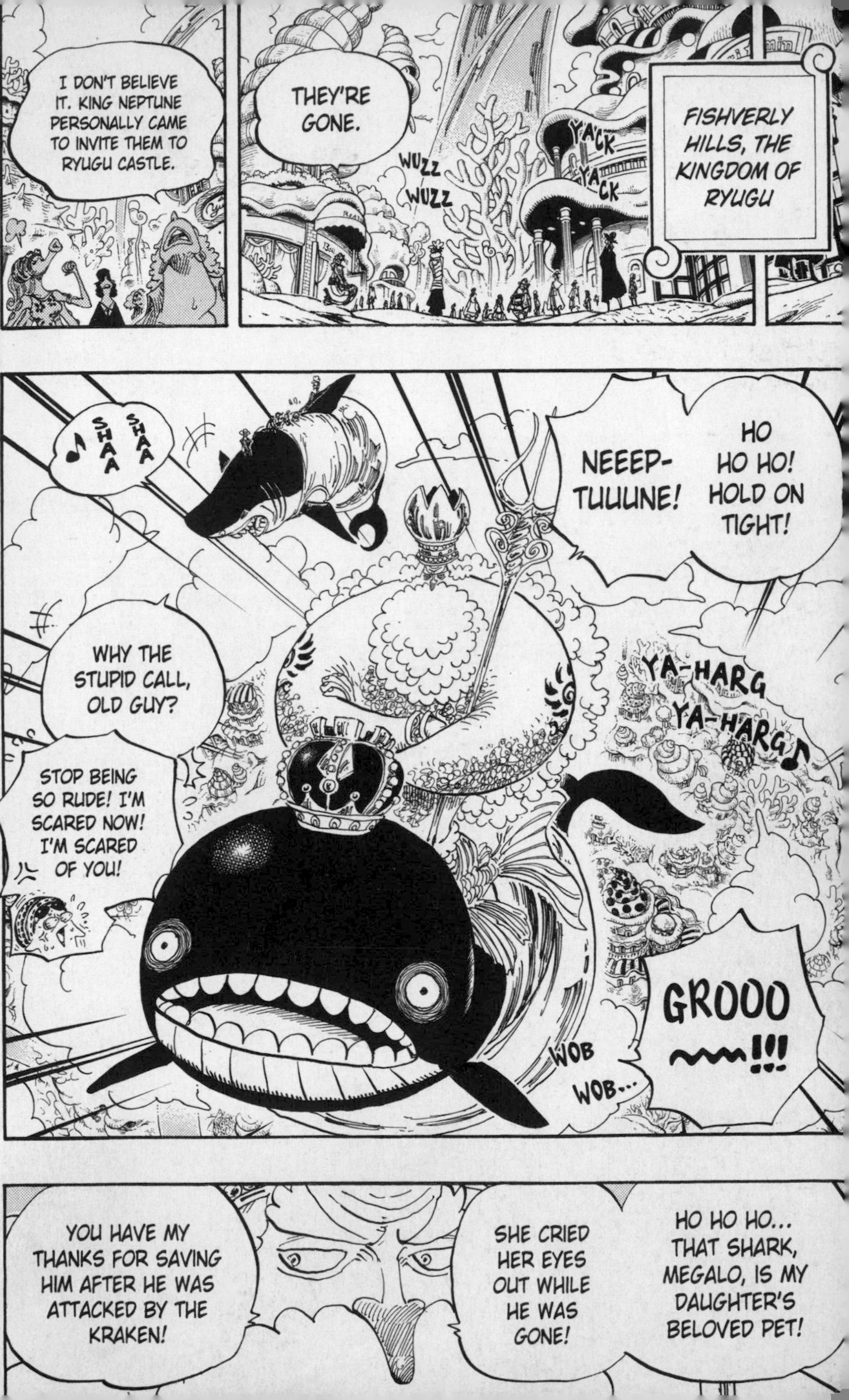
FISHVERLY HILLS, THE KINGDOM OF RYUGU
YACK YACK
WUZZ WUZZ
THEY'RE GONE.
I DON'T BELIEVE IT. KING NEPTUNE PERSONALLY CAME TO INVITE THEM TO RYUGU CASTLE.
HO HO HO! HOLD ON TIGHT!
NEEEP-TUUUNE!
♪ SHAA SHAA
YA-HARG YA-HARG ♪
WHY THE STUPID CALL, OLD GUY?
STOP BEING SO RUDE! I'M SCARED NOW! I'M SCARED OF YOU!
GROOO ~~~!!!
WOB WOB...
HO HO HO... THAT SHARK, MEGALO, IS MY DAUGHTER'S BELOVED PET!
SHE CRIED HER EYES OUT WHILE HE WAS GONE!
YOU HAVE MY THANKS FOR SAVING HIM AFTER HE WAS ATTACKED BY THE KRAKEN!

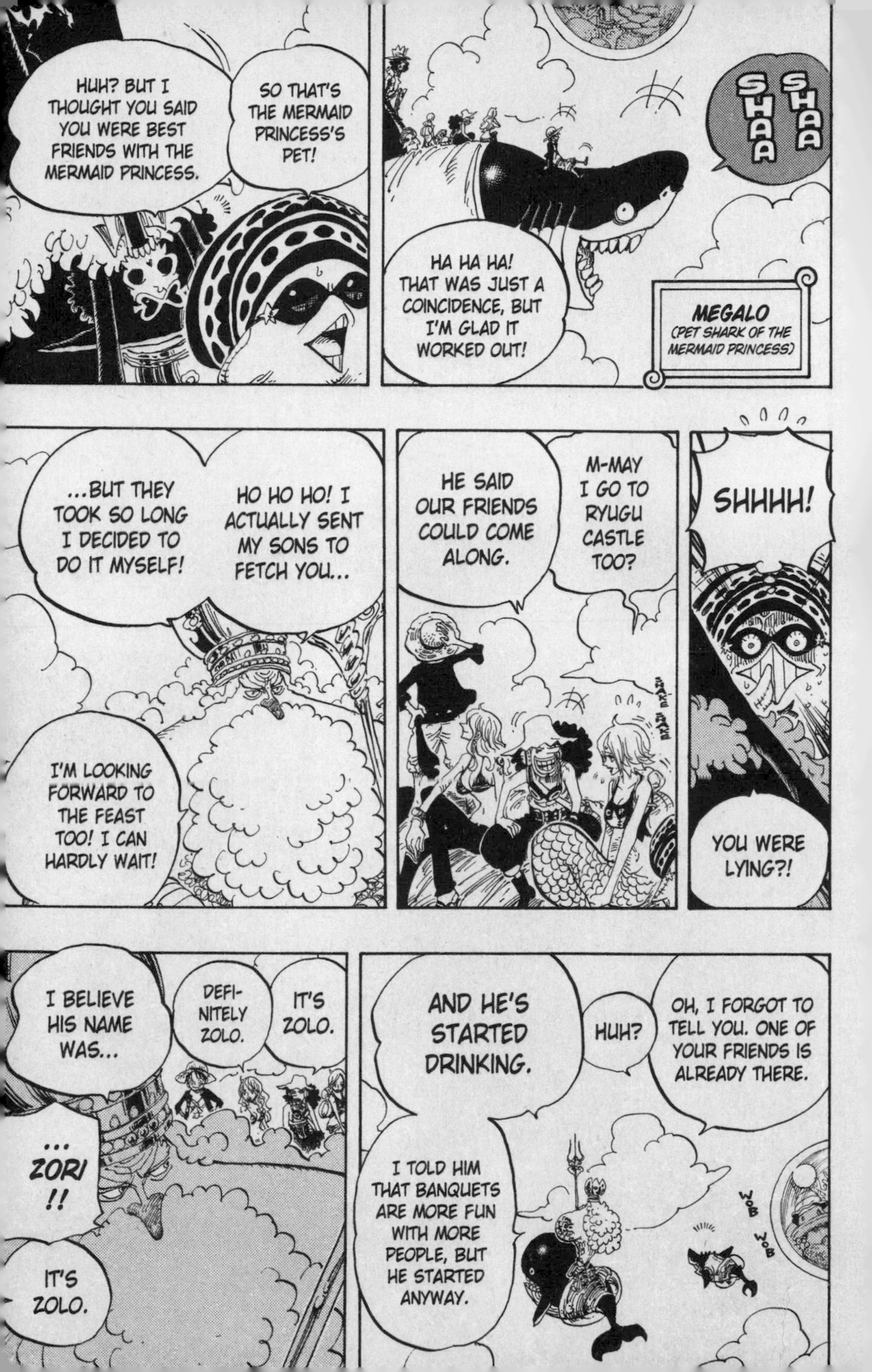
SHAA SHAA
HA HA HA! THAT WAS JUST A COINCIDENCE, BUT I'M GLAD IT WORKED OUT!
MEGALO
(PET SHARK OF THE MERMAID PRINCESS)
SO THAT'S THE MERMAID PRINCESS'S PET!
HUH? BUT I THOUGHT YOU SAID YOU WERE BEST FRIENDS WITH THE MERMAID PRINCESS.
SHHHH!
YOU WERE LYING?!
M-MAY I GO TO RYUGU CASTLE TOO?
HE SAID OUR FRIENDS COULD COME ALONG.
SHAKE SHAKE
HO HO HO! I ACTUALLY SENT MY SONS TO FETCH YOU...
...BUT THEY TOOK SO LONG I DECIDED TO DO IT MYSELF!
I'M LOOKING FORWARD TO THE FEAST TOO! I CAN HARDLY WAIT!
OH, I FORGOT TO TELL YOU. ONE OF YOUR FRIENDS IS ALREADY THERE.
HUH?
AND HE'S STARTED DRINKING.
I TOLD HIM THAT BANQUETS ARE MORE FUN WITH MORE PEOPLE, BUT HE STARTED ANYWAY.
WOB WOB
IT'S ZOLO.
DEFI-NITELY ZOLO.
I BELIEVE HIS NAME WAS...
...ZORI!!
IT'S ZOLO.

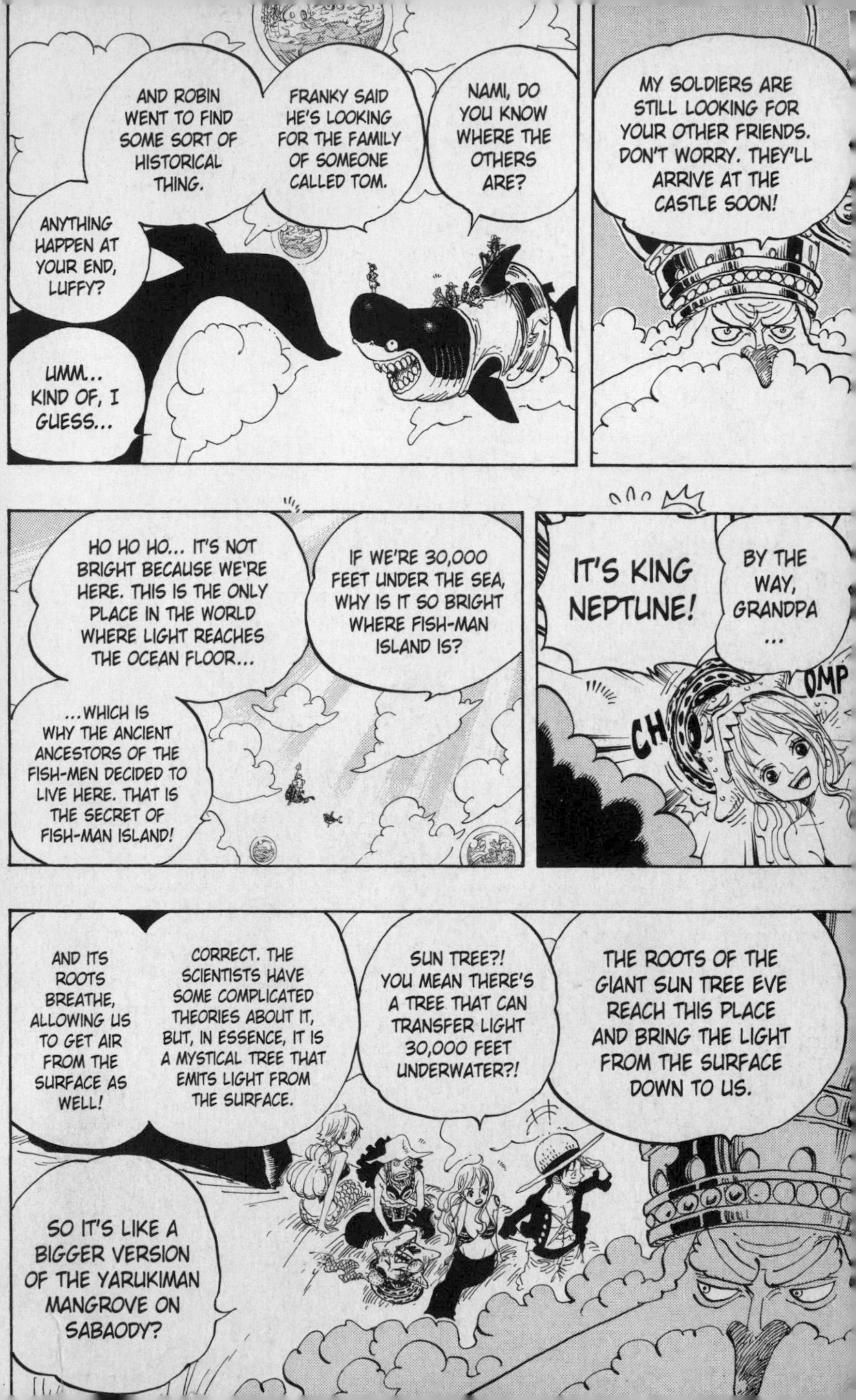
MY SOLDIERS ARE STILL LOOKING FOR YOUR OTHER FRIENDS. DON'T WORRY. THEY'LL ARRIVE AT THE CASTLE SOON!
NAMI, DO YOU KNOW WHERE THE OTHERS ARE?
FRANKY SAID HE'S LOOKING FOR THE FAMILY OF SOMEONE CALLED TOM.
AND ROBIN WENT TO FIND SOME SORT OF HISTORICAL THING.
ANYTHING HAPPEN AT YOUR END, LUFFY?
UMM... KIND OF, I GUESS...
BY THE WAY, GRANDPA ...
IT'S KING NEPTUNE!
OMP
CH
IF WE'RE 30,000 FEET UNDER THE SEA, WHY IS IT SO BRIGHT WHERE FISH-MAN ISLAND IS?
HO HO HO... IT'S NOT BRIGHT BECAUSE WE'RE HERE. THIS IS THE ONLY PLACE IN THE WORLD WHERE LIGHT REACHES THE OCEAN FLOOR...
...WHICH IS WHY THE ANCIENT ANCESTORS OF THE FISH-MEN DECIDED TO LIVE HERE. THAT IS THE SECRET OF FISH-MAN ISLAND!
THE ROOTS OF THE GIANT SUN TREE EVE REACH THIS PLACE AND BRING THE LIGHT FROM THE SURFACE DOWN TO US.
SUN TREE?! YOU MEAN THERE'S A TREE THAT CAN TRANSFER LIGHT 30,000 FEET UNDERWATER?!
CORRECT. THE SCIENTISTS HAVE SOME COMPLICATED THEORIES ABOUT IT, BUT, IN ESSENCE, IT IS A MYSTICAL TREE THAT EMITS LIGHT FROM THE SURFACE.
AND ITS ROOTS BREATHE, ALLOWING US TO GET AIR FROM THE SURFACE AS WELL!
SO IT'S LIKE A BIGGER VERSION OF THE YARUKIMAN MANGROVE ON SABAODY?

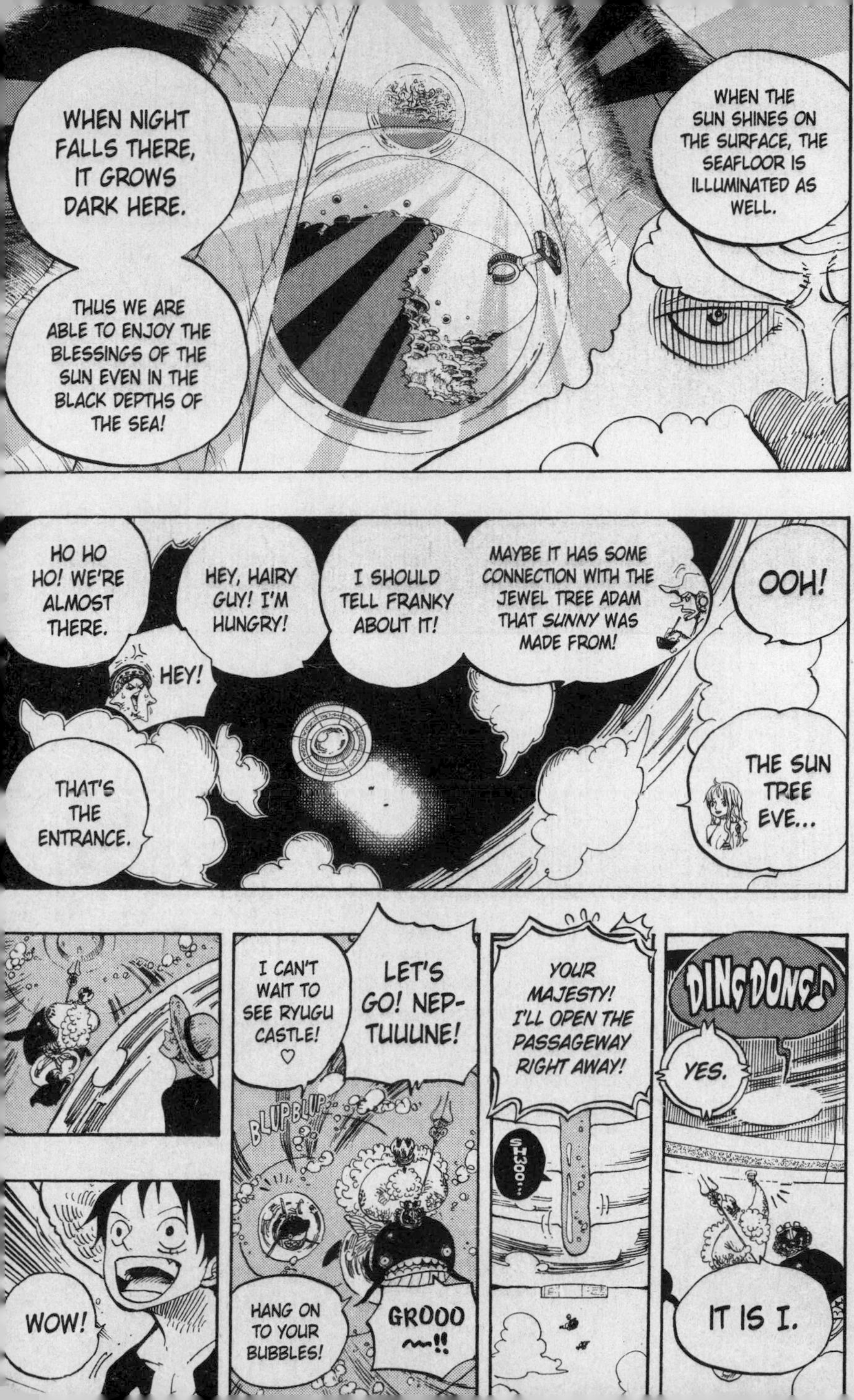
WHEN THE SUN SHINES ON THE SURFACE, THE SEAFLOOR IS ILLUMINATED AS WELL.
WHEN NIGHT FALLS THERE, IT GROWS DARK HERE.
THUS WE ARE ABLE TO ENJOY THE BLESSINGS OF THE SUN EVEN IN THE BLACK DEPTHS OF THE SEA!
OOH!
MAYBE IT HAS SOME CONNECTION WITH THE JEWEL TREE ADAM THAT *SUNNY* WAS MADE FROM!
I SHOULD TELL FRANKY ABOUT IT!
HEY, HAIRY GUY! I'M HUNGRY!
HO HO HO! WE'RE ALMOST THERE.
HEY!
THE SUN TREE EVE...
THAT'S THE ENTRANCE.
DING DONG♪
YES.
IT IS I.
YOUR MAJESTY! I'LL OPEN THE PASSAGEWAY RIGHT AWAY!
SHOOO...
LET'S GO! NEP-TUUUNE!
I CAN'T WAIT TO SEE RYUGU CASTLE! ♡
BLUPBLUP
GROOO~~!!
HANG ON TO YOUR BUBBLES!
WOW!

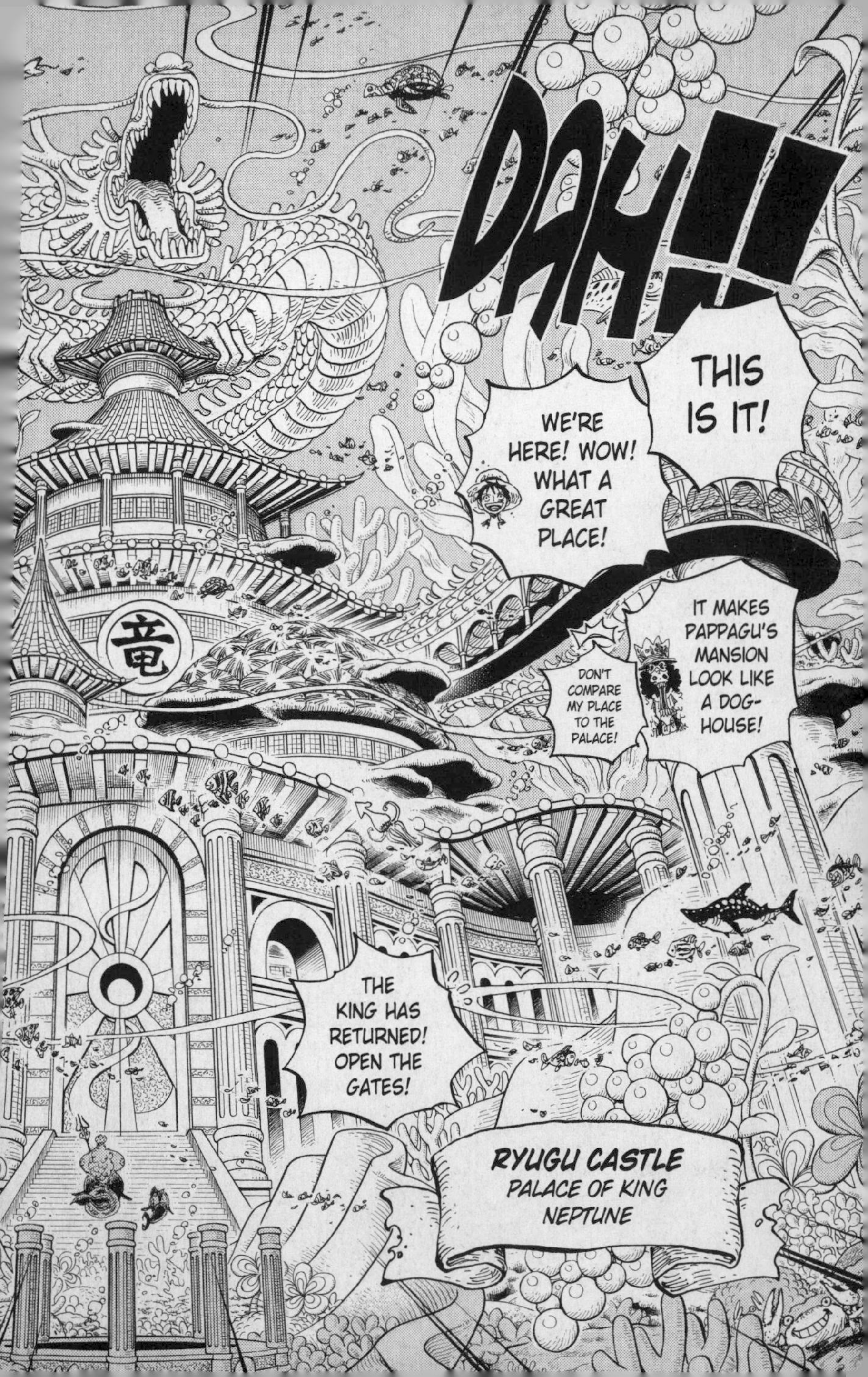
DOH!!
THIS IS IT!
WE'RE HERE! WOW! WHAT A GREAT PLACE!
IT MAKES PAPPAGU'S MANSION LOOK LIKE A DOG-HOUSE!
DON'T COMPARE MY PLACE TO THE PALACE!
竜
THE KING HAS RETURNED! OPEN THE GATES!
RYUGU CASTLE
PALACE OF KING NEPTUNE

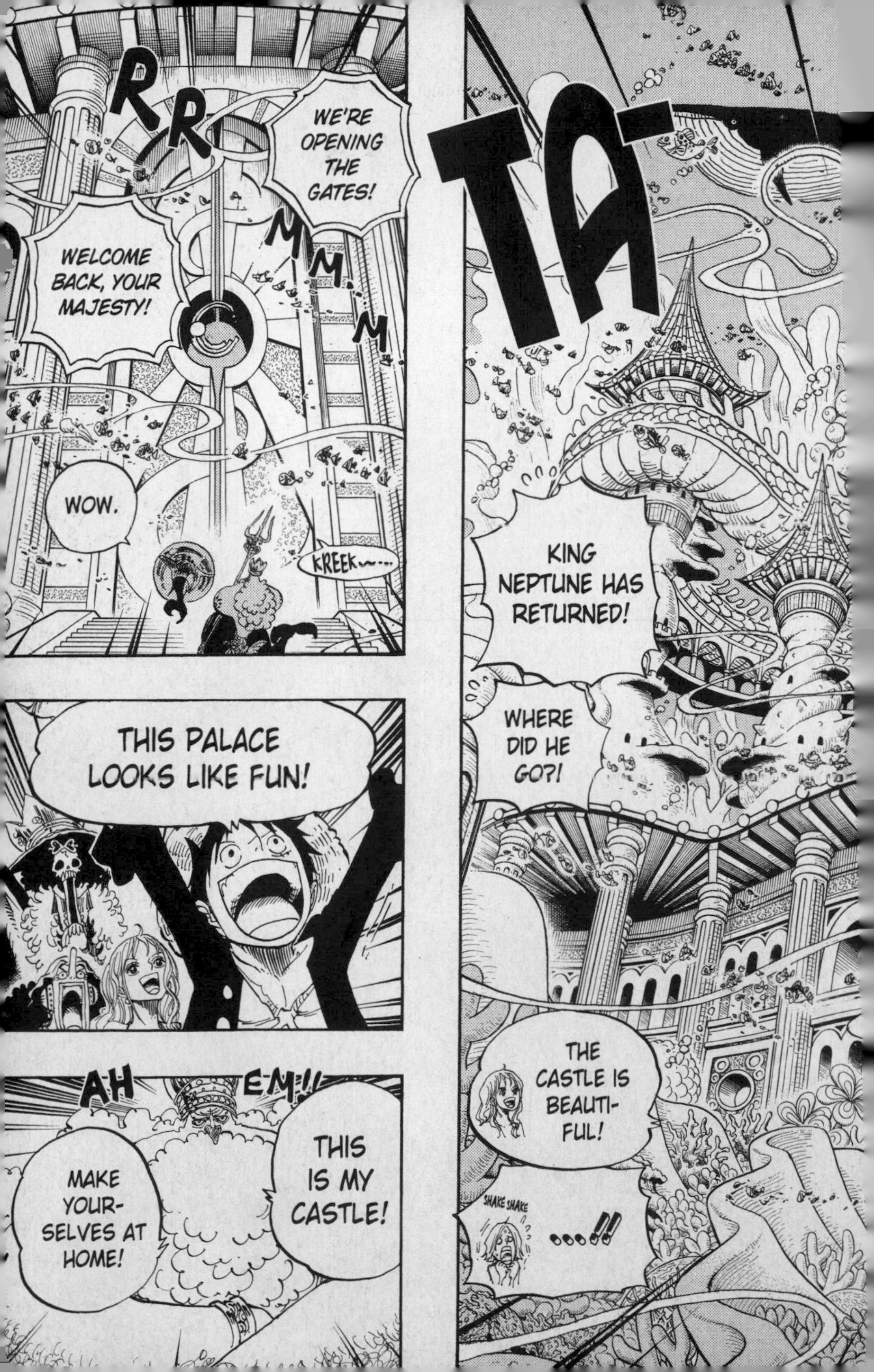
TA
KING NEPTUNE HAS RETURNED!
WHERE DID HE GO?!
THE CASTLE IS BEAUTIFUL!
SHAKE SHAKE
...!!
WE'RE OPENING THE GATES!
RRR
WELCOME BACK, YOUR MAJESTY!
MMMM
KREEK~...
WOW.
THIS PALACE LOOKS LIKE FUN!
AHEM!!
THIS IS MY CASTLE!
MAKE YOURSELVES AT HOME!

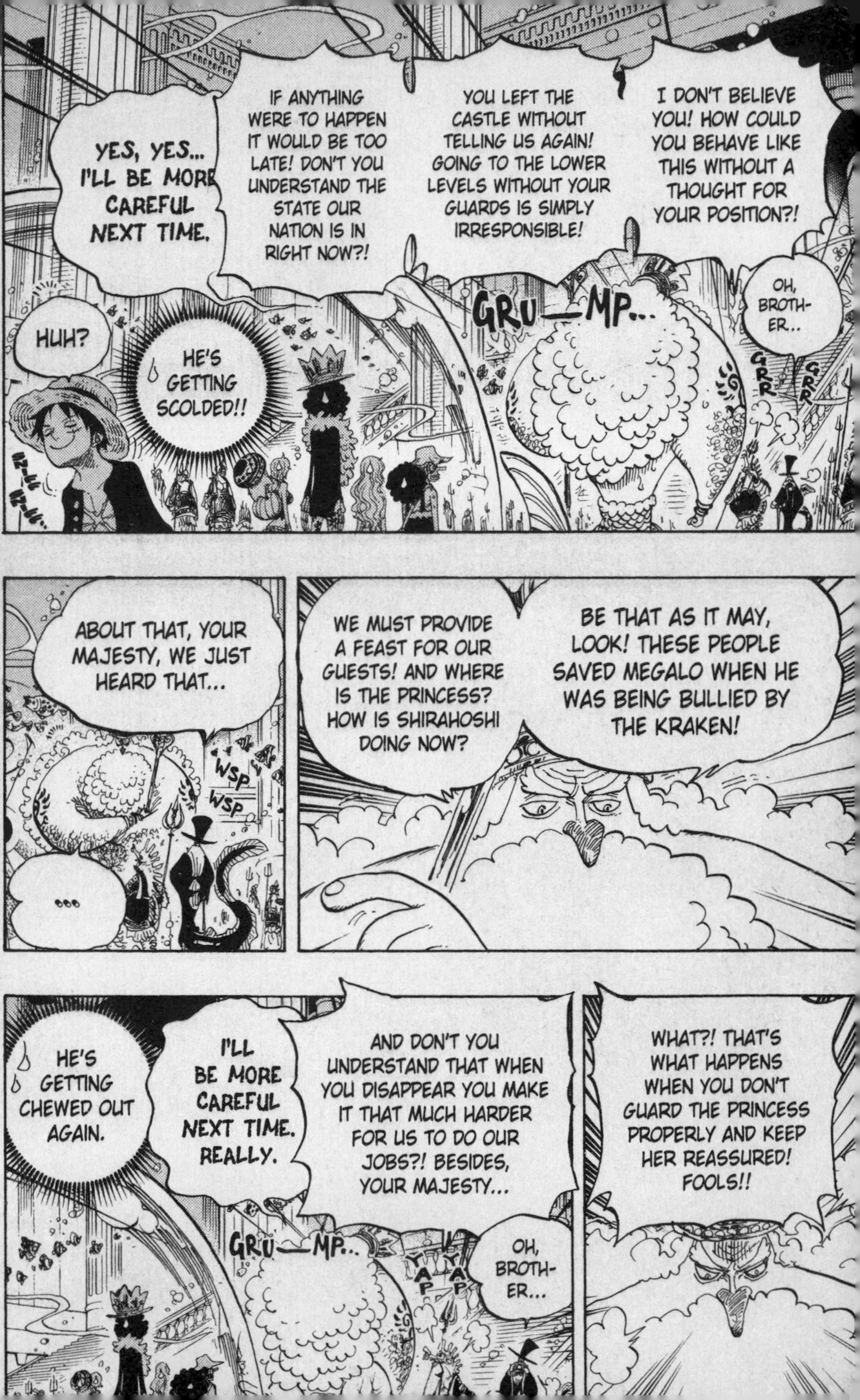
I DON'T BELIEVE YOU! HOW COULD YOU BEHAVE LIKE THIS WITHOUT A THOUGHT FOR YOUR POSITION?!
YOU LEFT THE CASTLE WITHOUT TELLING US AGAIN! GOING TO THE LOWER LEVELS WITHOUT YOUR GUARDS IS SIMPLY IRRESPONSIBLE!
IF ANYTHING WERE TO HAPPEN IT WOULD BE TOO LATE! DON'T YOU UNDERSTAND THE STATE OUR NATION IS IN RIGHT NOW?!
YES, YES... I'LL BE MORE CAREFUL NEXT TIME.
OH, BROTH-ER...
GRR GRR
GRU—MP...
HE'S GETTING SCOLDED!!
HUH?
SNIFF SNIFF...
BE THAT AS IT MAY, LOOK! THESE PEOPLE SAVED MEGALO WHEN HE WAS BEING BULLIED BY THE KRAKEN!
WE MUST PROVIDE A FEAST FOR OUR GUESTS! AND WHERE IS THE PRINCESS? HOW IS SHIRAHOSHI DOING NOW?
ABOUT THAT, YOUR MAJESTY, WE JUST HEARD THAT...
WSP WSP
...
WHAT?! THAT'S WHAT HAPPENS WHEN YOU DON'T GUARD THE PRINCESS PROPERLY AND KEEP HER REASSURED! FOOLS!!
AND DON'T YOU UNDERSTAND THAT WHEN YOU DISAPPEAR YOU MAKE IT THAT MUCH HARDER FOR US TO DO OUR JOBS?! BESIDES, YOUR MAJESTY...
I'LL BE MORE CAREFUL NEXT TIME. REALLY.
HE'S GETTING CHEWED OUT AGAIN.
OH, BROTH-ER...
YAP YAP
GRU—MP...

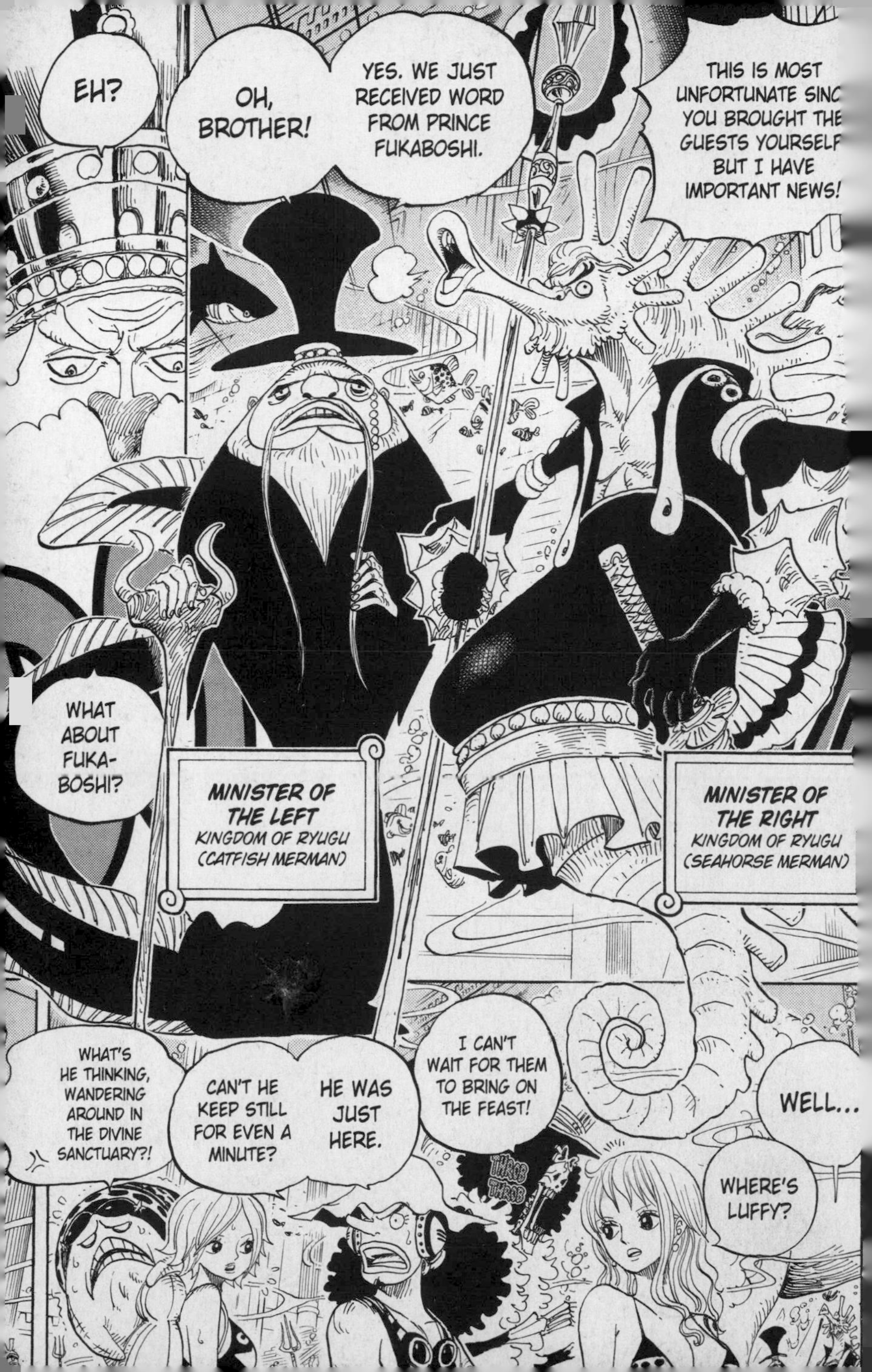
THIS IS MOST UNFORTUNATE SINC YOU BROUGHT THE GUESTS YOURSELF BUT I HAVE IMPORTANT NEWS!
OH, BROTHER!
YES. WE JUST RECEIVED WORD FROM PRINCE FUKABOSHI.
EH?
MINISTER OF THE RIGHT
KINGDOM OF RYUGU
(SEAHORSE MERMAN)
MINISTER OF THE LEFT
KINGDOM OF RYUGU
(CATFISH MERMAN)
WHAT ABOUT FUKA-BOSHI?
WELL...
WHERE'S LUFFY?
THROB THROB
I CAN'T WAIT FOR THEM TO BRING ON THE FEAST!
HE WAS JUST HERE.
CAN'T HE KEEP STILL FOR EVEN A MINUTE?
WHAT'S HE THINKING, WANDERING AROUND IN THE DIVINE SANCTUARY?!

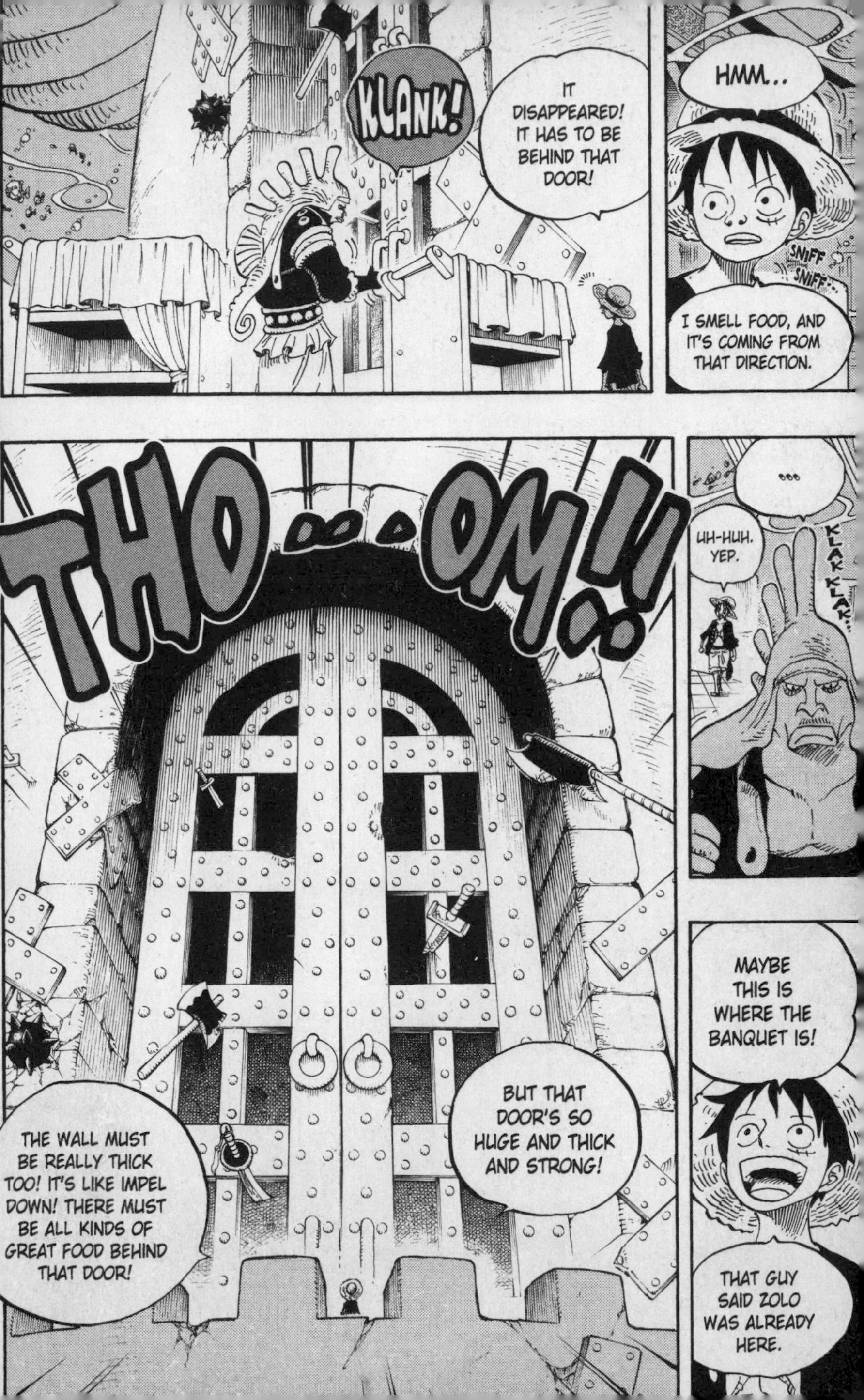
HMM...
SNIFF SNIFF...
I SMELL FOOD, AND IT'S COMING FROM THAT DIRECTION.
IT DISAPPEARED! IT HAS TO BE BEHIND THAT DOOR!
KLANK!
...
UH-HUH. YEP.
KLAK KLAK...
MAYBE THIS IS WHERE THE BANQUET IS!
THAT GUY SAID ZOLO WAS ALREADY HERE.
THO...OM!!
BUT THAT DOOR'S SO HUGE AND THICK AND STRONG!
THE WALL MUST BE REALLY THICK TOO! IT'S LIKE IMPEL DOWN! THERE MUST BE ALL KINDS OF GREAT FOOD BEHIND THAT DOOR!

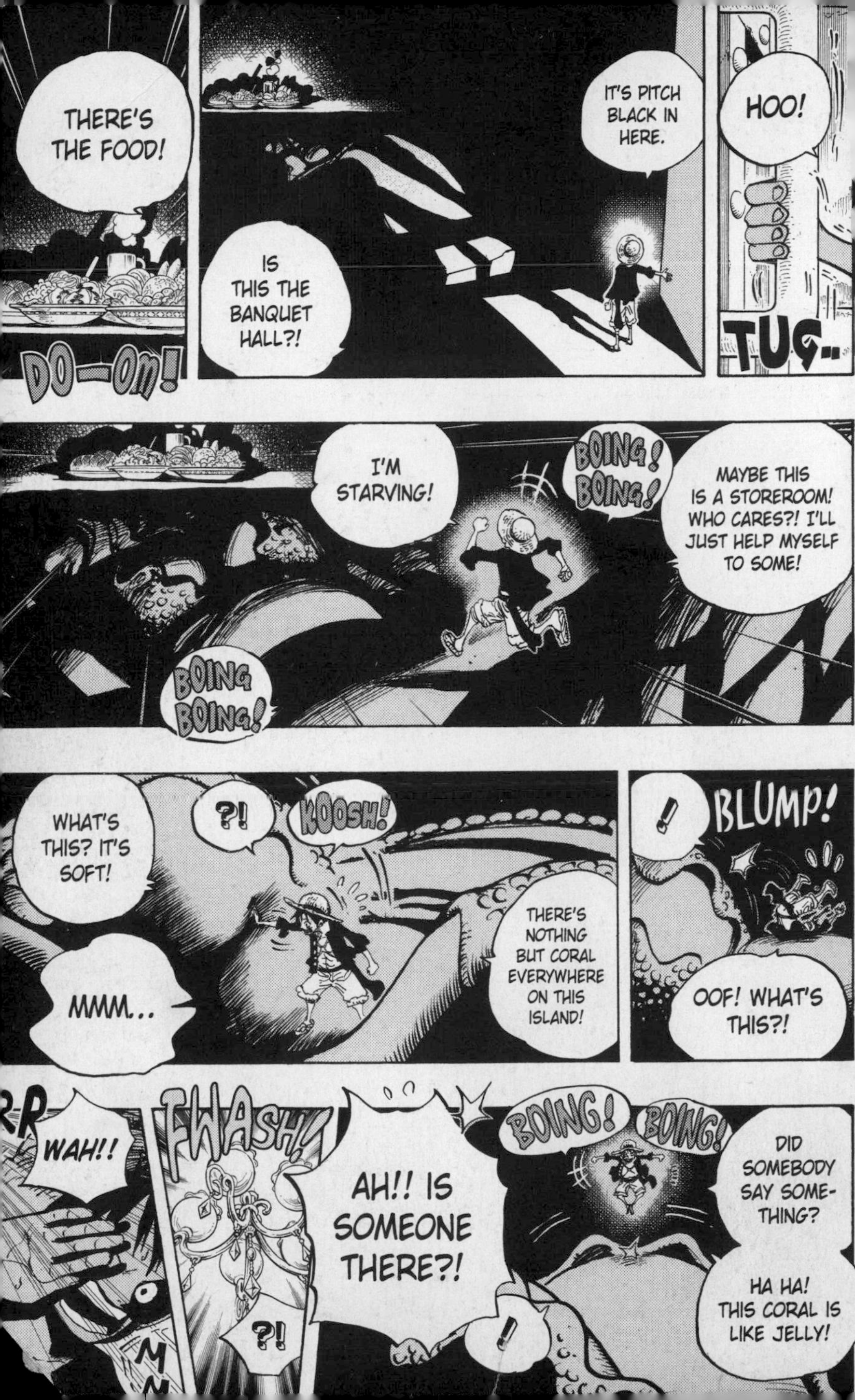
HOO!
TUG..
IT'S PITCH BLACK IN HERE.
IS THIS THE BANQUET HALL?!
THERE'S THE FOOD!
DO-OM!
MAYBE THIS IS A STOREROOM! WHO CARES?! I'LL JUST HELP MYSELF TO SOME!
BOING! BOING!
I'M STARVING!
BOING BOING!
BLUMP!
!
OOF! WHAT'S THIS?!
KOOSH!
?!
THERE'S NOTHING BUT CORAL EVERYWHERE ON THIS ISLAND!
WHAT'S THIS? IT'S SOFT!
MMM..
BOING! BOING!
DID SOMEBODY SAY SOME-THING?
HA HA! THIS CORAL IS LIKE JELLY!
AH!! IS SOMEONE THERE?!
!
FWASH!
?!
WAH!!

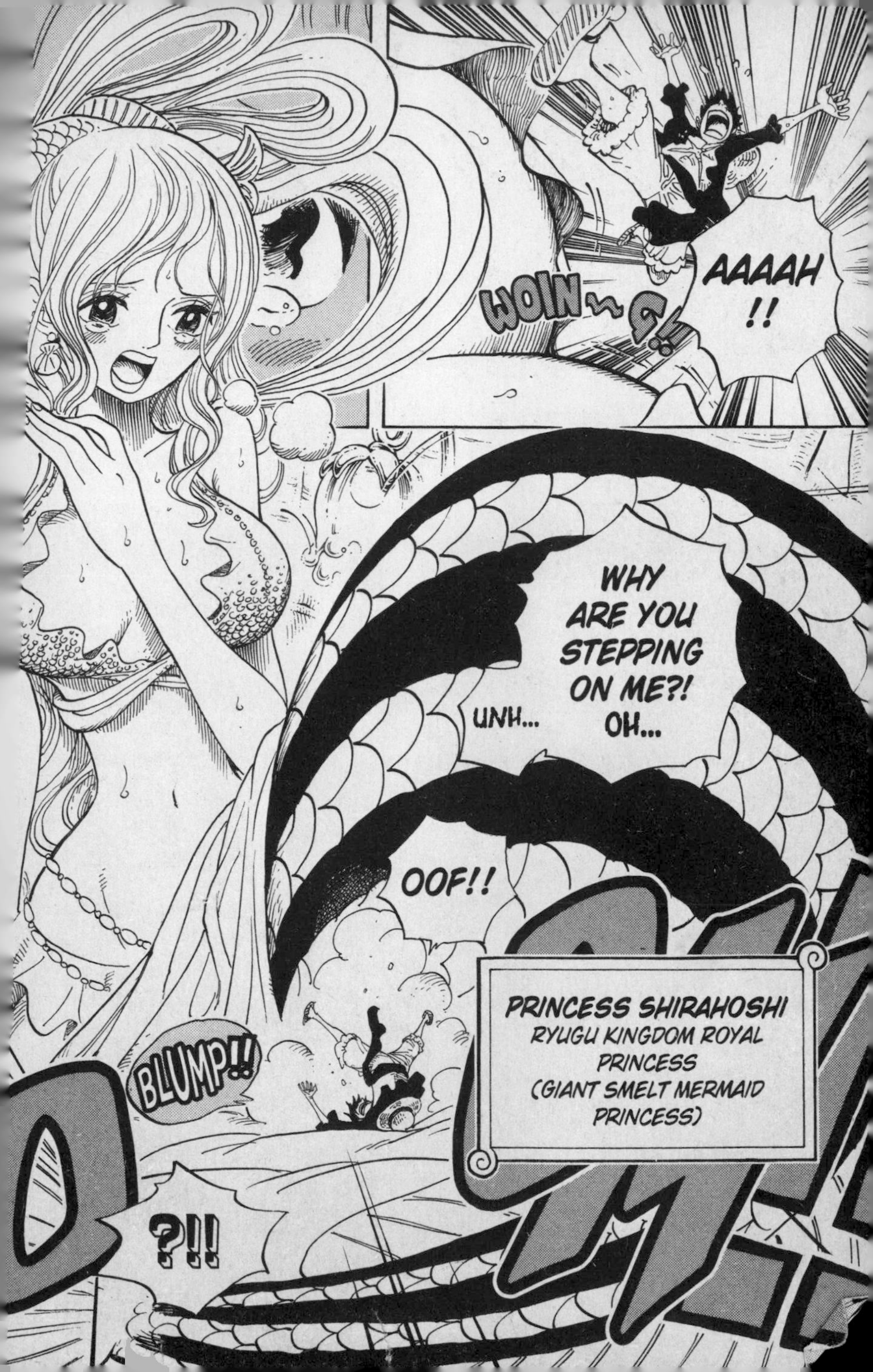
AAAAH!!
WOIN~G!!
WHY ARE YOU STEPPING ON ME?! OH...
UNH...
OOF!!
BLUMP!!
PRINCESS SHIRAHOSHI
RYUGU KINGDOM ROYAL PRINCESS
(GIANT SMELT MERMAID PRINCESS)
?!!

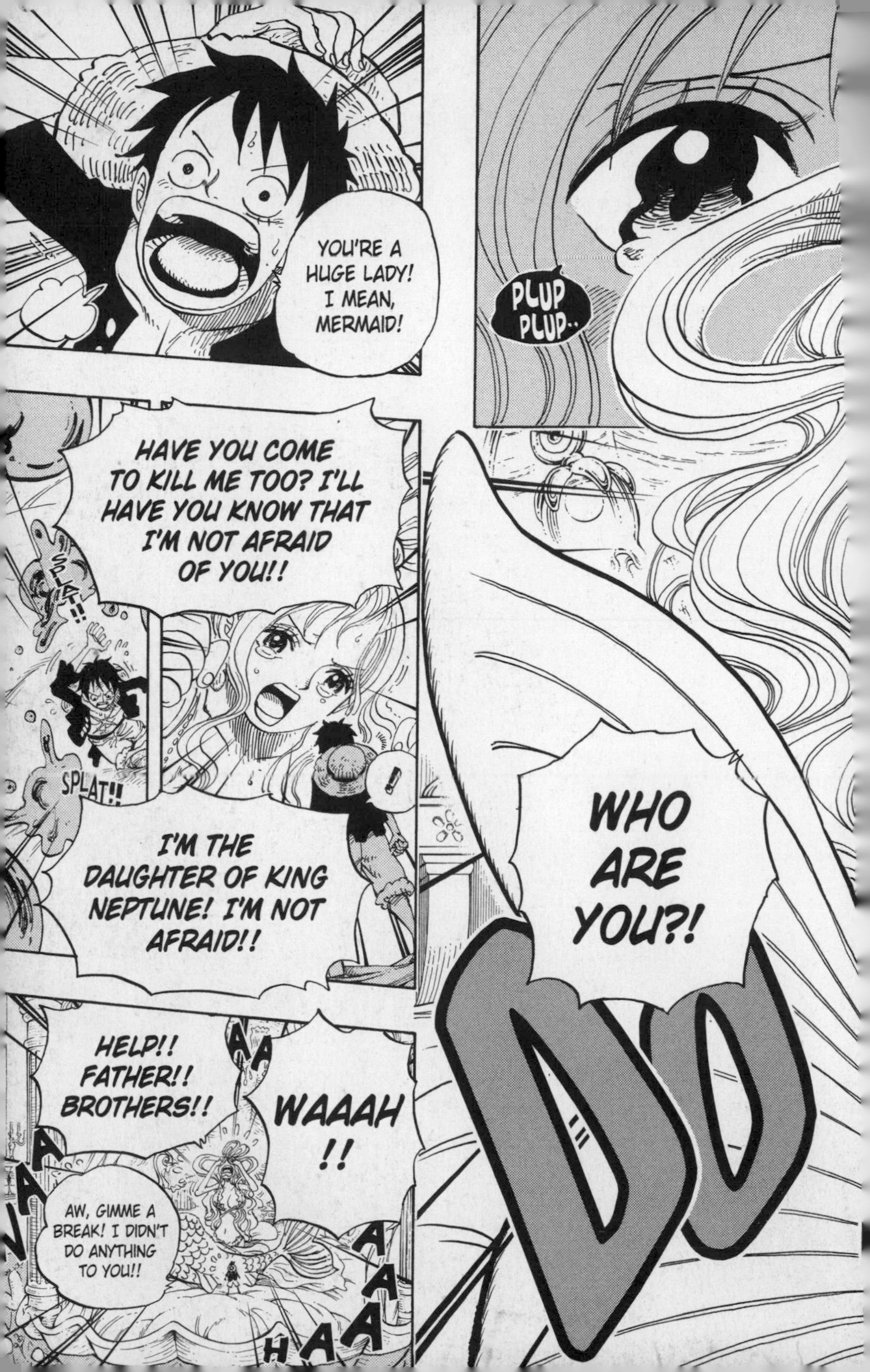
PLUP PLUP..
YOU'RE A HUGE LADY! I MEAN, MERMAID!
WHO ARE YOU?!
DO
HAVE YOU COME TO KILL ME TOO? I'LL HAVE YOU KNOW THAT I'M NOT AFRAID OF YOU!!
SPLAT!!
SPLAT!!
!
I'M THE DAUGHTER OF KING NEPTUNE! I'M NOT AFRAID!!
HELP!! FATHER!! BROTHERS!!
WAAAH!!
AW, GIMME A BREAK! I DIDN'T DO ANYTHING TO YOU!!

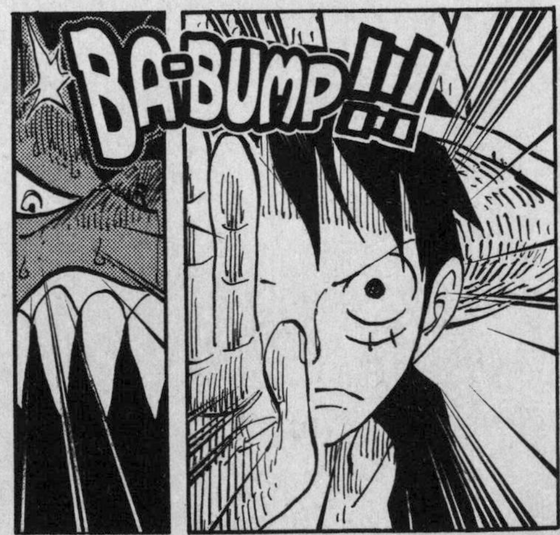
BA-BUMP!!!

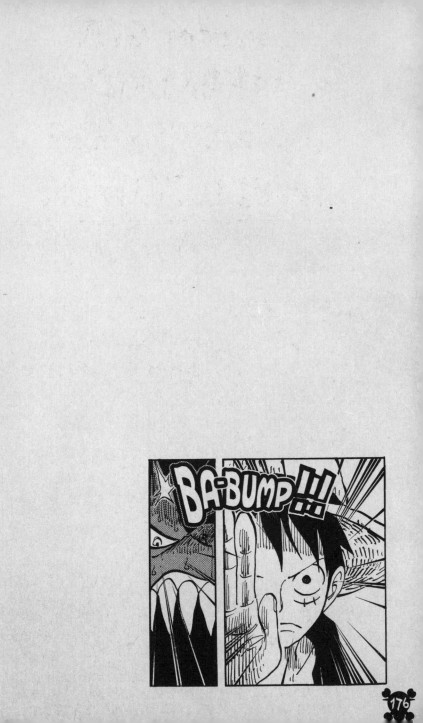

Chapter 613:
MERMAID PRINCESS OF SHELL TOWER

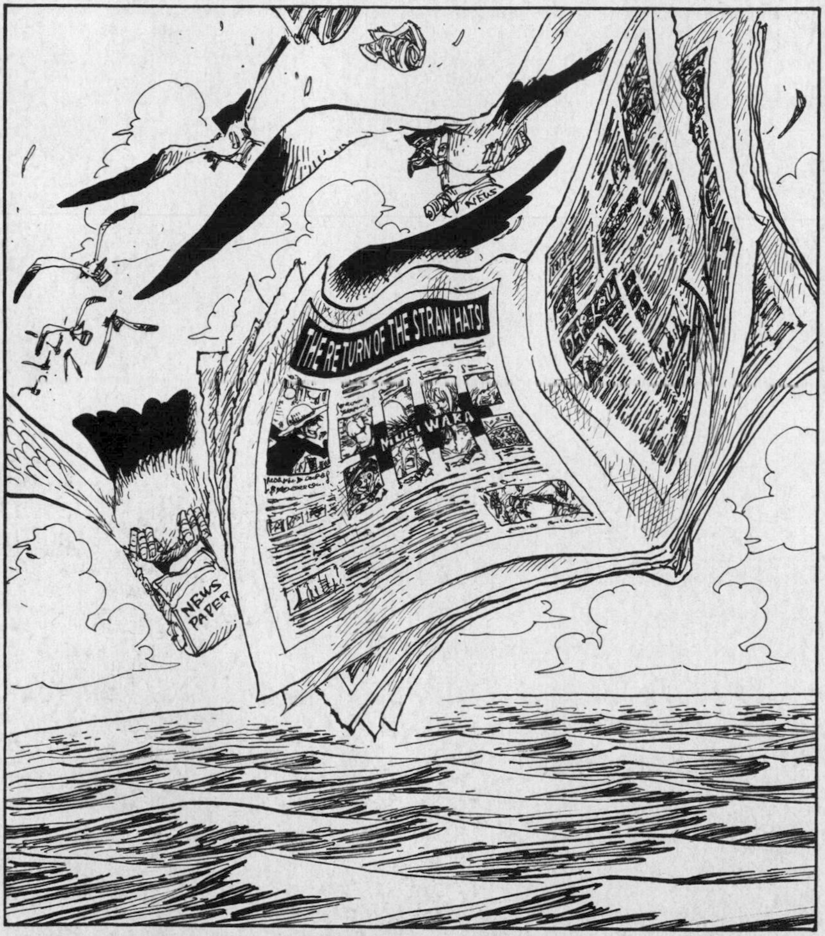
THE RETURN OF THE STRAW HATS!
MUGIWARA
NEWS
NEWS PAPER

LIMITED COVER SERIES, NO.19: DECKS OF THE WORLD, VOL. 1: "NEWS COO ACROSS THE SEAS"

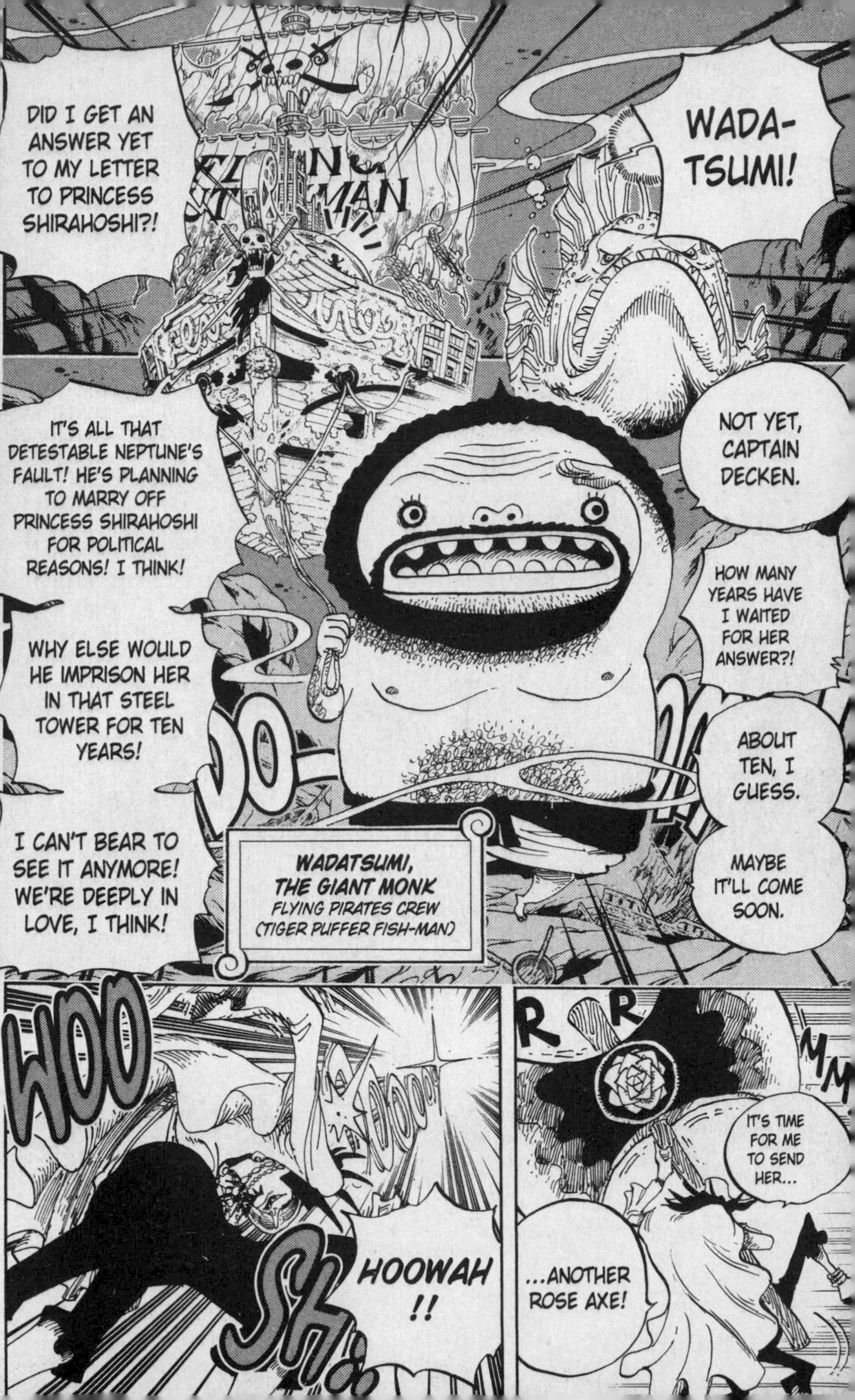
WADA-TSUMI!
DID I GET AN ANSWER YET TO MY LETTER TO PRINCESS SHIRAHOSHI?!
NOT YET, CAPTAIN DECKEN.
IT'S ALL THAT DETESTABLE NEPTUNE'S FAULT! HE'S PLANNING TO MARRY OFF PRINCESS SHIRAHOSHI FOR POLITICAL REASONS! I THINK!
HOW MANY YEARS HAVE I WAITED FOR HER ANSWER?!
WHY ELSE WOULD HE IMPRISON HER IN THAT STEEL TOWER FOR TEN YEARS!
ABOUT TEN, I GUESS.
MAYBE IT'LL COME SOON.
I CAN'T BEAR TO SEE IT ANYMORE! WE'RE DEEPLY IN LOVE, I THINK!
WADATSUMI, THE GIANT MONK
FLYING PIRATES CREW
(TIGER PUFFER FISH-MAN)
R R
MM
IT'S TIME FOR ME TO SEND HER...
...ANOTHER ROSE AXE!
WOO
HOOWAH !!
SH

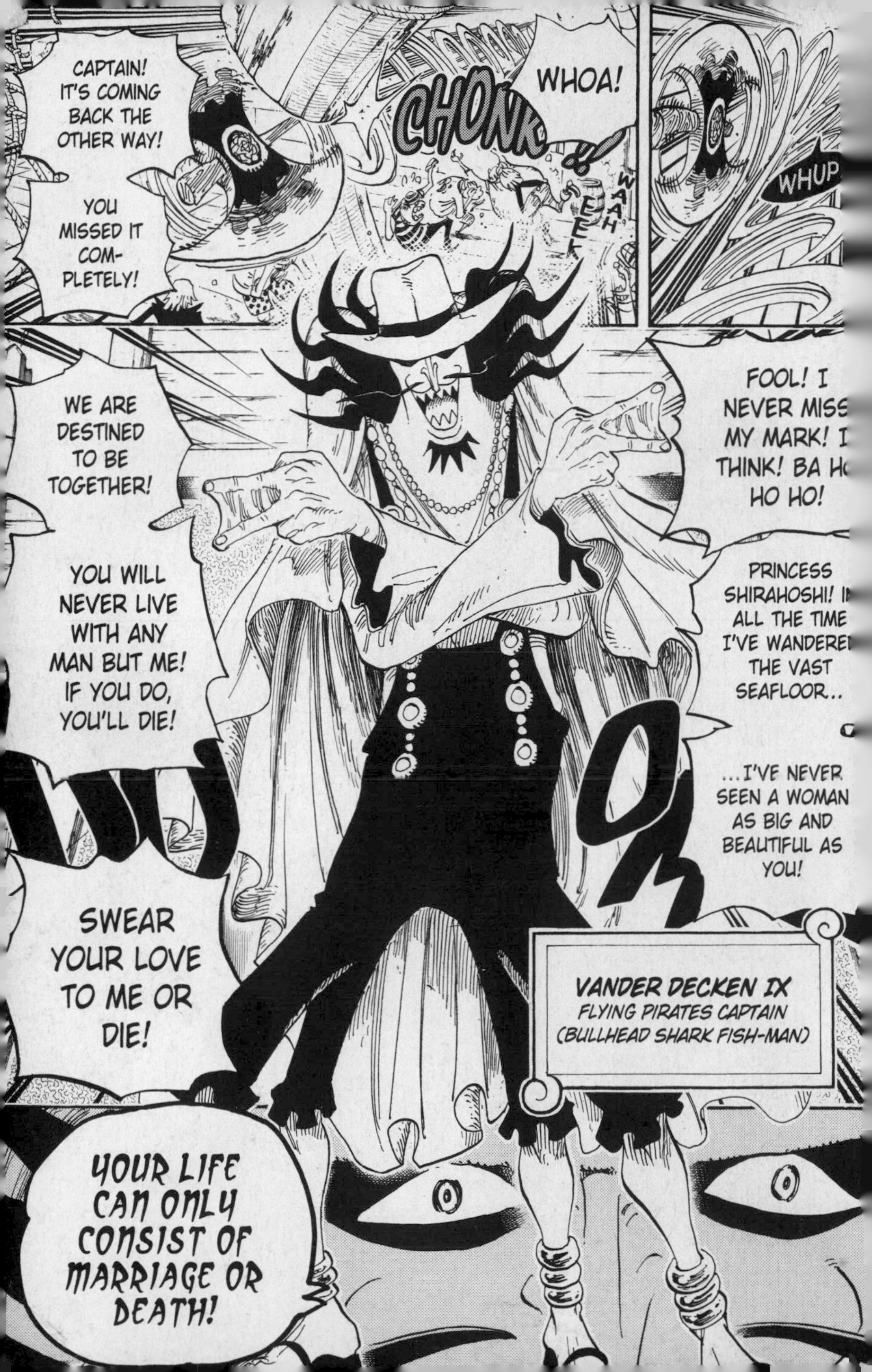
WHUP
WHOA!
CHONK
WAAH
EEK
CAPTAIN! IT'S COMING BACK THE OTHER WAY!
YOU MISSED IT COM-PLETELY!
FOOL! I NEVER MISS MY MARK! I THINK! BA HO HO HO!
PRINCESS SHIRAHOSHI! IN ALL THE TIME I'VE WANDERED THE VAST SEAFLOOR...
...I'VE NEVER SEEN A WOMAN AS BIG AND BEAUTIFUL AS YOU!
VANDER DECKEN IX
FLYING PIRATES CAPTAIN
(BULLHEAD SHARK FISH-MAN)
WE ARE DESTINED TO BE TOGETHER!
YOU WILL NEVER LIVE WITH ANY MAN BUT ME! IF YOU DO, YOU'LL DIE!
SWEAR YOUR LOVE TO ME OR DIE!
YOUR LIFE CAN ONLY CONSIST OF MARRIAGE OR DEATH!

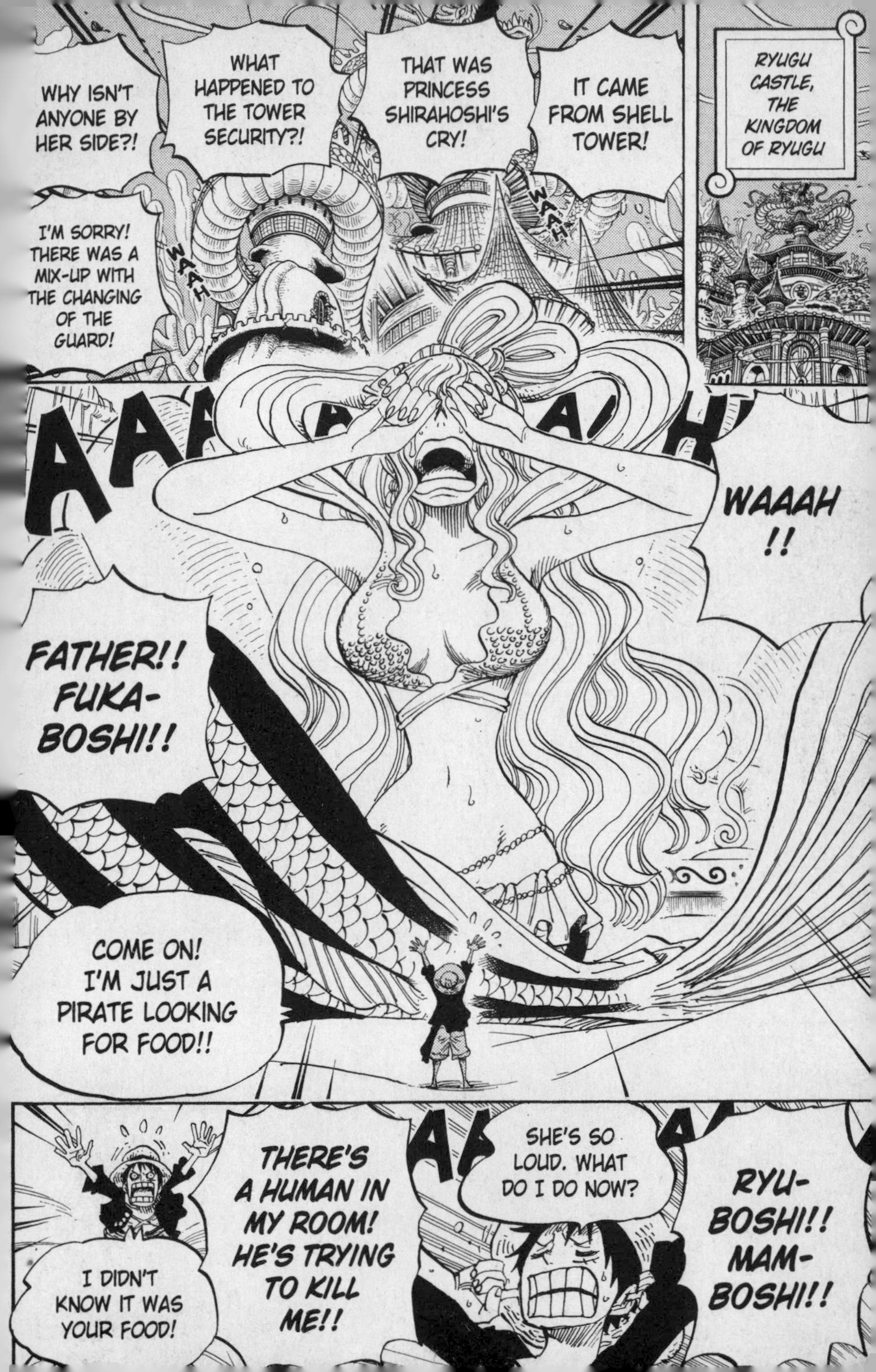
RYUGU CASTLE, THE KINGDOM OF RYUGU
IT CAME FROM SHELL TOWER!
THAT WAS PRINCESS SHIRAHOSHI'S CRY!
WAAH
WHAT HAPPENED TO THE TOWER SECURITY?!
WHY ISN'T ANYONE BY HER SIDE?!
WAAH
I'M SORRY! THERE WAS A MIX-UP WITH THE CHANGING OF THE GUARD!
WAAAH !!
FATHER!! FUKA-BOSHI!!
COME ON! I'M JUST A PIRATE LOOKING FOR FOOD!!
RYU-BOSHI!! MAM-BOSHI!!
SHE'S SO LOUD. WHAT DO I DO NOW?
THERE'S A HUMAN IN MY ROOM! HE'S TRYING TO KILL ME!!
I DIDN'T KNOW IT WAS YOUR FOOD!

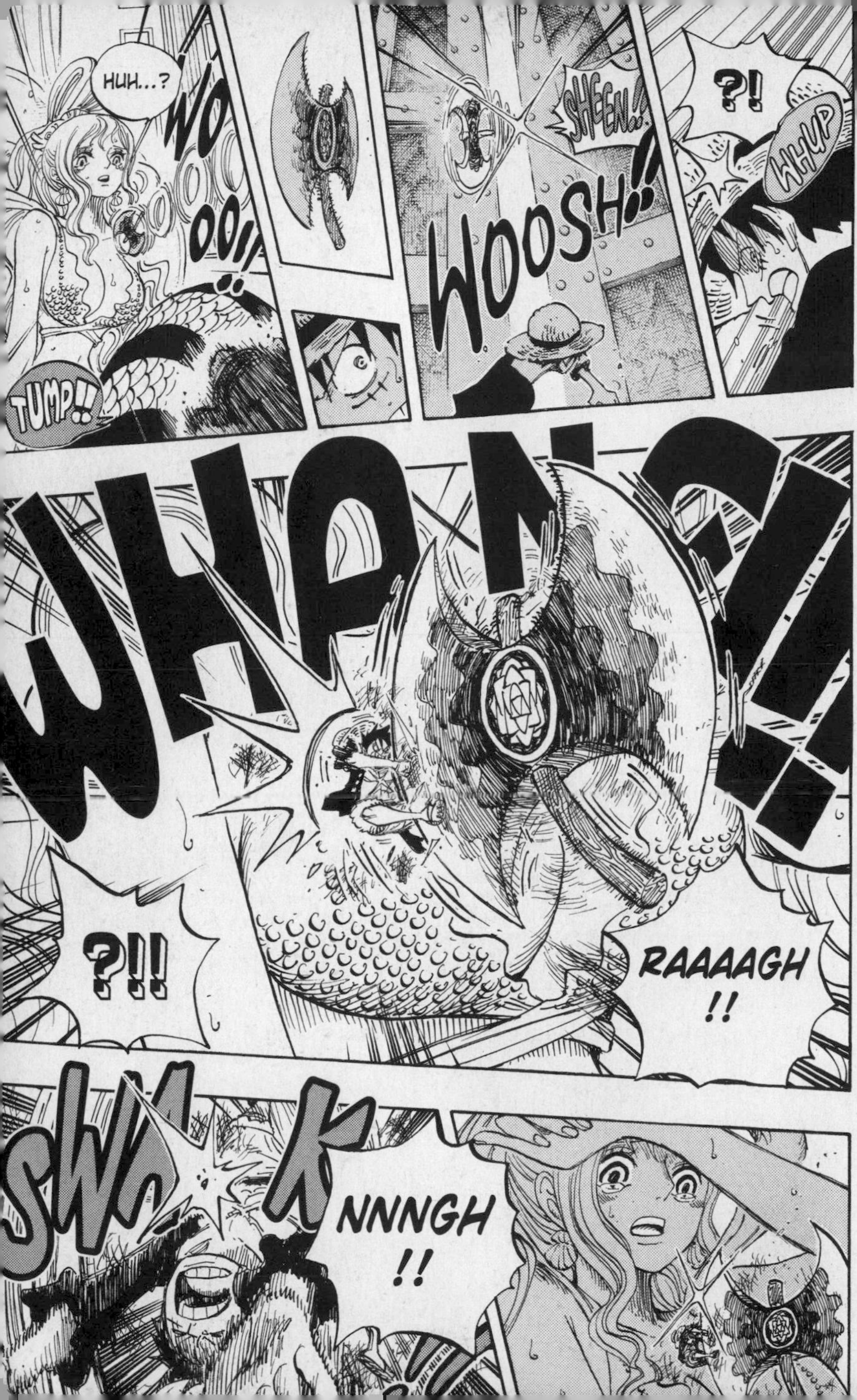
?!
WHUP
SHEEN..!!
WOOSH..!!
HUH...?
WOOOO!!
TUMP!!
WHANG!!
RAAAAGH!!
?!!
SWAK
NNNGH!!

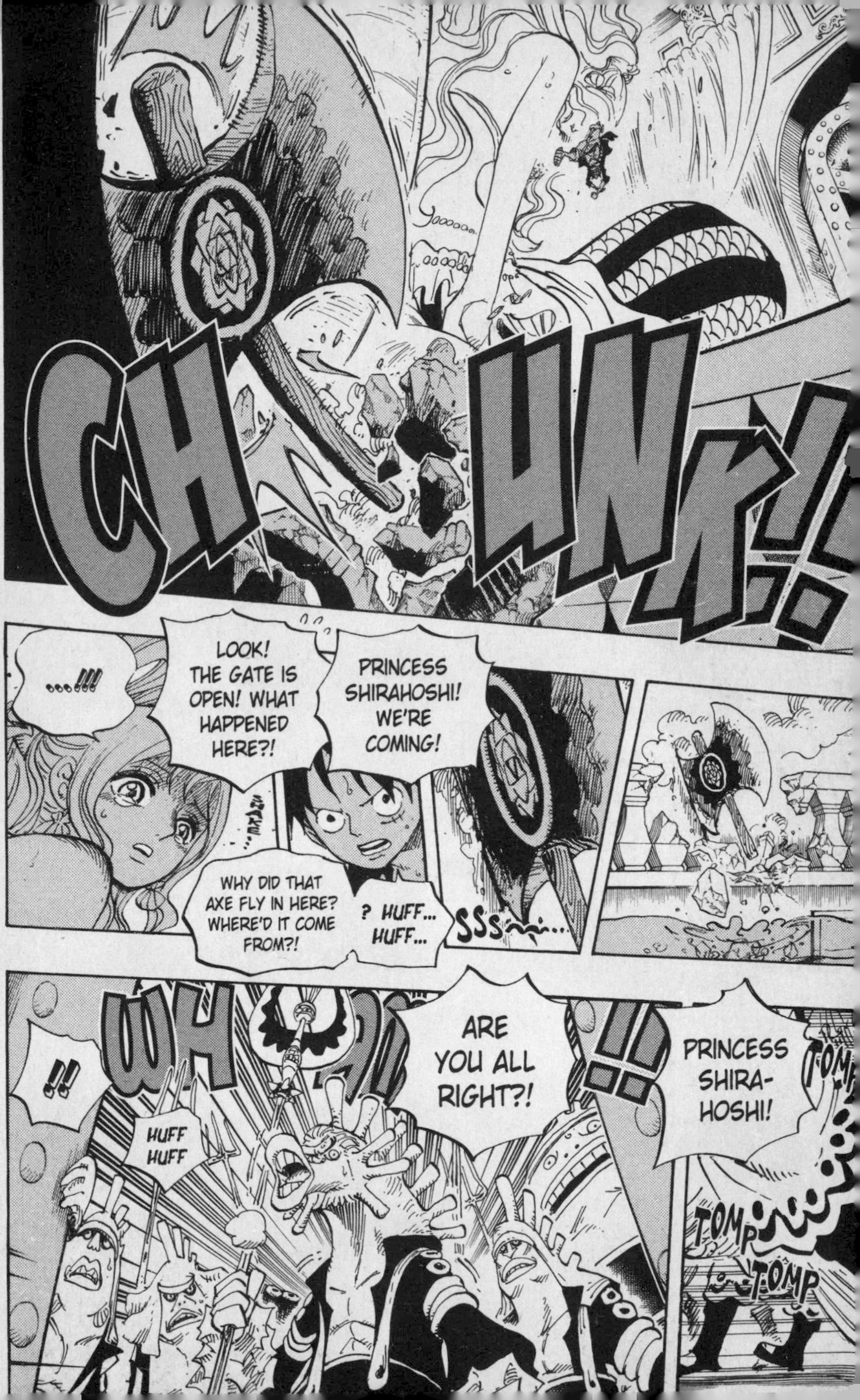
CHUNK!!
SSS~...
PRINCESS SHIRAHOSHI! WE'RE COMING!
? HUFF... HUFF...
LOOK! THE GATE IS OPEN! WHAT HAPPENED HERE?!
...!!!
WHY DID THAT AXE FLY IN HERE? WHERE'D IT COME FROM?!
TOMP
PRINCESS SHIRA-HOSHI!
TOMP TOMP
!!
ARE YOU ALL RIGHT?!
HUFF HUFF
!!

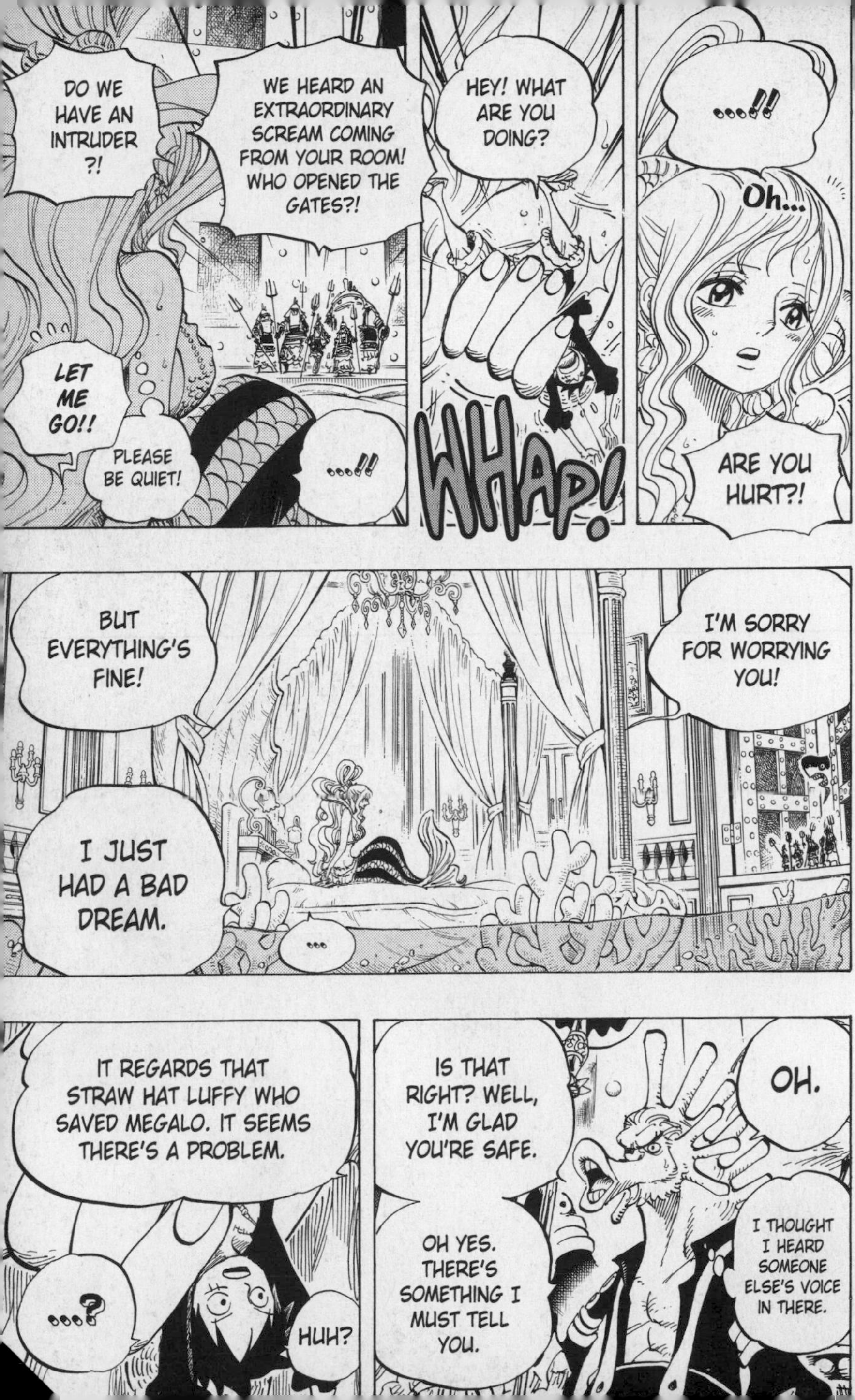
...!!
Oh...
ARE YOU HURT?!
HEY! WHAT ARE YOU DOING?
WHAP!
WE HEARD AN EXTRAORDINARY SCREAM COMING FROM YOUR ROOM! WHO OPENED THE GATES?!
DO WE HAVE AN INTRUDER?!
...!!
LET ME GO!!
PLEASE BE QUIET!
I'M SORRY FOR WORRYING YOU!
BUT EVERYTHING'S FINE!
I JUST HAD A BAD DREAM.
...
OH.
IS THAT RIGHT? WELL, I'M GLAD YOU'RE SAFE.
I THOUGHT I HEARD SOMEONE ELSE'S VOICE IN THERE.
OH YES. THERE'S SOMETHING I MUST TELL YOU.
IT REGARDS THAT STRAW HAT LUFFY WHO SAVED MEGALO. IT SEEMS THERE'S A PROBLEM.
HUH?
...?

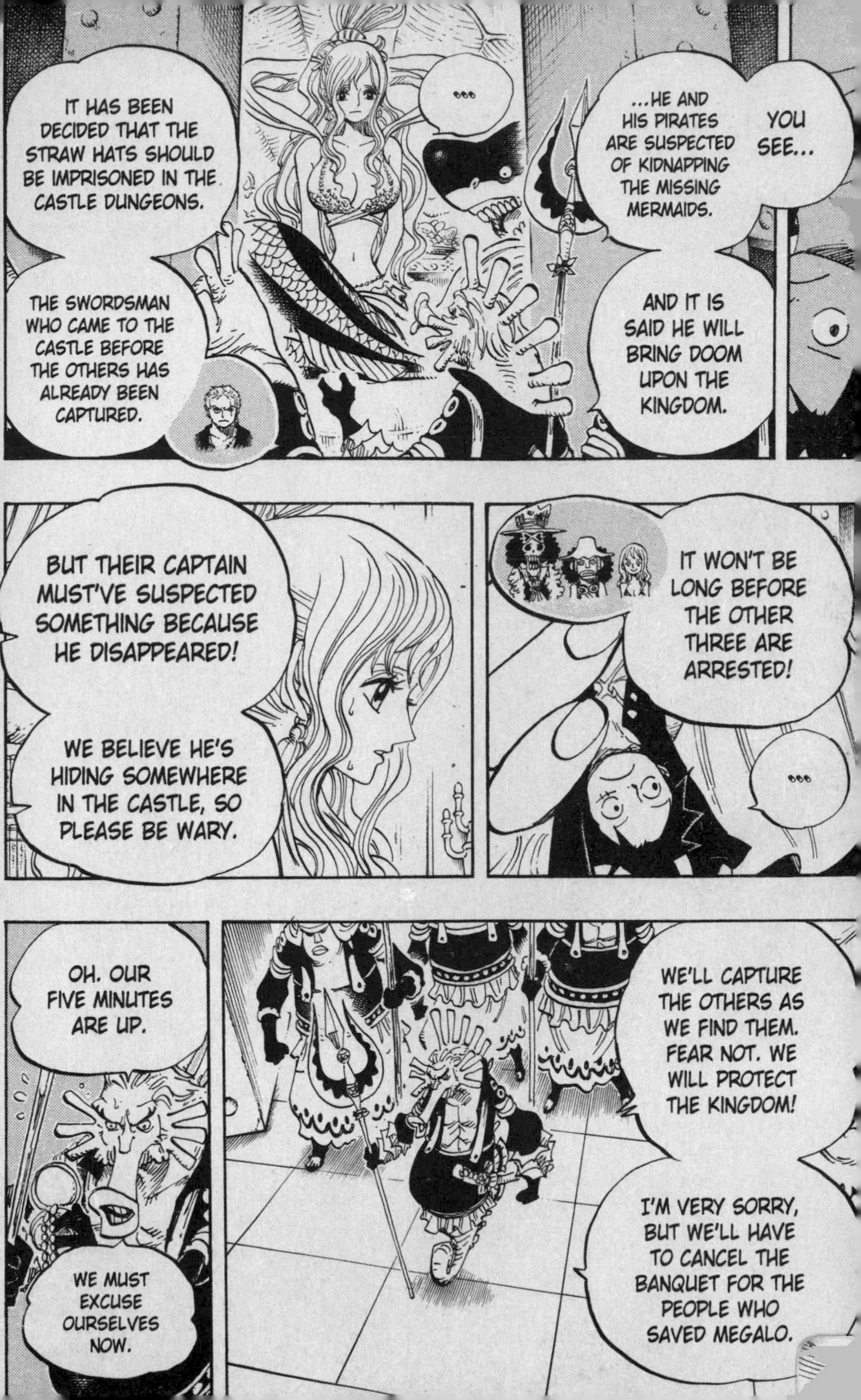
YOU SEE...
...HE AND HIS PIRATES ARE SUSPECTED OF KIDNAPPING THE MISSING MERMAIDS.
AND IT IS SAID HE WILL BRING DOOM UPON THE KINGDOM.
...
IT HAS BEEN DECIDED THAT THE STRAW HATS SHOULD BE IMPRISONED IN THE CASTLE DUNGEONS.
THE SWORDSMAN WHO CAME TO THE CASTLE BEFORE THE OTHERS HAS ALREADY BEEN CAPTURED.
IT WON'T BE LONG BEFORE THE OTHER THREE ARE ARRESTED!
...
BUT THEIR CAPTAIN MUST'VE SUSPECTED SOMETHING BECAUSE HE DISAPPEARED!
WE BELIEVE HE'S HIDING SOMEWHERE IN THE CASTLE, SO PLEASE BE WARY.
WE'LL CAPTURE THE OTHERS AS WE FIND THEM. FEAR NOT. WE WILL PROTECT THE KINGDOM!
I'M VERY SORRY, BUT WE'LL HAVE TO CANCEL THE BANQUET FOR THE PEOPLE WHO SAVED MEGALO.
OH. OUR FIVE MINUTES ARE UP.
WE MUST EXCUSE OURSELVES NOW.

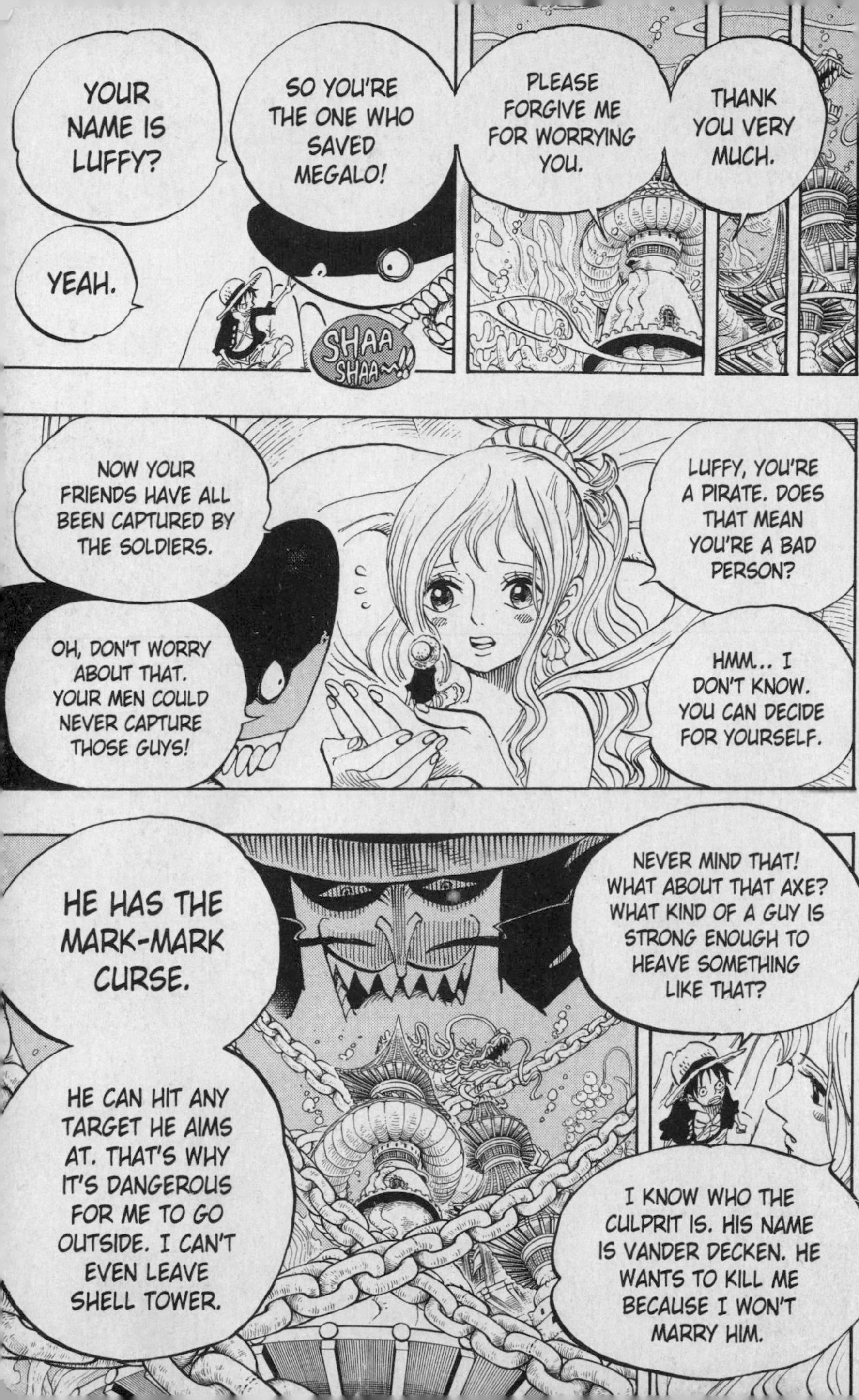
THANK YOU VERY MUCH.
PLEASE FORGIVE ME FOR WORRYING YOU.
SO YOU'RE THE ONE WHO SAVED MEGALO!
YOUR NAME IS LUFFY?
YEAH.
SHAA SHAA~!!
LUFFY, YOU'RE A PIRATE. DOES THAT MEAN YOU'RE A BAD PERSON?
HMM... I DON'T KNOW. YOU CAN DECIDE FOR YOURSELF.
NOW YOUR FRIENDS HAVE ALL BEEN CAPTURED BY THE SOLDIERS.
OH, DON'T WORRY ABOUT THAT. YOUR MEN COULD NEVER CAPTURE THOSE GUYS!
NEVER MIND THAT! WHAT ABOUT THAT AXE? WHAT KIND OF A GUY IS STRONG ENOUGH TO HEAVE SOMETHING LIKE THAT?
I KNOW WHO THE CULPRIT IS. HIS NAME IS VANDER DECKEN. HE WANTS TO KILL ME BECAUSE I WON'T MARRY HIM.
HE HAS THE MARK-MARK CURSE.
HE CAN HIT ANY TARGET HE AIMS AT. THAT'S WHY IT'S DANGEROUS FOR ME TO GO OUTSIDE. I CAN'T EVEN LEAVE SHELL TOWER.

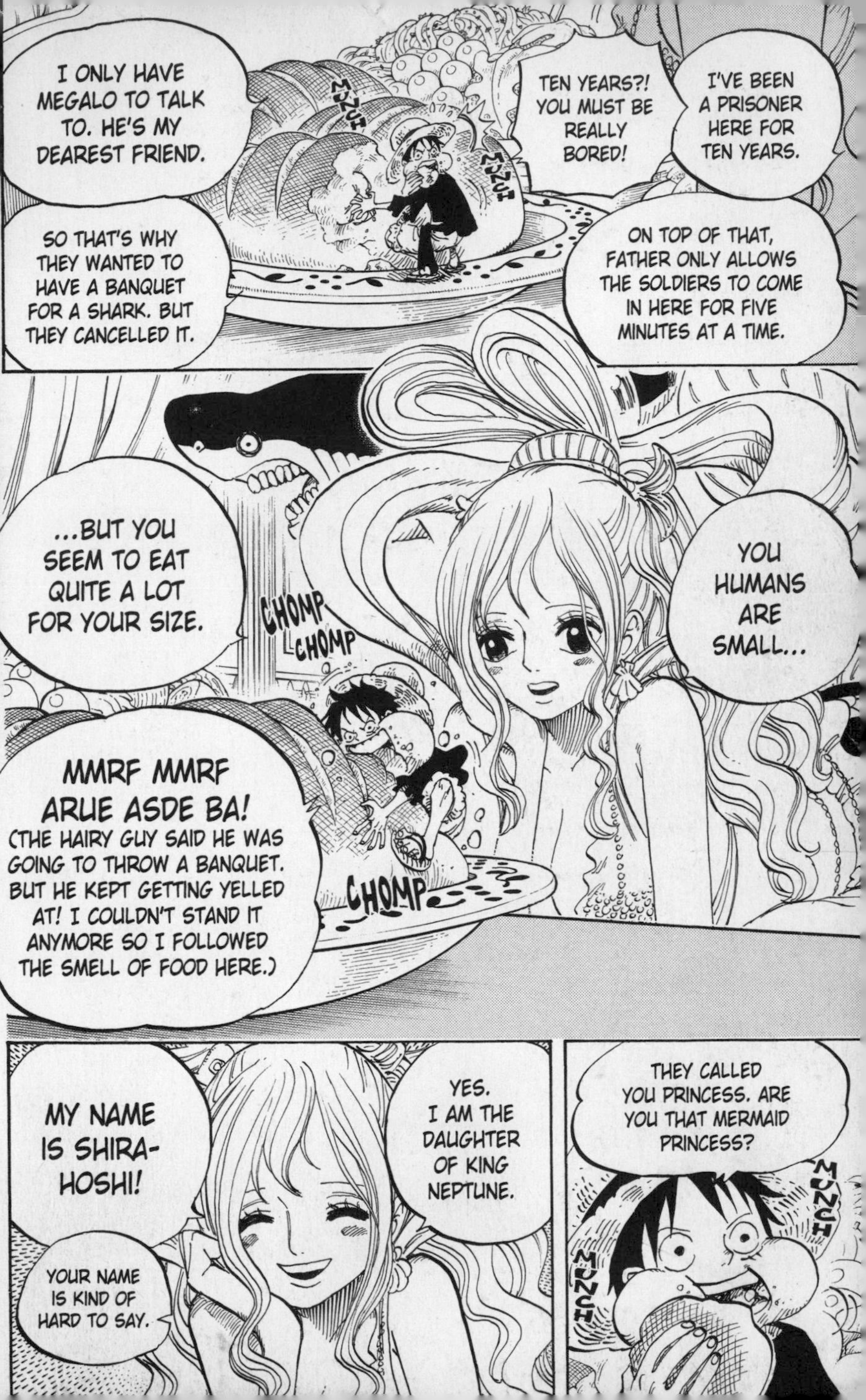
I'VE BEEN A PRISONER HERE FOR TEN YEARS.
TEN YEARS?! YOU MUST BE REALLY BORED!
ON TOP OF THAT, FATHER ONLY ALLOWS THE SOLDIERS TO COME IN HERE FOR FIVE MINUTES AT A TIME.
MUNCH
MUNCH
I ONLY HAVE MEGALO TO TALK TO. HE'S MY DEAREST FRIEND.
SO THAT'S WHY THEY WANTED TO HAVE A BANQUET FOR A SHARK. BUT THEY CANCELLED IT.
YOU HUMANS ARE SMALL...
...BUT YOU SEEM TO EAT QUITE A LOT FOR YOUR SIZE.
CHOMP
CHOMP
MMRF MMRF ARUE ASDE BA!
(THE HAIRY GUY SAID HE WAS GOING TO THROW A BANQUET. BUT HE KEPT GETTING YELLED AT! I COULDN'T STAND IT ANYMORE SO I FOLLOWED THE SMELL OF FOOD HERE.)
CHOMP
THEY CALLED YOU PRINCESS. ARE YOU THAT MERMAID PRINCESS?
MUNCH
MUNCH
YES. I AM THE DAUGHTER OF KING NEPTUNE.
MY NAME IS SHIRAHOSHI!
YOUR NAME IS KIND OF HARD TO SAY.

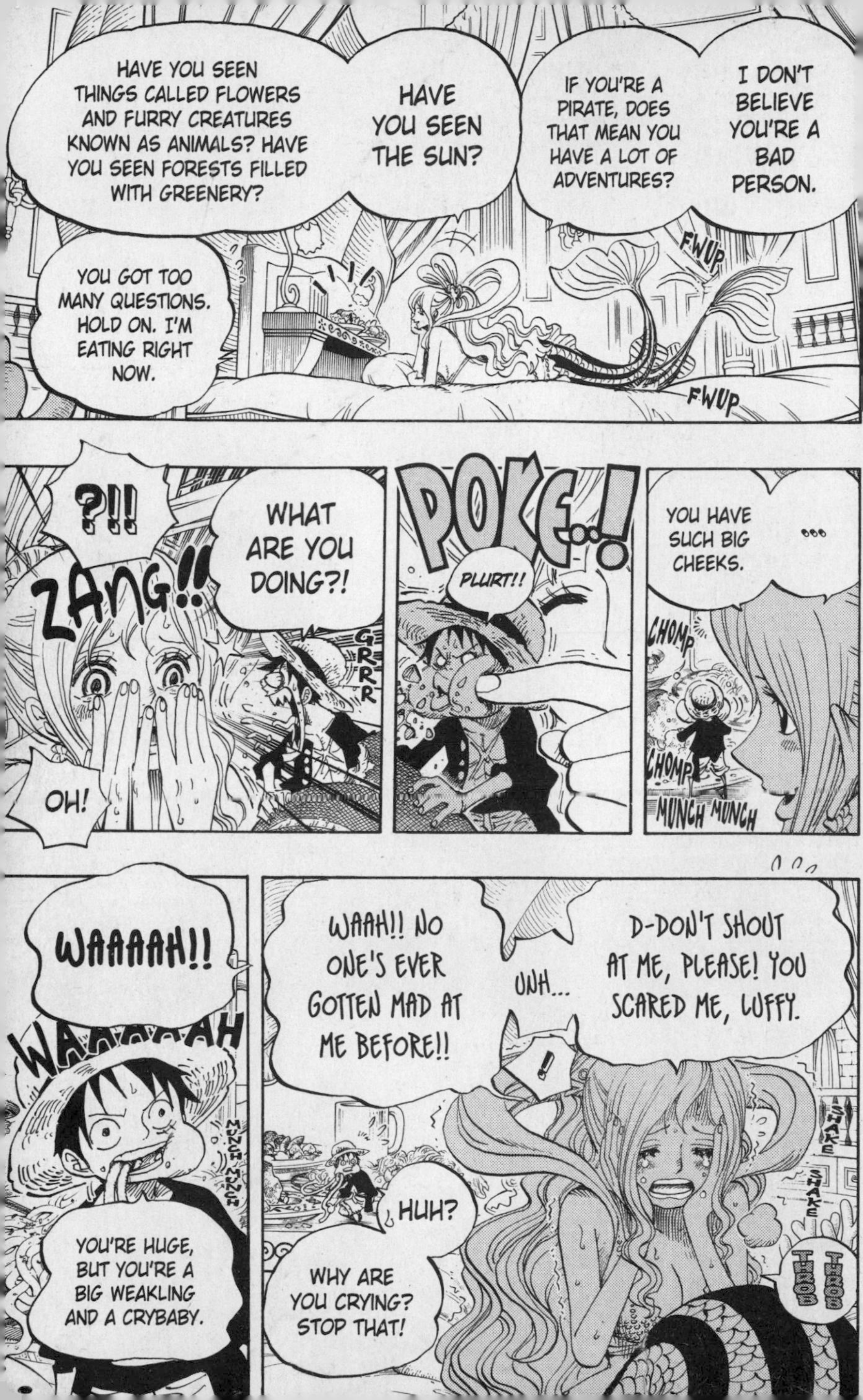
I DON'T BELIEVE YOU'RE A BAD PERSON.
IF YOU'RE A PIRATE, DOES THAT MEAN YOU HAVE A LOT OF ADVENTURES?
HAVE YOU SEEN THE SUN?
HAVE YOU SEEN THINGS CALLED FLOWERS AND FURRY CREATURES KNOWN AS ANIMALS? HAVE YOU SEEN FORESTS FILLED WITH GREENERY?
FWUP
FWUP
YOU GOT TOO MANY QUESTIONS. HOLD ON. I'M EATING RIGHT NOW.
...
YOU HAVE SUCH BIG CHEEKS.
CHOMP
CHOMP
MUNCH MUNCH
POKE..!
PLURT!!
WHAT ARE YOU DOING?!
GRRR
?!!
ZANG!!
OH!
D-DON'T SHOUT AT ME, PLEASE! YOU SCARED ME, LUFFY.
UNH...
WAAH!! NO ONE'S EVER GOTTEN MAD AT ME BEFORE!!
!
SHAKE
SHAKE
THROB THROB
HUH?
WHY ARE YOU CRYING? STOP THAT!
WAAAAH!!
WAAAAAH
MUNCH MUNCH
YOU'RE HUGE, BUT YOU'RE A BIG WEAKLING AND A CRYBABY.

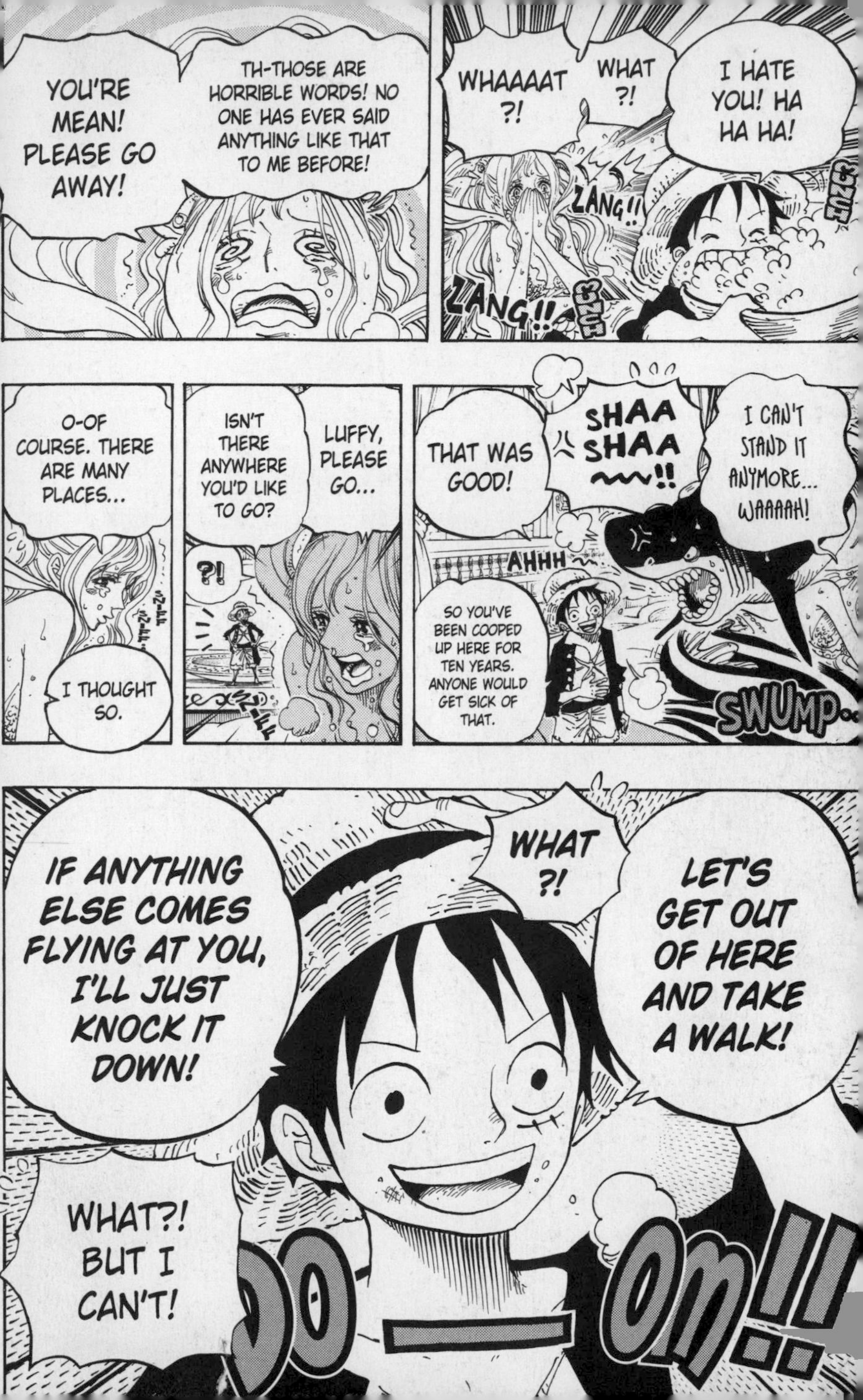
I HATE YOU! HA HA HA!
WHAT ?!
WHAAAAT ?!
ZANG!!
ZANG!!
TH-THOSE ARE HORRIBLE WORDS! NO ONE HAS EVER SAID ANYTHING LIKE THAT TO ME BEFORE!
YOU'RE MEAN! PLEASE GO AWAY!
I CAN'T STAND IT ANYMORE... WAAAAH!
SHAA SHAA ~~!!
THAT WAS GOOD!
AHHH
SO YOU'VE BEEN COOPED UP HERE FOR TEN YEARS. ANYONE WOULD GET SICK OF THAT.
SWUMP..
LUFFY, PLEASE GO...
ISN'T THERE ANYWHERE YOU'D LIKE TO GO?
?!
SNIFF
O-OF COURSE. THERE ARE MANY PLACES...
SNIFF SNIFF
I THOUGHT SO.
LET'S GET OUT OF HERE AND TAKE A WALK!
WHAT ?!
IF ANYTHING ELSE COMES FLYING AT YOU, I'LL JUST KNOCK IT DOWN!
WHAT?! BUT I CAN'T!
DOO—OM!!

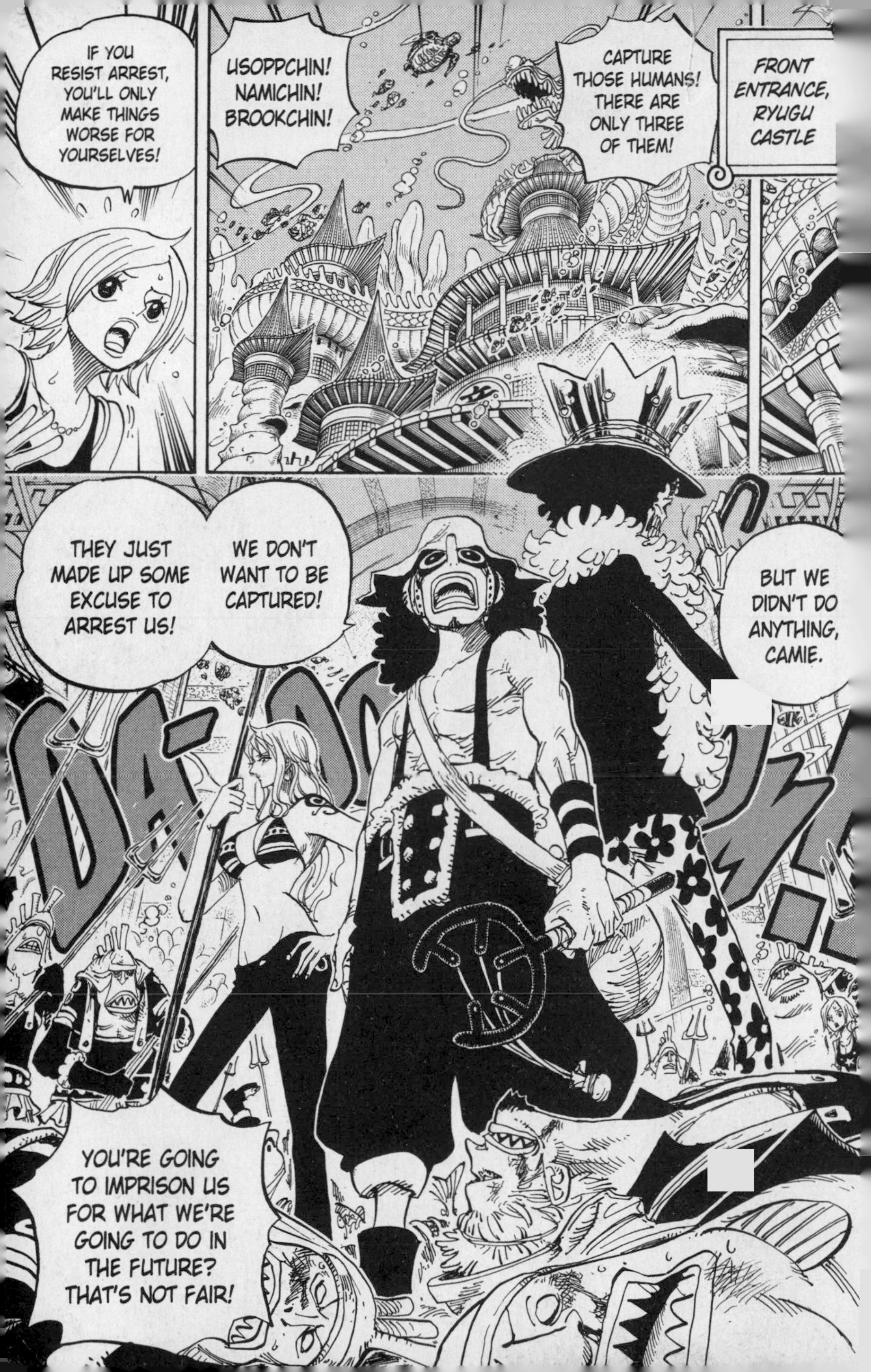
FRONT ENTRANCE, RYUGU CASTLE
CAPTURE THOSE HUMANS! THERE ARE ONLY THREE OF THEM!
USOPPCHIN! NAMICHIN! BROOKCHIN!
IF YOU RESIST ARREST, YOU'LL ONLY MAKE THINGS WORSE FOR YOURSELVES!
BUT WE DIDN'T DO ANYTHING, CAMIE.
WE DON'T WANT TO BE CAPTURED!
THEY JUST MADE UP SOME EXCUSE TO ARREST US!
YOU'RE GOING TO IMPRISON US FOR WHAT WE'RE GOING TO DO IN THE FUTURE? THAT'S NOT FAIR!

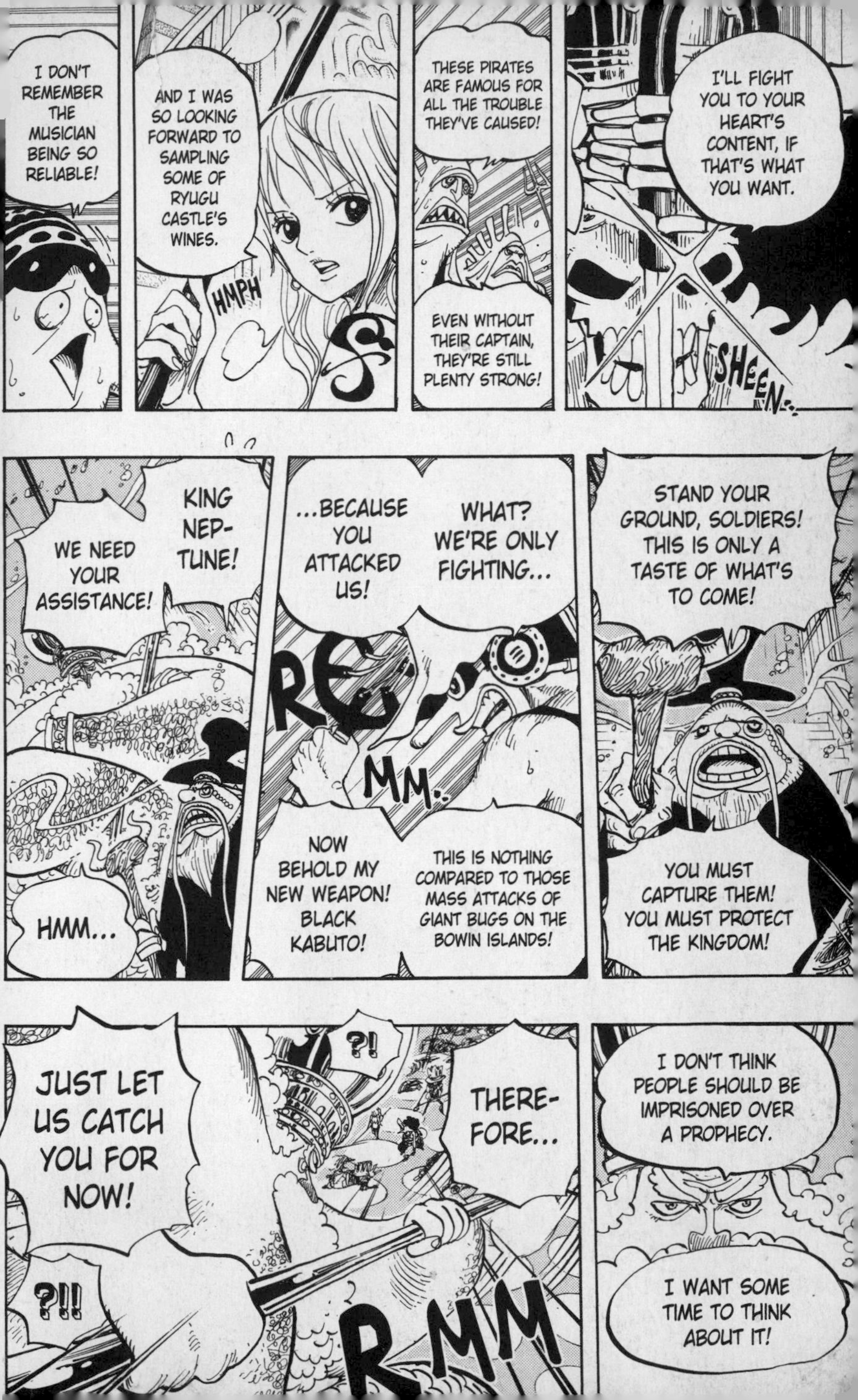
I'LL FIGHT YOU TO YOUR HEART'S CONTENT, IF THAT'S WHAT YOU WANT.
SHEEN...
THESE PIRATES ARE FAMOUS FOR ALL THE TROUBLE THEY'VE CAUSED!
EVEN WITHOUT THEIR CAPTAIN, THEY'RE STILL PLENTY STRONG!
AND I WAS SO LOOKING FORWARD TO SAMPLING SOME OF RYUGU CASTLE'S WINES.
HMPH
I DON'T REMEMBER THE MUSICIAN BEING SO RELIABLE!
STAND YOUR GROUND, SOLDIERS! THIS IS ONLY A TASTE OF WHAT'S TO COME!
YOU MUST CAPTURE THEM! YOU MUST PROTECT THE KINGDOM!
WHAT? WE'RE ONLY FIGHTING...
...BECAUSE YOU ATTACKED US!
REMM..
THIS IS NOTHING COMPARED TO THOSE MASS ATTACKS OF GIANT BUGS ON THE BOWIN ISLANDS!
NOW BEHOLD MY NEW WEAPON! BLACK KABUTO!
KING NEP-TUNE!
WE NEED YOUR ASSISTANCE!
HMM...
I DON'T THINK PEOPLE SHOULD BE IMPRISONED OVER A PROPHECY.
I WANT SOME TIME TO THINK ABOUT IT!
THERE-FORE...
?!
RMM
JUST LET US CATCH YOU FOR NOW!
?!!

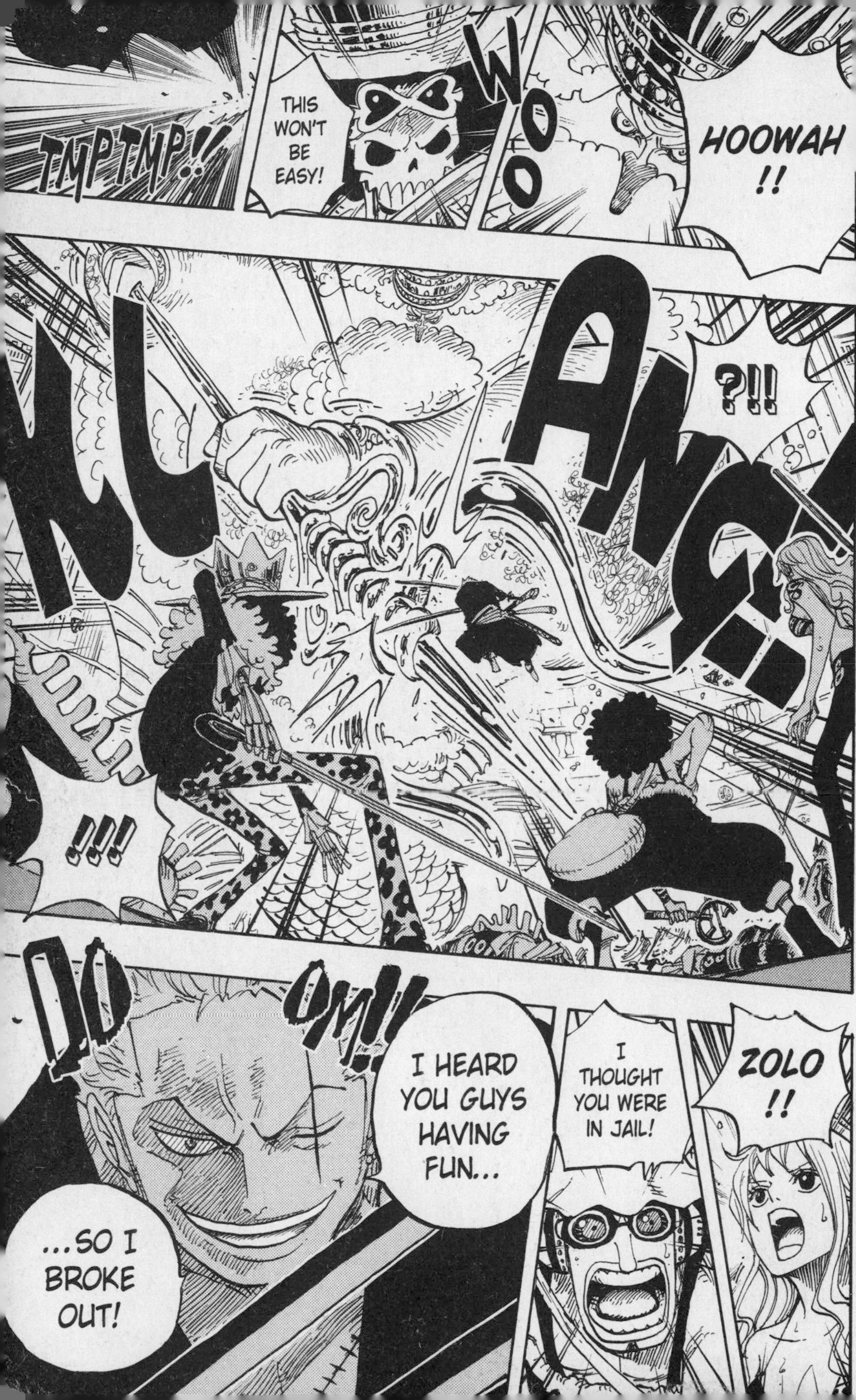
HOOWAH !!
WOOO
THIS WON'T BE EASY!
TMP TMP!!
?!!
!!!
ZOLO !!
I THOUGHT YOU WERE IN JAIL!
DOOM!!
I HEARD YOU GUYS HAVING FUN...
...SO I BROKE OUT!

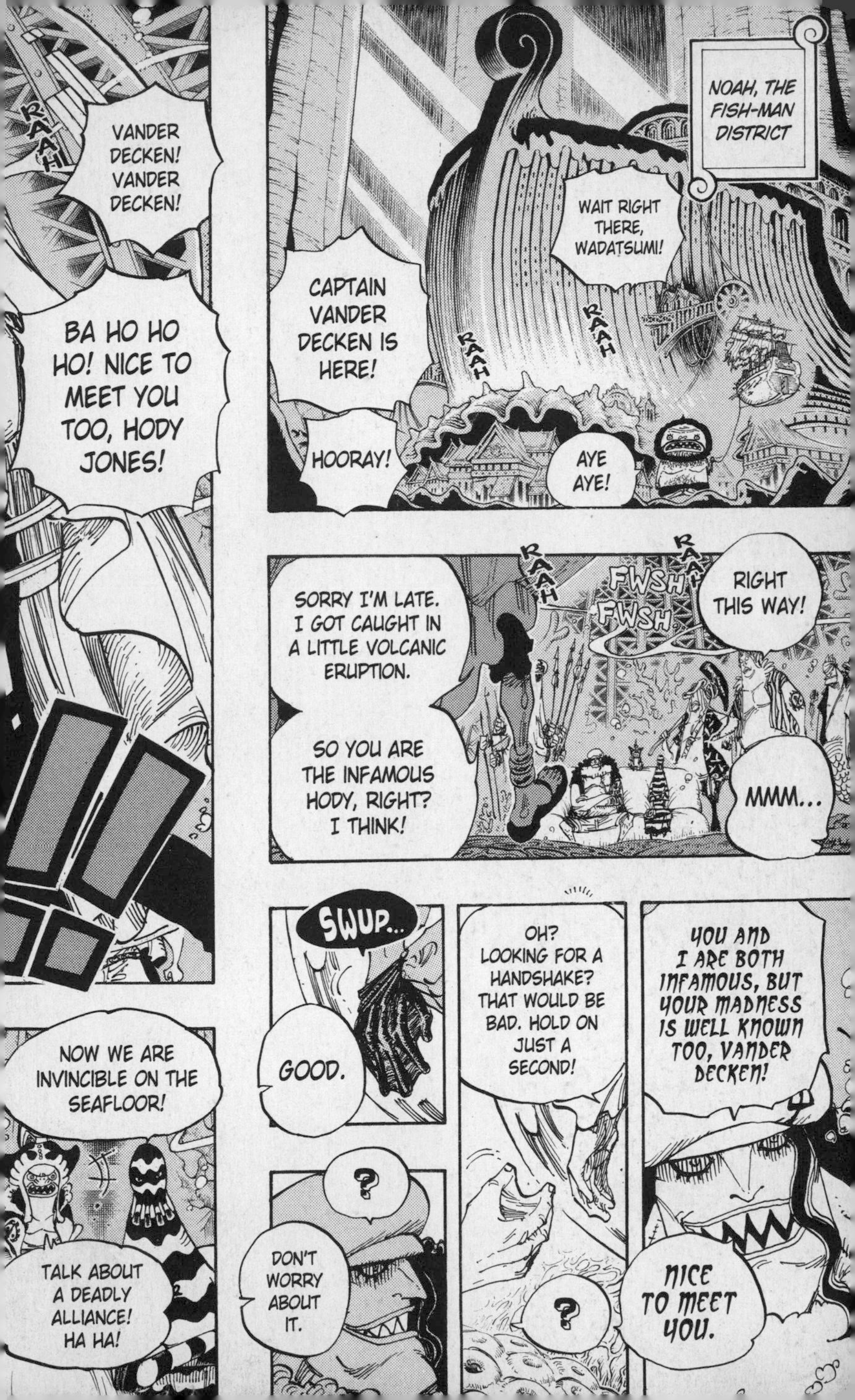
NOAH, THE FISH-MAN DISTRICT
WAIT RIGHT THERE, WADATSUMI!
RAAH
RAAH
CAPTAIN VANDER DECKEN IS HERE!
AYE AYE!
HOORAY!
RAAH
RAAH
FWSH FWSH
RIGHT THIS WAY!
SORRY I'M LATE. I GOT CAUGHT IN A LITTLE VOLCANIC ERUPTION.
MMM...
SO YOU ARE THE INFAMOUS HODY, RIGHT? I THINK!
YOU AND I ARE BOTH INFAMOUS, BUT YOUR MADNESS IS WELL KNOWN TOO, VANDER DECKEN!
NICE TO MEET YOU.
OH? LOOKING FOR A HANDSHAKE? THAT WOULD BE BAD. HOLD ON JUST A SECOND!
?
SWUP...
GOOD.
?
DON'T WORRY ABOUT IT.
RAAH
VANDER DECKEN! VANDER DECKEN!
BA HO HO HO! NICE TO MEET YOU TOO, HODY JONES!
NOW WE ARE INVINCIBLE ON THE SEAFLOOR!
TALK ABOUT A DEADLY ALLIANCE! HA HA!

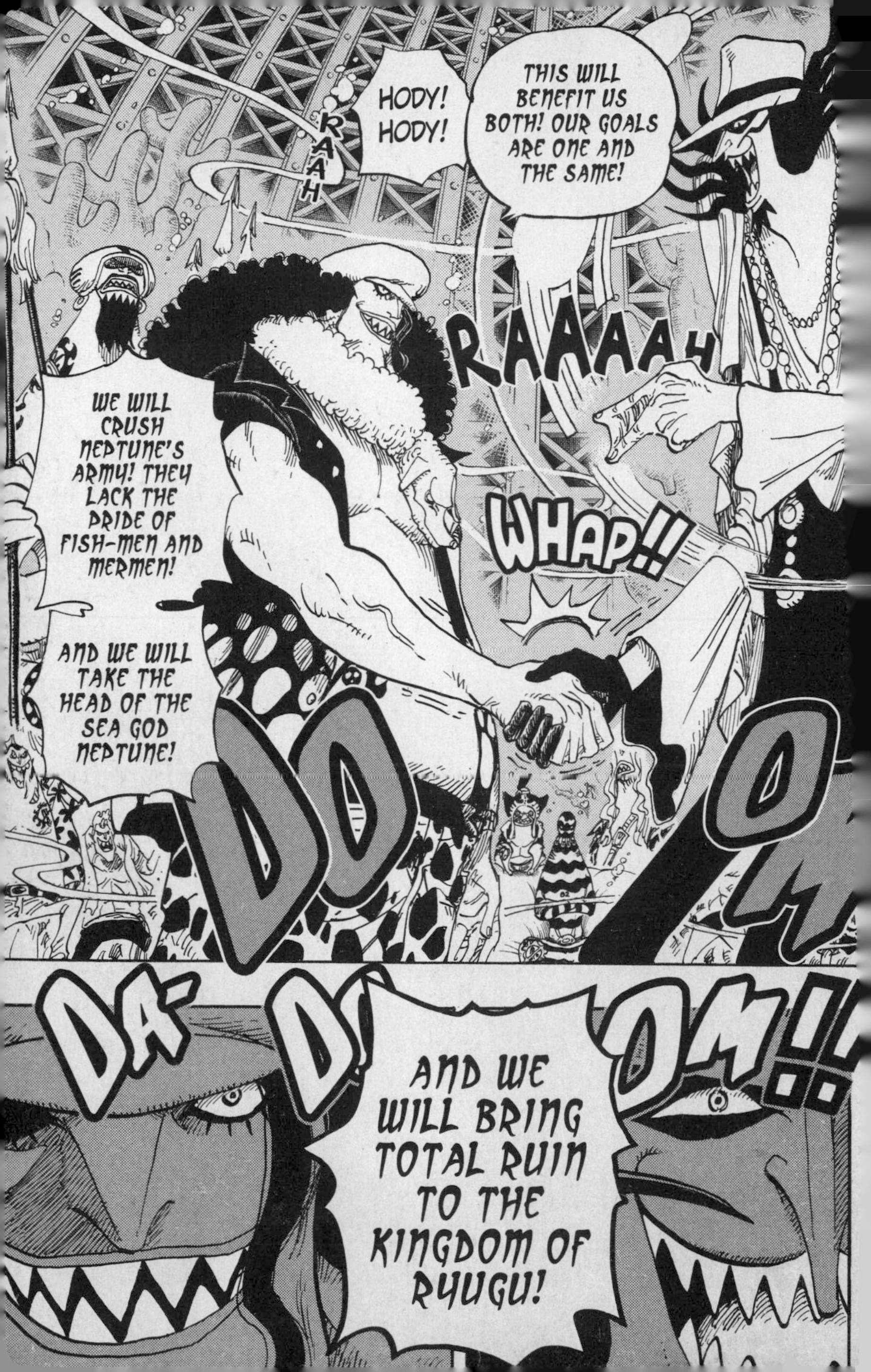
THIS WILL BENEFIT US BOTH! OUR GOALS ARE ONE AND THE SAME!
HODY! HODY!
RAAH
RAAAAH
WHAP!!
WE WILL CRUSH NEPTUNE'S ARMY! THEY LACK THE PRIDE OF FISH-MEN AND MERMEN!
AND WE WILL TAKE THE HEAD OF THE SEA GOD NEPTUNE!
DA-
OM!!
AND WE WILL BRING TOTAL RUIN TO THE KINGDOM OF RYUGU!

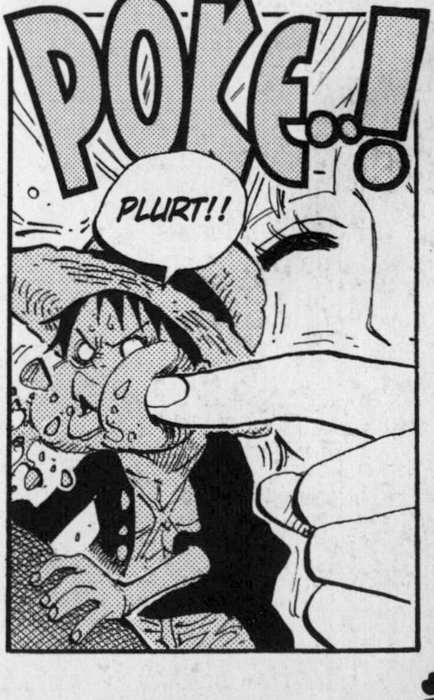
POKE...!
PLURT!!

Chapter 614:

TOO LATE NOW

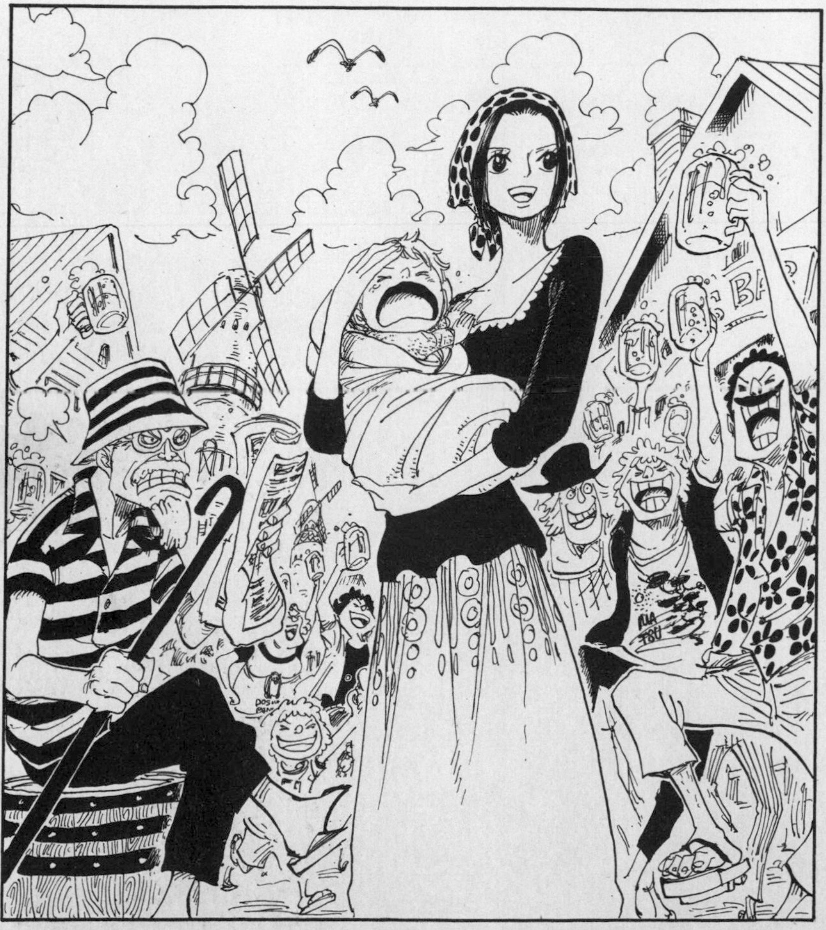

DECKS OF THE WORLD, VOL. 2: "WINDMILL VILLAGE"

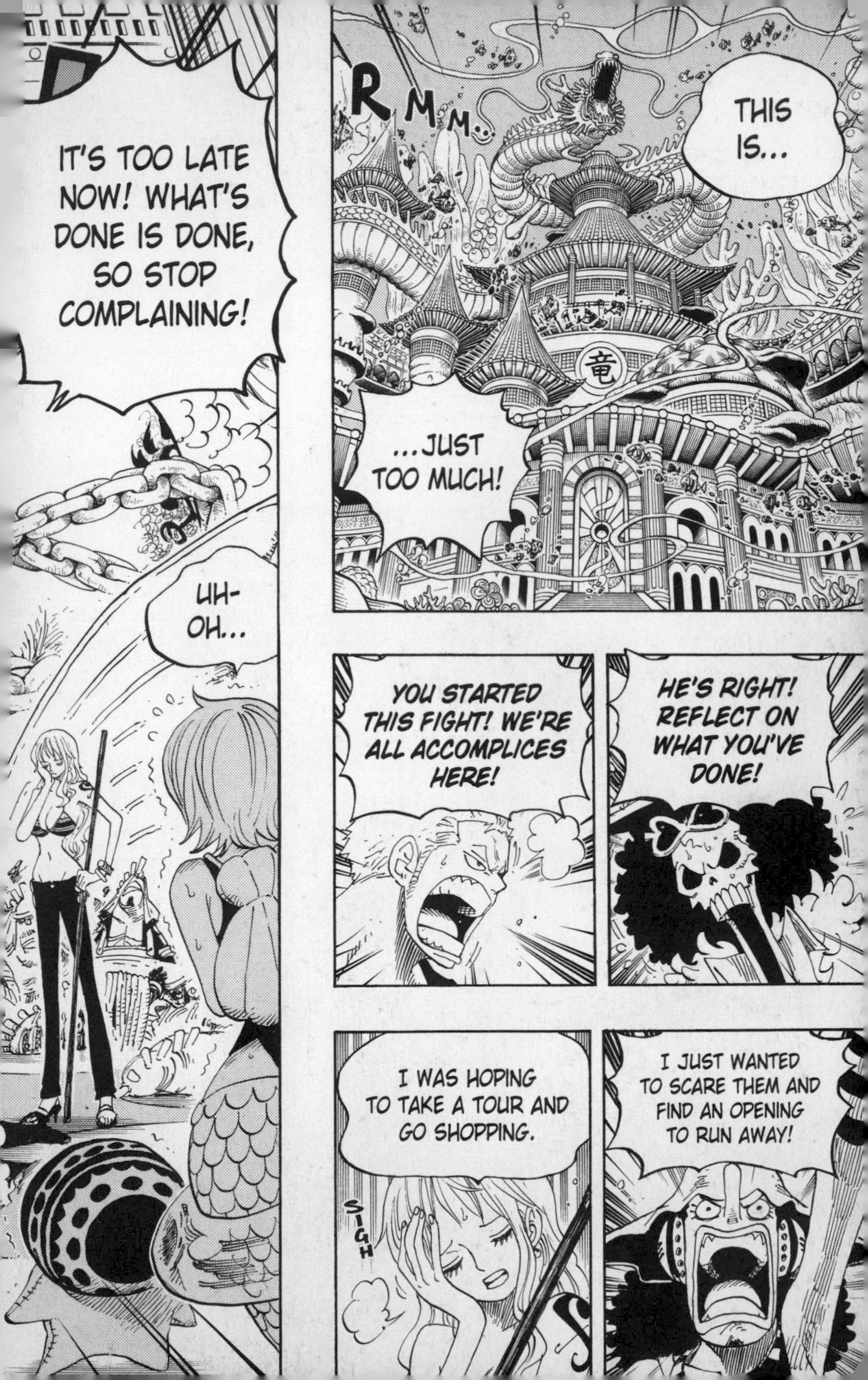
RMMM...
THIS IS...
...JUST TOO MUCH!
HE'S RIGHT! REFLECT ON WHAT YOU'VE DONE!
YOU STARTED THIS FIGHT! WE'RE ALL ACCOMPLICES HERE!
I JUST WANTED TO SCARE THEM AND FIND AN OPENING TO RUN AWAY!
I WAS HOPING TO TAKE A TOUR AND GO SHOPPING.
SIGH
IT'S TOO LATE NOW! WHAT'S DONE IS DONE, SO STOP COMPLAINING!
UH-OH...

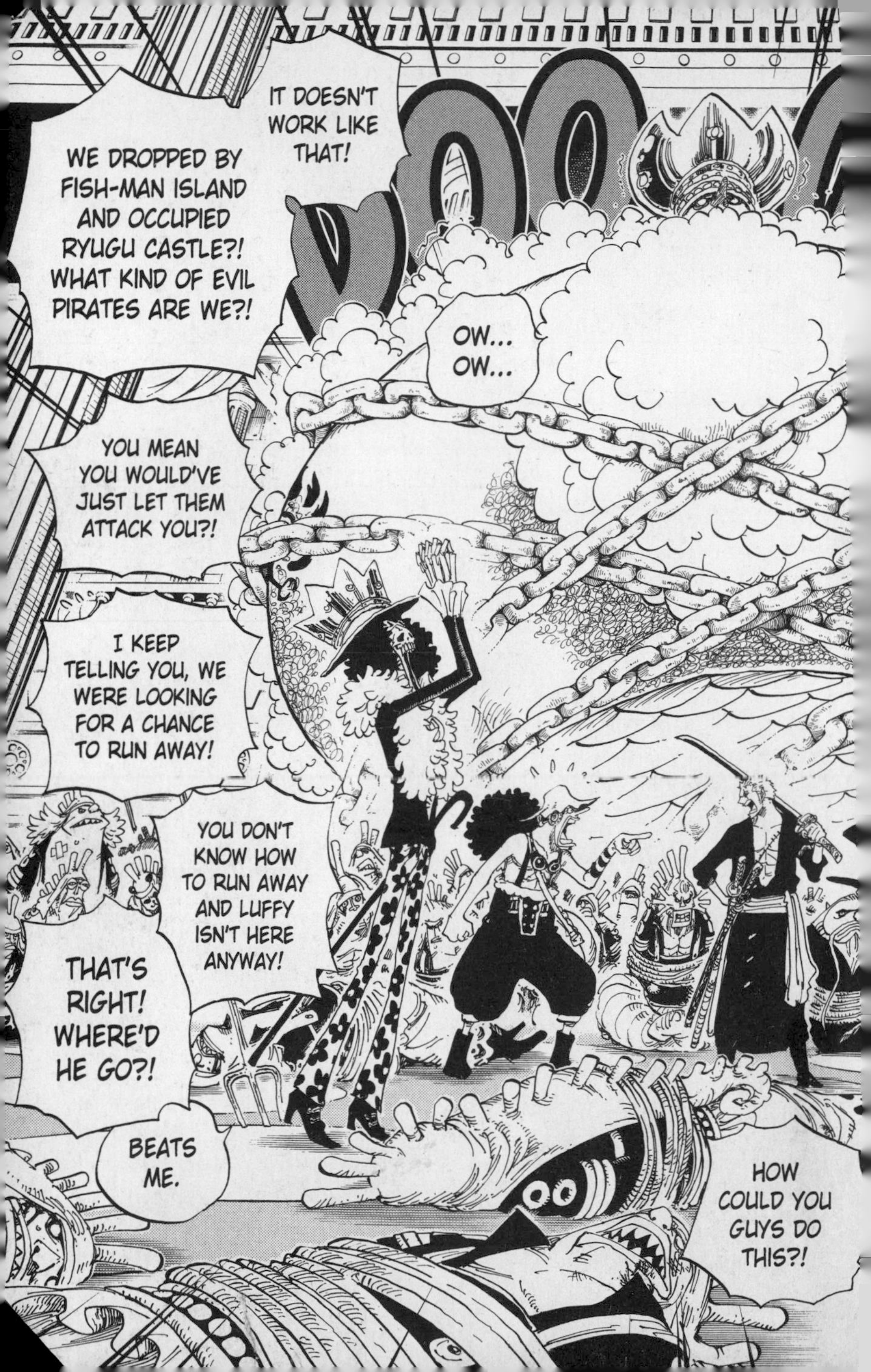
IT DOESN'T WORK LIKE THAT!
WE DROPPED BY FISH-MAN ISLAND AND OCCUPIED RYUGU CASTLE?! WHAT KIND OF EVIL PIRATES ARE WE?!
OW... OW...
YOU MEAN YOU WOULD'VE JUST LET THEM ATTACK YOU?!
I KEEP TELLING YOU, WE WERE LOOKING FOR A CHANCE TO RUN AWAY!
YOU DON'T KNOW HOW TO RUN AWAY AND LUFFY ISN'T HERE ANYWAY!
THAT'S RIGHT! WHERE'D HE GO?!
BEATS ME.
HOW COULD YOU GUYS DO THIS?!

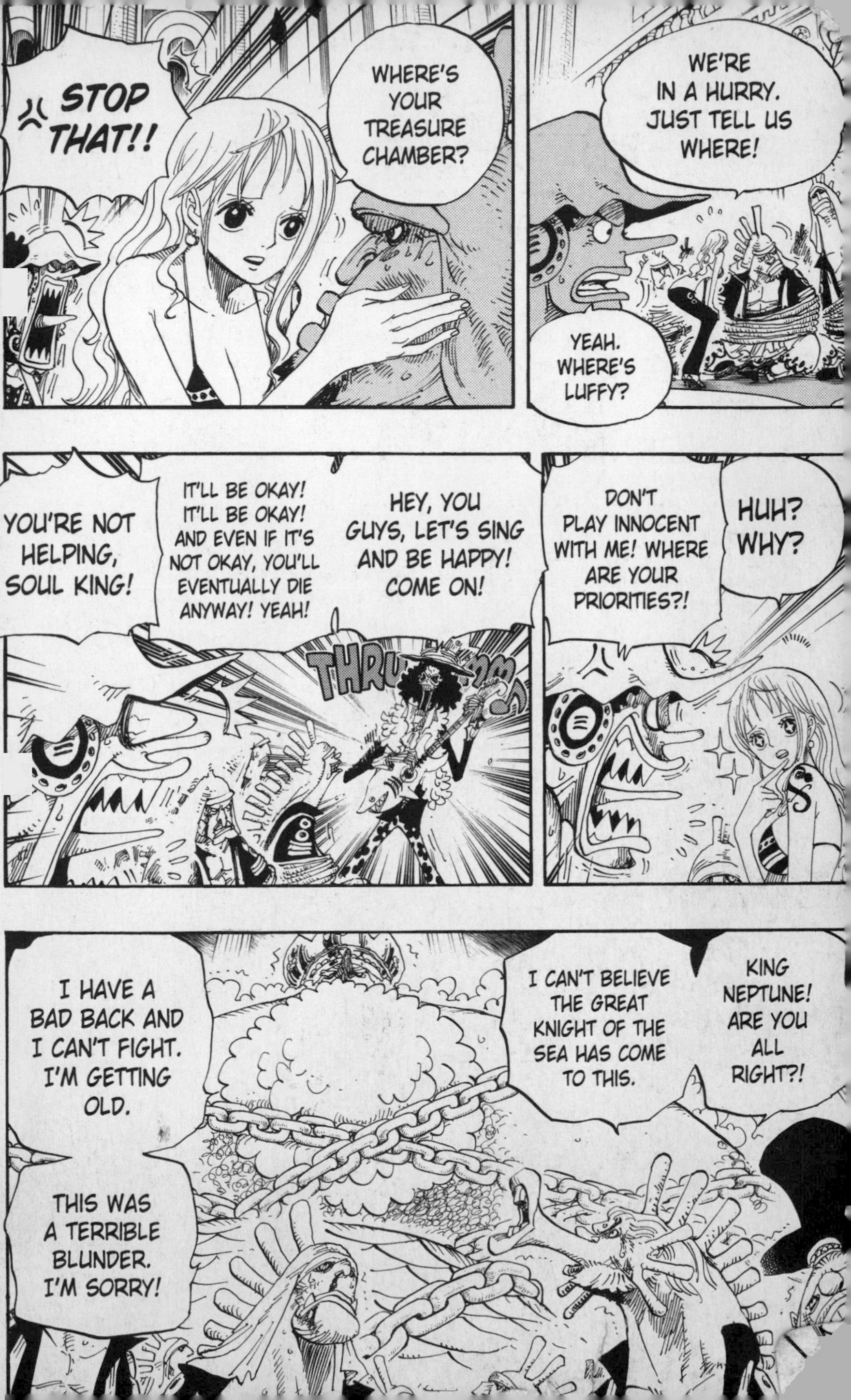
WE'RE IN A HURRY. JUST TELL US WHERE!
YEAH. WHERE'S LUFFY?
WHERE'S YOUR TREASURE CHAMBER?
STOP THAT!!
HUH? WHY?
DON'T PLAY INNOCENT WITH ME! WHERE ARE YOUR PRIORITIES?!
HEY, YOU GUYS, LET'S SING AND BE HAPPY! COME ON!
IT'LL BE OKAY! IT'LL BE OKAY! AND EVEN IF IT'S NOT OKAY, YOU'LL EVENTUALLY DIE ANYWAY! YEAH!
YOU'RE NOT HELPING, SOUL KING!
KING NEPTUNE! ARE YOU ALL RIGHT?!
I CAN'T BELIEVE THE GREAT KNIGHT OF THE SEA HAS COME TO THIS.
I HAVE A BAD BACK AND I CAN'T FIGHT. I'M GETTING OLD.
THIS WAS A TERRIBLE BLUNDER. I'M SORRY!

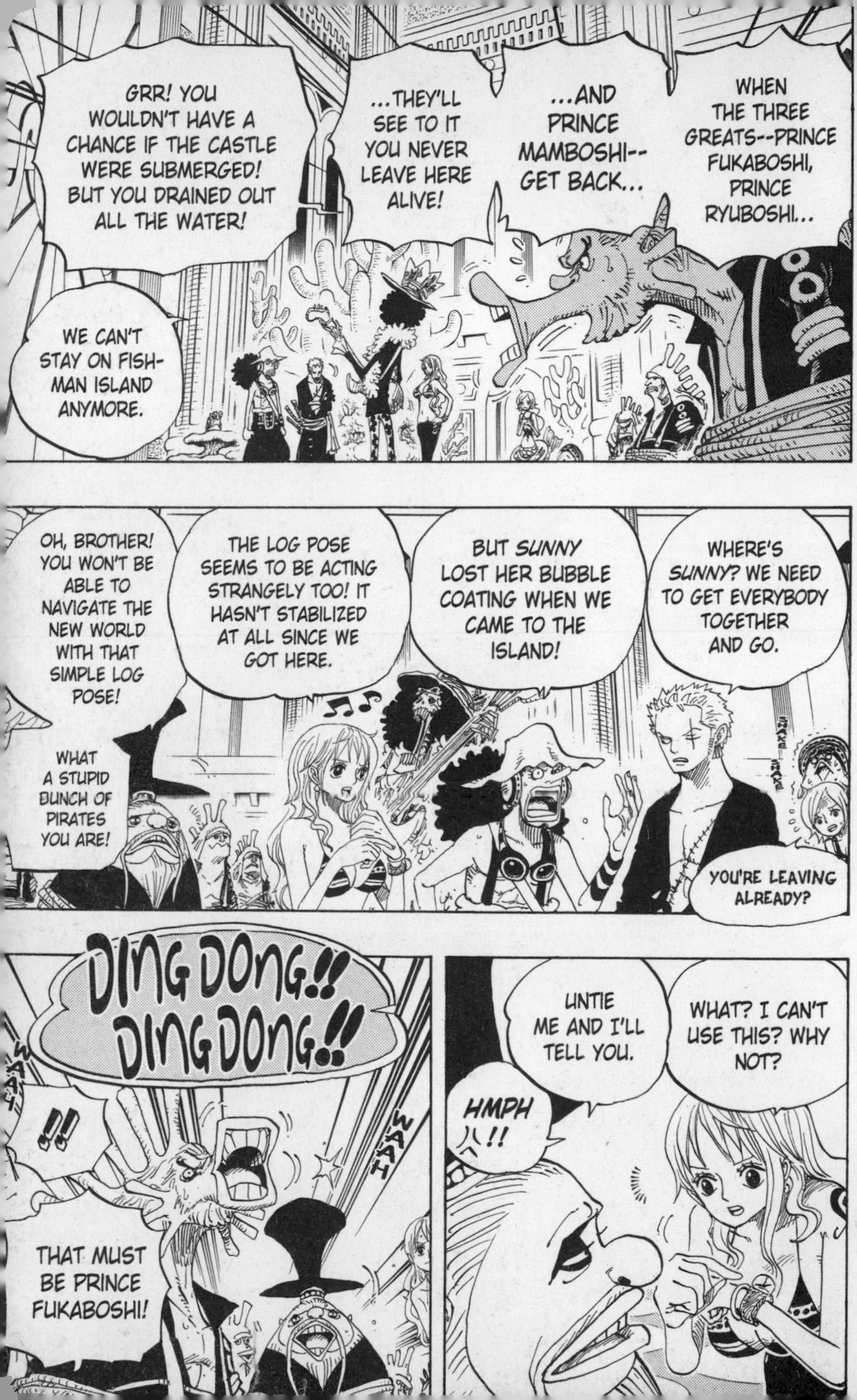
WHEN THE THREE GREATS--PRINCE FUKABOSHI, PRINCE RYUBOSHI...
...AND PRINCE MAMBOSHI-- GET BACK...
...THEY'LL SEE TO IT YOU NEVER LEAVE HERE ALIVE!
GRR! YOU WOULDN'T HAVE A CHANCE IF THE CASTLE WERE SUBMERGED! BUT YOU DRAINED OUT ALL THE WATER!
WE CAN'T STAY ON FISH-MAN ISLAND ANYMORE.
WHERE'S *SUNNY*? WE NEED TO GET EVERYBODY TOGETHER AND GO.
SHAKE SHAKE
BUT *SUNNY* LOST HER BUBBLE COATING WHEN WE CAME TO THE ISLAND!
THE LOG POSE SEEMS TO BE ACTING STRANGELY TOO! IT HASN'T STABILIZED AT ALL SINCE WE GOT HERE.
OH, BROTHER! YOU WON'T BE ABLE TO NAVIGATE THE NEW WORLD WITH THAT SIMPLE LOG POSE!
WHAT A STUPID BUNCH OF PIRATES YOU ARE!
YOU'RE LEAVING ALREADY?
WHAT? I CAN'T USE THIS? WHY NOT?
UNTIE ME AND I'LL TELL YOU.
HMPH 八!!
DING DONG!! DING DONG!!
WAAH
WAAH
!!
THAT MUST BE PRINCE FUKABOSHI!

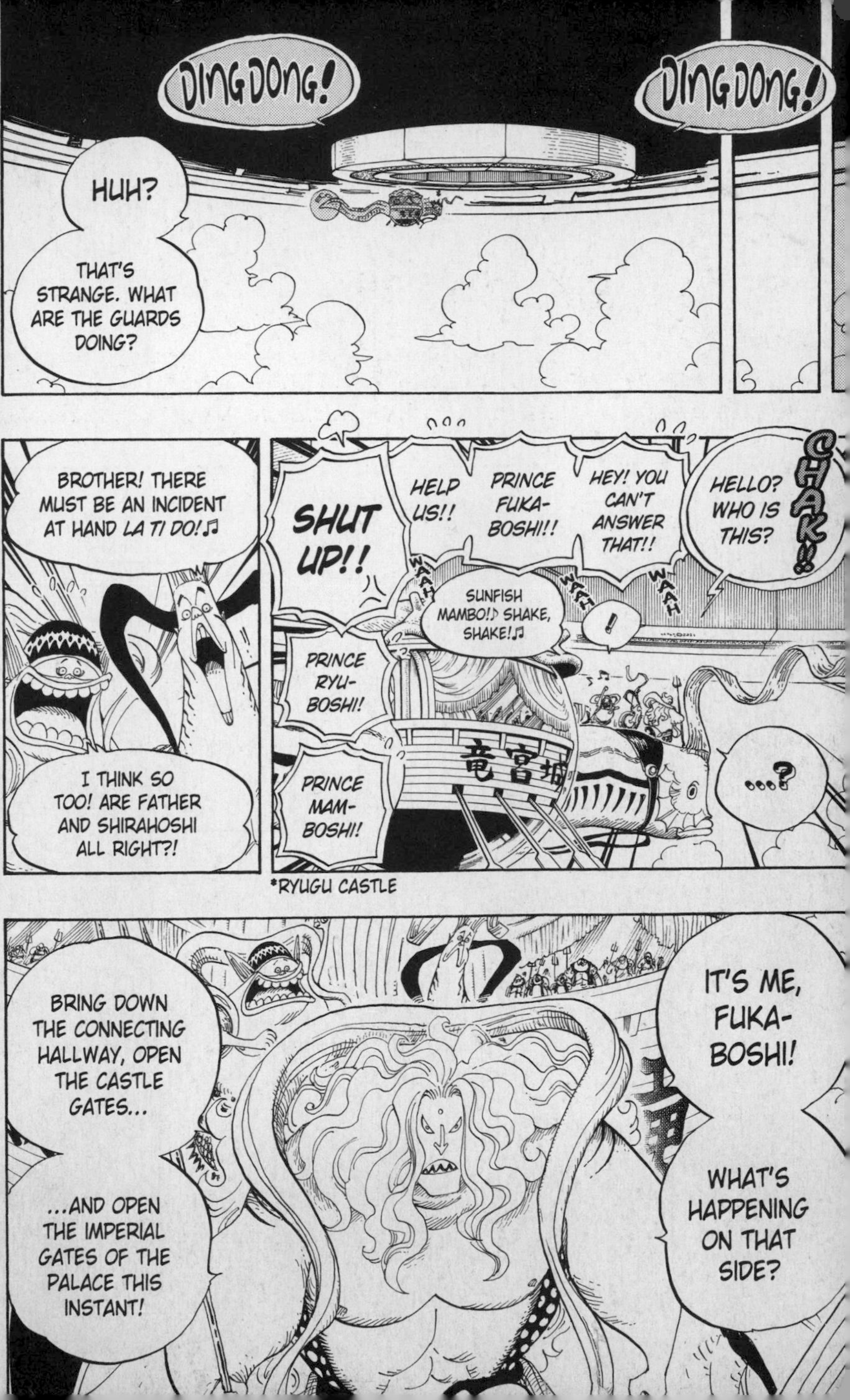
DING DONG!
DING DONG!
HUH?
THAT'S STRANGE. WHAT ARE THE GUARDS DOING?
CHAK!!
HELLO? WHO IS THIS?
HEY! YOU CAN'T ANSWER THAT!!
WAAH
WAAH
PRINCE FUKA-BOSHI!!
HELP US!!
WAAH
SHUT UP!!
SUNFISH MAMBO!♪ SHAKE, SHAKE!♫
!
...?
PRINCE RYU-BOSHI!
PRINCE MAM-BOSHI!
竜宮城
BROTHER! THERE MUST BE AN INCIDENT AT HAND LA TI DO!♫
I THINK SO TOO! ARE FATHER AND SHIRAHOSHI ALL RIGHT?!
*RYUGU CASTLE
IT'S ME, FUKA-BOSHI!
WHAT'S HAPPENING ON THAT SIDE?
BRING DOWN THE CONNECTING HALLWAY, OPEN THE CASTLE GATES...
...AND OPEN THE IMPERIAL GATES OF THE PALACE THIS INSTANT!

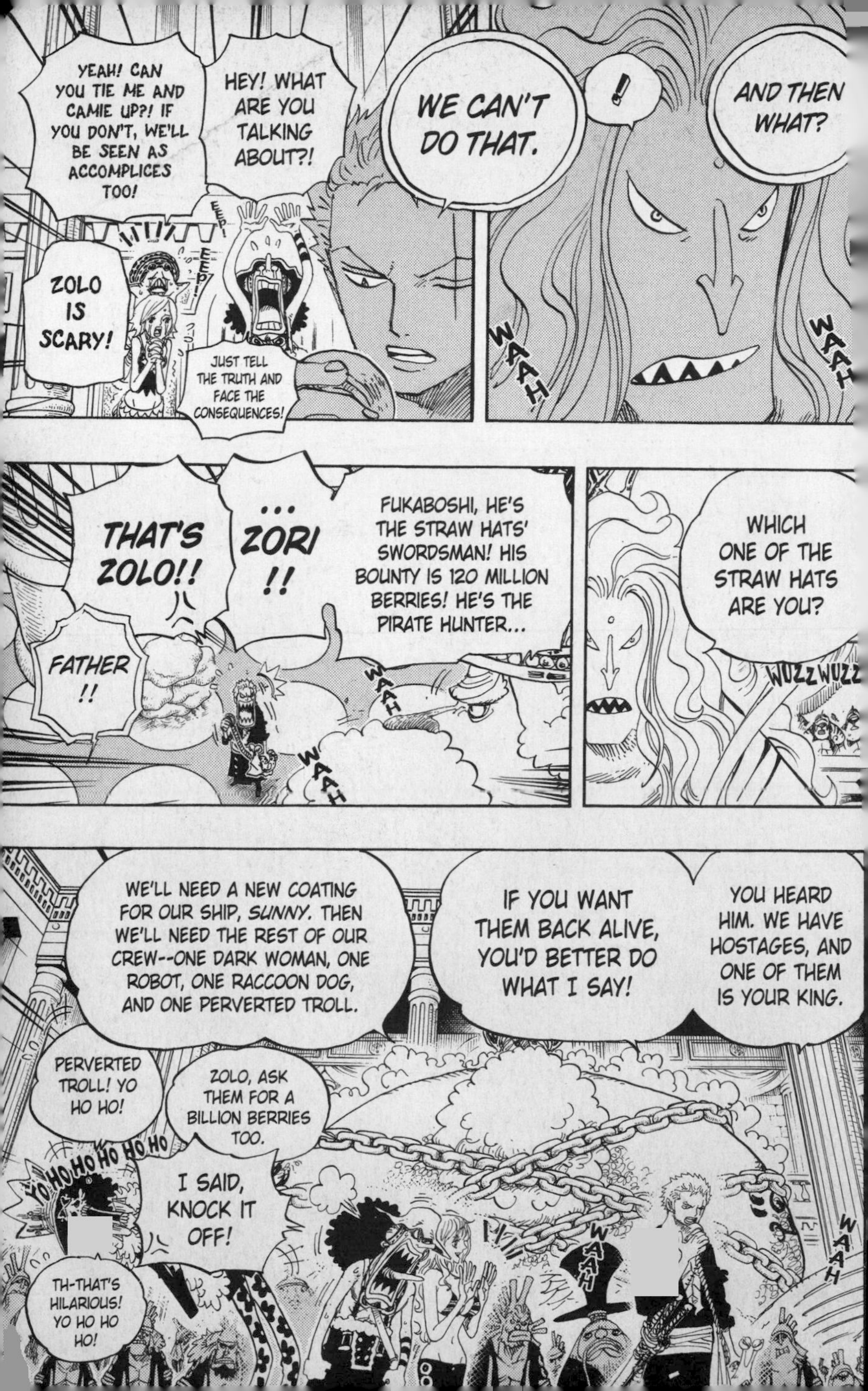
AND THEN WHAT?
!
WAAH
WAAH
WE CAN'T DO THAT.
HEY! WHAT ARE YOU TALKING ABOUT?!
YEAH! CAN YOU TIE ME AND CAMIE UP?! IF YOU DON'T, WE'LL BE SEEN AS ACCOMPLICES TOO!
EEP! EEP!
ZOLO IS SCARY!
JUST TELL THE TRUTH AND FACE THE CONSEQUENCES!
WHICH ONE OF THE STRAW HATS ARE YOU?
WUZZWUZZ
FUKABOSHI, HE'S THE STRAW HATS' SWORDSMAN! HIS BOUNTY IS 120 MILLION BERRIES! HE'S THE PIRATE HUNTER...
...ZORI!!
THAT'S ZOLO!!
FATHER!!
WAAH
WAAH
YOU HEARD HIM. WE HAVE HOSTAGES, AND ONE OF THEM IS YOUR KING.
IF YOU WANT THEM BACK ALIVE, YOU'D BETTER DO WHAT I SAY!
WE'LL NEED A NEW COATING FOR OUR SHIP, *SUNNY*. THEN WE'LL NEED THE REST OF OUR CREW--ONE DARK WOMAN, ONE ROBOT, ONE RACCOON DOG, AND ONE PERVERTED TROLL.
WAAH
WAAH
ZOLO, ASK THEM FOR A BILLION BERRIES TOO.
PERVERTED TROLL! YO HO HO!
YO HO HO HO HO HO
I SAID, KNOCK IT OFF!
TH-THAT'S HILARIOUS! YO HO HO HO!

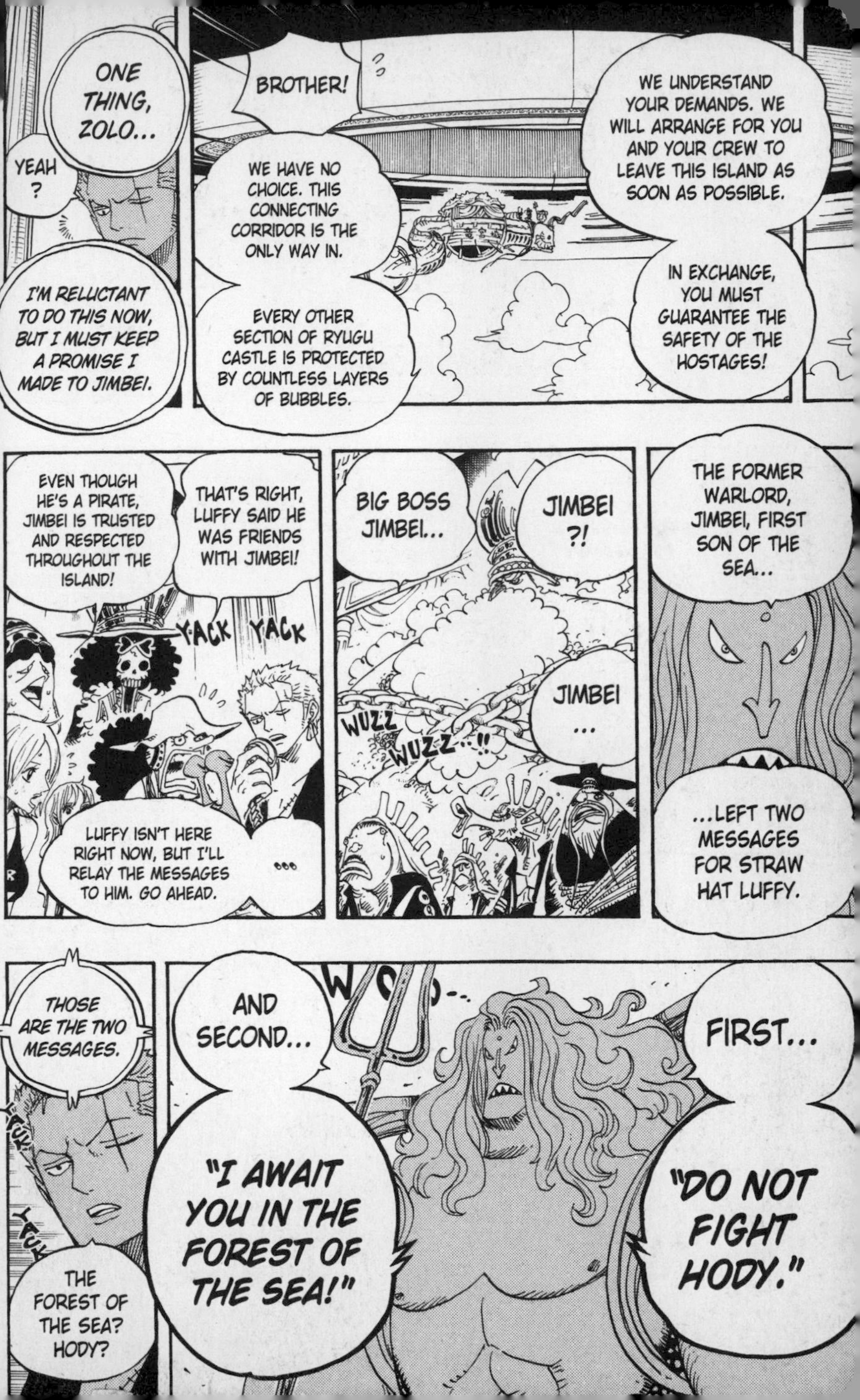
WE UNDERSTAND YOUR DEMANDS. WE WILL ARRANGE FOR YOU AND YOUR CREW TO LEAVE THIS ISLAND AS SOON AS POSSIBLE.
IN EXCHANGE, YOU MUST GUARANTEE THE SAFETY OF THE HOSTAGES!
BROTHER!
WE HAVE NO CHOICE. THIS CONNECTING CORRIDOR IS THE ONLY WAY IN.
EVERY OTHER SECTION OF RYUGU CASTLE IS PROTECTED BY COUNTLESS LAYERS OF BUBBLES.
ONE THING, ZOLO...
YEAH?
I'M RELUCTANT TO DO THIS NOW, BUT I MUST KEEP A PROMISE I MADE TO JIMBEI.
THE FORMER WARLORD, JIMBEI, FIRST SON OF THE SEA...
...LEFT TWO MESSAGES FOR STRAW HAT LUFFY.
JIMBEI?!
BIG BOSS JIMBEI...
JIMBEI...
WUZZ
WUZZ..!!
THAT'S RIGHT, LUFFY SAID HE WAS FRIENDS WITH JIMBEI!
EVEN THOUGH HE'S A PIRATE, JIMBEI IS TRUSTED AND RESPECTED THROUGHOUT THE ISLAND!
YACK YACK
LUFFY ISN'T HERE RIGHT NOW, BUT I'LL RELAY THE MESSAGES TO HIM. GO AHEAD.
...
FIRST...
"DO NOT FIGHT HODY."
AND SECOND...
"I AWAIT YOU IN THE FOREST OF THE SEA!"
THOSE ARE THE TWO MESSAGES.
YACK
YACK
THE FOREST OF THE SEA? HODY?

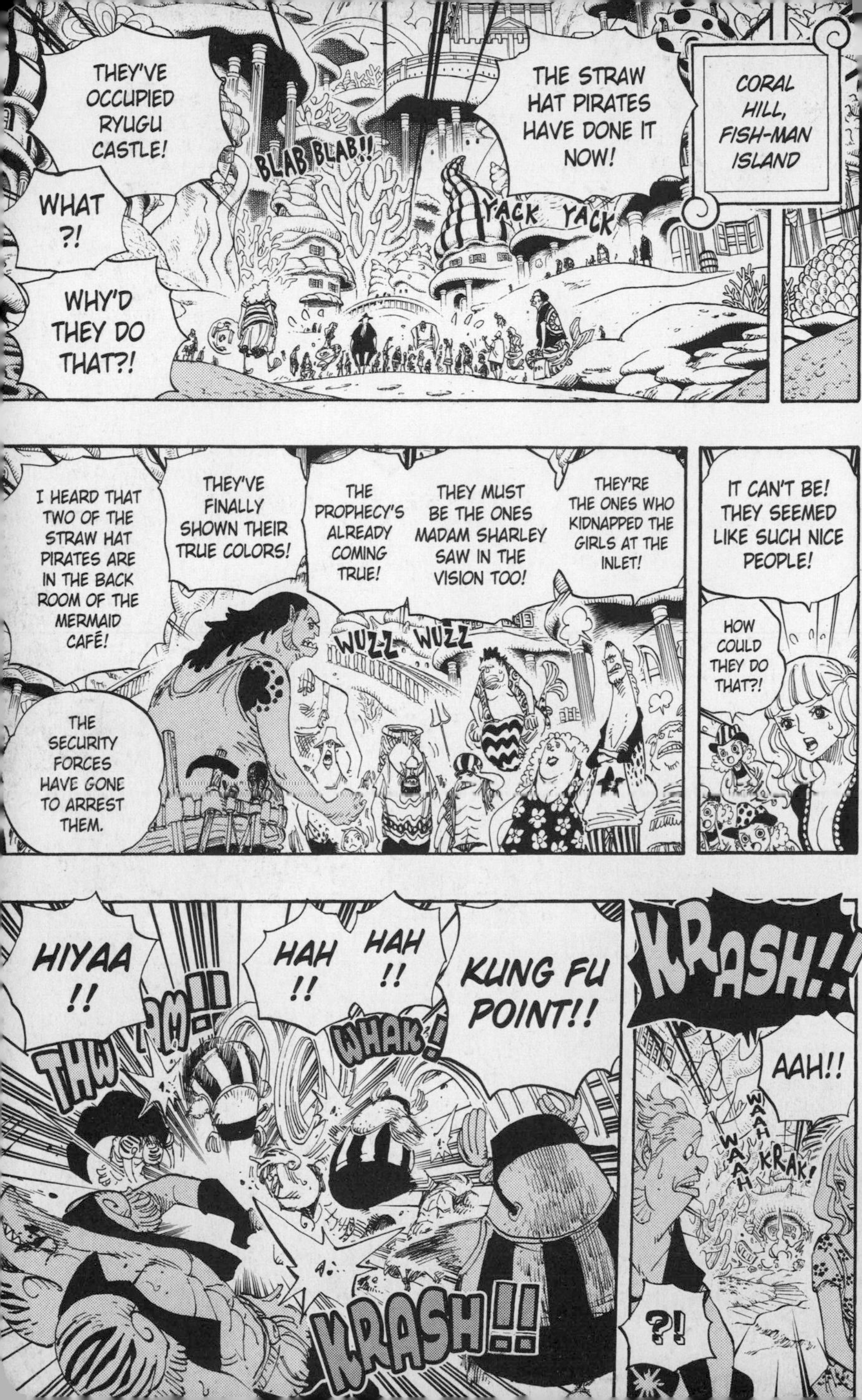
CORAL HILL, FISH-MAN ISLAND
THE STRAW HAT PIRATES HAVE DONE IT NOW!
YACK YACK
BLAB BLAB!!
THEY'VE OCCUPIED RYUGU CASTLE!
WHAT?!
WHY'D THEY DO THAT?!
IT CAN'T BE! THEY SEEMED LIKE SUCH NICE PEOPLE!
HOW COULD THEY DO THAT?!
THEY'RE THE ONES WHO KIDNAPPED THE GIRLS AT THE INLET!
THEY MUST BE THE ONES MADAM SHARLEY SAW IN THE VISION TOO!
THE PROPHECY'S ALREADY COMING TRUE!
THEY'VE FINALLY SHOWN THEIR TRUE COLORS!
I HEARD THAT TWO OF THE STRAW HAT PIRATES ARE IN THE BACK ROOM OF THE MERMAID CAFÉ!
WUZZ WUZZ
THE SECURITY FORCES HAVE GONE TO ARREST THEM.
KRASH!!
AAH!!
WAAH WAAH
KRAK!
?!
KUNG FU POINT!!
HAH!!
HAH!!
WHAK!
HIYAA!!
KRASH!!

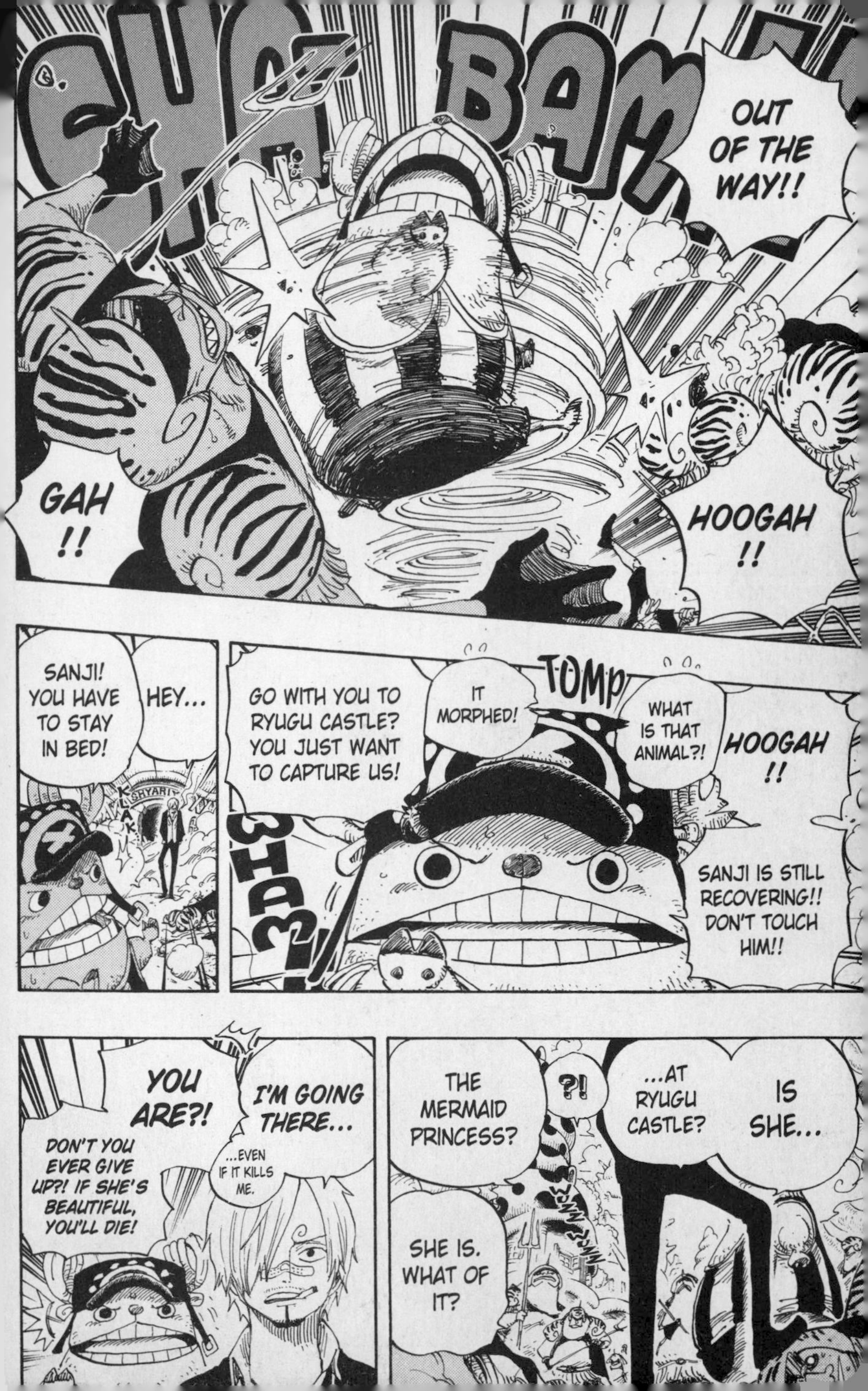
OUT OF THE WAY!!
BAM
HOOGAH !!
GAH !!
HOOGAH !!
WHAT IS THAT ANIMAL?!
TOMP
IT MORPHED!
GO WITH YOU TO RYUGU CASTLE? YOU JUST WANT TO CAPTURE US!
SANJI IS STILL RECOVERING!! DON'T TOUCH HIM!!
WHAM
HEY...
SANJI! YOU HAVE TO STAY IN BED!
IS SHE...
...AT RYUGU CASTLE?
?!
THE MERMAID PRINCESS?
SHE IS. WHAT OF IT?
I'M GOING THERE...
...EVEN IF IT KILLS ME.
YOU ARE?!
DON'T YOU EVER GIVE UP?! IF SHE'S BEAUTIFUL, YOU'LL DIE!

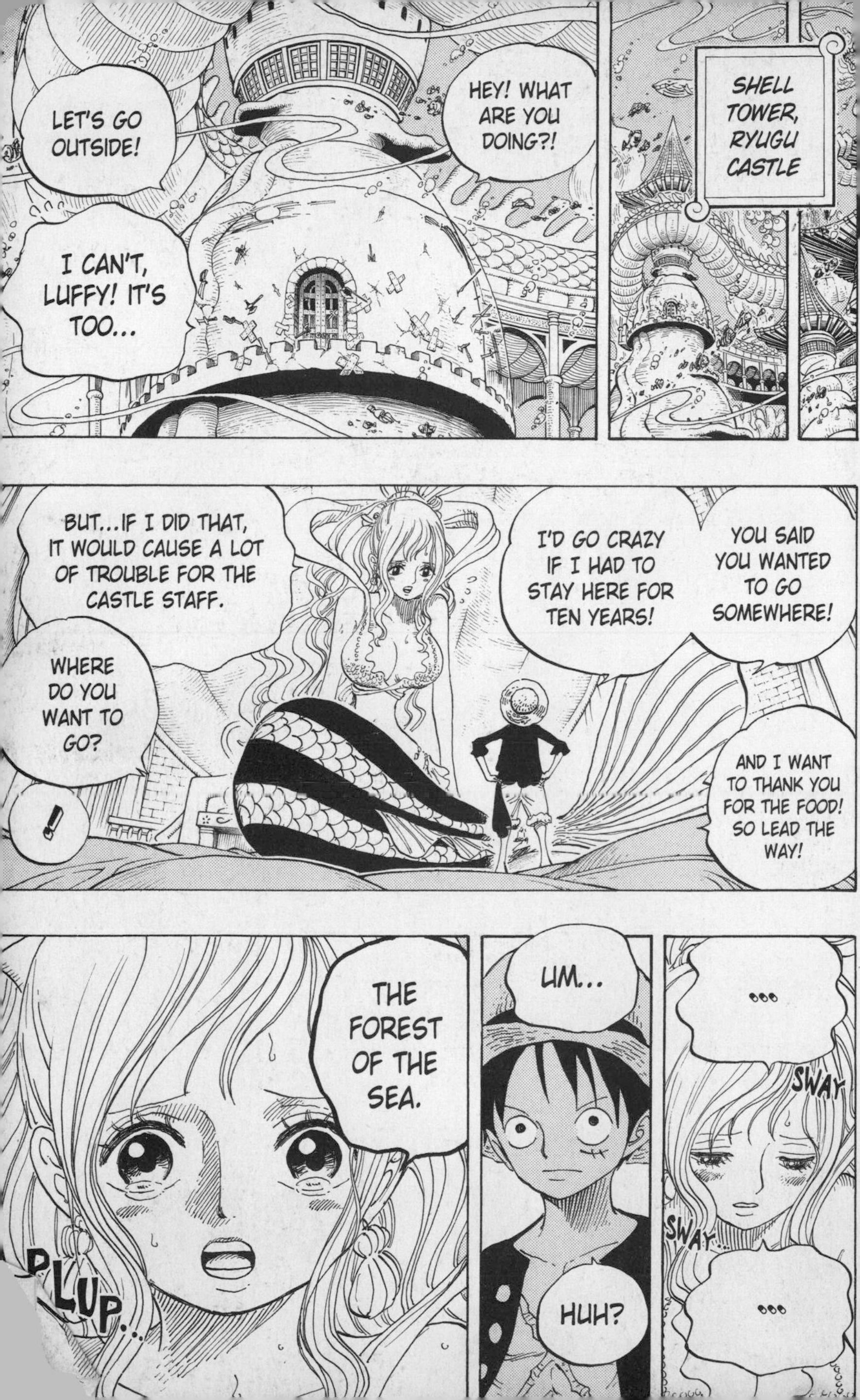
SHELL TOWER, RYUGU CASTLE
HEY! WHAT ARE YOU DOING?!
LET'S GO OUTSIDE!
I CAN'T, LUFFY! IT'S TOO...
YOU SAID YOU WANTED TO GO SOMEWHERE!
I'D GO CRAZY IF I HAD TO STAY HERE FOR TEN YEARS!
AND I WANT TO THANK YOU FOR THE FOOD! SO LEAD THE WAY!
BUT...IF I DID THAT, IT WOULD CAUSE A LOT OF TROUBLE FOR THE CASTLE STAFF.
WHERE DO YOU WANT TO GO?
!
...
SWAY
SWAY...
...
UM...
HUH?
THE FOREST OF THE SEA.
PLUP...

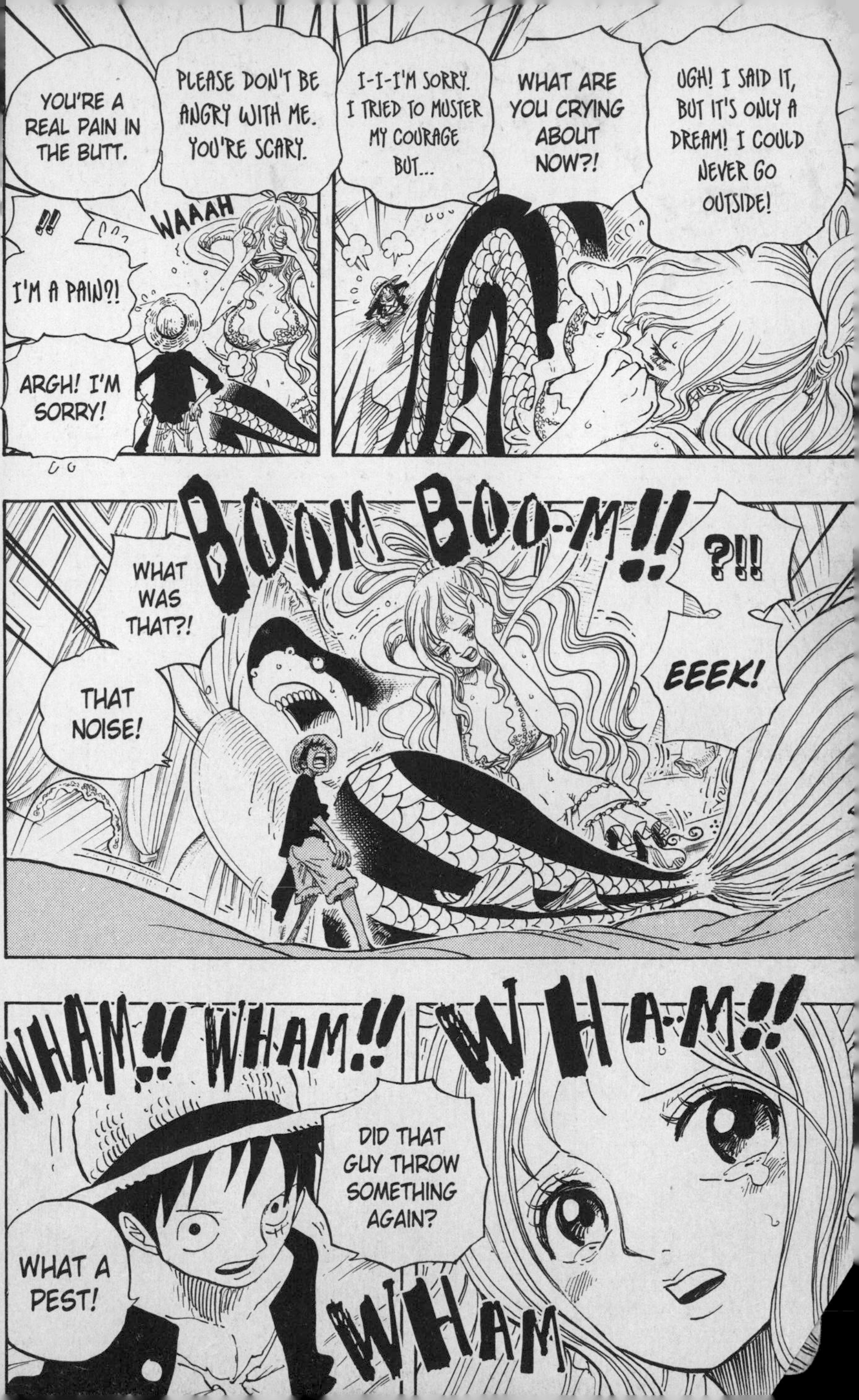
UGH! I SAID IT, BUT IT'S ONLY A DREAM! I COULD NEVER GO OUTSIDE!
WHAT ARE YOU CRYING ABOUT NOW?!
I-I-I'M SORRY. I TRIED TO MUSTER MY COURAGE BUT...
PLEASE DON'T BE ANGRY WITH ME. YOU'RE SCARY.
YOU'RE A REAL PAIN IN THE BUTT.
WAAAH
!!
I'M A PAIN?!
ARGH! I'M SORRY!
BOOM BOO-M!!
?!!
WHAT WAS THAT?!
EEEK!
THAT NOISE!
WHAM!!
WHAM!! WHAM!!
DID THAT GUY THROW SOMETHING AGAIN?
WHAT A PEST!
WHAM

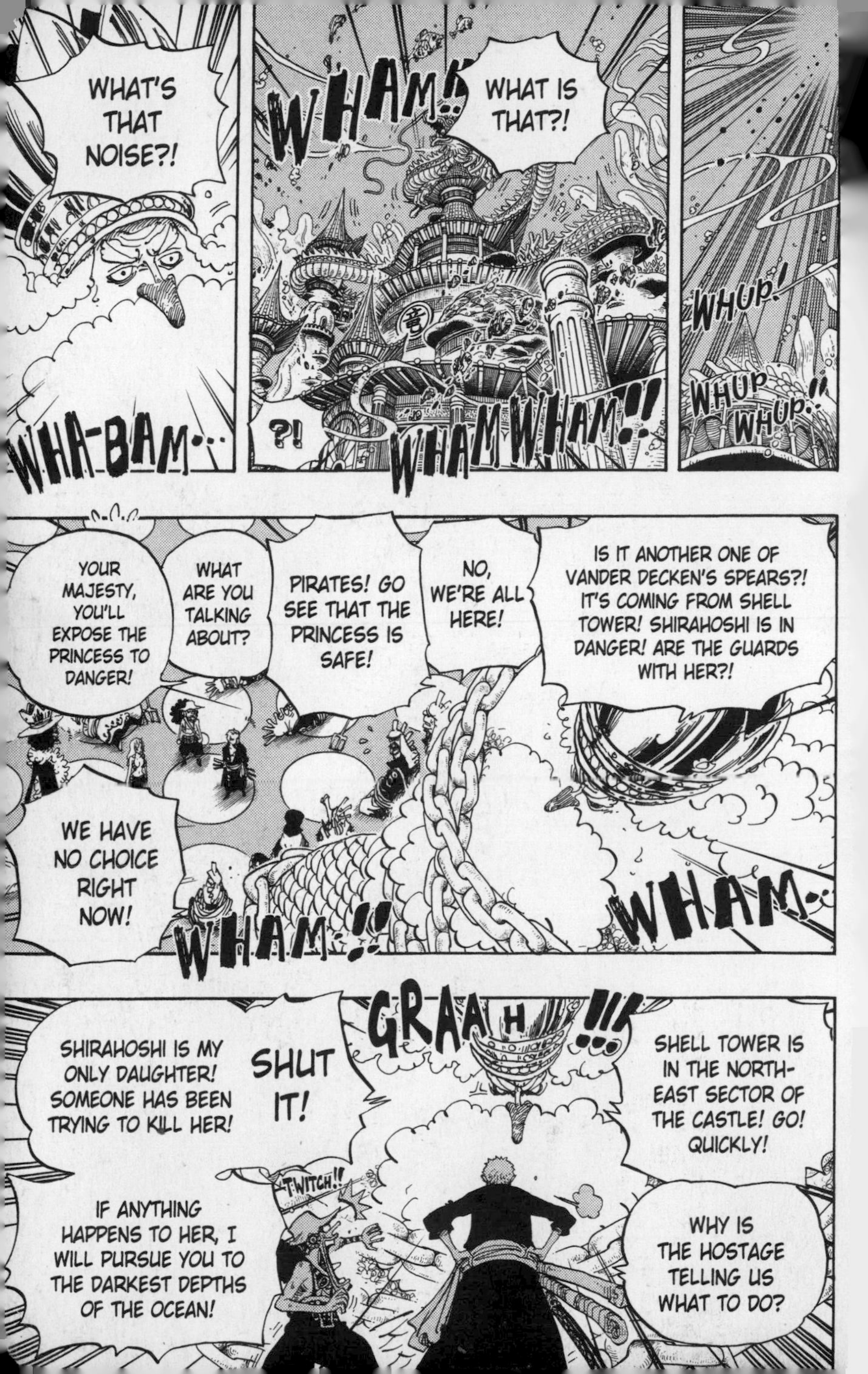
WHUP!
WHUP WHUP!!
WHAM!!
WHAT IS THAT?!
?!
WHAM WHAM!!
WHAT'S THAT NOISE?!
WHA-BAM...
IS IT ANOTHER ONE OF VANDER DECKEN'S SPEARS?! IT'S COMING FROM SHELL TOWER! SHIRAHOSHI IS IN DANGER! ARE THE GUARDS WITH HER?!
NO, WE'RE ALL HERE!
PIRATES! GO SEE THAT THE PRINCESS IS SAFE!
WHAT ARE YOU TALKING ABOUT?
YOUR MAJESTY, YOU'LL EXPOSE THE PRINCESS TO DANGER!
WHAM...
WE HAVE NO CHOICE RIGHT NOW!
WHAM!!
GRAAH!!!
SHELL TOWER IS IN THE NORTH-EAST SECTOR OF THE CASTLE! GO! QUICKLY!
SHUT IT!
SHIRAHOSHI IS MY ONLY DAUGHTER! SOMEONE HAS BEEN TRYING TO KILL HER!
WHY IS THE HOSTAGE TELLING US WHAT TO DO?
TWITCH!!
IF ANYTHING HAPPENS TO HER, I WILL PURSUE YOU TO THE DARKEST DEPTHS OF THE OCEAN!

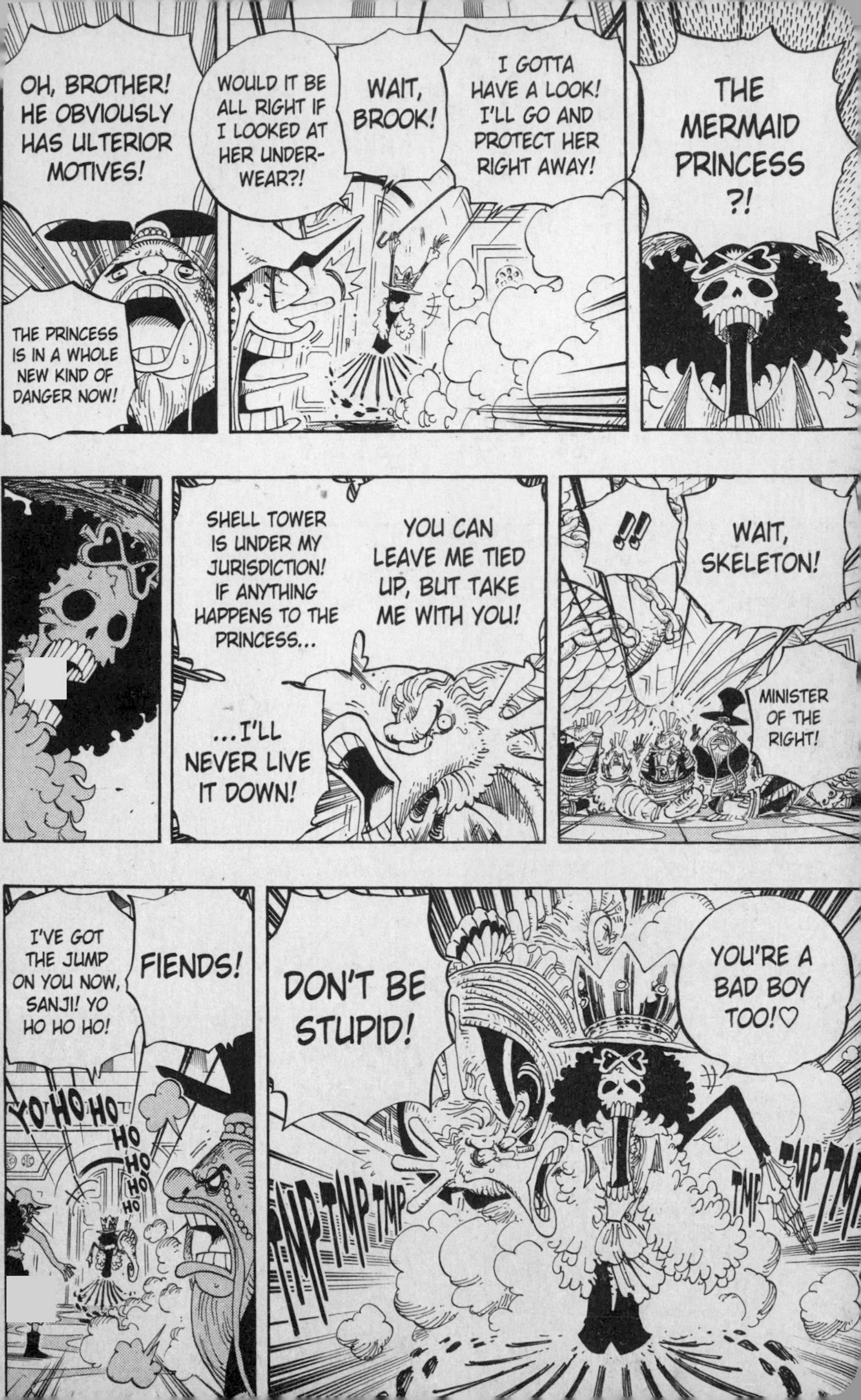
THE MERMAID PRINCESS ?!
I GOTTA HAVE A LOOK! I'LL GO AND PROTECT HER RIGHT AWAY!
WAIT, BROOK!
WOULD IT BE ALL RIGHT IF I LOOKED AT HER UNDER-WEAR?!
OH, BROTHER! HE OBVIOUSLY HAS ULTERIOR MOTIVES!
THE PRINCESS IS IN A WHOLE NEW KIND OF DANGER NOW!
WAIT, SKELETON!
!!
MINISTER OF THE RIGHT!
YOU CAN LEAVE ME TIED UP, BUT TAKE ME WITH YOU!
SHELL TOWER IS UNDER MY JURISDICTION! IF ANYTHING HAPPENS TO THE PRINCESS...
...I'LL NEVER LIVE IT DOWN!
YOU'RE A BAD BOY TOO!♡
DON'T BE STUPID!
TMP TMP TMP
TMP TMP TMP
FIENDS!
I'VE GOT THE JUMP ON YOU NOW, SANJI! YO HO HO HO!
YO HO HO HO HO HO HO HO

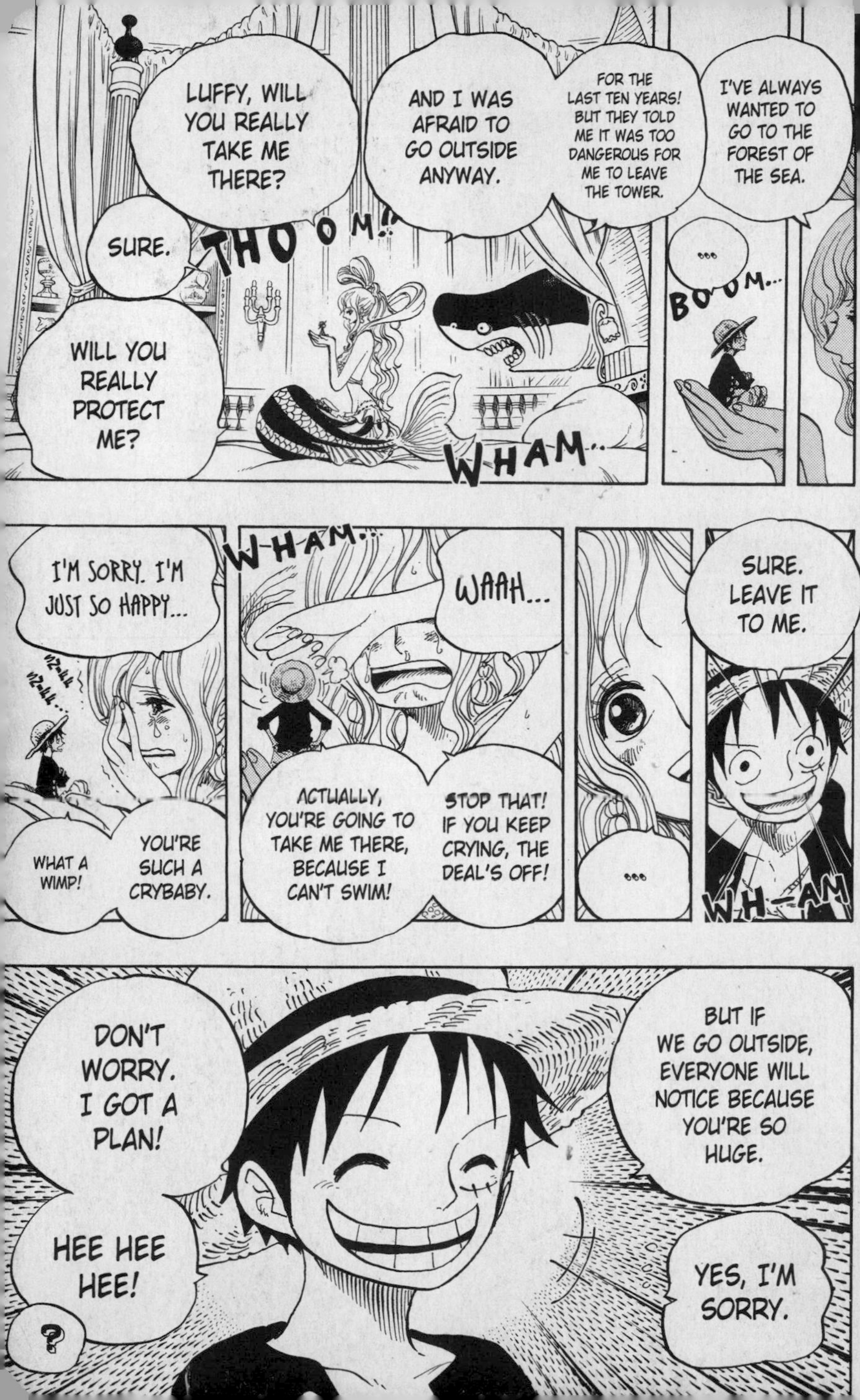

I'VE ALWAYS WANTED TO GO TO THE FOREST OF THE SEA.
...
BOOM...
FOR THE LAST TEN YEARS! BUT THEY TOLD ME IT WAS TOO DANGEROUS FOR ME TO LEAVE THE TOWER.
AND I WAS AFRAID TO GO OUTSIDE ANYWAY.
LUFFY, WILL YOU REALLY TAKE ME THERE?
THOOM!!
SURE.
WILL YOU REALLY PROTECT ME?
WHAM...
SURE. LEAVE IT TO ME.
WH-AM
...
WAAH...
STOP THAT! IF YOU KEEP CRYING, THE DEAL'S OFF!
ACTUALLY, YOU'RE GOING TO TAKE ME THERE, BECAUSE I CAN'T SWIM!
WHAM...
I'M SORRY. I'M JUST SO HAPPY...
YOU'RE SUCH A CRYBABY.
WHAT A WIMP!
BUT IF WE GO OUTSIDE, EVERYONE WILL NOTICE BECAUSE YOU'RE SO HUGE.
YES, I'M SORRY.
DON'T WORRY. I GOT A PLAN!
HEE HEE HEE!
?

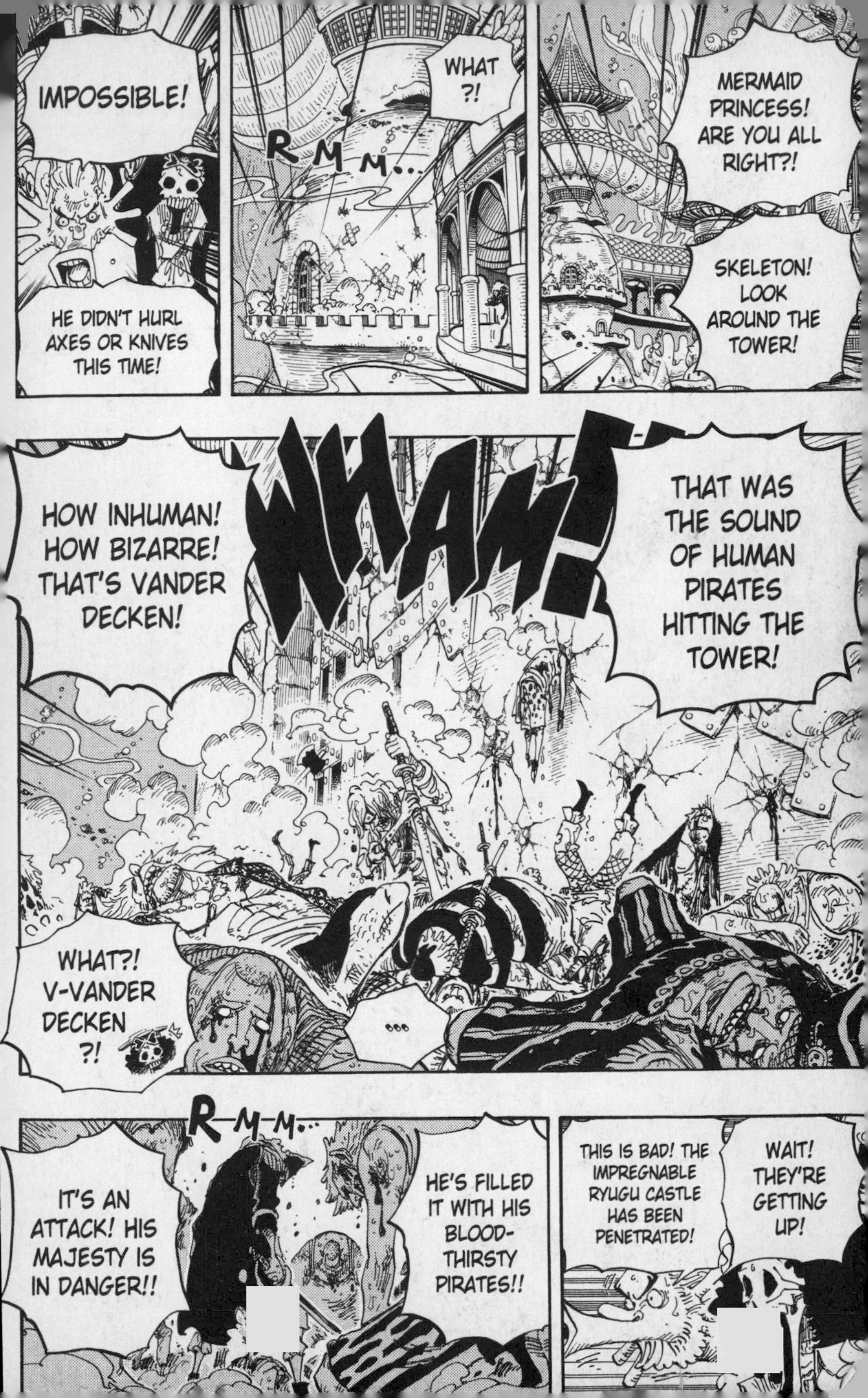
MERMAID PRINCESS! ARE YOU ALL RIGHT?!
SKELETON! LOOK AROUND THE TOWER!
WHAT ?!
RMM...
IMPOSSIBLE!
HE DIDN'T HURL AXES OR KNIVES THIS TIME!
THAT WAS THE SOUND OF HUMAN PIRATES HITTING THE TOWER!
WHAM!
HOW INHUMAN! HOW BIZARRE! THAT'S VANDER DECKEN!
...
WHAT?! V-VANDER DECKEN ?!
WAIT! THEY'RE GETTING UP!
THIS IS BAD! THE IMPREGNABLE RYUGU CASTLE HAS BEEN PENETRATED!
R-M-M...
HE'S FILLED IT WITH HIS BLOOD-THIRSTY PIRATES!!
IT'S AN ATTACK! HIS MAJESTY IS IN DANGER!!

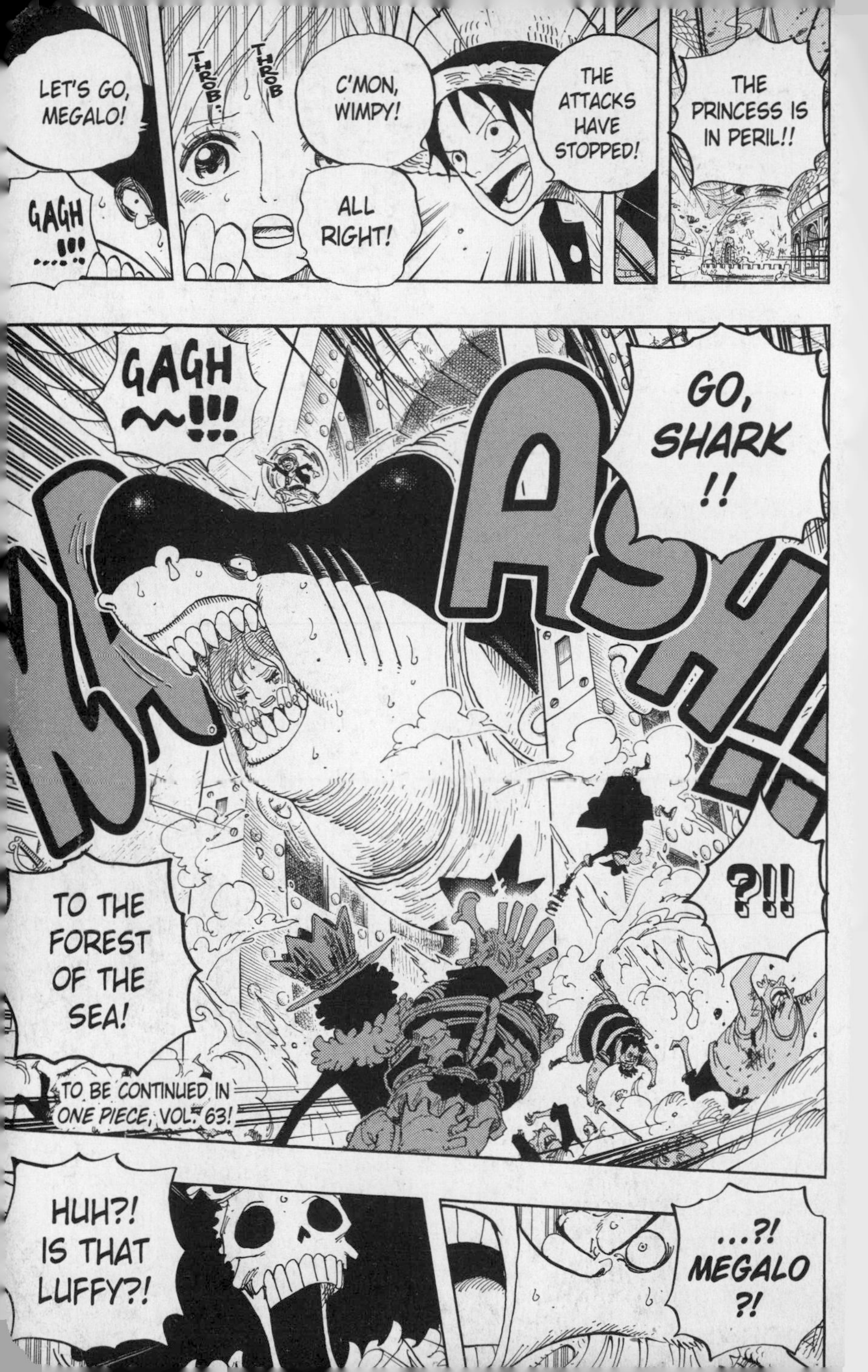
THE PRINCESS IS IN PERIL!!
THE ATTACKS HAVE STOPPED!
THROB THROB
C'MON, WIMPY!
ALL RIGHT!
LET'S GO, MEGALO!
GAGH ...!!!
GO, SHARK!!
GAGH ~!!!
WASH!!
?!!
TO THE FOREST OF THE SEA!
TO BE CONTINUED IN ONE PIECE, VOL. 63!
...?! MEGALO ?!
HUH?! IS THAT LUFFY?!

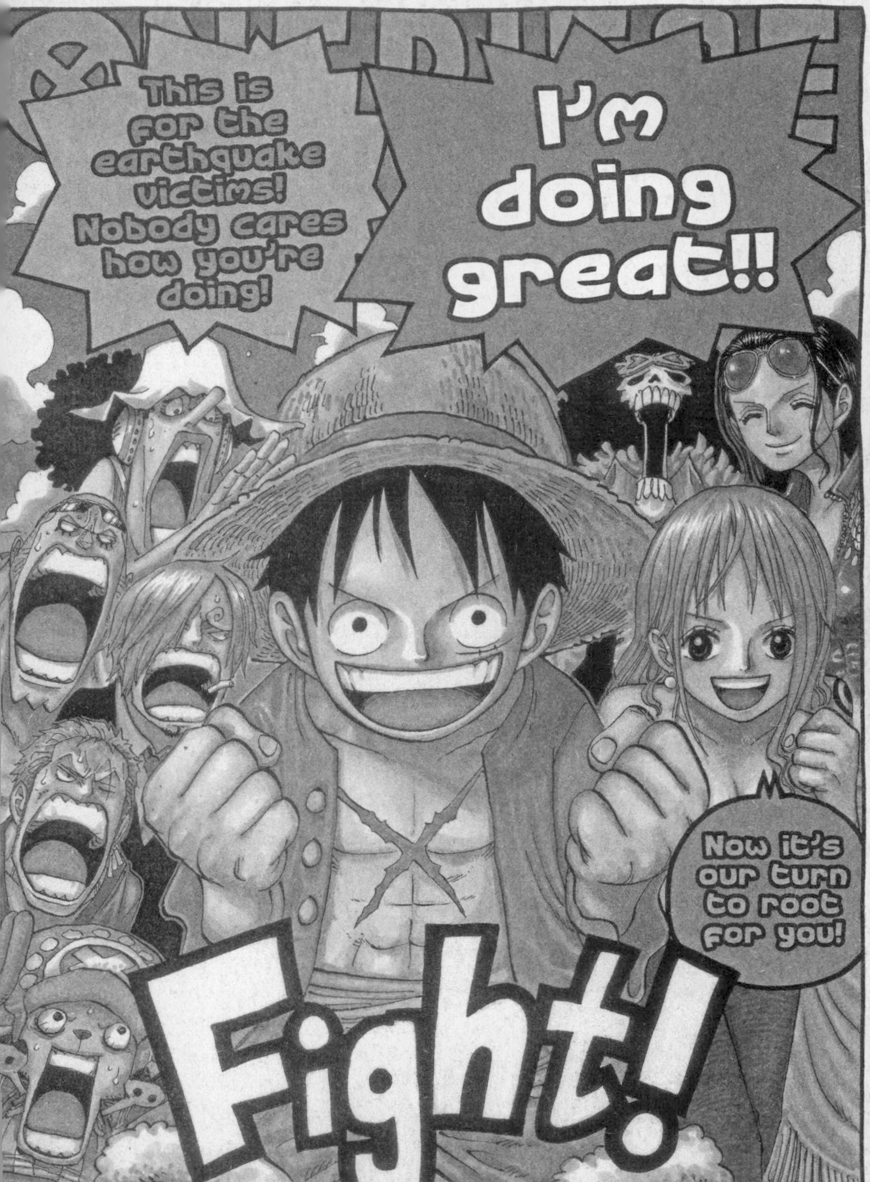
I'm doing great!!
This is for the earthquake victims! Nobody cares how you're doing!
Now it's our turn to root for you!
Fight!

HIS IS DEDICATED TO THOSE AFFECTED BY THE MARCH 2011 TOHOKU EARTHQUAKE AND TSUNAMI.
IS ILLUSTRATION WAS ORIGINALLY PLACED ON THE COVER OF THE BOOK UNDER THE DUST JACKET.

COMING NEXT VOLUME:

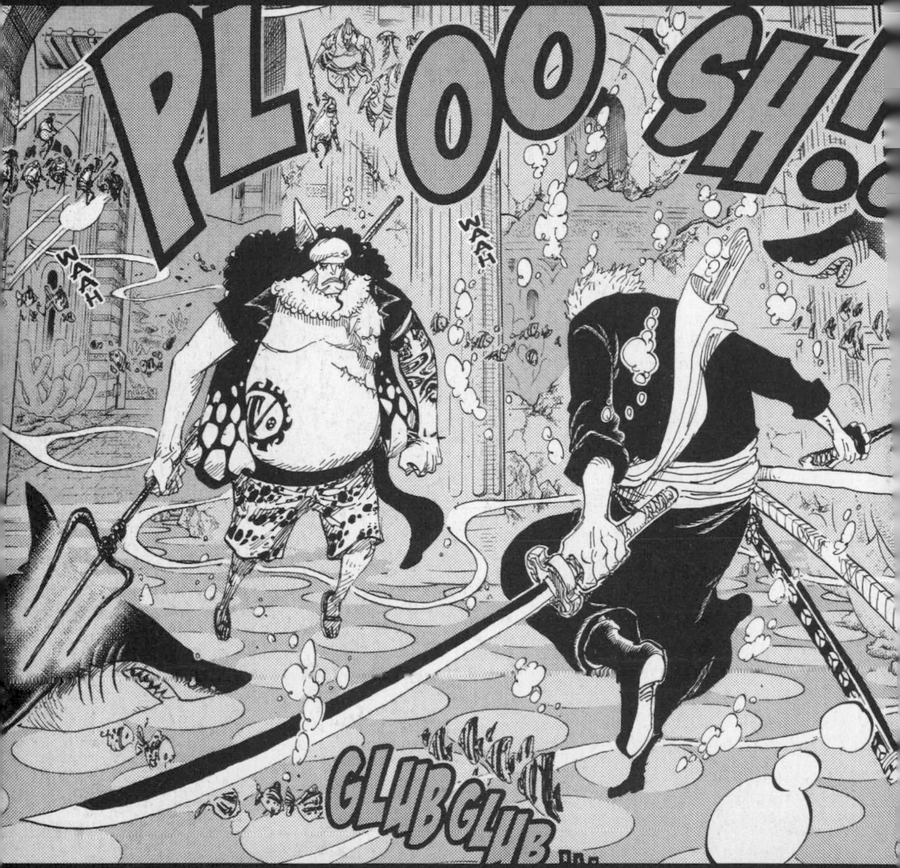
PLOOSH
WAAH
WAAH
GLUB GLUB

Luffy and Princess Shirahoshi head to the Forest of the Sea. But waiting there is an old friend who reveals a shocking story! Meanwhile, Hody Jones and his allies make their move to take over Ryugu Kingdom. But what is the source of the hatred that drives them…?

ON SALE JULY 2012!

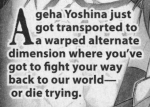

STORY BY TSUGUMI OHBA
ART BY TAKESHI OBATA

From the creators of *Death Note*

The mystery behind manga making REVEALED!

Average student Moritaka Mashiro enjoys drawing for fun. When his classmate and aspiring writer Akito Takagi discovers his talent, he begs to team up. But what exactly does it take to make it in the manga-publishing world?

Bakuman, Vol. 1
ISBN: 978-1-4215-3513-5
$9.99 US / $12.99 CAN *

Manga on sale at store.viz.com

Also available at your local bookstore or comic store

You're Reading in the Wrong Direction!!

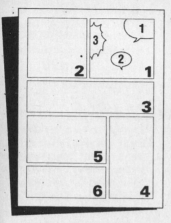

Whoops! Guess what? You're starting at the wrong end of the comic!

...It's true! In keeping with the original Japanese format, **One Piece** is meant to be read from right to left, starting in the upper-right corner.

Unlike English, which is read from left to right, Japanese is read from right to left, meaning that action, sound effects and word-balloon order are completely reversed...something which can make readers unfamiliar with Japanese feel pretty backwards themselves. For this reason, manga or Japanese comics published in the U.S. in English have sometimes been published "flopped"— that is, printed in exact reverse order, as though seen from the other side of a mirror.

By flopping pages, U.S. publishers can avoid confusing readers, but the compromise is not without its downside. For one thing, a character in a flopped manga series who once wore in the original Japanese version a T-shirt emblazoned with "M A Y" (as in "the merry month of") now wears one which reads "Y A M"! Additionally, many manga creators in Japan are themselves unhappy with the process, as some feel the mirror-imaging of their art skews their original intentions.

We are proud to bring you Eiichiro Oda's **One Piece** in the original unflopped format. For now, though, turn to the other side of the book and let the journey begin...!

—Editor